Nonverbal Behavior in Interpersonal Relations

Seventh Edition

VIRGINIA PECK **Richmond**

University of Alabama at Birmingham

JAMES C. **McCroskey**

M & R Training and Consulting

Birmingham, AL

MARK L. **Hickson III**

University of Alabama at Birmingham

Allyn & Bacon

Boston   Columbus   Indianapolis   New York   San Francisco   Upper Saddle River
Amsterdam   Cape Town   Dubai   London   Madrid   Milan   Munich   Paris   Montreal   Toronto
Delhi   Mexico City   São Paulo   Sydney   Hong Kong   Seoul   Singapore   Taipei   Tokyo

Editor in Chief, Communication: Karon Bowers
Editorial Assistant: Stephanie Chaisson
Editor: Toni Magyar
Marketing Manager: Blair Tuckman
Project Coordination: Electronic Publishing Services Inc., NYC
Text Design and Electronic Page Makeup: TexTech
Art Director, Cover: Anne Nieglos
Cover Design: Anne Bonanno Nieglos/Ilze Lemesis
Cover Illustration: Shutterstock
Image Asset Supervisor: Annette Linder
Senior Manufacturing Buyer: Mary Ann Gloriande

For permission to use copyrighted material, grateful acknowledgment is made to the
copyright holders on p. 345, which are hereby made part of this copyright page.

Library of Congress Cataloging-in-Publication Data

Richmond, Virginia P.
  Nonverbal behavior in interpersonal relations / Virginia Peck Richmond,
James C. McCroskey, and Mark L. Hickson III. — 7th ed.
    p. cm.
  Includes bibliographical references and index.
  ISBN 978-0-205-04230-2
  1. Body language.   2. Interpersonal relations.   I. McCroskey, James C.
  II. Hickson, Mark.   III. Title.
  BF637.N66R53 2011
  153.6'9—dc22   2010047142

Allyn & Bacon
is an imprint of

www.pearsonhighered.com   ISBN-13: 978-0-205-04230-2
                            ISBN-10:   0-205-04230-9

16 2019

CONTENTS

CHAPTER 7
Space and Territoriality   126

CHAPTER 8
Environment and Physical Surroundings   147

CHAPTER 9
Touch and Communication   174

CHAPTER 13
Teacher-Student Nonverbal Relationships 252

PREFACE

onverbal communication generates scholarly investigations in a wide variety of academic disciplines and involves many scholarly models. This book is a unique blend of social scientific and humanistic study and represents what we believe constitutes the area of nonverbal communication today. We have attempted to integrate the knowledge drawn from these diverse disciplines and orientations, while avoiding devotion to a specific scholarly approach.

Popular writers in the field often overgeneralize research findings, and such generalizations too often find their way into nonverbal communication classes. In addition, many nonverbal communication classes were developed as virtually content-free experiential courses. Such misrepresentations have not been conducive to generating respect for this area of study. Despite that, the study of nonverbal communication is having a significant impact on other disciplines such as psychology, sociology, social work, family relations, law, law enforcement, political science, and education. And we are just getting started!

The teaching of nonverbal communication is plagued by a dilemma. On one hand, we know that all of the categories of nonverbal behavior interact to create communicative impact. On the other hand, to understand all of these behaviors, it seems necessary to look at the individual categories of behavior one by one. Thus, most textbooks and course instructors choose between some type of variables approach and a functional approach. The former leads to an excellent understanding of the individual behaviors that make up nonverbal communication but to little understanding of how they interact. The latter leads to an excellent understanding of the complexity of nonverbal communication but to little understanding of the components of this complex communication system.

In this introductory textbook, we have attempted to resolve that dilemma by including chapters devoted to the individual categories of nonverbal behavior as well as chapters that examine all of those variables in specific contexts. Through this combined functions–variables–contexts approach, we hope you will develop a full and well-rounded perspective of the role of nonverbal behavior in human communicative relationships.

NEW TO THIS EDITION

In this current edition, we have fourteen chapters. Each chapter has been reviewed and updated by the authors to streamline information for students, and each has familiar as well as new content including over 100 new references in addition to new biological information. An extensive new photo program has also been designed that includes more vibrant and modern photographs to depict the concepts discussed throughout the textbook. We worked hard to incorporate, throughout each chapter, a closer focus on the world around us—not just the North American culture, but other cultures as well. With our increasingly global communities in both the classroom and in the real world, this shift in cultural focus to a broader view allows us to meet the needs of all students. With greater diversity in our classrooms, comes the extreme need for us to focus on the entirety of "the world around us."

ACKNOWLEDGMENTS

We would like to thank our editors and others who have been generous with their expertise. We thank Allyn & Bacon for its continued support and encouragement.

We appreciate the ideas of many teachers and students who have used and commented upon the first six editions of this book. Specifically, we would like to thank the following instructors who reviewed the previous edition and offered feedback for this one: Rachel L. DiCioccio, University of Rhode Island; Susan K. Minton, Lindsey Wilson College; Melissa Newman, Dallas Baptist University; Caroline S. Parsons, Clemson University; Candy Pettus, Dallas Baptist University; Marshall Prisbell, University of Nebraska at Omaha; Monica C. Rothschild-Boros, Orange Coast College; and Avinash Thombre, University of Arkansas, Little Rock. Many of their suggestions are reflected in modifications in this edition. We have included more citation references (both classic and contemporary) in this edition. We also have included extensive citations of references for each chapter at the end of the book for those who want to pursue a given topic more fully. We have cited the works of several of our colleagues who have written books appropriate for advanced study in this field. We hope that when you read this introductory book, you will be motivated to move on to their excellent works.

Virginia Peck Richmond

James C. McCroskey

Mark L. Hickson III

CHAPTER 1

Communication and Nonverbal Behavior

Interpersonal relationships are a central fact of our existence as human beings in modern society. Although there may have been a time when one person could be fully self-sufficient, that time has now passed. Our existence is dependent on others. We must relate to others to survive. Throughout the relationships we encounter during our life spans, the role of communication is the process that makes us human.

Human communication is the process of one person stimulating meaning in the mind of another person (or persons) by means of verbal and/or nonverbal messages. Because we have devoted several other books to explaining the nature of this process in considerable detail, we will not attempt to do so in this text. Our focus in this book is on the role of nonverbal behaviors as messages in human communication.

Our concern, then, is with **nonverbal communication**—the process of one person stimulating meaning in the mind of another person or persons by means of nonverbal messages (McCroskey, 2001; McCroskey & Richmond, 1996; Richmond & McCroskey, 2001).

MYTHS ABOUT NONVERBAL COMMUNICATION

For much of the history of the study of human communication, the nonverbal component was ignored (Andersen, 1999; Ruesch & Kees, 1971). As increased attention has been directed toward this aspect of communication, several myths have developed that have led to considerable confusion. Let us examine a few of these myths.

1. *Nonverbal communication is nonsense. All communication involves language. Therefore, all communication is verbal.* This is the traditional myth held by many persons who center their attention on language and consider language and communication as virtually interchangeable terms. However, nonverbal behavior with potential for communicative impact is always present in oral interactions. We cannot even talk on the phone without introducing nonverbal elements into our message. The sounds of our voices are there, and no two people's voices are exactly alike. Therefore no two people, even saying the same words, are sending the same message. Their voices cause the messages to differ from each other. In live interaction, of course, many more nonverbal messages are present. Nonverbal communication is not nonsense. Nonverbal behavior affects all oral communication situations. We wave, we wink, we hold hands without saying a word.

2. *Nonverbal behavior accounts for most of the communication in human interaction.* This myth is an overreaction to the falsity of the first myth. Early research into nonverbal communication, conducted in both laboratory and field settings, indicated that a large portion of the variability in meaning communicated was a function of nonverbal rather than verbal messages. Although this research conclusively showed the falsity of the traditional myth, it was overinterpreted by many later scholars. Many authors have commonly quoted this early research to conclude that 65 to 93 percent of all meaning communicated is attributable to nonverbal elements (Birdwhistell, 1970; Mehrabian & Ferris, 1967; Mehrabian & Weiner, 1967; Philpot, 1983). Indeed, such results were found to be the case in the studies cited. What is typically ignored, however, is that these early studies were specifically designed to prove the first myth incorrect, and the human interaction studied was not typical of all interaction. Therefore, some subsequent generalizations about the impact of all nonverbal behavior are unjustified. Although nonverbal elements dominate communication in many circumstances, in others nonverbal elements have far fewer significant effects. Therefore, both verbal and nonverbal elements are important in most human interaction, and the meaning

communicated usually depends on the interaction of the two, not on either element alone.

3. *You can read a person like a book.* Besides being the title of a popular book, this myth is held by many individuals who have never studied nonverbal communication. Human behavior is not structured like a language. It is highly variable and idiosyncratic for each individual. Although there are identifiable patterns, these are not nearly strong enough to tell us what a given nonverbal behavior means in all situations. Often nonverbal behavior cannot be translated into definitions that apply to verbal behavior with any degree of confidence. When a baby smiles, it may be that the baby is happy; it may also be that the baby has gas. When an adult smiles, it may be that the person is pleased; it may also be that the person is concealing anger or hatred. Read at your own risk!

4. *If a person does not look you in the eye while talking to you, he or she is not telling you the truth.* This myth is a variant of the previous myth and represents a whole range of myths about nonverbal behavior that we all learned as children. Many of our nonverbal behaviors are subject to our control. Where we direct our gaze is one of those behaviors. Because we learn that people think we are not telling the truth if we don't look them in the eye, we learn to look at them whether we are telling the truth or not. Some research shows that liars are more likely to look someone in the eye than to look away. The best con artists will always look you in the eye—while they are getting you to give them your money!

5. *Although nonverbal behavior differs from person to person, most nonverbal behaviors are natural to all people.* This myth is one that not everyone accepts when it is verbalized but one that almost all of us behave as if we believe. We assume that how we behave nonverbally is normal and that any substantial deviation from that pattern is not normal. This tendency is particularly problematic when we encounter people from another culture. People from different cultures learn different nonverbal behaviors, and all perceive their own as normal. There are also meaningful differences between males and females, between older people and younger people, and among people from various ethnic groups. "Normal" is dependent on one's cultural surroundings.

6. *Nonverbal behavior stimulates the same meanings in different situations.* This myth assumes that nonverbal behaviors are meaningful in themselves. In other words, a handshake or wrinkling one's nose means the same thing in different contexts. This is untrue. Meanings are in people's minds, not nonverbal behaviors. The meaning attributed to nonverbal behavior by others is always influenced by the context in which the behavior occurs. We should never attempt to draw inferences based solely on nonverbal information without considering the entire verbal and nonverbal context. Context must always be considered when attempting to explain communication based on nonverbal behavior.

Gestures and Sign Language

Students often ask the question whether the signing used by deaf speakers is included in the study of nonverbal communication. In this article, Adam Kendon provides an historical account of the concept of signing versus gesturing. The issue has circulated around those who teach linguistics for some time now. Vico used what he called "mute signs" as the basis for why he thought language itself began with gestures. In the United States, Thomas Gallaudet started the first school for the deaf in Connecticut in 1817. Throughout the first half of the nineteenth century, such schools teaching from a French as well as an English model were established. In 1872, a book by Charles Darwin, *Expression of the Emotions in Man and Animals*, drew some attention. Critics of Gallaudet's "manualist" approach referred to it as primitivism. Much of the

concern involved where language came from as opposed to how we use language. Ferdinand de Saussure suggested that the two should be separated. Others have indicated that sign language should be considered different from nonverbal communication (gestures) because sign language was first based on a written form of language. Kendon expresses the view of what he calls "alternate sign languages." Systems used in monasteries, baseball games, and noisy factories are examples. Our concern is with nonverbal communication, including gestures, and we would note that signers often gesture with their faces and other parts of their bodies aside from their hands.

Kendon, A. (2008). Some reflections on the relationship between 'gesture' and 'sign.' *Gesture, 8,* 348–366.

NONVERBAL VERSUS VERBAL MESSAGES

Throughout the almost 5,000 years of recorded history relating to the study of human communication, research and teaching about communication has centered on verbal messages. Not until the eighteenth century did communication scholars began to extend serious attention to the role of nonverbal behavior. By the mid-twentieth century, the study of nonverbal behavior and communication became the focus of intense interest in many scholarly disciplines, from anthropology to communication and from architecture to psychology. A difficult issue facing scholars of nonverbal communication has been the drawing of meaningful and clear distinctions between what is verbal and what is nonverbal. Such clear distinctions have been elusive. Although we cannot provide an absolute distinction between verbal and nonverbal messages, we can draw several less-than-perfect distinctions that will help you to see some of their differences.

The Linguistic Distinction

Verbal messages clearly depend on language, but nonverbal messages do not necessarily depend on the presence of any language. This has led some to suggest that nonverbal communication is simply "communication without words." Of course, much (if not most) nonverbal behavior exists in the presence of spoken words, so this distinction oversimplifies the matter. Nevertheless, the distinction is relevant. Verbal messages depend on language, and language is an arbitrary system of coding meaning so that it may be understood by people who share a common language. Most nonverbal behavior is not part of an arbitrary coding system. Emblems (a type of gesture we consider in Chapter 3) are an exception to this general rule. Similarly, some languages depend solely on nonverbal behavior, and these languages are also arbitrary systems of coding meaning. Some examples are American Sign Language (the gestural language of the hearing-impaired), drum languages in parts of Africa, smoke languages of American Indian tribes, the whistling language of the Canary Islands, semaphore (flag language), and the Morse code for telegraphic communication. Currently, there are many books for various cultures (e.g., Greek, Italian, U.S., and Japanese) that code and classify certain nonverbal behaviors with definite meanings. These books are useful when traveling to different cultures because they tell us what a behavior means to people in another culture. Although there are many exceptions, it is still useful to realize that most verbal messages rely on a language, whereas many nonverbal messages do not.

The Continuity Distinction

Verbal messages are discontinuous—that is, we say some words, then we stop saying words, then we say some more, then we stop, and so on. Nonverbal messages are continuous. Nonverbal behavior never stops. Even when we are asleep, our bodies continue to send nonverbal messages. The absence of behavior sends a message just as much as the presence, if not more so. (Have you ever received the silent treatment?) This fact has led us to this grammatically imperfect but thought-provoking comment: When you are in the presence of another human being, you cannot not communicate.

Although the continuity distinction has fewer exceptions than the linguistic distinction, it is also less than perfect. Nonverbal messages may be considered continuous only if we take them as a whole. Individual nonverbal messages indeed do stop. Gestures begin and end. Eye contact begins and ends. Vocal tones begin and end. Touch begins and ends. Smiles begin and end. However, it is best to think of nonverbal behavior as a package of simultaneous messages rather than as the discrete messages of gesture, voice, touch, and so on. In this sense, the continuity distinction is an important one.

The Processing Distinction

In recent years, much has been made of how the human brain processes incoming information. Early research in the United States provided strong evidence that most people process verbal stimuli on the left side of the brain while processing nonverbal stimuli on the right side of the brain. This suggests that verbal and nonverbal communication are really two separate and distinct communication systems. Subsequent research, however, has cast considerable doubt on this distinction. Humans are not all alike. Left-handed people do not consistently follow the pattern of right-handed people. Thus the processing distinction has not led to the insights researchers had hoped for. It is quite possible that as neurophysiological research advances, we will find important distinctions in the area of processing, but those findings have not yet appeared.

In conclusion, we find ourselves unable to make an absolute distinction between verbal and nonverbal messages. We appreciate the feeling of a member of the U.S. Supreme Court when he found himself unable to define pornography. He begged off by saying, "I know it when I see it." We believe we know what nonverbal messages are when we see them. We hope that by examining the various categories of nonverbal behavior in upcoming chapters, you will be able to do so as well—if you cannot already.

The Outcome Distinction

Verbal messages serve primarily a content or cognitive function. Nonverbal messages serve primarily an affective, relational, or emotional function. The content of what we say is communicated by the verbal message. Both types of messages (verbal and nonverbal) are important to the success of the communication between persons. If we expect others to develop positive attitudes about/toward us, our verbal communication alone may not accomplish this. If we ignore the verbal content of our messages, however, then others may not understand what it is we are trying to convey. Both the nonverbal and verbal components of communication are often necessary for a receiver to get the entire message and understand the meaning behind it.

The Absolute Distinction

Verbal messages generally have an explicit intent or meaning. Nonverbal messages convey an implicit or questionable meaning. Increasingly, nonverbal behaviors have less implicit meaning. This is because of the education taking place in many cultures about the various meanings that often exist behind a nonverbal movement or expression. However, it is unlikely that nonverbal messages will ever be truly explicit (one meaning for one message). Likewise, verbal messages will most likely remain structured and explicit.

INTENTIONALITY AND NONVERBAL COMMUNICATION

We have used the terms *nonverbal behavior* and *nonverbal communication*, but we have not distinguished between them. **Nonverbal behavior** is any of a wide variety of human behaviors that also have the potential for forming communicative messages. Such nonverbal behavior becomes nonverbal communication if another person interprets the behavior as a message and attributes meaning to it. We can engage in nonverbal behavior whether we are alone or someone else is present. We can engage in nonverbal communication only in the presence of one or more people who interpret our behavior as messages and assign meaning to those messages. At a mundane level, we can engage in the nonverbal behavior of scratching ourselves when we are alone. If we do so in the presence of another person and that person interprets our scratching as a message and as showing that we are nervous, for example, we have engaged in nonverbal communication, even if we are not aware of having done so.

For human communication to exist, whether verbal or nonverbal, a source must send a message and a receiver must receive and interpret that message. Sometimes we send messages intentionally and sometimes accidentally. Sometimes receivers perceive our verbal and nonverbal behavior as messages, and sometimes they do not. Figure 1.1 illustrates these distinctions.

In Box 1 of Figure 1.1, the source engages in nonverbal behavior with the intention of sending a message to the receiver, and the receiver interprets the behavior as a message. When this occurs, it is nonverbal communication. This does not mean that the receiver has interpreted the message the way the source intended, but communication has occurred whether or not the intended meaning was stimulated. Therefore the source engages in a behavior with intent to send a message; a receiver receives and interprets the behavior as a message. For example, the source smiles with intent to send a greeting to a receiver; the receiver interprets the smile as a message.

In Box 2 of Figure 1.1, the source has sent an intentional message (the smile), but the receiver did not interpret it as a message. Therefore no nonverbal communication has occurred. This can happen when the receiver simply misses the message (is looking the other way, for example) or does not recognize the behavior as a message. The latter may be illustrated by the case of one partner

		Source	
		Behaves to Send Message	Behaves with No Intent to Send Message
R e c e i v e r	**Interprets Behavior as Message**	1 Nonverbal Communication	3 Nonverbal Communication
	Does Not Interpret Behavior as Message	2 Nonverbal Behavior	4 Nonverbal Behavior

FIGURE 1.1

Nonverbal Behavior and Nonverbal Communication

kicking the other partner under the table to signal that it is time to leave, but the one kicked simply thinks it was accidental behavior and ignores it.

Box 3 of Figure 1.1 represents **accidental communication.** This is probably the most common type of nonverbal communication, and it is this that often causes a communication crisis. A person behaves by smiling, for instance, and others attribute meaning to the behavior without the source even being aware of it. For example, people simply observing the smile might assume that the source was making fun of them, smiling about something funny, smiling because he or she got away with something, or smiling out of a desire to know them better. Often people behave without considering the behavior's message potential for others. For example, a person may arrive a few minutes late for a meeting and think nothing of it. Other people in the meeting, however, may interpret this nonverbal behavior as showing lack of respect for them or a lack of interest in the meeting.

Box 4 of Figure 1.1 represents unintentional behavior that does not result in communication. The source engages in nonverbal behavior but the receiver pays no attention to it. Unfortunately, people who have not studied nonverbal communication tend to overestimate the proportion that falls in this category. They often are insensitive to the accidental messages that they are sending and how receivers are responding to them. Much of the information that belongs in the Box 3 category is thought to belong in Box 4. It does not. This lack of understanding of the communicative potential of nonverbal behavior is what this book is designed to reduce.

CULTURE AND NONVERBAL COMMUNICATION

As we note throughout this book, the communicative potential of nonverbal behavior is heavily influenced by culture. We learn to behave in certain ways through our exposure to our culture. Similarly, our culture teaches us how to interpret the messages generated by other people's nonverbal behavior. Every culture has its own unique way of communicating nonverbally. Thus a nonverbal behavior in one culture may send a strong message in that culture but have little or no message potential in another culture. Similarly, the meanings of nonverbal messages may differ sharply from one culture to another. Sometimes virtually opposite meanings may be stimulated by the same behavior in two different cultures.

This book is written principally from the vantage point of the general U.S. culture. We do not apologize for this ethnocentric approach. To understand the relationship between nonverbal behavior and nonverbal communication, one must work within some cultural framework, because little if any nonverbal behavior has a pan-cultural communicative impact. Once one develops an understanding of nonverbal communication in one culture, one can learn about nonverbal communication in other cultures. Without an understanding of nonverbal communication in one's own culture as well as the culture of the person with whom you are communicating, extensive accidental communication is probable.

FUNCTIONS OF NONVERBAL MESSAGES

Nonverbal communication does not occur in a void. In most circumstances, nonverbal communication occurs jointly with verbal communication. Moreover, although single nonverbal behaviors can send independent messages, more typically nonverbal messages are composed of groups of nonverbal behaviors. Receivers may interpret the various messages independently, but usually they are interpreted together as a message system. Sometimes we draw most of the meaning from the verbal messages, sometimes we draw most from the nonverbal messages, and sometimes the meaning we draw comes from the combined impact of both verbal and nonverbal messages. Whether verbal or nonverbal messages are dominant depends on the situation. As noted earlier, it is not possible to draw a valid generalization across all situations about the relative importance of verbal and nonverbal messages.

It is useful to examine the six major functions of nonverbal messages in relation to verbal messages in communication. Such an analysis will demonstrate how verbal and nonverbal messages often are highly interrelated. These six functions are *complementing, contradicting, accenting, repeating, regulating,* and *substituting*.

Complementing

Some nonverbal messages are consistent with accompanying verbal messages. A nonverbal message that complements the verbal message adds to, reinforces, clarifies, elaborates, or explains the intended meaning of the verbal message. Consider, for example, two people in love. One person says to the other, "I love you." These words alone will probably be well received by the other person. However, if the words are sent in a pleasant voice, accompanied by a long, warm embrace, the message is even stronger. In another vein, consider the person who says, "I'll make your life miserable!" Such a remark might upset us, but it would be much more upsetting if the person who said it were towering over us, yelling in a loud voice, and shaking a fist at us.

Contradicting

Instead of complementing the verbal message, some nonverbal messages contradict, dispute, counter, or are in conflict with the verbal messages. Consider, for example, the employee who has just been reprimanded by a supervisor. The supervisor says, "Tell me you won't make that mistake again." The employee says the words: "I won't make that mistake again," but does so with an extreme pout or sneer or whine while looking down at her or his desk. Would you believe that this employee won't make the mistake again? Most people would not. People tend overwhelmingly to believe the nonverbal rather than the verbal message when the two are contradictory. The exceptions to this are younger children. By about age twelve, children learn most adult nonverbal norms and accept the nonverbal over the verbal message when the mes-

Nonverbal behavior can speak volumes!

sages are in conflict. Typically, younger children have not learned this norm. If a parent whose child walked onto a clean carpet with muddy feet said, "That was really smart, Billy," Billy might take his parent at his or her word and engage in the behavior again in the future, believing that it makes him appear smart.

The latter illustration is an example of sarcasm. People often use sarcasm to make a point. Inherent in the use of sarcasm is the presentation of nonverbal messages that contradict the verbal messages. One must make sure that the nonverbal message clearly contradicts the verbal message if one wants the sarcasm to be understood. Even mature adults sometimes fail to sense the contradiction, and the sarcasm is lost on them. This, of course, is much more common in communication with young children.

Accenting

Nonverbal messages can be used to accent, enhance, emphasize, or highlight a verbal message. Pausing before speaking tends to make what is said next appear more important. Speaking louder than usual highlights the verbal message. Similarly, touching someone while talking emphasizes what is said. In contrast, we can accent a verbal message negatively by presenting it unenthusiastically. When messages are presented in such a way, people tend to think of them as unimportant and quickly forget them. You can probably think of an instructor or boss you have had who treated some material this way. The likelihood of your remembering the content of these messages is low.

Repeating

A nonverbal message that serves the function of repeating, reiterating, or restating the verbal is one that could stand alone if the verbal were not present. Such messages usually are emblems and are discussed in more detail in Chapter 3. As an example, however, consider the case in which you are ordering two tacos at a fast-food restaurant. You are likely to say you want two tacos and simultaneously hold up two fingers. The nonverbal repeats the verbal.

Regulating

Verbal interactions are coordinated through regulation and direction. Such regulation and management are accomplished primarily through nonverbal messages. These regulatory nonverbal messages include looking at or away from the other person, raising a finger while pausing to show that you have not finished speaking, raising or lowering the inflection of your voice, and so on. For example, when we wish to signal that it is the other person's turn to talk, we finish our current statement with a lowered inflection, look directly at the other person, and stop gesturing. Such nonverbal behavior regulates or manages the flow of verbal messages.

Substituting

Substitution occurs when nonverbal messages are sent instead of verbal messages. Waving at or beckoning toward another person is a common example. Glaring at another person may communicate the same thing as saying something negative. Often we let people know that we are angry with them by not sending them any verbal messages. Our nonverbal message of absence from their presence can express the same meaning, and it doesn't give them a chance to talk back!

These six functions do not always occur independently. It is quite possible for complementing, repeating, and accenting to occur simultaneously. Nonverbal messages can serve to accomplish a variety of functions. Sometimes these functions can be accomplished with a single nonverbal behavior, but more commonly a group of different behaviors is used to accomplish a given function. Sometimes more than one function is accomplished simultaneously. Sometimes verbal communication is involved, and sometimes it is not. In short, although verbal messages can sometimes stand virtually alone, as can individual nonverbal messages, more commonly there is interaction between nonverbal behavior and verbal behavior to produce meaning in the minds of others.

For the most part, verbal messages serve primarily a content function, whereas nonverbal messages serve primarily an affective or relational function. The cognitive content of what we are sending to others usually is sent primarily via verbal messages. The affective or relational meaning is sent primarily via nonverbal messages. This relational, emotional, or affective meaning often is called **nonverbal immediacy.** When one person is nonverbally immediate with another person, the other person often has a feeling of physical or psychological closeness to the immediate person. Although verbal messages can have an impact on immediacy, nonverbal messages usually have a much greater impact. We consider immediacy in greater detail in a later chapter.

CATEGORIES OF NONVERBAL MESSAGES

Individual nonverbal behavior serves as a communicative message only within a context and often in the company of many other nonverbal behaviors as well as verbal messages. Communication as a whole is a process that involves a variety of messages within a given context. It is a dynamic, ongoing, interactive process, not a linear one. If you turn the light switch on, the light comes on. If you step on the brake, the car slows. If you press a key on a computer keyboard, a function takes place. These are linear processes.

Communication is not like these linear processes. The same verbal or nonverbal behaviors do not always produce the same outcome. Messages are processed by receivers within contexts. Therefore it is rare that different receivers in different contexts interpret the same messages in the same way.

It is important to keep this in mind in reading this book. We will divide nonverbal behavior into several categories and examine each category in some detail. Nonverbal messages generated by each category do not exist in isolation but rather in the company of messages from other categories—verbal messages, contexts, and people functioning as message receivers. Although we discuss some effects of messages in each category, we must remember that these effects are influenced by more than the message from the given category alone. We hope that this structure helps you to understand how the parts work together to produce the total communicative effect.

This structure is outlined in the following text. At this point, we need to consider the various categories of nonverbal messages that are considered in detail in the following chapters: *physical appearance, gesture and movement, face and eye behavior, vocal behavior, space, touch, environment,* and *time.*

Physical Appearance

The first message we send to anyone with whom we come in contact is conveyed by our physical appearance. If that message is deplored by the other person, he or she may not even consider further communication. There are many aspects of physical appearance that produce potential messages, including body size, body shape, facial features, hair, skin color, height, weight, and the clothing and objects we wear. Each of these can have an important impact on our communication with others.

Gesture and Movement

The study of the communicative aspects of gesture and bodily movement is known as **kinesics** (Birdwhistell, 1970). This research focuses on the movements of hands and arms, posture, torso, and bodily movements (such as bending or walking). Messages generated by this type of behavior have often been called *body language,* but this term is a misnomer. Although the body is sending messages, such messages do not form a linguistic system (the gestural language of the hearing-impaired is an important exception) and thus do not represent a language in any normal sense of that term. Viewing all bodily movements and gestures as if they constituted a language may lead a person to believe that he or she can learn the meaning of the language and thus read people—this is not the case.

Face and Eye Behavior

The study of the communicative aspects of eye behavior is known as **oculesics.** Because it is virtually impossible to separate the messages sent by the eyes and those sent by the face (such as raising an eyebrow), we prefer to consider these together. These messages have a major influence on expressing emotions and regulating interactions between people.

Vocal Behavior

The study of the communicative aspects of the voice is known as **vocalics** or **paralanguage.** Characteristics of the voice and its use, including the accent with which we speak and the dialect we use, have a major impact on how verbal messages are received. Some researchers argue that more of the meaning in interpersonal communication is stimulated by vocalic messages than by the verbal messages themselves. While this may not always be true, it certainly is true much of the time.

Space

The study of the communicative aspects of space is known as **proxemics.** There are two important areas in this research—territoriality (claiming or marking space) and use of personal space (interactive space). Each has an important bearing on the kinds of messages we send as we use space. There is reason to believe that our basic approach to space is at least partly instinctual. Nevertheless, humans differ greatly in their use of space and, as a result, send different nonverbal messages.

Touch

The study of the communicative aspects of touch is known as **haptics.** Touch has been called the most potent nonverbal message in communication. Although this may not be universally true, it is generally true in the United States, where touch is so commonly forbidden. Touch, in this culture at least, sends a potent message, one that can rarely be ignored. Although touching is often taboo in this culture, it is less so in many other cultures.

Environment

Researchers in many disciplines have examined the impact of environment on human behavior and on communication behavior specifically. Because environment is not human behavior per se, it may seem strange to include this category in a book on nonverbal behavior. However, because environment can have a major influence on communication and we can exert considerable control over our environment through our behavior, we have chosen to include it. In relating environment to communication, we look at such things as architecture, interior spatial arrangements, music, lighting, color, temperature, and scent. The limited research involving the study of the communicative aspects of scent and smell has been called **olfactics.** If beauty is in the eye of the beholder, then scent is in the nose of the sniffer. People react differently to scents and smells. Often we send important nonverbal messages through our use of scents and smells. American society shows its concern with this nonverbal category by spending millions of dollars annually on deodorants and perfumes.

Time

The study of the communicative aspects of time is called **chronemics.** Few cultures are as dependent upon time as is our culture. Our use of time sends strong messages about how we feel about ideas and people. For example, if you are late for a meeting or class, a negative message is usually attached to your behavior. Because most people in this culture are so time-bound, they fail to realize what their responses to time might communicate to others. It has been said that time talks. "Time shouts" might be a more accurate statement.

Glossary of Terminology

Accidental communication occurs when people behave and others attribute meaning to the behavior without the sender intending it.

Chronemics is the study of the communicative aspects of time.

Haptics is the study of the communicative aspects of touch.

Human communication is the process of one person stimulating meaning in the mind of another person (or persons) by means of verbal and/or nonverbal messages.

Kinesics is the study of the communicative aspects of gestures and bodily movements.

Nonverbal behavior is any of a wide variety of human behaviors that also have the potential for being interpreted as a communicative message.

Nonverbal communication is the process of one person stimulating meaning in the mind of another person (or persons) by means of nonverbal messages.

Nonverbal immediacy refers to an individual's nonverbal behavior that causes another person to have a feeling of physical or psychological closeness to that individual.

Oculesics is the study of the communicative aspects of eye behavior.

Olfactics is the study of the communicative aspects of scent and smell.

Proxemics is the study of the communicative aspects of space.

Vocalics or paralanguage is the study of the communicative aspects of the voice.

CHAPTER 2

Physical Appearance

Students at Ramkhamhaeng University in Bangkok, Thailand.

Source: Photo by C. Price Walt

Many of us develop opinions about people we meet based on how they look, what they wear, whether we think they are attractive, and what objects they use to adorn their bodies or accessorize their clothing. Nonverbal messages based on physical appearance may be as important as any nonverbal messages we receive from other people. They may even be more important.

- First, these appearance-based messages are generally the first received.
- Second, these appearance messages initially have a strong influence on our willingness or unwillingness to communicate with another.

- Third, these appearance messages have a strong influence on how the relationship might develop.
- Fourth, these appearance messages are often used to make initial judgments about another person.
- Fifth, the initial judgments made about another person may or may not be representative of the person.

Simply put, if we see someone who looks like us or is appealing to us, we have a greater likelihood of approaching that person, communicating with him or her, and beginning a relationship. In this culture, we are less likely to approach people who look too different from us. In this chapter, we discuss the significance of physical appearance as it influences our perceptions of attractiveness and our perceptions of others.

ATTRACTIVENESS

When someone says that a person is attractive, what do they really mean? Do people possess something called attractiveness? Is it a characteristic of certain individuals? Is singer Beyoncé attractive? Is Denzel Washington attractive? In our culture, we think of **attractiveness** as a perception based on the physical attributes and features of the people we are considering. Attractiveness is something we perceive in someone else and they in us. It does not exist on its own. Attractiveness or nonattractiveness is in the eye of the beholder (Berscheid & Walster, 1969, 1971, 1972, 1978; Cash & Janda, 1984; Dion, Berscheid & Walster, 1972; Feingold, 1992; Lewis & Bierly, 1990; McCroskey & Richmond, 1996; McCroskey, Wrench & Richmond, 2003; Mottet & Richmond, 2002; Richmond, 2002; Richmond & Hickson, 2002; Richmond & McCroskey, 2000; Stone, Singletary, & Richmond, 1999; Walster, Aronson, Abrahams, & Rohmann, 1966).

Types of Attractiveness

Wilson and Nias (1999) state that "most people find beauty more powerful than they will admit" (p. 101). They continue by suggesting that most people, when asked what qualities they look for in a friend or lover, include such things as intelligence, sense of humor, caring, honesty, and warmth. However, the body of research and evidence about physical attractiveness concludes that physical attractiveness may be the single most important factor in determining whom we choose as our friends, dates, lovers, and coworkers. Initially, personality may not count in the early development of relationships; it is beauty and physical attractiveness that counts (Bixler & Nix-Rice, 1997; Heilman & Stopeck, 1985; Morris, 1985; Richmond, 1996; Sabatelli & Rubin, 1986; Walster, Aronson, Abrahams, & Rohmann, 1966; Widgery & Ruch, 1981).

Generally, attractiveness is the degree to which we perceive another person as someone with whom we would want to associate. *Attraction* is a term drawn from the field of physics. Some entities are magnetically drawn to each other. While magnetic forces do not draw people together, the analogy is a good one. We even sometimes refer to an individual as having a magnetic personality.

People are, indeed, psychologically drawn to one other (Mehrabian, 1971a, 1971b; Richmond, 2002). From this perspective, three different types of attractiveness were identified many years ago by McCroskey and McCain (1974). These three types of interpersonal attractiveness still hold true today.

The first type, the one with which we are primarily concerned here, is **physical attractiveness.** This type of attractiveness refers to the degree to which we perceive another person as attractive because of her or his physical attributes. While some people may prefer to look at the face first to determine attractiveness, others look at the body first, and still others scrutinize the entire package from head to toe. Although writers on nonverbal communication have had difficulty explaining the forces involved in physical attractiveness, clearly this type of attractiveness plays a important role in determining our interactions with others, particularly with strangers (Andersen, 1999; Henley, 1977; Widgery & Ruch, 1981; Morris, Gorham, Cohen, & Huffman, 1996). We usually prefer to converse with strangers whom we perceive to be good-looking, pretty, or handsome. People often attempt to avoid contact with those they find physically unattractive.

The second type of attractiveness is **social attractiveness.** Social attractiveness is the degree to which we perceive another person as someone with whom we would like to play, fraternize, associate, or socialize.

The final type of attractiveness is **task attractiveness.** This is the degree to which we perceive another person as someone with whom we would like to work, conduct business, or have as a coworker or teammate.

Although perceptions of physical attractiveness are distinct from perceptions of social and task attractiveness, this does not mean these are totally unrelated perceptions. Often, particularly during initial encounters, we perceive another person as physically appealing and then see him or her as socially or task attractive as well. On the other hand, we tend to judge physically unattractive persons as undesirable to socialize or work with. Although these are initial impressions, they often affect future interactions with new acquaintances as well as decisions regarding future communication. Perceptions of social and task attractiveness may change over time. These changes may occur despite the physical attraction. However, in a newly formed relationship, physical attractiveness may determine one's level of task or social attraction for another. Furthermore, we may find some people less than attractive, but as we begin to socialize or work with them, they take on a better appearance in our eyes. In conclusion:

- Initially, physical attractiveness may determine whether a person will approach another person.
- Initially, physical attractiveness may affect whether communication with another person takes place.
- Initially, physical attractiveness may affect what type of communication occurs.
- Generally, we like physically attractive people more than physically unattractive people.

Redefining Hijab

According to Droogsma, some American women object to Muslim women wearing a veil or headscarf in the United States. The hijab serves as a means of identifying the women with Muslim culture. The women who wear the hijab are viewed by others as wearing the veil as a sign of weakness and submission to their husbands. However, the wearers perceive the hijab as loyalty to their culture. In a sense, it makes them appear more authentic and not for their appearance of "womanhood." Because they do not adapt to American fashion, they feel that they are freer. Understanding a culture depends in part on understanding their dress.

Droogsma, R. A. (2007). Redefining hijab: American Muslim women's standpoints on veiling. Journal of Applied Communication Research, *35, 294–319.*

- As social and task attractiveness begin to emerge as important types of attractiveness, the impact of the physical appearance of another person may dissipate.
- As social or task attractiveness begins to become a part of the relationship, the person may actually seem more or less physically attractive to us.

However, in this culture, we should remember that often our baser instincts rule whom we approach and whom we do not approach. When we need directions to the mall, are we going to approach the average good-looking person on the street or the sweaty, smelly, red-faced, homely person? Nine times out of ten we will approach the more attractive of the two.

What Is Attractive Today May Be Out Tomorrow

What features we consider attractive are highly dependent on cultural and historical influences, as well as current trends (Gudykunst & Kim, 1992; Hall, 1984). In North American culture, recent trends for women suggest that the well-toned, athletic, superthin, almost emaciated look is in, whereas earlier generations found the ample, buxom, plump look more appealing. Recent trends for men suggest that the well-toned, tall, masculine look is in, whereas the well-fed look was more attractive in the past (Feingold & Mazzella, 1998; Henig, 1996; Johnston, 1994; Jourard & Secord, 1955; Kalick, Zebrowitz, Langlois & Johnson, 1998; Kaltenbach, 1991; Reyes, 1993; Singh, 1964; Stark, 1986; Walker, 1963).

Americans spend more money on cosmetic surgery than any other group in the world. Americans seem to spend much of their time worrying about appearance and impressing others. This keeps people such as Joya Paterson in business. Paterson holds seminars on guidelines for purchasing the correct bra. She suggests that 85 percent of women wear the wrong bra. Her seminars focus on figuring out each woman's body size and cup size, trying on the bra, and studying it. American women want comfort in their bras as well as a fit that enhances their appearance. Although leaders of the clothing industry may fear that the American public will sooner or later stop spending small fortunes on clothing and accessories, it has not happened.

Hairstyles for men and women change constantly and, we suspect, will continue to change as people's ideas of physical attractiveness evolve. Fair skin was once not only a mark of beauty but also a significant sign of social status. Only wealthy women and men could afford to stay inside. Now, tanned skin has become a sign that one has leisure time to sunbathe and travel to warm places. Recently, among health-conscious individuals, fair skin has become attractive again. The concern about skin cancer caused by exposure to the sun has influenced the culture's perception of what is attractive.

During the 1920s, American women went to great lengths to make their chests appear flat and their hips small. In more recent times, padded bras and breast implants have been used to enhance the breasts. By the 1990s, American men were receiving hair transplants, including on their chests, so that they would appear more masculine. Men and women are having liposuction to remove fat. Teenagers are begging parents for a new nose instead of a bicycle for Christmas.

Physical attractiveness depends on culture as well. In one culture, men appreciate women whose necks have been stretched to twelve inches and whose noses or lips are pierced with wooden jewelry. Many Afghan and Pakistani women are expected to cover their beauty, only showing eyes and eyebrows. The Chinese once believed that a woman's small feet were a sign of fertility. Therefore, from infancy, Chinese females would have their feet tightly bound to thwart growth. Although such binding is no longer common in most areas of China, small-footed women are still seen as attractive by many Chinese. In a few African cultures, people bind their heads to flatten them, stretch their lips with wooden plates, and scar their bodies in various places to make them more appealing. Many cultures consider body piercing and tattooing attractive.

In the United States, such appearances have been considered to be "low class" and ugly until recently. In the 1950s, for example, operators of tattoo parlors often refused a woman's request for service unless she was over 21 years old, married, and accompanied by her husband (Vevea, 2008). Today the variety and sophistication of tattoos is phenomenal. From prison tattoos, which prisoners use to show their rebellion against the uniformity of clothing, to women's preferences for tattoos with personal meanings to entire bodies used as canvases, today's younger population is much more accepting of tattoos. In every culture at different times, the need to be attractive has driven people to get their bodies shaped, sucked, pulled, twisted, nipped, tucked, or pushed into multiple shapes for the sake of appearance, group identification, status, likeableness, and popularity. Although it would be easy to laugh at these behaviors in other cultures and to muse about the lack of sophistication of such people, we must take care, for the last laugh may be on us. Such manipulation of the body is common in the United States. Breast implants, breast reductions, face-lifts, hair implants, liposuction, and other forms of plastic surgery; high-heeled pumps, body enhancers, padded bras, and skin-tight clothing; shaved legs, faces, and underarms; pierced lips, eyebrows, noses, and tongues are all examples of ways Americans have penalized their bodies and endured unnecessary pain to make themselves more appealing, well-liked, popular, and acceptable. Our phobia of unshaven underarms on women causes howls of laughter from people in most other parts of the world. Our culture is also addicted to diets, diets, and more diets, or the "healthy lifestyle" as it is commonly known today. If the diets and healthy life changes do not work, there's always liposuction! During the last decade in the United States, liposuction has become the most popular plastic surgery for both men and women. At one time, most of these self-mutilations were almost exclusively engaged in by women. Today they are just as likely to be engaged in by men. We can hardly make fun of other cultures and the things they do to their bodies to be more attractive. Maybe we should be laughing at each other—or just ourselves.

Why, then, is attractiveness so important? Why do we go to such extreme lengths to be perceived as attractive? The answer lies in the nonverbal messages our appearance communicates to others. Others use our appearance as an

Body piercing is becoming common in the American culture.

important source of information about us. They attribute to us certain characteristics, predict our social behavior, and make judgments about our success, competence, and character in our professional and personal lives. Think for a moment about your own reactions. When you see someone who is physically attractive, do you automatically make certain judgments about that person? In a class focusing on nonverbal communication, one young man responded anonymously to this question in this way:

> I tend to judge a book by its cover and a person by his or her looks. When I see somebody who is unattractive I tend to lose interest in wanting to meet them. Sometimes I even try to avoid them. In brief, it seems like these men and women don't care much about what other people think about them. Unattractive people also tend to be sloppy. I wonder sometimes how they think they are going to get by in this world. I know they can't help the way they look, but they could at least stay at home.

A female student in the same class, in response to the same question made the following observations:

> The way a person looks says a lot about them. I find myself being more interested in people (especially men) I think are attractive. They seem more sure of themselves and confident. They don't get as nervous around other people because they don't have to be self-conscious about their looks. Since they have more experience around lots of other people, they probably know more about how to act at parties.

Although these are responses selected to represent extreme views, they represent the views of many people.

Image Fixation

Image fixation (IF) is a long-term view a person has about her or his image or body. IF is an often painful preoccupation with one's physical appearance and attributes (body shape, size, height, weight, and so on). This syndrome can begin to become more important than other issues in a person's life. The person with high IF is constantly comparing her or his appearance to that of others. You can almost hear that person saying, "If only I could be prettier or taller, then. . . ." Please complete the questionnaire in Figure 2.1 (Richmond, 2000). Compute your score to determine how much you focus on your own appearance.

The concepts of image fixation and **appearance obsession** are similar. Both are associated with excessive attention to our own appearance. Our self-perceived physical attractiveness is related to our self-esteem. Our opinion of ourselves is strongly affected by how we look. Trying to measure up to unreasonable standards determined by others (media, significant others, etc.) may make us insecure, self-conscious, and depressed, and perhaps may even lead to physical health problems (Johnston, 1994).

Directions: This instrument is composed of twenty statements concerning feelings about your perception of your physical image. Please indicate the degree to which each statement applies to you by marking whether you (5) Strongly agree; (4) Agree; (3) are Undecided; (2) Disagree; or (l) Strongly disagree. Work quickly; record your first impression.

_____ **1.** I think my life would improve if my body were better looking.

_____ **2.** I am not sensitive to other people's comments about my weight.*

_____ **3.** I would like to have cosmetic surgery.

_____ **4.** I starve or do not eat at least one day a week.

_____ **5.** I am comfortable around attractive persons of my age/sex.*

_____ **6.** I am constantly comparing my body and face to my peers.

_____ **7.** I am not sensitive to other people's comments about my general appearance.*

_____ **8.** Several times each week, I feel I look fat.

_____ **9.** I berate myself about my general physical appearance.

_____ **10.** Most of the time, I think I look good in my clothes.*

_____ **11.** I change clothes constantly in order to get the "right" look.

_____ **12.** I often buy new clothes for comfort more than appearance.*

_____ **13.** I feel good about my overall appearance.*

_____ **14.** I am not sensitive to other people's comments about my height.*

_____ **15.** I will avoid social situations if I feel I do not have the right body or clothing.

_____ **16.** I wear big clothes to hide my appearance defects.

_____ **17.** When I look in the mirror, I like how I look.*

_____ **18.** I would not trade bodies with any one of my friends.*

_____ **19.** Comments from peers about what is the "right" look make me want to change my appearance.

_____ **20.** I find myself focusing more on who I am than how I look.*

IF Scoring: **Step 1:** Add items without an asterisk (items 1, 3, 4, 6, 8, 9, 11, 15, 16, 19)

Step 2: Add items with an asterisk (items 2, 5, 7,10, 12, 13, 14, 17, 18, 20)

Step 3: 60 + (Score from Step 1) - (Score from Step 2)

Your final score can range from 20 to 100.

Interpretation: High scores = higher levels of dissatisfaction with image or high image fixation.

FIGURE 2.1
Image Fixation Questionnaire

IT'S A FACT. Physical attractiveness is prized in the North American culture and other cultures. There is nothing wrong with wanting to look good, but when we become obsessed with our appearance or develop image fixation, then our focus is on how we look and not on what we have to offer others.

IMPACT OF AN APPEARANCE OBSESSION. More women than men have IF syndrome; however, men are catching up. Often people preoccupied with their images can experience a variety of negative feelings, including frustration, depression, embarrassment, shame, helplessness, and insecurity as well as mood swings. They are easily wounded by others when hurtful or demeaning comments are made about their bodies or general appearance, and they often feel unattractive even when they are widely considered attractive.

A PROFILE OF THE "IF" PERSON. Image fixators (IFs) have some common behaviors that set them apart from people who have a normal IF. High IFs are those who engage in some of the following behaviors: chronic dieting, "yo-yo" dieting, excessive exercise, excessive shopping, excessive appearance-checking, constant self-improvement, plastic surgery, weighing themselves once or several times a day, avoidance of social events that emphasize looks or bodies, and reliance on fashion to soothe. While there is some support for the idea that if you look good, you will feel good, the IF person places the emphasis on looking good to feel good.

Judgments Generated

Most of us regularly judge people by their appearance. Research in this area also suggests that we make relational decisions based upon a person's physical attractiveness. People who are rated as more attractive are often judged to be more socially desirable in many ways. Attractive people are perceived to be more successful in their careers, more sexually active, happier about their life situations, more responsive, sensitive, interesting, competent, and even better at persuading others. Sometimes we go so far as to perceive attractive persons as holding more prestigious jobs, having more friends, and having better marriages. In education, attractive students are viewed by teachers as more outgoing, educationally prepared, intelligent, and social, and as having parents who are more interested in their education. In business, attractive persons are more likely to be hired, evaluated positively, promoted, and socially accepted and less likely to be fired. In health care, attractive patients may receive more attention, care, and communication from physicians and nurses than unattractive patients. In summary, attractive persons generally fare better in our culture than unattractive persons (Dion, Berscheid, & Walster, 1972; Feiman & Gill, 1978; Moore, Hickson, & Stacks, 2010; Mehrabian, 1971a; Raiscot, 1983, 1986; Schlenker, 1980; Shriver, 2002; Tanke, 1982).

Attractiveness: A Double-Edged Sword?

Many of us assume that attractive women are frequently being asked for dates and attractive men seldom have trouble finding women to accompany them to movies, parties, and other social functions. Although these perceptions are often true, sometimes they are not. Studies of extremely attractive males and females show that they are often lonely and rejected by members of the opposite sex. They are seen as too attractive, or, as one person put it, too good to be true. We may see them as "out of our league." Clearly, many of our perceptions of others based on their physical attractiveness may prove to be correct. However, we sometimes completely misperceive the situation. Examples of the drawbacks of great attractiveness include stories told by Miss America candidates who report missing their senior proms because no one asked them, or by prominent athletes with classic good looks who describe being consistently turned down for dates in high school.

Perceptions of physical attractiveness are associated with many personality characteristics. One study asked subjects to rate attractive and unattractive persons on a variety of personality variables. The attractive people were judged as warmer, more genuine, sincere, mentally stable, sociable, and affable. Most of these perceptions are positive and desirable. Thus, one would expect that great attractiveness should produce only positive outcomes. However, to the highly attractive person, life is not always a bed of roses. Many report having to overcome the negative judgments of others. For example, highly attractive persons could be viewed as incompetent, non-social, or stuffy. Whether attractive or unattractive, we sometimes find ourselves stereotyped in ways that significantly influence our interactions with others.

Another major issue related to attractiveness involves interaction behavior itself. We have seen from the preceding discussion how attractiveness affects perceptions. Now let's consider the effects of attractiveness on interaction in different contexts.

Effects of Attractiveness

EDUCATIONAL SETTING. In the educational environment, scholars have found some interesting relationships between physical attractiveness and student-teacher interaction. Attractive students receive higher grades than their less attractive counterparts. Observations in classrooms show that teachers engage in fewer interactions with unattractive students and initiate more communication and respond to their more attractive students more readily. Not only do we see such behavior from teachers, but classmates are also less likely to communicate with the less attractive classmates. In early grades, the physically unattractive student begins to experience the value our culture places on good looks. Others have reported that even misbehavior in the classroom is interpreted differently depending on a child's attractiveness. Teachers generally perceive the unattractive child as a chronic behavior problem, whereas the attractive child is more likely to be judged to have a temporary problem. We should stress here that teachers usually do not engage in such behavior maliciously. They, like others, are not immune to the stereotypes and expectations many persons have of others' physical appearance. This does not, however, negate the significance of the impact that teachers' actions and reactions have upon their students' successes or failures

(Aiken, 1963; Dion, Berscheid, & Walster, 1972; Richmond, 1996; Singh, 1964; Wilson & Nias, 1999). In addition, Richmond (2002) has reported that teachers portray different images depending on how they are dressed. Those who dress more formally are viewed as competent, organized, prepared, and knowledgeable. Teachers who dress casually or informally (but not sloppy) are seen as friendly, outgoing, receptive, fair, and flexible (see also Frymier & Wanzer, 2006).

PERSUASIVE SETTING.   We stated earlier that physically attractive people often are perceived as more persuasive. Attractive people have greater success at getting others to do what they want them to do. Attractive women, in particular, are better at changing the attitudes of males. Important work has shown that attractiveness even pays off in the American court system. Not only are attractive persons more likely to be found innocent of charges brought against them, but when they are found guilty, their chances of receiving lighter sentences are better. With these kinds of results, it is no mystery why most actors in television commercials are physically appealing people. Their job is to get us to buy their products. Sales-training consultants place great stress on an attractive physical appearance. They realize the impact that first impressions have on a potential customer's decision to purchase a product. For example, many major pharmaceutical companies make sure their sales representatives are not only task and socially attractive but also physically attractive. These companies know that the physically attractive person has a better chance of getting her or his foot in the door of an office or hospital than an unattractive person (Berscheid & Walster, 1978; Efran, 1974; Hewitt & German, 1987; Mills & Aronson, 1965; Walster, Aronson, Abrahams, & Rohmann, 1966; Widgery & Ruch, 1981).

The results of an interview with a manager of a regional office of a life insurance company and one of her employees in a large city in California illustrate the impact of attractiveness in that setting. At a luncheon engagement one day, this manager introduced a young man the manager claimed was her best salesperson. The young sales agent had a striking appearance: blond, tanned, tall, and lean, with a most charming smile. His resemblance to a younger Robert Redford was remarkable. Because the young man had been a life insurance salesman for only a short time, the interviewer was curious about the salesman's quick success with a product that is usually quite difficult to sell. The agent's response was not surprising.

> I sell only to women. When marketing individual policies, I either identify households run by single women or make sure the wife is present when I give my sales pitch to her husband. When selling group policies, I try to find companies that have women in charge of such decisions. After that, my job is easy.

This young sales agent was not arrogant or self-centered, but he did realize that his best asset at guaranteeing success was his physical attractiveness to women.

Before jumping to the conclusion that only women are susceptible to such influences, be assured that males are equally susceptible. How else can we explain the effectiveness of advertisements for male-oriented products that prominently display female models? Many, many alcohol and cigarette ads feature attractive and appealing women (Myers & Biocca, 1999).

INTERVIEW SETTING. Physically attractive people seem to have an edge on other people when it comes to interviewing for a job. Many researchers have suggested various types of people who they claim have the big advantage during job interviews. According to Molloy (1975, 1978, 1983, 1988), the first type is the beautiful person. He suggests that people who are good-looking have a three-to-four-times-greater chance of being hired for almost any position, whether it is keyboarding, computer repair, sales, or management. Looks alone do not guarantee you a job, but when all else is considered, they generally help. Whether in business or social contexts, we seem to want to be surrounded by the beautiful people. Some nonverbal scholars have even suggested that one important consideration for executives when choosing a secretary is the candidate's potential to decorate the office environment with her or his appearance (Henley, 1977; Keenan, 1976; Keenan & Wedderburn, 1975; Richmond, 1996; Sterrett, 1978; Webster, 1964; Young & Beier, 1977).

DATING AND MARRIAGE. Our perceptions of physical attractiveness have an important influence on dating and marriage decisions as well. When people are asked by researchers whether they would marry a person they would rank low on physical attributes, the results are interesting. The results show that men would more likely reject women who are not good-looking, but women do not seem quite as concerned about the physical appearance of potential marriage partners. In contemporary culture, however, it is much more acceptable for women to talk about the physical attractiveness of men than it was fifty years ago. Another interesting finding in the research literature is that men are reported to want partners who are more attractive than they perceive themselves to be; whereas, women would marry men who are similar to them in attractiveness (Walster, Aronson, Abrahams, & Rohmann, 1966; Wilson & Nias, 1999).

Because such general preferences could lead to constant conflicts if everyone shared the same standards of judgment for physical attractiveness, we are left to speculate about the importance of self-esteem in such decisions. We should stress that in hiring, dating, and marriage decisions, physical attractiveness is not always the number-one priority. However, sometimes it is. Studies have shown that, within the context of a blind date between college students, physical attractiveness was the primary predictor of whether those involved said they liked their date. Subsequent research revealed that perceptions of a date's attractiveness also predicted whether the partner would want to ask the person out again. As the relationship develops, attractiveness gradually takes a backseat to other considerations. Of course, if the perception of attractiveness is not there in the first place, the relationship may not continue long enough for those other considerations to come into play (Berscheid & Walster, 1978).

THE MATCHING HYPOTHESIS. The matching hypothesis suggests that, even though men and women might be attracted to people more attractive than themselves, most people select to date or choose partners considered to be in the same attractiveness category as they are. Often you see couples who look like they belong together or who are the perfect match. Why, then, do people seem mismatched at times? Remember, attractiveness is in the eye of the beholder; therefore, Heather or Jon may perceive themselves as more attractive than others do. Thus, in relational development stages, Heather and Jon are not daunted by persons who are more attractive; rather, they seek them out and date them. Some attractive persons do not view themselves to be as attractive as others do and therefore often date less attractive persons. What then is the perfect match? No one knows. However, in our culture, people often comment when others seem mismatched. For example, if Jennifer Aniston had married Willie Nelson, what would people have said?

Physical attractiveness has a substantial impact on our communication with other persons. These powerful nonverbal messages influence our decisions about approaching or avoiding others, dating or not dating, marrying or not marrying, hiring or not hiring; they also influence our expectations about the future success of others. Let's now turn to a discussion of the particular aspects of physical appearance.

PERSONAL BODY CONCEPT

Ask yourself these questions:

- What parts of others' bodies do I think are the most important?
- Are they the same as the ones I focus on in myself, in terms of my satisfaction with my own body?
- Is there any relationship between the two categories?

Skin color need not hinder positive communication.

It should not surprise you that the body parts you find most important in judging attractiveness in others may also be the ones you are either extremely satisfied with or dissatisfied with in yourself.

How you feel about your body has an impact on your self-concept as a whole. Your **personal body concept** is the perception you have of how attractive your body is, and what you perceive to be the particular attributes of your body. The importance of the personal body concept to our discussion of nonverbal communication is twofold: First, the concept is developed through of our communication with others; second, it influences our communication with others. Let's look at these factors more closely.

The thoughts and feelings we have about our own bodies did not simply materialize in our minds at some magic age. Personal body concept, whether positive or negative, develops gradually. The influencing factors involve our interactions with other people, particularly if those people are important to us. Significant others provide us with many verbal and nonverbal messages that communicate the feelings and attitudes they have about our bodies. We eventually incorporate their judgments into our judgments of ourselves.

Research indicates the significant impact that peer and parental judgments have on children's personal body concepts. One study has shown that children with predominantly negative concepts about their own attractiveness and abilities received negative messages from their parents. Let us consider an illustration. Ten-year-old Scottie was not an attractive child. He was quite plump, his nose was too large, and he had greasy, limp hair. Scottie's parents were often self-conscious about his appearance while they were with friends and acquaintances. One day, Scottie overheard his parents lamenting to a neighbor, "We are afraid Scottie will never be very popular, given the way he looks. He's not at all athletic-looking, you know. We constantly worry that the other kids at school will tease him about his weight. On top of that, his grandfather makes us so angry when he refers to Scottie as having the biggest cheeks on the block."

Feelings of inadequacy are influenced by our communication, and they also affect future interactions. Scottie's feelings about his body will eventually affect his communication behavior. He may choose to withdraw from or avoid associations with peers at school for fear that they will ridicule him. His feelings may influence his decisions about sports, leisure activities, friends, dating, and even his career choice.

Satisfaction with our bodies is important to both our self-esteem and our interpersonal relationships. One does not have to be movie-star attractive to be satisfied with the appearance and attributes of one's body. One rule does tend to hold true, however: The more satisfied people are with their bodies (regardless of their actual appearance) the better their chances of being happy about themselves. This satisfaction, in turn, probably contributes to healthier interactions with others (Berscheid, Walster, & Bohrnstedt, 1973; Cortes & Gatti, 1965; Gashin & Simmons, 2002; Haseltine, 2002; Henig, 1996; Johnston, 1994; Jourard & Secord, 1955; Korda, 1975; McCroskey, Larson, & Knapp, 1971; Knapp & Vangelisti, 2000; Richmond, 1996; Sheldon, 1940, 1942, 1954; Walker, 1963; Wells & Siegel, 1961).

NONVERBAL MESSAGES OF BODY SHAPE AND SIZE

Whether you realize it or not, the general shape and size of your body communicate nonverbal messages. Figure 2.2 is a self-description survey about your body. Follow the instructions and work your way through the survey.

Many writers have shown that a person's body shape and general temperament are closely related. Sheldon (1940, 1942, 1954) is usually credited with originating this idea. Sheldon believed that there are three classifications of body types, and worked to develop a method called **somatotyping** to categorize individuals into one of three major types. There has been considerable criticism of some of Sheldon's experimental methods, his original conceptualization of temperament, and some of his mathematical calculations, but others have taken Sheldon's work and improved on it, and many writers on nonverbal communication now think there is merit to his work.

The first general body type is called the **endomorph.** Persons who are endomorphs have rounded, oval-shaped bodies, are usually heavy (though not necessarily obese), and are often described as pear-shaped. The second type is the **mesomorph.** Mesomorphs are characterized by a triangular body shape that is broad at the shoulders and tapers to the hips. Their shape is firm and muscular in appearance, with all the curves and angles in the right places, at least for U.S. culture. They are frequently described as athletic in appearance. The third type is the **ectomorph.** Ectomorphs are characterized as bony, thin, and tall. They have a fragile-looking physique, flat chest, and underdeveloped muscular tone. (See Figure 2.3.)

Can you think of anyone you know who fits into one of the three categories? What about yourself? Oprah Winfrey, the title characters in *Mike & Molly*, and Santa Claus have endomorphic characteristics. Clement C. Moore (1823) in his famous poem, "A Visit from Saint Nicholas," illustrated clearly what an endomorphic body shape is: "a broad face and a little round belly that shook when he laughed like a bowl full of jelly."

Clint Eastwood, Denzel Washington, Harrison Ford, Sylvester Stallone, Mel Gibson, Michael Jordan, and Candice Bergen are appropriate examples of the mesomorph. Calista Flockhart, Paris Hilton, Tobey Maguire, and Uma Thurman have ectomorphic features.

Return to the body type survey in Figure 2.3. This inquiry has been used in several studies investigating the relationship between body type and temperament. Cortes and Gatti (1965) developed this instrument and found that the subjects chose adjectives to describe themselves that were highly associated with their body types. In Figure 2.4, you will find three columns listing the adjectives found on the body type survey. Place a check mark beside each adjective you chose earlier. After checking the adjectives, count the number of checks for each column and write the totals underneath. You should have three numbers. These numbers should add up to 21.

From these three numbers, you can now determine your general temperament or psychological type. Let us take you through a couple of examples. Michelle checked 3 adjectives in the first column, 14 adjectives in the second

Purpose: To demonstrate how body type affects behavior and communication.

Directions: Fill in each blank with a word from the suggested list following each statement. For any blank, three in each statement, you may select any word from the list of twelve immediately below. An exact word to fit you may not be in the list, but select words that seem to fit most closely the way you are.

1. I feel most of the time _____, _____, and _____.

calm	relaxed	complacent
anxious	confident	reticent
cheerful	tense	energetic
contented	impetuous	self-conscious

2. When I study or work, I seem to be _____, _____, and _____.

efficient	sluggish	precise
enthusiastic	competitive	determined
reflective	leisurely	thoughtful
placid	meticulous	cooperative

3. Socially, I am _____, _____, and _____.

outgoing	considerate	argumentative
affable	awkward	shy
tolerant	affected	talkative
gentle-tempered	soft-tempered	hot-tempered

4. I am rather _____, _____, and _____.

active	forgiving	sympathetic
warm	courageous	serious
domineering	suspicious	soft-hearted
introspective	cool	enterprising

5. Other people consider me rather _____, _____, and _____.

generous	optimistic	sensitive
adventurous	affectionate	kind
withdrawn	reckless	cautious
dominant	detached	dependent

6. Underline one word out of three in each of the following lines that most closely describes the way you are:
   (a) assertive, relaxed, tense
   (b) hot-tempered, cool, warm
   (c) withdrawn, sociable, active
   (d) confident, tactful, kind
   (e) dependent, dominant, detached
   (f) enterprising, affable, anxious

Source: Cortes, J. B., and Gatti, F. M. (1965). "Physique and Self-Description of Temperament," *Journal of Consulting Psychology, 29,* 432–439. Copyright © 1965 by the American Psychological Association. Reprinted with permission.

FIGURE 2.2
Body Type Survey

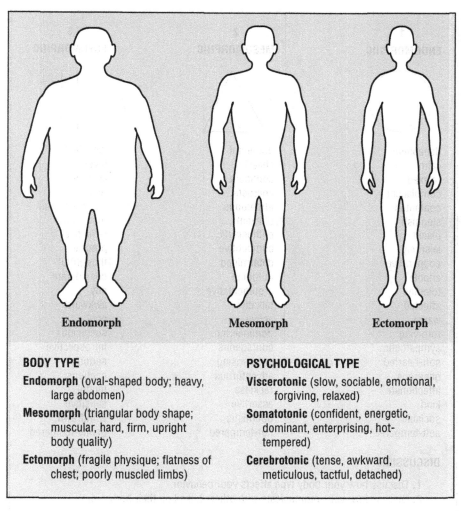

| **Endomorph** | **Mesomorph** | **Ectomorph** |

BODY TYPE

Endomorph (oval-shaped body; heavy, large abdomen)

Mesomorph (triangular body shape; muscular, hard, firm, upright body quality)

Ectomorph (fragile physique; flatness of chest; poorly muscled limbs)

PSYCHOLOGICAL TYPE

Viscerotonic (slow, sociable, emotional, forgiving, relaxed)

Somatotonic (confident, energetic, dominant, enterprising, hot-tempered)

Cerebrotonic (tense, awkward, meticulous, tactful, detached)

FIGURE 2.3
Sheldon's System and Body Types

column, and 4 in the third. Her overall temperament score is 3/14/4. Mike checked 11 adjectives in the first column, 5 in the second, and 5 in the third. His overall temperament score is 11/5/5.

According to Sheldon's theory, endomorphs have a corresponding psychological type called **viscerotonic.** The viscerotonic psychological type is characterized by the self-descriptors in column 1 of Figure 2.4. In other words, endomorphs tend to characterize themselves as slow, sociable, submissive, forgiving, relaxed, and so on. Mesomorphs have a corresponding psychological type called **somatotonic.** The somatotonic type is described as dominant, confident, energetic, competitive, assertive, hot-tempered, enthusiastic, and opti-

1 **ENDOMORPHIC**	**2** **MESOMORPHIC**	**3** **ECTOMORPHIC**
dependent	dominant	detached
calm	cheerful	tense
relaxed	confident	anxious
complacent	energetic	reticent
contented	impetuous	self-conscious
sluggish	efficient	meticulous
placid	enthusiastic	reflective
leisurely	competitive	precise
cooperative	determined	thoughtful
affable	outgoing	considerate
tolerant	argumentative	shy
affected	talkative	awkward
warm	active	cool
forgiving	domineering	suspicious
sympathetic	courageous	introspective
soft-hearted	enterprising	serious
generous	adventurous	cautious
affectionate	reckless	tactful
kind	assertive	sensitive
sociable	optimistic	withdrawn
soft-tempered	hot-tempered	gentle-tempered

DISCUSSION

1. Discuss how your body type affects your behavior.
2. Discuss how you communicate with others based on their body types.

Source: Cortes, J. B., and Gatti, F. M. (1965). "Physique and Self-Description of Temperament," *Journal of Consulting Psychology, 29,* 432–439. Copyright © 1965 by the American Psychological Association. Reprinted with permission.

FIGURE 2.4
Body Type Self-Descriptors

mistic. The ectomorphic type is associated with the **cerebrotonic** psychological type represented by adjectives such as tense, self-conscious, meticulous, precise, sensitive, awkward, and withdrawn.

Michelle, having a temperament score of 3/14/4, would have a somatotonic psychological type and more than likely have mesomorphic physical features. By contrast, Miles's score of 11/5/5 would indicate that he has a viscerotonic psychological type and an endomorphic body.

Individuals' body shapes correspond with one's own psychological self descriptions. A major question is this: Do others perceive certain psychological characteristics in persons who are endomorphs, mesomorphs, and ectomorphs? According to the results of one well-designed study using silhouette drawing, we make psychological judgments of others based on body shape. We describe them similarly as they describe themselves. In this study, the researchers showed 120 adults the silhouettes of the three body types and asked them to rate the drawings on several adjectives. The results showed that the endomorph was rated as older, shorter, more warm-hearted, more talkative, weaker, lazier, and more old-fashioned. The mesomorph was perceived as taller, younger, stronger, more adventurous, more masculine, better looking, more mature, and more self-reliant. Finally, the ectomorph was seen as more tense and nervous, more ambitious, thinner, younger, quieter, more inclined to be difficult, more suspicious of others, less masculine, and more stubborn (Wells & Siegel, 1961).

Our culture values the mesomorphic body more than the other two types, although recent trends would show that ectomorphs are beginning to gain ground in positive social judgments. The mesomorph has many physical features we rate as physically attractive. As such, we often assume they are socially and task attractive as well. That is, we perceive them during initial encounters as more likely to be sociable and desirable as coworkers. Although we tend to perceive endomorphs as socially attractive at the outset, we rarely indicate that they are physically attractive or task attractive. Ectomorphs are more likely to be seen as task attractive, particularly because we consider them meticulous, precise, and considerate. However, they are not typically perceived as socially attractive during initial interactions because we characterize them as detached and more inclined to be difficult.

Our discussion about the correspondence between body shape and temperament has important implications for our communication with others. The relationship between the two is not airtight. Nonetheless, social impressions based on body type do exist, and these impressions are at least somewhat accurate. Moreover, the fact that any correspondence exists at all is more than likely a function of our interactions with others. We stereotype people by the sizes and shapes of their bodies. We develop expectations about the personalities and behaviors of endomorphs, mesomorphs, and ectomorphs and then interact with them as if they possessed the qualities we expect. As suggested earlier, people develop their self-concepts partly by how others respond to them. If we expect oval-shaped endomorphs to be lazy and submissive, then we may communicate with them consistent with those expectations. We contribute to their self-concepts, and they often submit to the roles we force on them. They may accept others' evaluations of them as their own evaluations.

Nonverbal Messages of Height, Weight, and Skin Color

HEIGHT. Taller is preferred, particularly where males are concerned. Our culture values height in men, and height is only slightly less valued in women. The military and law enforcement agencies have only recently begun to relax the height standards for their recruits. Surveys reveal that the overwhelming majority of male executives in the Fortune 500 companies are more than six feet tall. Women want tall, dark, and handsome men. We tell our children to stand tall. The taller of the two presidential candidates has won almost every election since 1900.

Height is often associated with power and dominance. People with a height advantage can tower over others and may appear to be overpowering and dominating the other individual during conversations. It is not difficult to imagine the power and authority a tall supervisor communicates while reprimanding a short subordinate. Shorter men have reported that one major reason they refuse to date tall women is their fear that the women may dominate the relationship. Taller individuals may have a general advantage in persuading others and influencing their behavior.

In a study investigating the interpersonal impact of height, one person was introduced to different groups of students. With each introduction, the person introduced was ascribed a different status (student, lecturer, doctor, professor). The results revealed that the students distorted the height of the person introduced depending upon that individual's ascribed role. In short, the higher the ascribed status, the higher the students' judgments of height (Guerrero, DeVito, & Hecht, 1999; Feingold & Mazzella, 1998).

WEIGHT. At any one time, approximately 75 to 80 percent of women in the United States feel unhappy about their weight and want to be thinner. In addition, most of these women either are on some type of diet or have dieted in the past. The heavy, overweight woman is the most maligned individual in our culture. Heavy women are perceived to be slow, unattractive, and perhaps even lazy. Often they are not even viewed as jolly, as overweight men often are. Furthermore, the range between the ideal weight and the weight perceived to be overweight is much smaller for women than for men. Therefore most women in the United States spend a lifetime attempting to stay slim. It is no wonder that anorexia nervosa and bulimia are so common today. Generally, in this culture, when a woman's weight increases, her self-esteem decreases, and the pressure is strong for that woman to lose weight (Guerrero, DeVito, & Hecht, 1999; Feingold & Mazzella, 1998).

This is not to suggest that men do not also suffer from weight consciousness. They do. More than ever, men are enrolling in diet courses and workout programs to stay slim, virile, and young-looking. In this culture, slim and trim (despite gender) are associated with success, good self-concept, physical wellbeing, and acceptability. Overweight is associated with apathy, sluggishness, physical slowness, unattractiveness, and perhaps even mental slowness (Guerrero, DeVito, & Hecht, 1999; Feingold & Mazzella, 1998).

SKIN COLOR. Another body dimension that has the potential to communicate is skin color. Much attention has been given to racial and ethnic issues in the last century. Prejudices and stereotypes are perpetuated and individuals categorized solely on the color of their skin. The 1960s saw our culture take strides against the negative images that have so long burdened African Americans. The cry came forth that "Black is beautiful," and the rally revolved around the color of skin. Civil rights leader Martin Luther King, Jr. painted a powerful picture for the vast crowd in Washington, D.C., in 1963, when he spoke these words: "I have a dream that one day my little children will not be judged by the color of their skin, but by the content of their character." Unfortunately, that dream is yet to be fully realized. To decide just how far we have yet to go, respond quickly to the following questions: What color skin do people have who are good at math? Good at basketball? Good at dancing? Good at leading others? Good at surgery? Good at football? Good at computers? How many of your friends do you think would give the same answers you did?

Recently the prejudice has been even greater toward individuals from the Middle East. Because of the tragedy of 9/11, many Americans discriminate against anyone with skin of a medium-brown color, whether they are from the Middle East or even India or Pakistan. In many ways, the prejudice is similar to that portrayed during World War II against Japanese Americans, who were blamed for the actions of their ancestral homeland.

Nonverbal Messages of Hair

If anything changes with the times, it is how people wear their hair. In the past, the fashion for males was the crewcut or flattop; at another time it was wearing hair very long and stringy. For many years, females stiffened their hair with sticky sprays, wore it up, and had "big hair." At another time, most of them wore their hair very long and in a ponytail. Students today might be heard saying, "I wouldn't be caught dead looking like that." Their children and/or grandchildren will look back to the styles of today and make the same statement their parents are making now.

Hairstyles have much to do with our perceptions of attractiveness and social competence. Hairstyles give us cues about social norms. Nonverbal messages of hair result from hair color, hair length, facial hair, and hair manipulation.

HAIR COLOR. With little effort you can probably address several stereotypes associated with hair color. Sally is a blonde woman. Does she really have more fun? Mark has coal-black hair. Is he really more mysterious? Do redheads have hot tempers? Maybe not, but that does not mean we don't think so. It seems most of us perceive red hair as tempestuous, brown hair as wholesome, and black hair as sultry; but, the blondes still have all the fun. A survey completed years ago showed that most men prefer to have blondes for their mistresses but would rather marry a brown-haired woman. Another survey showed that most women would prefer their men to have hair (color was not an issue), but a significant minority preferred bald men.

HAIR LENGTH. Length of hair has been associated with perceptions of credibility. One study asked subjects in two different classrooms to assess a speaker's credibility. The speaker was the same man for each of the two classes of students. For one class, the speaker's hair was arranged to make it appear long; in the other, his hair was arranged to appear short. On the credibility dimensions of competence and dynamism, the speaker was rated significantly higher with short hair. Some writers have suggested that this study may indicate that men are perceived as less serious and less mature when wearing longer hair. Think of all the U.S. presidents who had long hair! Obviously, perceptions based on hair length vary with the times.

Career and job placement personnel have suggested that long hair on men is detrimental to their chances of being hired, contending that the longer the hair, the fewer the job opportunities. Women, as well, may influence their chances for jobs by the length of their hair. Contrary to some popular notions, women who enhance their sex appeal for the office may create feelings of resentment from their female coworkers and perpetuate perceptions of incompetence and low intelligence among the men. In short, one popular writer may have been right when he warned that long hair on women may work wonders in the bedroom but is a real killer in the boardroom. For this reason, many women who have long hair wear their hair up for work and down after work.

FACIAL HAIR. People's perceptions of facial hair on men has led to many interesting conclusions. The more hair a man has on his face, the more likely he is to be evaluated as mature, masculine, good-looking, dominant, courageous, industrious, self-confident, and liberal. Studies have shown that both men and women describe clean-shaven men as youthful. By women only, bearded men are perceived as mature, sophisticated, masculine, and more sexually appealing. Men, however, suggest that they feel less tense with clean-shaven men than with bearded men. It seems that perceptions of facial hair differ depending on the sex of the perceiver. Women may find beards a more positive characteristic, whereas men may perceive them as cues that stimulate withdrawal and avoidance, possibly the result of apprehension or fear. However, men with beards in this culture sometimes are perceived as hiding something (Kalick, Zebrowitz, Langlois, & Johnson, 1998).

HAIR MANIPULATION. Hair manipulation may also create strong social impressions. Consider Yolanda for a moment. She sits in a dimly lit lounge. She soon spots Sid across the room at another table. Sid has been watching her for some time, seemingly waiting for an opportunity to get acquainted. Finding him to her liking, Yolanda runs her fingers through her hair, intermittently curling the ends around a finger. What do you think will happen?

Such hair manipulations are called "preening behavior" and, according to some experts, this behavior is usually engaged in while in the presence of members of the opposite sex. Preening behavior is a nonverbal cue to potential courtship partners, informing them that it is all right to approach and possibly engage in more intimate interaction. It is, of course, quite possible that individuals perform this behavior out of habit or as adaptive behavior while anxious or nervous. In such cases, hair manipulations may be misinterpreted as approach messages or perhaps even invitations for sexual interaction. Other examples of hair manipulation include beard stroking, chewing on one's hair, pulling of the arm hair, and brushing hair away from the eyes.

APPEARANCE AND DRESS

How we dress communicates a great deal of information about us. The fabrics, colors, textures, and styles adorning our bodies send messages about what we think, who we are, our relationship to others, our values, attitudes, preferences, goals, and aspirations. Think about the money, time, and effort you spent choosing clothing. You probably had specific reasons for buying a particular pair of shoes, suit, or sweater. Often we communicate highly intentional messages with our clothes. Prostitutes, for example, know the signals they send; they dress the part so that potential clients can easily identify them (check out the movie *Pretty Woman*). These signals eliminate what may be a waste of time for both client and prostitute (Molloy, 1988; Fischer-Mirkin, 1995; Sybers & Roach, 1962).

We intentionally clothe our law enforcement officers and military personnel in readily identifiable uniforms. Law enforcement and the military go to great pains to publish and enforce their rules for tailoring for success for both men and women. Personnel in these positions who do not tailor for success are not likely to be promoted or recommended for promotion (Bickman, 1974; Gundersen, 1987, 1990; Rosencranz, 1962; Singer & Singer, 1985; Tenzel & Cizanckas, 1973).

Those of us who are not assigned a dress code still attempt to dress for success. For example, we take great pains and fuss over details before job interviews. The youthful high school English teacher wears a jacket and tie to offset his baby face. After all, he is only a few years older than his senior students, and he wants to give the impression of status and competence.

These are obvious examples of how people intentionally encode specific meaning into their dress. However, the vast majority of our messages of dress are not nearly as deliberate as these examples suggest. Many of our dress cues are transmitted without our awareness. Similarly, we receive many messages from others without realizing that their clothing stimulated the meaning. During the 1960 presidential election, Richard Nixon and John Kennedy held a series of presidential debates. In one of those debates, millions of television viewers saw Nixon in a gray suit that, on the black-and-white TV sets of those days, provided little contrast to the drab gray background. Kennedy, on the other hand, contrasted quite well in his dark suit, so well that several commentators have attributed much of his success in that debate to the fact that his clothing allowed him to stand out, creating a favorable impression with the viewers. Those who work for candidates pay quite a bit of attention to dress. In 2004, George W. Bush wore a light-blue tie in the first debate. Many newspapers reported that he had lost the debate. A few weeks later, Bush had changed to the type of red (power) tie that his opponent, John Kerry, had worn in the first debate.

Consider for a moment society's preoccupation with designer clothing during the past three decades. By being clothing-conscious, people have made the following popular at one time in our clothing history: Izod and Polo shirts, designer jeans, Gucci loafers, Tommy Hilfiger clothes, Christian Dior ties, The Gap clothing, and the list could go on and on. Surely we are aware of the acceptance and the perceptions of social competence that resulted from adorning our bodies with this fashionable wear. Are we always conscious, however, of the perceptions we may be creating in others? An anonymous source once complained, "My, my, ye all in equal attire! Do you not think in unison as well?" Is conformity what we are trying to communicate?

Why Do People Dress the Way They Do?

According to Morris (1985), one reason we dress the way we do is for *comfort and protection*. This hardly needs a lengthy explanation. The act of protecting our bodies from the elements evolved when human beings began to move about the world, traveling into areas where climatic conditions required more protection than their bodies alone could supply.

Concealment is a second function of dress. Morris notes that the loincloth is culturally the most widespread of all garments. Comfort, protection, and concealment probably satisfy the basic human motivations, the drive for survival and shelter, and the psychological comfort of modesty. Recent thinking, however, leads us to conclude that protection and concealment may not be the primary reasons we wear clothing. Many cultures, for example, do not conceal their bodies to satisfy standards of modesty. People in some cultures do not clothe their bodies even though they live in taxing weather conditions. This would indicate that other motivations influence the wearing of clothing.

Morris claims that the third function of clothing is *cultural display*. He suggests it is impossible to wear clothing without transmitting social signals. When our dress serves this function, our clothes become important sources of information about us. Articles of clothing are essentially sociocultural badges communicating our social and economic status, morality, educational background, trustworthiness, level of sophistication, level of success, and social background. Researchers Sybers and Roach (1962) summarized the sociocultural messages of dress as follows: "Clothing serves as a symbol of our status; if we fail to dress as expected, we tend to believe that our occupational mobility is negatively affected; we feel that we have to dress according to our job to impress other people; and we feel that others associate our clothing choices with our socioeconomic status, goals, and satisfaction."

CLOTHING CHARACTERISTICS AND PERSONALITY. Is it possible that our clothing reveals messages about our characteristics and personality? Does our use of dress give any clues about what characteristics are a part of our social and psychological orientations? According to many writers, it does (Aiken, 1963; Bixler, & Nix-Rice, 1997; Compton, 1962; Fischer-Mirkin, 1995; Henley, 1977; Hewitt & German, 1987; Knapp & Hall, 1992; Korda, 1975; Molloy, 1988; Rosencranz, 1962; Rosenfeld & Plax, 1977; Taylor & Compton, 1968; Thourlby, 1980). Let's review several studies that have investigated the relationships between the characteristics of wearers and the actual clothing they wear.

Compton (1962) was interested in establishing an association between the characteristics of individuals and their preferences for particular clothing designs and colors. Her research showed that people who preferred saturated colors and deep shades tended to be outgoing, forward, and sociable. Individuals who preferred small fabric designs, on the other hand, were more interested in making a good impression. Compton concluded that people choose colors, fabrics, and designs consistent with the ideal image they hold of themselves. Our clothing choices, then, allow us to conform to that perfect picture. Thourlby (1980) suggests that there are ten decisions we might make about another person based solely on clothing choice. These are:

1. Economic level
2. Educational level
3. Trustworthiness
4. Social position
5. Level of sophistication
6. Economic background
7. Social background
8. Educational background
9. Level of success
10. Moral character

Rosencranz (1962) studied the clothing attitudes of married women. The results showed that women who were high in dress awareness usually belonged to many organizations, were in the upper social classes, had better verbal skills, were more educated, and married white-collar men with higher-than-average incomes. According to Rosencranz, the upper classes of society probably place a great deal of emphasis on the physical appearance of their members, thus making clothing awareness a high priority. It would also seem that women in upper socioeconomic brackets have the time and financial resources to focus more attention on their dress.

Fortenberry, McLean, Morris, and O'Connell (1978) as well as Gorden, Tengler, and Infante (1990); Gross (1990); Henley (1977); and Kaiser (1999), and others have studied the influence of formal attire versus casual attire on perception. It seems that formal attire commands more respect, attention, and cooperation. Formal attire often results in our being perceived as more credible by others. However, casual attire may lead to perceptions of approachability despite perhaps indicating lower respect, attention, and compliance. Perhaps designating casual Fridays is not always the best move for some organizations.

Casual versus formal attire may not send the best message from a novice employee to customers. Kiddie (2009) found that the number of companies allowing casual dress decreased from 53 percent in 2002 to 38 percent in 2006 (p. 352). Peluchette and Karl (2007) found that employees felt business attire indicated that one was authoritative, competent, and trustworthy. Previously some researchers indicated that casual clothing increased productivity, with Apple, Inc. as the prototypical case. Regardless of higher productivity, though, trends in the past few years have been toward moving back to business attire, probably to increase credibility with clients. Such is especially the case for marketing professionals (Esterling, Leslie, & Jones, 1992). Perhaps, then, work clothing is different depending on whether one's primary job is working in the office or communicating with customers.

One of the more famous and extensive studies relating clothing to wearer characteristics is that of Aiken (1963). This researcher was interested in whether clothing selections were associated with personality traits. Aiken's classic survey questionnaire was developed to identify five dimensions of clothing selection. In brief, people select their articles of clothing because:

1. They have an interest in dress.
2. They are concerned about economy in dress.
3. They use their clothing for decoration.
4. They dress for conformity.
5. They dress for comfort.

Essentially, the Aiken study attempted to determine what personality traits best predicted how individuals select their clothing.

Using only females in the investigation, Aiken found that women with an interest in dress were conventional, conscientious, compliant before authority, persistent, suspicious, insecure, tense, and stereotyped in thinking. Women who were concerned about economy in their clothing selection scored as more responsible, alert, efficient, precise, intelligent, conscientious, and controlled. Those who used their dress for decoration were conscientious, conventional, stereotyped, nonintellectual, sympathetic, sociable, and submissive. Women who dressed for conformity were characterized as more socially conscientious, moral, traditional, and submissive, and exercised restraint. These women also emphasized economic, social, and religious values and tended to de-emphasize aesthetic values. Finally, Aiken found that women who chose their clothing for the sake of comfort were self-controlled, socially cooperative, sociable, thorough, and deferent to authority.

Follow-up investigations appear to confirm Aiken's original findings. Notable among these studies is that of Rosenfeld and Plax (1977). A major improvement here is that the researchers used both female and male respondents in exploring the relationships between four clothing orientations and personality characteristics. The first clothing orientation was *clothing consciousness*. People who have a high clothing consciousness would, for example, feel that it is important for others to always notice what they wear.

The second dimension or orientation toward clothing was *exhibitionism*. Those scoring high in exhibitionism would, for instance, approve of skimpy bathing suits and actually prefer and enjoy wearing them. This group might wear inappropriately revealing clothing to the formal work setting.

The third dimension identified by Rosenfeld and Plax was *practicality*. Subjects who responded very agreeably to such statements as, "When buying clothes, I am more interested in practicality than beauty" would score high on this dimension.

The fourth dimension, *designer,* referred to the degree to whic would love to be a clothing designer. In Table 2.1, we have proviueu uw results of the Rosenfeld and Plax study. Listed are the personality characteristics for both females and males who were either high or low on the four clothing orientations.

POPULARITY, LIKING, AND HOMOPHILY. Some people dress as they do to enhance their popularity or because they feel that others will like them better. Can our clothing affect others' feelings about us? Creating *homophily* with others can be quite beneficial to our interpersonal relationships. **Homophily** is perceived similarity in appearance, background, attitudes, and values. Some experts suggest that similarity in appearance (in the clothing we wear) may ease perceptions of similarity in other ways as well. One thing seems to hold true: We tend to like people more whom we perceive to be similar to us, and this includes similarity in dress.

Conforming to the dress of others is related to our desire to be liked and accepted. Additionally, people do like us and accept us more based on how we dress. Popularity and liking are related to clothing. Research shows that for women, wearing the right clothing is more important than either personality or looks when aspiring to become popular. The women studied also considered clothing the most important factor in describing the attributes of popular women.

RANK AND STATUS. We suggested earlier that clothing serves as a symbol of our status. Dressing formally rather than casually increases perceptions of status. In many situations, we can enhance or minimize our status with others by the clothes we wear. Some writers report that dress is the most important consideration during initial business encounters. If our dress suggests we are of a higher status than our customers, then we may not be approached. If our dress is below the standard of our customers, then we might be perceived as not worthy of the job or position (Bixler & Nix-Rice, 1997; Fischer-Mirkin, 1995; Hewitt & German, 1987; Molloy, 1988; Nix-Rice, 1996; Richmond, 1996; Rosencranz, 1962; Rosenfeld & Plax, 1977; Sybers & Roach, 1962; Taylor & Compton, 1968).

The young and inexperienced classroom teacher finds that if he wears a tie and coat, or if she wears a dress suit or blazer with a skirt, students will behave differently toward him or her. Think about your own college instructors for a moment. If you attend a large university, chances are good that some of your teachers have been graduate teaching assistants—you remember them. They are more than likely the most formally dressed or the most informally dressed instructors you will ever have. Why? Many of them are only two or three years older than you and have been well coached by their own professors about the importance of creating a perceived status differential in your minds. They are told, and rightly so, that higher-status clothing often engenders more respect. Others are of the opinion that dressing more informally makes them appear to be one of the group, and they think they will create more homophily with their students.

Clothing serves as a symbol of rank, power, or status.

Source: Photo by C. Price Walt

Some experts suggest that clothing is important in the business world when it comes to giving messages of rank and status. The expensive-looking tailored suit, we are told, denotes upper-level management. However, in business, it is often recommended that a person should dress like the people one position above the one they hold. This is thought to make others perceive you as a more likely candidate for your next promotion.

POWER AND SUCCESS. Closely related to rank and status are the nonverbal messages of power and success. In the world of high finance and big business, corporate men and women struggle daily to achieve the rewards that come with the successful climb up the ladder. Popular writers have stressed the importance of the symbols of power and success that are necessary in our places of business. According to various sources, the man's business suit is designed to send powerful messages of authority and credibility. Writers suggest that darker suits create perceptions of more authority. However, solid black, navy, or gray tailored business suits may communicate too much power. And although dark blue and gray pinstripes are acceptable, solid colors are strongly recommended.

Other writers have stressed the importance of the navy-blue, charcoal, or black skirted suit for career women. Businesswomen, however, need to avoid imitating the dress of their male counterparts. This could be seen as a threat

CLOTHING CONSCIOUSNESS

High Females: inhibited, anxious, compliant before authority, kind, sympathetic, loyal to friends

High Males: deliberate, guarded, deferential to authority, custom, and tradition

Low Females: forceful, independent, dominant, clear thinking, low motivation for heterosexual relationships, low motivation to manipulate others

Low Males: aggressive, independent, did not believe people are easily manipulated

EXHIBITIONISM

High Females: radical, detached from interpersonal relationships, high opinion of self-worth

High Males: aggressive, confident, outgoing, unsympathetic, unaffectionate, moody, impulsive, low self-concept regarding familial interactions

Low Females: timid, sincere, accepting of others, patient, feelings of inferiority, low motivation for heterosexual relationships

Low Males: believe people are easily manipulated, guarded against revealing themselves, low self-concept regarding familial interactions

PRACTICALITY

High Females: enthusiastic, outgoing, clever, confident, guarded against revealing themselves, feelings of superiority, no desire to lead

High Males: dissatisfied, cautious, rebellious, inhibited, also had little motivation for sustaining relationships, gaining recognition from authority figures, or making friends

Low Females: detached, self-centered, independent

Low Males: analytical, serious, forceful, success oriented, mature

DESIGNER

High Females: stereotyped in thinking, irrational, uncritical, expressive, ebullient, quick

High Males: conforming, demanding, irritable, cooperative, sympathetic, warm, helpful, sought encouragement, worried about their behavior

Low Females: persistent, resourceful, clear thinking, efficient, when under pressure became easily disorganized, pessimistic about future in career

Low Males: egotistical, dissatisfied, adventurous, anxious, feelings of superiority, little motivation to make friends

FIGURE 2.5

Personality and Clothing Orientation

and eventually reduce the women's power and authority in the corporate office. Women are encouraged to model the highest level of female business attire. Additionally, a businesswoman may want to avoid wearing a sweater instead of a jacket. A sweater without a jacket may project the image of lower status. What one wears away from the work environment, of course, is another matter. Thus, although some clothing may make a woman more attractive, it may not enhance her value in the company. Some well-controlled research shows that attractiveness (at least after initial hiring) is not an asset to women employed above the clerical rank. Physical attractiveness was found to be negatively related to performance evaluations (Henley, 1977; Korda, 1975; Molloy, 1988; Fischer-Mirkin, 1995).

GROUP IDENTIFICATION.   Closely associated with popularity and liking, *group identification* is another reason people dress as they do. We are often told that if you want to belong to the group, you have to do what the group does. In other words, when in Rome, do as the Romans do (paraphrase of a quote by St. Ambrose).

Singer and Singer (1985) found that when police officers were in uniform, they were perceived to be more competent, reliable, and intelligent than when dressed casually. Hewitt and German (1987) found that a male Marine Corps sergeant and a male Navy lieutenant were perceived as more attractive and intelligent when in uniform than when dressed casually. It is clear that our dress illustrates who we are, the groups we belong to, and our attitudes. For example, when a group of antischool students wear T-shirts that say, "I don't do school," this says a lot about the group—not only to teachers but to other persons who observe this group-identification form of dress.

Try this small test: Go to a bank where you are not known, dress informally and somewhat sloppily, then attempt to cash a check. Watch the teller's reaction. Later, go back to the same bank dressed in a suit or formal attire and watch the reaction.

People have always sought to belong, to be identified with a certain group of individuals. The young man begs his parents to buy him a sports shirt with his favorite football team's colors or his favorite baseball player's jersey number. Young women imitate the fashions of famous actresses and models. On college campuses, men and women aspiring to become members of fraternities, sororities, and other groups attempt to prove themselves worthy by identifying with the clothing and actions of their potential brothers, sisters, and group peers. An older man once boasted that he could tell a Republican from a Democrat by the very clothing the person wore. Whether we know it or not, we wear the uniforms of the groups with which we associate (or aspire to associate). The clothing we wear communicates a great deal about our social and political attitudes.

Generalizations About Dress

We have discussed several important functions of clothing, including the fact that we use the dress of others to perceive and stereotype them in many ways.

Before we move on, it is necessary to outline important generalizations about judgments we make based on dress.

GENERALIZATION 1. The accuracy of our judgments about others based on dress varies as a function of what type of judgment we make. Researchers suggest greater accuracy is found in judging sex, age, nationality, socioeconomic status, identification of group, occupational status, and official status. In other words, we are generally much better at judging demographic characteristics based on dress. Less accuracy is found in judging personality, moods, values, and attitudes. That is, we are usually not as good at using the dress of others to evaluate psychological characteristics.

GENERALIZATION 2. Whether the dress of others influences our perceptions of them is in part a function of whether they are strangers or acquaintances. Basically, impressions based on dress tend to be most important during the initial and early stages of interaction. Two studies conducted by Hoult (1954) seem to support this rule. He asked subjects in the first study to rate male models on several social dimensions. The models receiving the lowest ratings were then instructed to dress up; those with the highest ratings were told to dress down. The models were then rated a second time, but Hoult found no change in the ratings. The clothing had no influence on social judgments. Upon realizing that his research might be confounded because the subjects were closely acquainted with the models, he conducted another study using models who were complete strangers to the subjects. The results of the second study showed that clothing did influence the ratings. The models who dressed up increased in social ranking, and those who dressed down lost ground in their ranking. This conclusion still holds true today.

GENERALIZATION 3. The perception we have of others is initially influenced by their dress. We judge others based on their dress. Often we decide whether to initiate interaction based on a person's dress and general physical appearance.

GENERALIZATION 4. If someone dresses similarly to us, we are more likely to approach her or him and initiate interaction. Again, the principle of homophily emerges. The more two people perceive themselves to be similar (based on dress), the more likely they are to communicate with one another.

GENERALIZATION 5. If a person wants to be recognized or identified as part of a group, he or she should wear clothing that denotes the group. If you want to be perceived as a serious businessperson, wear the standard, serious, business clothing.

GENERALIZATION 6. Clothing can denote our credibility level. When we are selecting clothing, we should always consider the level of credibility we want to achieve with others. How we dress may not predict how we act, but it can predict whether someone will interact with us. Suits for both men and women generally give an impression of higher credibility.

In short, when we know someone, her or his clothing has little influence on our perceptions. We see the real person even if the clothing is not consistent with that perception. With strangers, however, clothing takes on an extremely important role in our judgments. As with other physical appearance factors, the clothes of strangers are a rich source of information about them when no other source exists. If we don't know the real person, what we see is what we assume is real.

ARTIFACTS AND ACCESSORIES

Look at your body and dress. Search well. Do you find anything adorning, decorating, or identifying you other than your clothing? The accessories used to adorn our bodies and clothes are called personal **artifacts** and can tell as much about us as our dress. Jewelry, glasses, hats, purses, backpacks, briefcases, writing pens, and even smoking artifacts communicate to others the personality underneath it all. Amsbary, Vogel, Hickson, and Oakes (1994) found that students rated a person much higher in similarity to them, in credibility and in interpersonal attraction, when they were perceived as nonsmoking.

Many individuals are so closely identified with their personal artifacts that it is virtually impossible to divorce them. During World War II, General George S. Patton was as famous for his ivory-handled pistol and swagger stick as he was for his successful military campaigns. It is quite difficult to imagine General Douglas MacArthur without his aviator sunglasses and corncob pipe. Johnny Cash was associated with black clothing for many years. The character Ally McBeal was associated with her very short skirts. Many music stars are associated with certain pieces of adornment such as rings, glasses, and so on. Lisa Loeb is rarely seen without her trademark black-framed eyeglasses.

Professional image consultants do not hesitate to give guidelines for artifact choice. Molloy (1975) used an image IQ test in which he asked, "For which professions are bow ties acceptable?" The answer was waiters, clowns, college professors, and commentators. Almost all professions have personalized artifacts. For example, many groups have lapel pins, brooches, tie tacks, watches, and other badge-like artifacts that identify their status.

Quite common among the artifacts we use are our articles of jewelry. The type of watch you wear may say much more than you realize. A Timex may communicate a very different image than a Rolex. Both can transmit a strong signal about your socioeconomic status. Many image consultants have suggested that the amount and type of jewelry the businessperson wears can make or break her or his business image. The recommendation for the businessman is simple: no earrings, but do have a simple (preferably thin) gold watch and, if married, a wedding band. Any more is overdoing it. Although things may change in the future, for now, even one of those simple gold-post earrings is too many for the businessman!

As for businesswomen, adding more than simple earrings to the watch and wedding ring is going too far. The rule for women in business is usually four accessories: a watch, a wedding ring, and earrings (each counts as one accessory). Overdoing jewelry is a mistake many businesswomen make. Too much jewelry can be distracting during conversation (and may even make noises) and may suggest that you are of higher status than you actually are or that you are somewhat insecure with your status. In business, less is more when it comes to accessories (Fischer-Mirkin, 1995; Kaiser, 1999; Guerrero, DeVito, & Hecht, 1999).

The most prominent and probably the most researched artifacts of all are eyeglasses (Harris, 1991; Lyon, Rainey, & Bullock, 2002; Terry & Brady, 1976; Terry & Hall, 1989; Terry & Krantz, 1993; and Terry & Stockton, 1993). Since their invention, eyeglasses have been associated with particular personality characteristics. Studies have concluded that people who wear glasses are thought to be more intelligent, industrious, and honest. One study found that women who wear glasses are seen as more religious, conventional, and unimaginative. At least for women, general perceptions related to eyeglasses are somewhat negative. This may explain why a large percentage of all contact lens wearers are women and why more women than men elect eye surgery to correct their vision. Since the early 1980s, however, manufacturers of eyeglass frames have become highly imaginative with their products. Designer frames and other innovations, as well as the changing perceptions and uses of eyeglasses, allow wearers to express themselves in ways that were impossible only a few years ago.

Eyeglasses can also communicate messages by the way we manipulate them. People who wear glasses can send a variety of signals about their self-images and emotional states. Chewing on the temple tips, for example, is usually a sign of nervousness, tension, or stress. Deep concentration can be communicated when wearers touch the temple tips together. Boredom may be shown by the individual who continually folds and unfolds her or his glasses. Gesturing with one's eyeglasses while speaking can definitely emphasize a point. A person who pushes his or her glasses up on the forehead to look at another person directly may demonstrate honesty and willingness to be open. Resting glasses on the tip of the nose and looking over the top of the frames may send a message of control, power, or disbelief.

We have discussed just a few of the many artifacts that contribute to the social and cultural cues you transmit every day. Little things they may be. However, you should never dismiss the smallest lapel pin, the simplest necklace, or the plainest earrings in taking an inventory of the potential nonverbal messages you send others through your physical appearance. Others judge you by your artifacts as well as your clothing. Your artifacts communicate your self-image, your affiliations, and your social and political attitudes.

Glossary of Terminology

Appearance obsession   refers to the tendency to focus on one's appearance to an excessive level.

Artifacts   are accessories used to adorn our bodies and clothing.

Attractiveness   is the degree to which we perceive another person as someone with whom we would want to associate.

Cerebrotonic psychological type   is tense, awkward, meticulous, tactful, and detached.

Ectomorphs (ectos)   are bony, thin, tall people with a fragile-looking physique, flat chest, and underdeveloped muscle tone.

Endomorphs (endos) are people with rounded, oval-shaped bodies who are somewhat heavy (not necessarily obese) and are often described as pear-shaped.

Homophily refers to similarity between people.

Image fixation (IF) is a long-term, fixated view that a person has about her or his image or body.

Mesomorphs (mesos) are people with a triangular body shape that is broad at the shoulders and tapers to the hips. Their shape is firm and muscular in appearance with all the curves and angles in the right places, at least for U.S. culture.

Personal body concept is the perception you have of how attractive your body is and what you perceive to be the attributes of your body.

Physical attractiveness is the degree to which we perceive another person as attractive because of her or his physical attributes.

Social attractiveness is the degree to which we perceive another person as someone with whom we would like to socialize.

Somatotonic psychological type is confident, energetic, dominant, enterprising, and hot-tempered.

Somatotyping is a method used to categorize individuals into one of three major body types: endomorphic, mesomorphic, and ectomorphic.

Task attractiveness is the degree to which we perceive another person as someone with whom we would like to work or conduct business or have as a coworker or teammate.

Viscerotonic psychological type is slow, sociable, emotional, forgiving, and relaxed.

CHAPTER 3

Gesture and Movement

People in business learn to interpret quickly the many different gestures and body movements of others. Only the unsuccessful business people neglect the importance of gestures and body as they talk with potential clients. When we talk with our gestures and movements, many meanings can be generated. In introductory situations, a person must know the appropriate greeting for the context. To nod, bow, kiss, shake hands, smile, wave, touch cheeks, or rub noses are common greetings used throughout the world. Use an inappropriate gesture for greeting and the door may never open to you.

Answer the following questions and compare your answers with those of another person:

1. In this culture, what is the gesture for greeting?
2. What is the gesture for goodbye?
3. What is the gesture for "good job" or "well done"?
4. What is the gesture for agreement?
5. What is the gesture for disagreement?
6. What is the gesture for "I'm hungry"?
7. What is the gesture for "what time is it"?
8. What is the gesture for "I'm thirsty"?
9. What is the gesture for "come here"?
10. What is the gesture for "go away"?
11. What is the gesture for "I am really ticked off at you"?
12. What is the gesture for "I don't know"?

Gestures and body movements often convey the true feelings behind a person's words. The context in which the gesture or body movement is used often determines how it will be interpreted. For example, let's look at Don in the interviewing context.

Don felt uncomfortable, nervous, and anxious. He had never interviewed for a real long-term job in his life. His prior positions had all been part-time jobs. Never before had he wanted to impress someone so he could obtain a permanent, future-oriented job. He kept thinking: Will they like me? Did I remember to check my appearance? Do I look too young? Do I look confident? How should I appear? Don had spent much of the morning analyzing his appearance. He made sure his navy-blue business suit was acceptable, analyzed the fit of the jacket, his tie, and the fit of his slacks. He looked at his shoes to make sure they were polished, not scuffed. The longer he waited, the more he fidgeted, squirmed, and wiggled. What could go wrong? He had studied all the information he could obtain on the corporation he was interviewing with. Why was he worried?

He sat in an outer waiting room with several other applicants, all of whom looked much like him. The interviewer had been calling them in one at a time to meet with a committee. Sit up straight. Look alert. Look calm. Don't bite your nails. Stop running your hands through your hair. And stop drumming your fingers on the chair arm! Don then realized that he had been running his hands through his hair again, and his crossed leg was twitching rapidly. He folded his arms loosely across his chest, breathed deeply, and forced himself to sit calmly.

In the next chair, a well-dressed woman sat calmly reading a magazine. She slumped and yawned. A man to her right continually looked at his watch. Toward the other side of the room, Don noticed another woman pacing in front of a bulletin board. Occasionally, she flipped a posted notice or brochure, then looked anxiously down the hall where several interviewees had disappeared with the corporation representative. "Donald T. Smith," said a strong, serious, firm voice. Don turned to see the representative gesturing for him to follow. Don approached, smiled, extended a trembling hand, and bent from his waist. "Not nervous, are you Mr. Smith?" asked the representative. "Oh, no, no, sir . . . I mean madam . . . I mean ma'am. Not at all. Very good to meet you." Don bit his lower lip for fear that his general behavior and mannerisms had betrayed him.

Because of books and articles in mass circulation, body movements have become commonly known as body language (Argyle, 1975; Birdwhistell, 1970; Fast, 1970; Henley, 1977; Malandro & Barker, 1983). Although such writings have helped raise awareness of nonverbal behavior and of gesture and movement in particular, the movements, actions, gestures, motions, displays, twitches, swings, and sways of our bodies do not constitute a language. They are simply behaviors to which one may attribute some meaning. In short, they may communicate, but they do not do so like words (Richmond, 1996; Guerrero, DeVito, & Hecht, 1999).

Kinesics is the study of the communicative impact of body movement and gesture. In Chapter 1, we introduced the various functions of nonverbal communication: complementing, accenting, contradicting, repeating, substituting, and regulating. Our body movements convey many messages that serve these functions.

Kinesic behaviors include all gestures, head movements, eye behavior, facial expressions, posture, and movements of the trunk, arms, legs, feet, hands, and fingers. Researchers have studied these motions from many perspectives, but most nonverbal scholars today agree that it is virtually meaningless, and probably inappropriate, to study kinesic behaviors apart from their contexts. It is rare that a particular body movement symbolizes a specific message outside the restrictive environs of the context or culture where it occurs.

Consider Don's behavior in our example. Had you not known his particular situation, the impending interview, could you have assigned specific meaning to those behaviors? Probably not. Some would have guessed that he was bored, others that he was irritated. It is only because we understand his predicament that we know his behaviors are signs of nervousness and anxiety.

Besides the situation that provides context for body motions, it is also essential to understand that our culture, upbringing, ethnic and geographic origins, social status, and even educational background contribute to the meaning of gesture and movement. In our culture, how a man walks may lead some individuals to question his masculinity. In other cultures, the same gait would not. The "A-OK" sign North Americans use may indicate that all is well or fine in Buffalo, New York, or Dallas, Texas, but don't rely on the same interpretation in some Latino cultures, where the North American "A-OK" sign is equivalent to giving the middle finger. Decades of extensive research and formal observation have shown us the error of our ways when we attempt to categorize nonverbal human behavior. Crossing your legs and shifting away from another person while talking with him or her may not indicate that youare rejecting that person. You may simply be more comfortable in that position.

We would like to discuss gesture and movement in several ways. First, we present a section on the theoretical views of this area of nonverbal communication. Second, we present a discussion on the types or categories of gestures and movements. Third, the idea of posture is discussed in terms of its potential to communicate. Finally, we review the effects of gesture and movement on our communication with others.

A THEORETICAL LOOK AT GESTURE AND MOVEMENT

We have always known intuitively that body movements tell us much about another person. Gestures and movements illustrate and regulate our verbal dialogue. Through our bodily motions, we communicate our emotions, reinforce and accent our spoken words, and even contradict what we have said. It is only quite recently, however, that theorists and researchers have developed scientific ways of studying the kinesic behavior of humans. There are two general approaches to the study of kinesics. The first is the *structural* approach; the second, the *external variable* approach. As we will see, researchers from each perspective make different assumptions about the communicative potential of kinesic behavior (Birdwhistell, 1952, 1970; Dittman, 1971; Ekman, 1976; Ekman & Friesen, 1969a, 1969b, 1972, 1974; Johnson, Ekman, & Friesen, 1975; Knapp & Hall, 1992; Rogers, 1978; Richmond, 1996).

Structural Approach to Kinesics

The common thread among the writers who take the structural approach to kinesics is that they view communication as a structured system and presume

Nonverbal Matching in Consoling Behavior

The researchers looked at the concept of consoling behavior. Four confederates (two male and two female) were trained to act out nine combinations of nonverbal immediacy. Each combination was ranked as low, moderate, or high. The participants discussed an emotionally distressing event. Two hypotheses were supported and one was not. First, participants matched the confederate regardless of the immediacy condition. Second, women engaged in more immediacy matching than did men. Additionally, women displayed more emotional cues than men. Women matched higher with other women than with male confederates. Male-female and male-male dyads (pairs) tested similarly for matching. The third hypothesis, that matching and perceived liking for the helper, is moderated by manipulated levels of the helper was not supported. However, immediacy exerted a big effect on liking.

Jones, S. M., & Wirtz, J. G. (2007). Sad monkey, see, monkey do: Nonverbal matching in emotional support encounters. Communication Studies, 58, 71–86.

this system is independent of the specific behaviors people engage in during particular interactions. These scholars believe that all behavior should be presumed to be learned socially and to have communicative value. Birdwhistell (1952, 1970) is one of the most famous structuralist writers. He believed that the context in which behavior occurs is important, but that behavior can also be seen as meeting many criteria for language. In other words, there is an underlying structure to behaviors, a rule system that can be discovered. Behaviors can be broken into parts like sentences or words, and they can be categorized. Thus, Birdwhistell thought that it was meaningless to make distinctions between verbal and nonverbal communication. His linguistic approach to movements is widely known today and much debated.

Birdwhistell's (1952) method for studying body motions involved identifying the smallest and most basic units of behavior, called *allokines*. We usually cannot detect these microbehaviors in ongoing interaction with others. They are performed rapidly and usually must be detected by mechanical means such as video recorders or computers. Several allokines together compose larger units of behavior called *kines*. According to Birdwhistell, even kines may not be meaningful. A still larger unit of behavior, *kinemes*, is a combination of kines. These movement kinemes are the smallest sets of body movements to which differential meaning can be attributed. They are analogous to the linguistic unit of phoneme, which is the smallest phonetic unit in a language. Kinemes make up *kinemorphemes*, which are analogous to the linguistic unit of morpheme, the smallest meaningful unit of language, consisting of a word or word element. Thus Birdwhistell based his category system of behavior on a model taken from the categories of verbal communication (allophone, phone, phonemes, morphemes, semantics, syntax, and grammar).

Dittman (1971), a major critic of Birdwhistell's approach to the study of kinesics, rejects the belief that all nonverbal behavior can be treated in the same way we treat verbal language. According to Dittman, the basic hypothesis of kinesics as a communication system with the same structure as spoken language is not viable. He has claimed that all spoken language consists of discontinuous and discrete pieces of information. However, only certain body motions and gestures can meet this criterion. Many or most must be considered continuous and therefore cannot be treated or studied as a linguistic system. Dittman suggests that there is little evidence that movement elements are assembled into groupings based on any set of rules internal to the movements themselves. Other critics of Birdwhistell have cautioned that his approach may lead researchers to impose a structure on the body movements they observe that may not exist but which rather fits a presupposed model of the researchers.

However, it should be noted that Dittman and others strongly agree with Birdwhistell that gestures and movements are valuable sources of information. They would disagree that no distinction between verbal and nonverbal behavior can or should be made. As you probably have surmised, we find ourselves firmly in Dittman's corner in this controversy. The distinctions we noted in Chapter 1 between verbal and nonverbal behaviors are important. The stream of research based on the linguistic model has not been particularly useful for

ιding human communication and today has lost popularity among
:ation researchers.

External Variable Approach to Kinesics

Unlike Birdwhistell, most other researchers have taken an external variable
approach to the study of bodily motion. Ekman (1976) is one of the more
famous of these. He started by observing behavior experimentally and then
developed his theory based on his findings. Ekman and his colleagues were not
interested in microbehaviors that could not be seen by the naked eye. They
saw no real use in hypothesizing the existence of allokines and kines, because
these units had no significance in relation to social meaning and communication. Ekman and Friesen (1969a, 1969b) often stated that their interest in how
nonverbal behavior functions in social interaction required them to examine
molar units of behavior. According to Ekman and Friesen, any classification of
human gesture and movement should be based on motions that are easily seen
by any observer. If movements cannot be discerned by the average observer,
how can they consciously communicate? Of course they can't. However, there
could be a non-conscious impact. Ekman and Friesen (1969a, 1969b, 1972,
1974) were also interested in the type of information certain nonverbal acts
convey. Movements can convey idiosyncratic information or shared information. Movements and gestures that can be understood only in relation to one
individual generate idiosyncratic meaning. That is, the meanings of these nonverbal acts are seen as different if they are engaged in by different people
within the same group. Furthermore, knowledge of the particular circumstances surrounding such acts is essential to understanding them. Nonverbal
acts that generate shared meaning are those that most persons in a given group
or culture would interpret similarly. The middle finger and the victory sign
are examples of behaviors that generate shared meaning in U.S culture.
Conversely, one person may engage in a particular movement in response to
feelings of stress, such as stroking an arm or biting the fingernails, which stimulates no meaning in most others nearby; whereas, another observer (such as a
spouse) recognizes this behavior as a sign of anxiety. This would be idiosyncratic meaning.

In an extension of their idiosyncratic distinction, Ekman and Friesen distinguished between inborn and innate behavior versus behavior that is learned
through social interaction and cultural influences. We generally agree with
Ekman and Friesen that many gestures and movements are both inborn and
innate and that—as we grow, develop, mature, listen to and observe others,
and model others—we begin to develop or learn a rather sophisticated means
of communicating with people in our culture. Ekman and Friesen's kinesic system is a function of inborn tendencies and learned behaviors.

From their research and thinking, Ekman and Friesen devised the most
commonly accepted system to categorize gestures and movements. Let us now
turn to a discussion of the types of bodily motions using the categories they
developed.

TYPES OF GESTURE AND MOVEMENT

Gestures and movements of human beings may be separated into five different types: emblems, illustrators, regulators, affect displays, and adaptors (Ekman, 1976; Ekman & Friesen, 1969a, 1969b, 1972, 1974; Scherer & Ekman, 1982). The following discussion presents each type and describes its characteristics.

Emblems

The first type of body motion is called the emblem. **Emblems** are often referred to as the speech-independent gestures. Gestures must have several characteristics before they become classified as emblems:

- Emblems are gestures and movements that have a direct verbal translation.
- Emblems are known by most or all of a group, class, culture, or subculture.
- They can be used to stimulate specific meanings in the minds of other persons in place of verbal communication. Giving someone the finger or "A-OK" sign typically produces a precise shared meaning, and few in our culture would miss the message the gesture transmits. However, those who know American Sign Language (ASL) can communicate much more fully with an emblematic language based on gesture. This, of course, is a complete language system, not just unrelated gestures and movements.
- Emblems are used intentionally by the sender to communicate a specific message to an individual or group. Rarely do individuals unconsciously wave goodbye or raise their thumbs when standing along the roadside to signal for a passerby to pick them up.
- Users of emblems are aware of their actions and are in control of the movement or gesture. The sender, in essence, takes responsibility for the message.
- Emblems are often socially and culturally learned behaviors to which precise meaning can be attached.
- Emblems can be used, in many cases, to substitute for the spoken word.

Though generally classified as nonverbal behavior, emblems have more in common with verbal communication than any other nonverbal behavior. Besides having direct verbal translations and usually being used intentionally, emblems are socially learned in much the same manner as language. Furthermore, emblems are much like language itself. The meanings we assign to them are arbitrary, and the way we associate meaning with the action is highly similar to the way we associate meaning with words. Finally, as with words, emblems may stimulate entirely different meanings or no meanings at all in the minds of people from different cultures. Given the closeness of emblems to language, it may be better to think of nonverbal and verbal behavior as a continuum than as a dichotomy. Emblems would fall somewhere in the middle of the continuum, with verbal and nonverbal behavior representing the polar extremes:

Verbal behavior _____ *Emblems* _____ *Nonverbal behavior*

In our culture there are several common emblems that mean something completely different in other cultures. The "A-OK" sign, which is seen as positive in this culture, is an obscene gesture elsewhere; it is seen as a symbol for money in some cultures and as meaningless in others. Ekman and Kendon have suggested that certain cultures may have gestures in common for such words as *hello* and *goodbye*. Other candidates for gestures that may span a number of cultures are those signaling agreement, disagreement, dislike, like, hunger, thirst, lust, stop, go, uncertainty, tiredness or fatigue, happiness, sadness, and surprise. Other than the smile, there are very few universal gestures. In summary, for the most part, gestures should be interpreted within contextual and cultural confines.

Illustrators

Gestures and movements that are closely linked with spoken language and help to demonstrate what is being said are called **illustrators.** These are often referred to as speech-linked gestures. Like emblems, illustrators are usually intentional. Unlike emblems, however, they cannot stand alone and stimulate the same meaning of the verbal. That is, illustrators generate little or no meaning when they are not accompanying speech. Try turning down the volume on your television and observe the actions of the people on the screen. Unless you are an excellent lip-reader, you will find it extremely difficult to understand every action accurately. Seldom can we assign specific meaning to illustrative behavior without the accompanying speech. Illustrators usually make little sense without the words they accompany.

Illustrators generally come in four categories. The first category is gestures that are related to the speech referent or explanation. Such gestures are movements that illustrate the idea or spoken word, as when a person says, "I caught a fish this big!" and holds her or his hands far apart. Try generating your own examples of gestures related to a speech referent.

Category two comprises gestures that suggest the source's relationship to the speech referent or explanation. These gestures suggest the sender's acculturation or attitude to the referent. For example, a person might ask you how the big fish we caught tasted, and you might reply by saying it was so-so, while waving a hand back and forth in the "so-so" fashion. Or you might stick out your tongue and shake your head as you say, "It was awful."

Category three is gestures that punctuate, highlight, or emphasize a spoken word or message in conversation. For example, when we speak of three ideas, we might raise a different finger for each idea to punctuate or highlight that idea.

Category four is interaction gestures that help the source in organizing, managing, or directing the conversation. These tend to be gestures used in conjunction with speech, which signal when it is another person's turn to talk or remain quiet. For example, these can be head, hand, eye, or body movements that signal or punctuate speech.

Researchers and practitioners have found that illustrators are used more often in face-to-face interaction. This is because in face-to-face communication,

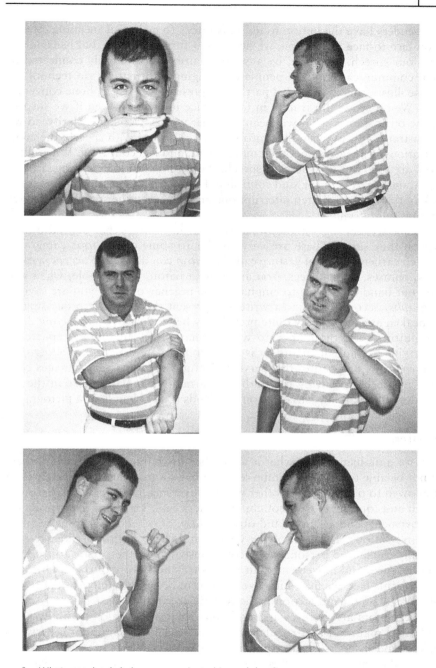

I What meaning is being communicated in each box?

we as senders have the option to use illustrators to make our meaning clearer. In non-face-to-face interaction, we need other forms of nonverbal behavior to clarify our speech. However, because illustrators are so closely connected to verbal communication, even people exchanging information via technology may use illustrators as a natural part of the presentation (e.g., phone conversations). We often use illustrators in face-to-face interaction even if we suspect that the other knows what we mean. In other words, we like to clarify, so we use illustrators. Last, when illustrators are used in sync with speech, the communication exchange is smoother, more fluent, and less confusing. When illustrators are used out of sync with speech, the communication exchange can be choppy, uneven, less fluent, and confusing. People will overlap in conversation, speak out of turn, and often interrupt one another when the speech illustrative pattern is out of sync.

Some writers suggest additional types of illustrators that depend on the function they serve. These are very similar to some of the four categories reviewed earlier. A type of gesture called a *baton* can be used to accent spoken words, phrases, or sentences. You are using a baton, for example, when you slam your hand on a table to emphasize the urgency of what you are saying. *Ideographs,* according to most writers, represent the cognitive processing of the speaker, and are usually quite prevalent when individuals are having difficulty putting their thoughts into words. Snapping your fingers repeatedly while trying to think of an answer is an example of an ideograph. *Pictographs* are movements or gestures that serve as pictures or drawings of images contained in speech. Drawing the outline of a male or female figure in the air while describing an attractive person to friends is an example of a pictograph.

Regulators

Think for a moment about what it would be like to interact daily with others and not be able to see them. Some research has shown that if interactants are not allowed to observe one another while conversing, the interaction becomes difficult and considerable miscommunication occurs. This happens because we use movements and gestures (and observe those of others) to help us regulate our conversations. This is also why we find it difficult at first to interact with a visually challenged person. We unconsciously expect the person to respond to our gestures and movements, but he or she is not aware of them. Once we recognize this fact, we may still have a problem because we have to figure out how to regulate the interaction without these nonverbal aids.

Regulators are gestures and body movements that, along with eye and vocal cues, maintain and regulate the back-and-forth interaction between speakers and listeners during spoken dialogue. Regulators are not nearly as intentional as emblems and illustrators. They are learned gradually and are an integral part of the communication socialization process. Usually, they are learned to such a degree that they become ingrained habits. We are rarely conscious of the behavior we use to control and regulate our conversations with other people.

Kendon and Ferber (1973) identified six stages of gene regulate or act in the regulative mode in greeting situations. T

1. Sighting, orientation, and initiation approach.
2. The distant salutation, or movements and gestures that ification and acknowledge that a greeting sequence has been initiated and who the participants are. Smiles, waves, head nods, and so on can all be part of this official acknowledgment stage.
3. The head dip, which signifies transitions between acts and shifts in psychological orientation. This stage may not be observed if the participant did not continue to pursue the other participant.
4. The approach, which assumes that the greeting process continues. In this step, the participants use several nonverbal behaviors that signify approach, such as moving toward one another, gazing, grooming, and extending one or both arms.
5. The final approach, where participants are less than ten feet apart. There is smiling, mutual gazing, and much face-to-face interaction.
6. The close salutation, when the participants of the greeting ceremony negotiate a standing position. They use ritualistic speech (Hi, how are you?) and if the situation calls for body contact (such as a handshake, shoulder slap, or embrace), it takes place here.

Consider the behavior(s) you use to cue others that you are finished talking. What particular actions are signals that you want to speak? That you do not want to speak?

Managing communication turn-taking is the primary function of regulators. It is necessary during our conversations to exchange roles as the sender and the listener. The goal, of course, is to switch those roles smoothly and fluidly. Communication **turn-taking behaviors** can be categorized into those that the speaker uses to maintain or yield her or his talking turn, and those that the listener uses to request or decline an invitation to talk (Duncan, 1972, 1974).

- **Turn-yielding cues** are given by speakers who wish to discontinue talking and give the listener the opportunity to take the speaking role. These movements may include direct body orientation, a forward lean, a beckoning gesture with the hand or head that says "come on, I'll listen to you now," and many eye and vocal cues (increased eye contact, raised inflection, or simply a long silent pause). Yielding cues can be seen as behaviorally putting on the brakes to communicating to your fellow interactants that you are coming to a verbal stop.
- **Turn-maintaining cues** are used by speakers who want to continue talking. They are especially observable when the listener is trying to interrupt. Keeping eye contact to a minimum, increasing the rate and loudness of speech, indirect body orientation, filled pauses, and halting gestures (holding your hand up with the palm facing the listener as a traffic officer

would while stopping traffic) are all examples of turn-maintaining cues. They communicate to the listener that you still have more to say.

- **Turn-requesting regulators** are used by the listener to signal the speaker that he or she would like to talk. Examples of requesting cues include raising the hand or index finger, an audible intake of breath, tensing and straightening of posture, or any other behavior that may get the speaker's attention. Vocally, we can use a throat-clearing sound or a stutter start to request a speaking turn. One writer has also suggested that requesting cues are used to hurry the speaker to the finish line. Rapid head nods that signal agreement or a rolling gesture with the hand may get the speaker to make her or his point much sooner than she or he normally would.
- **Turn-denying behaviors** are cues listeners use to signal that we decline our turn to speak. Sustaining a relaxed posture while remaining silent, slow and frequent, positive head nods, and positive vocal utterances such as "uh-huh, uh-huh" usually encourage the speaker to continue.

Communication turn-management cues can help direct, organize, and control the flow of conversation. These cues can also assist in the maintenance of smooth, fluid, in-sync speech.

Affect Displays

The fourth category of bodily motion is **affect displays**. These cues primarily involve facial expressions but also include a person's posture, the way he or she walks, limb movements, and other behaviors that provide information about her or his emotional state or mood. Affect displays indicate both one's emotional reactions to what is going on and the strength of those reactions.

It is quite possible for many or most people to portray an emotion they do not actually feel. Similarly, it is possible for many people to repress the expression of an emotion they feel would be inappropriate for others to be aware of. However, behaviors that reveal true emotional states are usually unintentional, even when we are aware of them. For instance, when we feel our knees shaking and see our hands trembling while experiencing fear or anxiety, we often cannot control them.

Adaptors

The fifth category of nonverbal behavior is the adaptor. **Adaptors** are highly unintentional behaviors that are usually responses to boredom or stress or are closely linked with negative feelings toward ourselves or others. These behaviors are vestiges of coping behavior that we learn very early in life. According to several writers, adaptors were once part of our efforts to cope with physical and emotional needs and the need to learn instrumental behavior. They are, in essence, behaviors that once allowed us to adapt to situational, social, and cultural influences. They can be described as leftovers of goal-directed behavior that later became automatic, habitual actions.

Quite often, behaviors that people use every day may actually be adaptors. Are you, for instance, aware when you pick your nose, tap your pen or pencil on your desk, pull at your earlobe, rub your arms, or fiddle with an object in your hand? Lip biting and nail biting are not generally well-accepted behaviors, but we often see people do them in front of total strangers. Chances are that such behaviors are adaptors.

Many researchers characterize adaptors as falling into three different types. **Self-adaptors** are nonverbal acts in which an individual manipulates her or his own body. Scratching, rubbing, and hair twisting are common self-adaptors. **Alter-directed adaptors** are movements that are designed to protect the individual from other interactants. Folding one's arms may indicate protection against some sort of verbal or nonverbal attack. Unconscious leg movements during interaction may represent a thinly repressed desire to keep others away.

Finally, there are **object-focused adaptors**. These acts include the unconscious manipulation of a particular object, such as tapping a pen, smoking, or twisting a ring around your finger. Some speakers feel it necessary to have a piece of chalk in hand while speaking.

While not contradicting the work of Ekman and his colleagues, Wachsmuth (2006) has explained some new elements of gesture theory. This work has been taking place in the area of neuroscience. Here the researchers believe that gestures are coverbal. That is, they believe that gestures arrive along the same pathways as verbal communication. Kelly, Kravitz, and Hopkins (2004) studied what happened when their subjects were forced to create messages with consistent and inconsistent verbal and nonverbal messages. They found that there were negative peaks (called the *N400 effect*) when there were contradictions between the verbal and the nonverbal. Similar N400 effects occurred when subjects made verbal misstatements such as "He spread his toast with socks" (Wachsmuth, 2006, p. 22). McNeill (2005) has subdivided gestures into four types:

1. **Deictic**—when the gesture accompanies the word, especially words like *here, there, I,* and *you* (Wachsmuth, 2006, p. 23).

2. **Iconic**—relating a gesture to an event, as when telling a story about a girl with an umbrella. Here the storyteller pretends to be carrying the umbrella.

3. **Metaphorical**—these gestures are similar to iconic ones, but they usually relate to more abstract things, such as "the next topic. . . ."

4. **Beats**—these gestures are related to the "poetry" or "music" of the message itself, such as pounding one's fist.

Wachsmuth (2006) has reported that there are three stages in the development of a message. In the preverbal stage, the person is trying to translate an idea into a message. In the second stage, the brain begins to construct the sentence. The third stage is the use of the lungs and vocal chords to produce the message. Contemporary researchers believe that the gestures are considered in stage one, where both the words and accompanying gestures are being created.

Carney, Hall, and Lebeau (2005) found that using gestures includes the attempt to create social power—to persuade. They found seventy different gestures, proxemic behaviors, and vocalic measures used to persuade. All of these researchers were looking for information about how gestures are used when people are telling the truth. However, there is also a significant amount of research regarding deception.

DECEPTION CUES

Many people believe that deception, for example, can sometimes be detected in body movements even though speakers may believe they have effectively concealed any cues that might give them away. Research on deception and movement indicates that people are better able to conceal lying cues in the movements of the face and head than in other body areas. In several studies, observers who observed only the body of the deceiver were slightly more likely to guess who was lying than observers who keyed in on the face and head. But don't assume that you can always catch liars. Even with videotape and unlimited time to review observations, observers' ability to detect deception by observing bodily movements is not meaningfully better than by chance guessing.

Caso, Maricchiolo, Bonaiuto, Vrij, and Mann (2006) tested the impact of forcing their subjects to lie. They interviewed subjects about the possession of an object. Then they were interviewed a second time, indicating that the researcher knew they had lied the first time and therefore showed suspicion. When there was suspicion, there was a decrease in deictic gestures and an increase in metaphoric gestures. There was also a decrease in self-adaptors. Their study took place with Italian subjects, and cultural factors may influence the kinds of gestures that occur when lying.

Some conclusions about detecting deception are needed at this juncture. As nonverbal encoders and decoders, we can safely conclude the following about deception:

- The particular behavior that is likely to show that one is lying depends on the characteristics of the lie, the liar, the receiver of the lie, and the context.
- Liars learn to control their head and facial movements (upper 12 inches of the human body) when deceiving, but it is difficult for them to control all nonverbal behavior.
- Leakage cues are not the same for everybody; they differ from person to person, context to context, and for different emotions.
- With most liars (deceivers) it is almost impossible to detect the lie. Many people are highly skilled deceivers and are effective liars who do not feel guilty about a lie, have convinced themselves that they are not lying, or are confident that the target of their lies will believe them.
- Attractive people are more likely to be able to convince others of untruths than unattractive people. The reasoning here is that attractive persons receive more opportunities to communicate, gain confidence in a variety of communication situations, and therefore can control their verbal and

nonverbal behavior more easily when lying. They are a¹
be given the benefit of the doubt by their listeners. T'
successful con artists.
- Children and adults who have honest-looking features and
  plays are often given the benefit of the doubt even if someone thinks the,
  are lying. People in this culture often say that the person can't be lying
  because he (or she) looks too honest.
- Deception is difficult to discern. We must be cautious in assuming that
  someone is lying because he or she has negative affect displays, or in assuming that someone is telling the truth because he has honest affect displays.

People who claim to be able to identify liars with high accuracy are lying
to you—or to themselves. Deception has been a major research topic of leading psychologists and communication scholars for several decades. With the
exception of a few very highly trained security officers, the ability of most people to detect liars, even those with specific training, is astoundingly low—
barely as good as flipping a coin. Accuracy is increased a little bit when the
potential liar is well-known by the observer—their idiosyncratic characteristics when lying are known. Looking for nonverbal behaviors in strangers is as
worthless as using a lie detector to identify liars. Both are based on myths in
our culture, which is why lie detector evidence is not usually permitted in criminal trials and testimony by involved observers is taken only with a large
"grain of salt." Face it. People will lie to you, and you will have no way of
knowing which ones are doing it. Becoming a nonverbal behavior expert will
not protect you, but it can give you a false sense of security (DePaulo, 1988;
DePaulo & Kirkendol, 1988; Goleman, 1999; McCroskey & Richmond,
1996; Richmond, 1996; Rosenfeld, 1966a, 1966b, 1982).

However, not all lying is criminal or bad, such as small social lies. These
small social lies occur in families, friendships, and business relations. Hall suggests it would be tactless and rude to call attention to social lies. Most social
lies involve simple politeness; they generally are meaningless and not hurtful
(DePaulo,1988; Goffman, 1959, 1967; Hall, 1996, 1998).

POSTURE

Heather walked into the office on Monday morning. She strolled to the coat
rack, hanging up her jacket and gloves. Checking her mailbox, Heather slowly
pulled out a pile of miscellaneous memos and letters, thumbed through them,
and dropped them on the edge of her desk. She then fell limply into her chair
and tossed her purse into the bottom desk drawer. After reading a note from
the boss taped to her word processor, she sighed and leaned over her desk to
begin work. Her coworker Janet glanced at Heather. Somewhat puzzled, Janet
thoroughly scrutinized her and asked, "Heather, are you feeling all right this
morning?" Heather paused, lifted her bent head slightly, and said, "I feel fine.
Why?" Dismissing the entire matter, Janet replied, "Oh, nothing. We'd better
get back to work."

Reading the above scenario, you are probably wondering why Janet seemed concerned. It may not be apparent to you that she was keying in on visible kinesic cues that Heather may not have been aware of transmitting. Janet was receiving messages from Heather's posture. This morning, Heather's shoulders were drawn downward. Her head was turned a bit downward, and she seemed to slump. As she slowly walked through the office, her feet seem to plod on the floor. Usually, Heather had a crisp and commanding stride. Not today. In Janet's mind, it was definitely a slow, painstaking gait.

As we said earlier, posture can be a rich source of information about emotional states and relationships. The way we walk, whether with a bounce or a saunter, sends messages to others. The way we sit can indicate interest or boredom. Our body orientation toward others during conversation may say much about our relationship with, orientation toward, and feelings about other persons. You can receive social signals from a person by the way he or she stands, lies, leans, lounges, reclines, or rests.

How Does Posture Communicate?

A leading writer on body movements and gestures, Mehrabian (1969a, 1969b, 1971, 1972), posits that there are two primary dimensions of posture through which we transmit messages about our attitudes. The first dimension is called *immediacy*. The concept of immediacy is discussed in depth in a later chapter. For now, the postural behaviors that represent an immediate attitude include direct body orientation, symmetric positioning, and forward leaning of the body (Richmond, 2002a).

The second dimension identified by Mehrabian is called *relaxation*. Relaxed behavior includes backward leaning of the body, reduced tension in the arms and legs, and asymmetry of positioning.

The basic idea of Mehrabian's work is that we can communicate an openness and willingness to communicate, along with a positive attitude, by exhibiting immediacy and relaxation in our postural positions. On the other hand, our posture can close out another person and shut off communication. Noncommunicative postural cues that reduce visibility and increase perceptions of distance tend to discourage interaction.

Scheflen (1964), another notable writer and researcher in the area of kinesics, contends that we can communicate with our posture in many ways. Scheflen divides all postures of interacting persons into three major categories: inclusive or noninclusive, face-to-face or parallel body orientation, and congruence or incongruence.

INCLUSIVE VERSUS NONINCLUSIVE. Postural cues in this category are acts or positions that either include or block out other people. Imagine you're at a party held by a social organization. It may be in a large hall or ballroom, and the attending crowd may be large. As you look around the room, you observe that small groups, or conversation pockets, have formed. You particularly notice a group of four people who are enjoying their private interaction immensely while virtually ignoring the other partygoers. With their posture, this little group has communicated to others that they are not included. You are well acquainted with each of the four but may hesitate to approach and become a part of their interaction because of the noninclusive postural cues they are transmitting.

FACE-TO-FACE VERSUS PARALLEL BODY ORIENTATION. This category refers primarily to the postural relationship between two people during conversation. Essentially, two people can engage in conversation while facing one another or while sitting or standing side by side. These postural orientations can tell a great deal about a relationship. For instance, the face-to-face position may indicate more formal or professional interaction. It may also suggest that each person feels a need to continually monitor the other. The face-to-face positioning also may be a sign of a more active interaction; whereas, the parallel orientation may indicate neutral or passive interaction.

CONGRUENCE VERSUS INCONGRUENCE. Scheflen's last category, congruence versus incongruence, refers to whether two people imitate or share a similar posture. If they share a similar posture and tend to imitate each other's positioning and movements, they are exhibiting congruent body positions. If there is a marked difference in the postures of interactants, they are engaging in incongruent body positioning.

When the postures of two people are congruent, this may signal agreement, equality, and liking between them. A primary message transmitted when postures are incongruent is that there is a status differential between the interactants. The higher-status individual exhibits a more relaxed posture with indirect orientation, backward leaning, and asymmetric leg and arm positions. The lower-status person usually maintains a more formal posture with direct orientation, forward leaning, more muscle tension, and straightened spine. Therefore people of perceived equal status, such as friends, may strive to maintain that equality through their posture, whereas those of different status, such as teachers and students, doctors and patients, supervisors and subordinates may exhibit postural cues that signal the inequality.

Communicative Potential of Posture

Many psychiatrists, therapists, and psychologists believe that attitudes, predispositions, and emotional states may be manifested as enduring postural patterns. They contend that the structure and orientation of the body seldom lie. Practitioners, such as some chiropractors, believe that our history of emotions, deep-rooted feelings, and personality can be identified by the way we hold our bodies, move our bodies, and exhibit tension in them.

As we noted in our Janet and Heather scenario earlier, the way we walk can betray our outlook on life, our attitudes, or even our emotions. It may even tell others a lot about our cultural or ethnic backgrounds. Others suggest that our stride is closely linked to our personality. We may be able to change others' perceptions of us by changing the pace or rhythm with which we walk.

It is not surprising that our posture is most effective at reflecting our gender. In fact, many behaviors that go into separating the boys from the girls can be seen in the way we hold, carry, and orient our bodies. For centuries, females in American culture have been socialized to exhibit shrinkage in their postures. Shrinkage cues include such things as the lowering of head and eyes, tilting the head to one side, and pulling the body and limbs inward to take up less space (knees and feet together and arms held closely to the trunk). Males, on the other hand, have been socialized to engage in expanding nonverbal acts. A stereotypical masculine posture is characterized by positions and movements that take up more space. Such expansive behavior includes such things as positioning the legs apart while standing or sitting, carrying arms away from the trunk, and taking longer strides.

It should be noted that individuals begin to develop the postures considered appropriate to their genders as early as infancy, leading some to believe that they are natural. While this may be partially true, our culture also influences our posture. As children, if we show indications of postural positions and movement that are typically associated with the other gender in our culture, we may be encouraged by our parents, teachers, peers, and other members of our culture to change our posture. Consider the stereotypes associated with males who exhibit the shrinking behavior generally accepted as feminine. How about the female who has the masculine expanding posture, walk, or body orientation? Some people around these individuals are likely simply to move away from such culturally inappropriate nonverbal displays. Others will express their displeasure openly.

MOVEMENT AND COMMUNICATOR STYLE

Norton (1983) published a comprehensive book on different styles of communicators. He defined **communicator style** as the way a person verbally and paraverbally interacts to signal how literal meaning should be taken, interpreted, filtered, or understood in the communicative process. To Norton, communicator style is what gives form to the content of messages. According to Norton, several verbal and nonverbal factors differentiate among the various styles. One of these factors is the different pattern of body movements and gestures that is used by different communicators. Norton suggests that the major types of communicator styles are *dramatic, dominant, animated, relaxed, attentive, open, friendly, contentious,* and *impression-leaving.* Let us consider the behaviors that go into each style.

The Dramatic Style

You probably know someone who is quite dramatic when he or she speaks. These individuals are usually masters at exaggeration, tell the most fascinating stories, and often have a rhythm to their voices. Dramatizing, according to Norton, is the most physically visible of all communicator styles. It is usually not enough for the dramatist to say something in an interesting way. He or she generally relies on a wide range of illustrative behaviors. Common illustrators that represent the dramatic style are pictographs, drawings of forms and figures in space, and moving dramatically from one location to another. In short, the world is a stage. An interesting characteristic of dramatic style is that the behavioral cues signal deviations from normal behavior. The abnormality of dramatic behavior is probably the major reason it successfully captures the interest of listeners. Additionally, perceptions of popularity, attractiveness, and status are often enhanced by the dramatic communicator style.

The Dominant Style

The dominant communicator uses nonverbal cues to dominate listeners. Some writers have likened the too-dominant style to a big stick that beats the listener into a submissive posture. Expansive body posture and movements that fill space are often associated with dominance. People who quickly approach fellow interactants are generally seen as dominant. Although these behaviors are more commonly used by males, females with dominant styles use them as well, along with more reciprocal eye contact. Research shows that dominant communicators are perceived as more confident, conceited, self-assured, competitive, forceful, active, and enthusiastic.

The Animated Style

The animated communicator engages in exaggerated bodily motions and gestures actively while speaking. Talk-show hosts Jay Leno and Jon Stewart illustrate the animated style well. Frequent and repetitive head nods and frequent smiles are commonly used with this style. In early work, Scheflen (1964) suggested that preening and intimate positioning are essentially animated behaviors that pervade courtship and dating.

The Relaxed Style

The relaxed communicator seems to remain collected and calm internally in anxiety-producing situations; he or she also manifests relaxation in posture, movement, and gesture. Rarely do relaxed speakers unconsciously engage in adaptive-type behaviors. They seem immune to nervous mannerisms and seldom allow their gestures to get out of control. Communicators with a relaxed style transmit a variety of messages. According to one investigation, a relaxed style communicates calmness, serenity, peace, confidence, and comfortableness. A lack of tension in the body and movements may also indicate self-assurance.

The Attentive Style

The attentive style of communication more adequately characterizes a style of listening to or receiving messages from others than a style of speaking. Some writers have referred to attentiveness as active listening. Norton contends that the attentive style is inversely related to the dominant and dramatic styles. Attentiveness is characterized by a more immediate posture, forward leaning, head nods that indicate agreement, a direct body orientation, and gestures that encourage the speaker to continue. These also are cues that signal interest and empathy. The attentive communicator can make the speaker feel that what he or she is saying is worth hearing.

The Open Style

Norton contends that the open communicator uses bodily activity that is expansive, unreserved, extroverted, and approach-oriented. Other characteristics of the open style include affable, friendly, frank, gregarious, nonsecretive, and conversational behaviors. The primary function of behavior used by open-style communicators is to signal to individuals that they can communicate openly and freely. Think for a moment about how difficult it would be to share your feelings with people who hardly looked at you, seemed more interested in a cup of coffee, positioned their body away from you, and folded their arms across their chests. Add to that a plethora of adaptors (tapping a cup with their fingers, playing with a napkin) that start just about the time you begin spilling your guts. Chances are that you would quickly become discouraged and change the topic of conversation to a less personal matter. The next time you find yourself easily revealing your intimate thoughts to a friend or acquaintance, check the person's behavior. Through openness in positioning and orientation, the person may have pulled it out of you.

The Friendly Style

Norton says that the friendly style ranges from an absence of hostility to signals of deep intimacy. To the extent that communicators strive to neutralize or avoid being perceived as hostile, they use a friendly style of communication. This style is closely related to both the open and attentive styles. Body movements that serve to reduce distance such as approach, forward leaning, and other immediacy behavior may help to create a friendly style. In addition, communicators with a friendly style continually confirm their fellow interactants wishes; often touch them in an affectionate, stroking manner; and behave in a way that positively and uniquely acknowledges the other interactants.

The Contentious Style

This style is similar to the dominant style, but it might better be thought of as aggressive dominance. People exhibiting this style are argumentative. They are likely to accompany their assertive tone of voice with forward leaning and a substantial amount of arm waving. They sound like they want to fight and often intimidate their less assertive interaction partners.

The Impression-Leaving Style

This is the least researched of the various communication styles and may be simply a combination of the others. The name refers to the impression a communicator projects or leaves—not just how the person is remembered after communication, but also whether the person leaves an impression at all.

GENERAL COMMUNICATOR STYLES

Norton's dimensions of communicator style have received considerable attention from many writers. However, others have suggested that some of these styles can be combined because they involve common communicative behavior. There are three general dimensions of communication style: *assertiveness, responsiveness,* and *versatility* (McCroskey & Richmond, 1996). Let's consider each in turn.

Assertiveness is a communicator's use of control and ability to maintain the interest and attention of listeners. Common to the assertive communicator are factors such as dominance, forcefulness, independence, presence, taking charge, and willingness to defend one's own beliefs. The assertive communicator is an initiator. He or she is actively engaged in maintaining the attention of others through a dynamic delivery, vocal variety, and frequent movements and gestures. The assertive style is a combination of the dramatic, dominant, animated, and contentious styles.

The communicator who uses a responsive style is characterized as emotional, understanding, sensitive, and approachable. Through her or his actions, the responsive communicator projects friendliness, warmth, sincerity, and tenderness. Responsive communicators are eager to soothe hurt feelings and often show sympathy to others. They are willing to be helpful through their liberal use of positive feedback and may continually reward others for open communication. The responsive style is a combination of the open, attentive, relaxed, and friendly styles.

The third general communication dimension is versatility. Highly versatile communicators are those who adapt to the communicative behavior of others. They often let others know of their willingness to be adaptive through an attentive posture. The versatile-communicator manager, for instance, can adapt her or his style of behavior and interaction to the needs of each employee. He or she uses dominating and assertive behavior with employees who require more control or direction, while using a more responsive style with those who need encouragement and supportive interaction. Behavior is flexible depending on the person or situation. The person who is capable of this communicator style projects a deliberately high or deliberately low level of all, or nearly all, of the styles described by Norton. Clearly, this individual has considerable communicative competence.

EFFECTS OF BODY MOVEMENTS AND GESTURES

In the final section of this chapter, we look at some effects of body movements on perceptions and interaction. Because the concept of communicator style is fresh in your mind, let's begin with a brief review of some studies that have been conducted in this area.

Communicator Style

Does the dramatic, animated, contentious, or versatile style affect people's perceptions of you in any way? Research shows that it does. For example, in one study the researchers were interested in whether students' perceptions of teachers' effectiveness were associated with perceived assertiveness, responsiveness, and versatility in the behavior of the teachers. They found that students who saw their teachers as assertive also reported a more positive attitude toward the class and had a greater behavioral commitment to the teacher and the subject matter. The authors suggested that teachers who use assertive behavior are well liked. Students who judged their teachers to be highly versatile and responsive also reported a more positive attitude and greater behavioral commitment (Richmond, 1996, 2002a, 2002b; Richmond, Smith, Heisel, & McCroskey, 2002). In another study, teachers who were perceived as more dramatic by their students were rated as more effective instructors. In brief, within the educational environment, more animated and lively styles of presenting material make it more interesting and provide a touch of entertainment. Similarly, teachers who use open and attentive positioning and encouraging movements can influence their students to view them as concerned and supportive (Richmond, 1996, 2002a, 2002b; Richmond, Smith, Heisel, & McCroskey, 2002).

Simplifying Encoding and Decoding

Many writers believe that the use of illustrative gestures actually helps us to more easily encode our thoughts into spoken words. The use of illustrative gestures can help us to decode speech. When you see someone who is having difficulty finding the right words, you probably notice that her or his gesturing increases considerably. Research tells us that, for one reason or another, the gesturing is aiding the speaker in her or his attempt to express.

Role of Illustrators in Decoding

Body movements can elaborate the meaning of verbal messages and provide a second way to process information. People who paint pictures with their gestures or visually place imaginary objects in the space around them while speaking are giving their listeners cues, which the listeners can process spatially and temporally while they are digesting the words. This may have important implications in the classroom. It is likely that students with dramatic teachers retain more class material and perform better on exams. One study was conducted to determine whether listeners who were provided visual cues by speakers were better at comprehending verbal messages. The results indicated that when listeners had the opportunity to see the speaker's body movements, their comprehension scores increased. Even when the speaker's lip and facial cues were hidden from the listeners' view, kinesic cues alone positively affected comprehension (Archer, 1991; Argyle, 1975; Krauss, 1998; Sousa-Poza & Rohrberg, 1977).

Positive and Negative Perceptions

We have already discussed many perceptions others have of us based on our bodily motions. We said, for instance, that open and attentive posture can affect perceptions of responsiveness and friendliness; closing ourselves off by blocking movements or indirect body orientation may produce perceptions of aloofness or an unwillingness to get too deeply involved. Other studies have shown that our positive or negative movements can influence others' judgments of our attractiveness. On the one hand, positive head nods and other approval-type gestures are positively related to attractiveness. On the other hand, people who use self-manipulation behaviors are generally rated as less attractive.

Research on Immediacy

Studies have shown that movement such as forward leaning, closer proximity, more openness of arms and body, more direct body orientation, and postural relaxation can influence whether a person likes you. Closely related to liking, perceptions of warmth can be enhanced with shifts in posture toward fellow interactants and keeping the hands still while smiling. You can, however, communicate a cold attitude by drumming your fingers, slumping in your chair, and moving your eyes as you look around the room (Richmond, 2002a).

As we conclude this chapter, it is important to note that gesture and movement are at the heart of the study of nonverbal communication. We have summarized many ways by which nonverbal messages are encoded into and decoded from the bodily actions of human beings. They provide particularly effective means for complementing, accenting, regulating, contradicting, and substituting for verbal utterances. Caution should be exercised, however, in assigning specific meaning to behavior without considering the context within which the nonverbal behavior occurs.

Glossary of Terminology

Adaptors are unintentional behaviors that are usually responses to boredom or stress or responses closely linked with negative feelings toward ourselves or others.

Affect displays are cues that involve primarily facial expressions but also include a person's posture, gait, limb movements, and other behaviors that provide information about her or his emotional state or mood.

Alter-directed adaptors are movements that are designed to protect an individual from other interactants.

Communicator style is the way a person verbally and paraverbally interacts to signal how one's literal meaning should be taken, interpreted, filtered, or understood in the communicative process.

Emblems are gestures and movements that have a direct verbal translation. Emblems are known by most or all of a group, class, culture, or subculture. They can be used to stimulate specific meanings in the minds of others in place of verbal communication.

Illustrators are gestures and movements that are closely linked with spoken language and help to illustrate what is being said.

Kinesics is the study of the communicative impact of body movement and gesture.

Object-focused adaptors are behaviors that include the unconscious manipulation of a particular object.

Regulators are gestures and movements that, along with eye and vocal cues, maintain and regulate the back-and-forth interaction between speakers and listeners during spoken dialogue.

Self-adaptors are nonverbal acts in which an individual manipulates her or his own body.

Turn-denying behavior is behavior we use to decline our turn to speak.

Turn-maintaining cues are used by speakers who want to continue talking.

Turn-requesting regulators are used by the listener to signal the speaker that he or she would like to talk.

Turn-taking behavior is behavior that the speaker uses to either maintain or yield her or his talking turn or that the listener uses to request or decline an invitation to talk.

Turn-yielding cues are given by speakers who wish to cease talking and give the listener the opportunity to speak.

CHAPTER 4

Facial Behavior

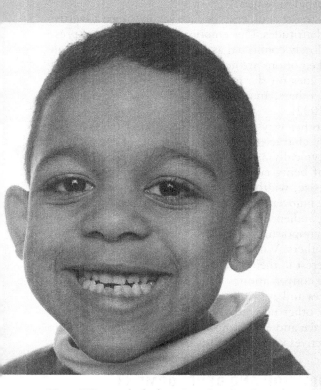

Nonverbal theorists imply that the study of facial expressions is the study of "emotion itself" (Darwin, 1998; Tomkins, 1962; Tomkins & McCarter, 1964). Experience and research have helped us to understand that the human face is a primary tool used for transmitting emotional expressions. The facial muscles provide such a complex repertoire of configurations that most of us, if we worked at it, could move our faces into more than a hundred different looks, much like Jim Carrey, the master of facial contortion and emotional expression.

IMPORTANCE OF FACIAL EXPRESSIONS

The major reason the face is so important in human communication is that it is usually visible during interaction. When you converse with others, where do you usually look? At their feet, legs, hands, shoulders, chests, or elbows? Maybe, but most of us look at the face, often to the exclusion of other parts of the body. When asked to describe an attractive man or woman, we generally begin with facial features. When we are engaged in serious dialogue with friends, acquaintances, and strangers, we turn to their faces for evidence that supports or contradicts their verbal messages.

The eyes are the windows to the soul, and the face is a marquee advertising one's emotions, moods, and attitudes. Our emotions and the facial expression of those emotions are so closely connected as to be inseparable. Although we believe that expressions and emotions are not totally linked, we do feel that people can find a plethora of cues on the faces of others that provide rich information about feelings self, others, and probably life itself (McCroskey & Richmond, 1986; Richmond, 2002).

The face is important in other ways as well. By looking at the face and eyes, we often infer personality characteristics. We can think of a variety of facial features that are stereotypically associated with certain personalities. Many performers complain of being typecast in television or movie roles because of the shape, profile, size, width, or narrowness of their faces. The crook, the family man, even the innocent victim must have the facial characteristics that convince the viewing audience of the role being played.

The face and eyes are also important because they help us to manage and regulate our interactions with others. With our faces, we can signal our disapproval, disbelief, or sincere interest in the messages of others. Our expressions can set the mood or tone of the conversation.

Expressions using our faces and eyes influence our day-to-day communication at least as much as any other nonverbal behavior. To develop a clear perspective on the role of the face and eyes in nonverbal communication, it is useful to examine some perspectives others have advanced.

PERSPECTIVES ON ACQUISITION AND DEVELOPMENT

The debate over whether facial expressions are innate, learned, or both is not new. Are our facial expressions somehow inherently linked with our feelings? Do we have to learn how to smile when we are happy, to frown when we are sad or angry? Are facial expressions a product of social and cultural influences, or is there something universal and innate about the way we express our feelings on our faces?

Perspective 1: Evolution and Natural Selection

Charles Darwin (1872), who is most famous for his theories of evolution, was interested in the facial expressions of animals. Darwin believed that expressive facial behaviors are essentially survival mechanisms and therefore evolved in much the same way as other physical characteristics. From this evolutionary perspective, facial expressions were acquired through the process of natural selection for establishing successful interaction. Long before the human species mastered the higher-level communicative skills required by verbal exchange, facial expressions allowed higher-order primates to transmit their feelings, attitudes, and emotional states.

Results of research are increasingly supportive of the hypothesis that some facial expressions are inborn characteristics of human beings. Even without access to that research, if one travels the world, one can see that the meanings of many facial expressions are successfully conveyed across cultural boundaries (Weitz, 1974). This is not true of other aspects of human behavior.

Eibl-Eibesfeldt (1970, 1972), a researcher in the area of expressive behavior, holds closely to the position that facial expressions are innate. Much of his claim is based on his observations of children who were born both deaf and blind. Eibl-Eibesfeldt's research has shown that the fundamental expressions of emotion (sadness, anger, disgust, fear, interest, surprise, and happiness) on the face can be observed in such individuals. Eibl-Eibesfeldt (1972) notes that deaf and blind children smile, sulk, cry, and show surprise and anger. The probability that they acquired these facial expressions by learning is practically nil, since they can neither see nor hear, the primary means by which humans learn (p. 305). In response to the argument that deaf and blind children may have acquired expressions similar to those of normal children through the sense of touch, Eibl-Eibesfeldt suggests that brain-damaged deaf and blind children also exhibit the typical or primary facial expressions. He states:

> It is difficult to imagine how they [blind and deaf brain-damaged children] could have learned social expressions without deliberate training. If anyone insists in such cases on the learning theory, the burden of proof for such an improbable hypothesis lie[s] on his [or her] side. It seems more reasonable to assume that the neuronal and motor structures underlying these motor patterns developed in a process of self-differentiation by decoding genetically stored information (p. 306).

Therefore, according to Darwin's and Eibl-Eibesfeldt's perspectives, some primary facial expressions are inherently linked with moods and feelings. They are innate products of the evolutionary process, and they are generally universal, whether you are Native American, South American, North American, European, Asian, African, or Indian. More recently, Patterson (2003) has supported the view that facial expressions of emotion are largely rooted in evolutionary theory.

Perspective 2: External Factors

Let's think about other possible influences before we accept this position as the only explanation for how we acquire our facial expressions. Although much research supports the view of innateness and many basic or primary facial expressions are similarly decoded in many cultures, there are probably external factors such as the environment, social rules, and culture that contribute to our facial behavior. Although the research does not support the theory that facial expressions are entirely learned, that does not mean that the learning perspective has no place in our understanding of facial expressions. From early childhood, most people are taught appropriate facial behaviors for given situations. For example, children are generally aware that it is proper to look somber and serious at funerals, not happy. As children grow and develop, they are taught by various role models what facial expression is appropriate for a certain emotion (Ekman, 1972; Ekman & Friesen, 1967). In fact, many of us even know how to smile with spontaneous enjoyment smiles as well as deliberate nonenjoyment smiles (Miles & Johnston, 2007; Forgas & East, 2008); Schmidt, Battacharya, & Denlinger, 2009).

Perspective 3: Innate and Learned

The other major perspective on the acquisition of facial expression is that such behaviors are both innate and learned. Many theorists hold to this position (Ekman & Friesen, 1969a, 1969b, 1975; Ekman, Friesen, & Ellsworth, 1972). Let us summarize what this position is.

It is generally accepted that there are primary facial expressions that, from the day we are born, are closely linked to our primary emotions: sadness, anger, disgust, fear, interest, surprise, and happiness. An effective and entertaining way to remember them is the acronym of **SADFISH**.

As Ekman and his colleagues continued their research on the expression of the emotions in the facial area, they felt that the emotion of disgust-contempt was a natural blend. However, Ekman and Friesen (1986) found later that contempt is a different emotion and has a different facial expression (see also Ekman & Heider, 1988). Walton (2004) has provided an interesting description of contempt: "To hold somebody in contempt is to regard them with scorn, and at the same time hardly to regard them at all. Contempt hovers between a desire to ignore the offending individual, and the desire to make it plain to him how worthless he is—in effect two quite different strategies" (p. 207). Many of us are aware of the concept of contempt in a court of law, usually where the witness will not answer a question posed to him or her, or when a participant does not give the judge the respect that is due. In everyday communication, perhaps we should think of contempt as the act of "dissing" someone, in today's vernacular.

The expression of contempt has received quite a bit of publicity over the past twenty years, primarily because of the negative effects of the emotion on marriage (Gladwell, 2005). As Hickson, Stacks, and Moore (2005) point out, there has historically been a difference of opinion between those researchers and others, including the views expressed in previous editions of this book. Here, however, we will add the expression of contempt without deleting any of our previous conclusions. Carrere and Gottman (1999) found that contempt was one of the major indicators to determine whether a married couple would obtain a divorce within the next fifteen years. They claimed that they could predict, with 95 percent accuracy, whether a divorce would occur based on analyzing only one hour of talk between husband and wife. Even with only fifteen minutes, the researchers claimed they could predict the future of the relationship with 90 percent accuracy. Later, one of their colleagues discovered that there was a high level of predictability with only three minutes of the couple's taped interactions. Gladwell (2005) and others have called these short analyses *thin slicing*. While Carrere and Gottman found gender differences in the expressions of most emotions, contempt was not one of them.

Thin slicing has not met with total agreement. LeGault (2006), for example, has indicated that what is really happening when researchers study a two-minute tape is that they are taking into consideration all that they have learned through years of watching thousands of hours of tape. Murphy (2005) has found that thin slicing results in "moderate to high positive correlations between the thin slices" (one-minute slice, total of two one-minute slices, total of three one-minute slices) and the full interaction (p. 235). She observed "the number of gestures, nods, self-touches, smiles, and time spent gazing at a partner" (p. 238). The total interactions were 15 minutes long. Unfortunately, Murphy does not provide us with the amount of training received by the judges of the thin slicing. Gladwell, however, has reported that Gottman has observed more than three thousand couples.

Whether the predictive numbers are as high as 95 percent may still be held in question, but there can be little doubt that there is an expression of the emotion of contempt. The transmission of that emotion, if perceived by the other person, can have long-term negative consequences. Considering the addition of contempt in our expression repertoire, we must create a new acronym, **SCADFISH.**

As we observe infants and young children, we see that they do spontaneously express the emotions they feel. As they grow older, however, they become socialized into the adult world of their culture. As with anything else, they learn certain facial display rules that they must follow in particular social situations. As this learning process begins to take hold, facial expressions and feelings become somewhat divorced. In short, we learn what is acceptable and what is unacceptable in terms of expressive behavior. For instance, it is natural to smile and laugh when something strikes us as funny. However, we soon learn that smiling and laughing at someone's off-key singing of "The Star-Spangled Banner" at a baseball game is a behavior that elicits a poke in the ribs from a friend or relative near you. We've learned rule number one: Thou shalt not smile at some things that are funny.

The culture-specific differences that eventually appear in our facial expressions arise primarily from three factors:

1. Cultures differ concerning circumstances that elicit certain emotions.

2. Cultures differ about the consequences that follow certain emotional expressions.

3. Different cultures have different display rules that govern the use of facial behavior, which their members must learn.

For instance, even today in the United States, men are discouraged from expressing extreme sadness or happiness. American males are expected to be more composed. Many are taught, "Big boys don't cry!" Consider other consequences that might befall the male who is too expressive. Females, on the other hand, are generally allowed to be more emotional than males, whether they feel extremely sad or tremendously happy. In other cultures, we may find the rules reversed. Some Arabic cultures view it as perfectly acceptable for their men to be overcome with joy and excitement at the reunion of an old friend or to weep openly when saddened or disappointed.

When a child is born, he or she generally exhibits the primary facial expressions. As one grows, develops, and comes into contact with a variety of communicators and communication situations, he or she learns to put the face on that others expect (Newcombe & Lie, 1995; Russell & Bullock, 1985; Wagner, MacDonald, & Manstead, 1986).

According to Haseltine (2002a), a forced smile does look fake. By studying the profiles of stroke patients, neurologists concluded "that the brain has two largely independent circuits for controlling smiles: one under conscious control of the cerebral cortex and another governed unconsciously by deep, primitive brain structures involved with emotions" (p. 88). Therefore, when we must smile for the camera, our smiles are often conscious and appear fake to others. When we smile because we find something or someone funny, the smile is an unconscious, more genuine smile. Additionally, the unconscious smile is a more genuine smile accompanied by the orbicularis oculi (skin around the eyes crinkles up). Genuine smiles encourage others to smile and convey an honest emotion. Fake smiles may make others think we do not mean what we are saying, or fake smiles could evoke a response of dislike or damage social bonding. Haseltine (2002b) confirms that facial symmetry is a

Real and Fake Smiles

One of the primary issues about decoding facial expressions is whether the emotion is real or fake. The authors of this study tested the hypothesis that whether we assess a smile as real or fake is dependent on our own mood at the time we are assessing. The participants judged how genuine the expression was as well as whether the emotion was positive or negative and how much confidence the decoder felt about his or her evaluation of the emotion. They found that when a receiver is in a positive mood, he or she increased the evaluation as genuine. When the participant was in a negative mood, he or she felt the smile was less genuine. This tells us that when we critique facial expressions of emotion, our own feelings affect what we see in others. For a test of your own ability to determine real and fake smiles, go to: http://www.bbc.co.uk/science/humanbody/mind/surveys/smiles/.

Forgas, J. P., & East, R. (2008). How real is that smile? Mood effects on accepting or rejecting the veracity of emotio nal facial expressions. Journal of Nonverbal Behavior, 32, 157–170.

big factor in determining whether people perceive us as attractive. Haseltine (2002c) confirmed that smiling can make us feel better. When we are amused, we smile more and this smiling can create a chain reaction in our brain that goes something like this—that when we see something funny, it elicits a conscious emotion that causes contractions of our facial muscles, which leads to a smile. When we are smiling, we may feel happier, and this happiness may be communicated to others.

FACIAL MANAGEMENT AND EXPRESSION OF EMOTION

We suggested earlier that some researchers believe that a study of the face and its expressions is a study of emotion itself. Although the face is a vital source of information about the type of emotion a person is experiencing, some writers claim that body tension is a better indicator of the intensity with which an emotion is felt. Furthermore, cultural and social influences may have taught us to divorce our emotions from our actual facial behavior (Ekman & Friesen, 1969a, 1969b; Harper, Wiens, & Matarazzo, 1978). Controlling our facial behavior is an ability we learn early in life. We master display rules that tell us how to show our emotions in various social settings. **Facial management techniques** are the concepts used to describe these prescribed or display behaviors.

Facial management techniques are not only learned early but often are learned so thoroughly they become habitual. That is, we learn them so well that they become automatic responses. We can modify facial expressions of primary emotions to the point that normally universal expressions can differ from culture to culture. In addition, social norms decide which facial management techniques are appropriate for each emotion when expressed by individuals of varying status, gender, age, and social role. Let's review the four most common facial management techniques: *masking, intensification, neutralization,* and *deintensification* (MIND) (Ekman & Friesen, 1969a, 1969b, 1975).

MASKING. The first facial management technique we learn to use under certain cultural or social influences is **masking.** This technique involves repression of the expressions related to the emotion felt and their replacement with expressions that are acceptable under the circumstances. Think for a moment how people feel when they lose a contest to another person. How do you think they really feel? How would you feel? Not too great, most likely. However, in American culture we are expected to show happiness and pleasure for the winner and to avoid any expressions of our own disappointment. That's part of being a good loser or a good sport. An elementary school principal recently told a story about a second-grade boy who had been sent to the office for telling an unacceptable joke during class. After several long minutes of talking with the young boy and explaining the inappropriateness of such behavior, the principal asked the boy if he had understood the situation. Looking puzzled, the boy asked, "Don't you want to hear the joke? It's a very good one." The boy proceeded to tell the joke, whereupon the principal scolded him. The circumstances dictated that the principal should show sternness, although he actually found the entire situation extremely humorous.

In some cultures, expression of negative emotions is more taboo than it is in others. This often causes communication problems when people from different cultures interact. When American businesspersons do not like something, it is considered appropriate that they express this displeasure. For Japanese businesspersons, the opposite is true. The Japanese are often considered masters of masking. Americans, then, have difficulty understanding how their Japanese counterparts are responding because the external expressions of emotion may always be positive or neutral. A friend of the authors returned from an unsuccessful trip to Japan with this comment: "There is no word in the Japanese language for 'no,' but there are a hundred words for 'yes.' Unfortunately they all really mean 'no.' " Clearly, he had learned about the art of masking in Japanese culture.

INTENSIFICATION. The **intensification** of our expressions is accomplished by exaggerating what we feel. Sometimes we have to build the external expression of the emotion far beyond what we feel in order to meet the expressed concern of others. Have you ever been in a situation where social pressures required that you exaggerate a facial expression? Consider the following scenario:

> Enrique's colleagues had decided to surprise him with a birthday party on a Friday evening following work. They had planned the party well in advance to ensure that Enrique could be there. Friday afternoon finally arrived, and Enrique decided to stay in the office and work for several more hours. Then his colleague Tim bounded into the office.
> "Let's go out."
> "No, I need to work for several more hours."
> "You usually don't work late on Fridays; let's go."
> "Nope, not tonight, Tim. I need to work."
> Tim then had to reveal the plan for the surprise party to Enrique. He was not overwhelmed with happiness. However, that evening, no one ever guessed that Enrique had been told because his face was filled with wonder, amazement, and happiness when everyone yelled, "Surprise!" He exaggerated his facial expression so that his colleagues would not be disappointed. Enrique felt pleased, but not nearly as joyous as his friends expected him to be. He intensified his expression to meet their expectations.

In some cultures, such as those of several Mediterranean countries, sadness or grief responses commonly are exaggerated. In others, such intensification would appear out of place. Similarly, some people habitually engage in intensification, such as those who employ a dramatic communication style, whereas others do not. Most of us who live in the United States find intensification an appropriate technique from time to time.

NEUTRALIZATION. You have probably heard someone described as a poker face. Chances are these seemingly emotionless individuals are engaging in the facial management technique called **neutralization.** When we neutralize our facial expressions, we essentially eliminate any expression of emotion. The poker player does not want her or his face to tell the world that he or she is holding a good hand. To express elation at this point would alert the other players, and they would fold. Conversely, the player does not want the disappointment of a bad hand of cards to show on his or her face, either. If the other players were to read her or his face and discern that the hand was weak, the player could no longer bluff them. Consequently, the successful poker player learns to neutralize all facial expressions and keep opponents confused.

It is not only in poker games that we may wish to neutralize our facial expressions. In many circumstances, we may experience emotions, knowing that expressing them might not be in our best interests. Although we cannot usually avoid feeling negative emotions such as fear or anger, we often can prevent undesirable reactions from others by neutralizing our expression of those emotions. When our expressions are neutralized, others are unaware that we are experiencing any emotion.

DEINTENSIFICATION. There are situations and social events that call for **deintensification**—that is, when we reduce the intensity of our facial expression of a particular emotion because circumstances require us to downplay how we truly feel. Usually, deintensification of expression occurs when we experience feelings that our culture has taught us are unacceptable. The British, as you may know, are well known for understating almost any emotion. In our culture, men are generally not permitted to express strong feelings of fear or sadness. At the funeral of a loved one, the American man is permitted to express some grief, but because he is expected to be strong for everyone else, he may deintensify those expressions to meet the expectations of his family members.

People in controlling positions—such as managers, instructors, physicians, and clergy—often find themselves in situations where it would be most inappropriate to express their emotions to the true extent to which they are felt. A manager might be outraged at the behavior of a subordinate during a departmental meeting but recognizes that expressing those emotions in that setting would be counterproductive. After the meeting ends, the manager might express his or her concern in a controlled manner, and the subordinate appropriately reprimanded. However, if the manager expresses his or her actual feelings during the meeting, the employee might be publicly humiliated and embarrassed. This would not help the supervisor and employee to communicate with one another in future settings.

The truly competent communicator knows what face to put forward in differing communication situations. Learning to control one's expression of emotion takes caring, skill, and practice.

Styles of Facial Expressions

Based on these facial management techniques, researchers (Ekman & Friesen, 1969a, 1969b; Ekman, Friesen, & Ellsworth, 1972; Ekman, Friesen, & Tomkins, 1971) devised a classification of various styles of facial expressions. The techniques we have discussed are often used during a particular situation at a particular time. However, Ekman (1972) contends that some people display a certain style of expression consistently, no matter what the circumstances may be. The styles identified by Ekman and Friesen represent enduring predispositions toward making certain emotional displays. Let's look at eight different styles that some people consistently use. Keep in mind that these facial behaviors are generally outside the conscious awareness of the people displaying them.

1. The *withholder style* is characterized by those who seldom have any facial movement. The face inhibits the display of actual feelings. We might say that withholders use the neutralizing display rule almost constantly.

2. The *revealer style* is essentially the reverse of the withholder style. Revealers always show their true feelings. They are often described as wearing their hearts on their sleeves, and they generally admit that they just cannot help expressing themselves. They often have a highly dramatic communication style.

3. The *unwitting expressor* often believes that he or she is doing a good job of masking true feelings when, in fact, he or she unknowingly leaks information about the actual emotion that is being experienced. This person is a poor neutralizer. Thus, he or she often is in trouble for expressing inappropriate emotions, such as laughing when someone else falls down or spills food.

4. *Blanked expressors* have ambiguous or neutral expressions even when they believe they are displaying their emotions. They think they have moved their faces into a smile, but the only thing that others see is blankness. For these people, the feeling of emotion and the expression of emotion are two unconnected phenomena.

5. The *substitute expressor* substitutes one emotional expression for another. The person may think that he or she is showing happiness but actually is expressing disgust. The substitute expressor will not believe it when told what her or his expression really communicates.

6. The *frozen-affect expressor* always manifests at least a part of a particular emotional expression. During a neutral state, frozen-affect expressors look naturally sad, happy, or angry under all circumstances. One emotion is carved forever in their faces. This person wears a permanent mask.

7. *Ever-ready expressors* tend to display one particular emotion as the initial response to almost any situation. They first smile, for example, whether

they are receiving good news or bad news. Whether the situation provokes anger, surprise, fear, or sadness, the ever-ready expressor's first response is always the same and is then followed by a more revealing expression.

8. *Flooded-affect expressors* flood their faces constantly with a particular emotion. These individuals never appear neutral. One person, for instance, may have an extreme look of fear all the time; even during situations that cause him or her to express happiness, the fearful expression does not fade completely. Any temporary expressions are generally tempered by the expression of fear.

Our discussion of facial management techniques and facial styles brings up an important point about the expression of emotion. We do not always express one emotion. In other words, our facial expressions are not purely ones of sadness, happiness, or disgust. Sometimes, we express two or three emotions simultaneously. At other times, we attempt to remain neutral in our expression, but one area of the face reveals our feelings. The following discussion addresses this issue.

PRIMARY AFFECT DISPLAYS AND COMMUNICATION

Ekman, Friesen, and Tomkins (1971) devised a way of locating and evaluating the facial expressions of individuals. Their technique is called the **Facial Affect Scoring Technique (FAST)**, and it separates the face into three areas: the lower face, including cheeks, nose, and mouth; the eyes and eyelids area; and the brows and forehead area. Designed for use with both still photographs and motion picture film, the FAST technique (see Figure 4.1) determines which emotions are being expressed in the three different areas. Based on the seven primary facial expressions that Ekman categorized (sadness, happiness, anger,

1. Eyebrows and forehead
2. Eyes and eyelids
3. Lower face: cheeks, nose, and mouth

FIGURE 4.1
Three Regions of Facial Analysis
Source: Photo by C. Price Walt

surprise, disgust, contempt, and fear), we can accurately classify where certain emotions are found in the face. As stated earlier, one new emotion has been added to the list, *interest.*

In considering the lower face, Desmond Morris (1985) suggests that the cheek is the region most likely to expose the true emotions of its owners. For it is here that emotional changes of color are most conspicuously displayed (p. 85). He further suggests that shame and embarrassment can be seen on the cheeks when two small points on the cheeks turn deep red. Cheeks are also indicators of anger. In anger, there is a different pattern of reddening. The red color spreads all over the cheeks and even to the top of the skull (although the cheeks of a truly aggressive person may turn very pale, almost white, because the blood is drained away from the skin). If a person is truly frightened, the color may drain from the cheeks, and the person's cheeks may look blanched. Of course, these displays are much more difficult to observe in people with dark skin.

The human mouth, Morris points out, "works overtime." Other animals use their mouths to bite, lick, suck, taste, chew, swallow, cough, yawn, snarl, scream, and grunt, but we have added to this list. We also use the mouth for talking, whistling, singing, smiling, laughing, kissing, and smoking. "It is hardly surprising that the mouth has been described as the battleground of the face," says Morris (p. 93). He goes on to suggest that the mouth is not only one of the busiest parts of the body but also one of the most expressive. The mouth can be used to express boredom, interest, erotic emotions, sadness, happiness, contempt, disgust, fear, anger, bodily needs, insubordination, surprise, and many other emotions. Because the mouth is such a focal point on the face, cultures have often modified, exaggerated, improved, reshaped, colored, stained, tattooed, or in other ways altered the appearance of the mouth. In fact, one of the first expressions we learn is the social smile. We are taught to smile at socially appropriate situations, thereby making others feel good and eliciting a smile from them. For example, we know to smile when being introduced to a stranger at a social gathering. We know to smile when someone is talking about an interesting topic, even if we do not care about the topic. We know to smile when someone is showing photos of their newborn infant.

The nose, according to Morris, is unique. "Other species have nothing quite like it" (p. 65). The nose can be seen as a resonator, a shield to protect the eyes against injury, a shield against water, a shield against dust and dirt, or an air filter. If we lose the use of our nose as a filter, we experience serious respiratory difficulty within a few days. The nose also aids us in scent. If we lose our scent function, we may cease to enjoy food and certain forms of entertainment. As with the mouth and cheeks, many cultures have gone to extreme lengths to change, reshape, or decorate the nose.

Morris says of the eyes and eyelids that "it has been estimated that 80 percent of our information about the outside world enters through these remarkable structures" (p. 49). We are visual animals. If we can see it, we are likely to remember it. "The entire primate order is a vision-dominated group, with the two eyes brought to the front of the head, providing a binocular view of the world" (p. 49).

As for the brows and forehead region, Morris suggests t brow like a human being, you have to be an intelligent animal i human brow, made up of forehead, temples, and eyebrows, was t of our ancestors' dramatic brain enlargement (p. 37). The brow region can express many messages. Lowering the eyebrows is a frown and can be a sign of displeasure. Raising the eyebrows can be a sign of interest, hence the term "an eye-opening experience." An extreme eyebrow raise can express surprise or fear or amazement, depending on the situation. Raising one eyebrow (the cocked eyebrow) while keeping one steady is a questioning expression. Knitted, or furrowed, eyebrows can be associated with chronic pain, headaches, anxiety, grief, or extreme frustration. Flashing eyebrows (eyebrows raised and lowered in a second) could mean acknowledgment, greeting, friendly recognition, surprise, or have a sexual connotation. Like the other areas of the face, this region can communicate multiple expressions and emotions.

Researchers in the area of facial expression have used the FAST and similar methods and found that some primary emotions can be judged accurately and consistently. No one area of an individual face is best at revealing an emotion. The information one gets from any particular area depends a great deal on the emotion being judged. Research in this area has revealed a number of interesting findings (Boucher & Ekman, 1975; Ekman & Friesen, 1975; Johnson, Ekman & Friesen, 1975; Kalick, Zebrowitz, Langlois, & Johnson, 1998).

- Sadness and fear are best identified from the eyes and eyelids area (67 percent of the time).
- Anger, however, is not accurately perceived from any one area alone. At least two areas of the face must be seen for anger to be judged accurately. Anger is usually expressed in the cheeks, mouth, brows, and forehead.
- Disgust often blends with surprise. Disgust can often be found in a number of places on the face. Often disgust is found in the lower region of the face.
- Happiness can be judged accurately 98 percent of the time from the lower face (when the corners of lips are drawn back and up in the lip-corner puller) and 99 percent of the time from the eyes and eyelids (crinkly eyes).
- Surprise is accurately identified from all three areas fairly well (brows/forehead, 79 percent; eyes/eyelids, 63 percent; and lower face, 52 percent).

Heisel, Williams, and Valencic (1999) have studied the following facial expressions and receivers' perceptions of 12 of the most commonly used emotions in U.S. culture: sadness, anger, disgust, fear, interest, surprise, happiness, distrust, confusion, contempt, guilt, and betrayal. Their results are similar to those of previous studies concerning facial expressions.

Katsikitis, Pilowksy, and Innes (1990) tested whether line drawings of faces generated by a computer produced the same responses in decoders as did the photographs from which the line drawings were derived. The computer-generated line drawings were of the mouth, nose, eyes, eyebrows, and facial outline and were not gender-specific. Twelve facial measures were generated by the computer. They were named End-Lip Raise, Mouth-Width, Mouth-Opening,

Mid-Top-Lip Raise, Mid-Low-Lip Raise, Top-Lip Thickness, Lower-Lip Thickness, Eye-Opening, Top-Eyelid/Iris Intersect, Lower-Eyelid/Iris Intersect, Inner-Eyebrow Separation, and Mid-Eyebrow Raise. These 12 represented landmark facial points relevant to emotional signals and were chosen because they accounted for a wide range of emotional expression. The subjects viewed the computer-generated images and the original photographs and made judgments. The conclusions of the researchers are as follows: The subjects, or judges, could recognize and decode facial expressions from computer-generated line drawings and real photographs with fairly equal ability. Human judges are attuned to the common emotions and the common expressions that correlate with these emotions, whether depicted by a computer-generated line drawing or a photograph. The subjects could reliably distinguish expressions of smiles from neutral looks, for example. Therefore—whether we see computer-generated, photographic, or

1. _____

2. _____

3. _____

Choose from the following:
sadness
happiness
anger
surprise
disgust
fear
interest
betrayal
guilt
contempt
confusion
distrust

FIGURE 4.2
Guess the Emotion

real-life portrayals of faces—most of us can fairly accurately judge the primary facial emotional expressions commonly used within this culture.

In their research, Tucker and Riggio (1988) found that the "ability to pose emotions was possibly facilitated in those individuals skilled in verbal expression" (p. 94). In other words, individuals with higher verbal ability could also portray emotions more readily. Or, conversely, they could mask emotions better. Much of this research warrants further examination.

Brownlow and Zebrowitz (1990) found that mature-faced spokespersons on television were viewed by judges as more expert than baby-faced spokespersons, although baby-faced spokespersons were viewed as more trustworthy than mature-faced spokespersons. Women were viewed as slightly more trustworthy than men, and men were viewed as slightly more expert than women by the judges. Therefore Brownlow and Zebrowitz conclude that the results of "this study reveal that actors' facial maturity and gender influence the type of commercial [messages] they are chosen to deliver" (p. 58). The relationship between baby-faced spokespersons and mature-faced spokespersons must be examined extensively before conclusions can be etched in stone. However, the results do affirm some past research on the effects of facial appearance on interviewer impressions and real-world experiences.

Emotional states can be invoked by facial expressions (Figure 4.2). A smile is often equated with happiness, a frown with doubt, downcast lips and eyes with sadness, an open mouth with surprise, contorted or wrinkled-up mouth and nose with repulsion or contempt, flared nostrils with anger, and widened eyes with fear. Some researchers suggest that if we were to mimic smiling and put on a happy face, we might actually feel better about ourselves. There is much agreement that the basic SCADFISH emotions and their corresponding facial expressions are almost universally recognized. However, elements of them are blended differently by different cultures. Our faces and the expressions we assume show the world what we think or feel about the world and perhaps even ourselves.

VARIATIONS OF FACIAL EXPRESSIONS

The facts seem to show that whether one area of the face best reveals an emotion depends on which emotion is being judged. Ekman (1972) contends that at any given time an individual may show two or more emotions—one in the lower face and another in the eyes, for example. These multiple facial expressions are called **affect blends.** When someone plays a nasty trick on you, you may respond by showing anger in the eyes and disgust in the lower face. When Enrique walked into his surprise birthday party in our earlier example, chances were he expressed both happiness and surprise simultaneously, but in different areas. Affect blends and partials, defined later, may be responsible for many cultural differences found in emotional expression. In one culture, sadness expressed at a funeral may be combined with expressions of fear, while in another culture the expression of sadness may be combined with anger. Although primary facial expressions may be universal, affect blends are not.

How we combine displays of affect is generally dictated by cultural and social constraints (Archer, Iritani, Kimes, & Barrios, 1983).

Partials involve revealing an emotion in only one area of the face while successfully controlling the other two areas. Emotional leakage may be the cause for partial facial expressions. For example, a basketball coach fearful of a loss tries to mask her fears with a calm appearance, but one area, a partial, leaks the true feeling. Therefore some of the more astute players might see the fear, but other players will not.

Affect blends appear on the face in several ways. These are emotions that wash or flow across the face, like seawater washing across the sand. One emotion appears in one area of the face, and another emotion appears in another area. An example of this type of blend would be raised eyebrows for surprise while the corners of the mouth are lifted into a smile to show happiness. Sometimes two emotions appear in one area of the face. Knapp and Hall

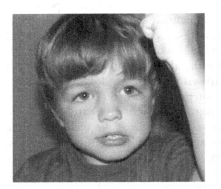 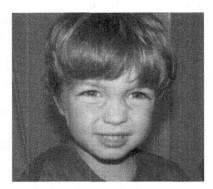

Small children can demonstrate different facial expressions of emotion.
Source: Photo by C. Price Walt

(1992) suggest that we sometimes show surprise and anger with the eyebrows, with one raised and one pulled down toward the eye. And a more complicated facial expression may be produced by muscle action associated with two emotions but containing specific elements of neither. When a coworker puts a whoopee cushion on your chair and you sit on it, you might respond by showing surprise in the lower region of the face and anger in the upper region. Astute observers of nonverbal communication will probably see both reactions and know that you were not pleased by the trick.

Micromomentary facial expressions are brief, fleeting expressions. They are usually not observable in normal conversation and can change so quickly that the naked eye may not detect or discern each emotion. But while people cannot pinpoint the actual micromomentary expression, they can get a feeling or a sense from it about the other person. When micromomentary facial expressions are recorded and then played back at a slow pace, one can often see the expressions of emotions that one might otherwise have missed. These brief, fleeting emotions can give another person an intuitive feeling about what another is truly feeling.

What can we conclude about our knowledge of facial behaviors?

1. We know that, at least in the U.S culture, negative facial behaviors are expressed less often than positive facial behaviors. It is not polite to look negative. Therefore we attempt to look positive even when the situation is negative.
2. We know that women smile more often than men.
3. We know that many of us have learned to skillfully control our expressions of emotion based upon the given situation.
4. We know that many of us put on a social smile when the situation demands that we do so.
5. Most of us have learned great control over the upper portion of our bodies (12 inches and up; upper shoulders, neck, and head). Therefore, we can mask what we truly think or feel.
6. Children are born with some innate facial expressions, but many other expressions are taught by parents.
7. By looking at various portions of the face, we may detect the true feeling of that person.
8. The human mouth works overtime.
9. At any given time, an individual may show two or more facial emotions.
10. Smiling is contagious. The more we smile, the more likely it is that another person will smile.

Glossary of Terminology

Affect blends are multiple simultaneous facial expressions.

Deintensification is the de-emphasizing or downplaying of the facial expression of emotion.

Facial Affect Scoring Technique (FAST) separates the face into three areas: the lower face, including cheeks, nose, and mouth; the eyes and eyelids area; and the brows and forehead area.

Facial management techniques are behaviors used to control facial expressions and are divided into four common types: masking, intensification, neutralization, and deintensification (MIND).

Intensification is an exaggeration of facial expressions.

Masking is the facial management technique that involves repressing the expression of the emotion actually felt and replacing it with expressions that are acceptable under the circumstances.

Neutralization is when people eliminate any facial expression of emotion.

Partials are emotional expressions revealed in only one area of the face.

SADFISH = surprise, anger, disgust, fear, interest, sadness, and happiness

SCADFISH = surprise, contempt, anger, disgust, fear, interest, sadness, and happiness.

CHAPTER 5

Eye Behavior

The study of eye behavior, eye contact, eye movement, and the functions of eye behavior is called **oculesics**. Of all of the features of the face, the eyes are probably the most important in human communication. The human eye can respond to 1.5 million simultaneous messages, and yet it is no bigger than a ping pong ball (Morris, 1985, p. 49). Approximately 80 percent of our information about the outside world enters through the eyes. Morris suggests that—despite all the talking, listening, movement, and touching we do—we are still visual animals. Some writers claim that the eyes provide signals concerning emotions, attitudes, and relationships when no other body cues may be found. The initial contact made between people usually is eye contact. If that contact is not pleasing to one or both of the individuals, it is quite possible that no additional contact will take place.

PROPERTIES AND FUNCTIONS OF EYE BEHAVIOR

There are three primary properties of eye behavior. The first property is *salience*. Because eye behavior, such as a direct gaze, has a high probability of being noticed, it is usually a much more salient interaction signal than most other bodily motions. That is, the behavior of our eyes plays an extremely important role in managing our interactions, eliciting the attention of others, and communicating our interest in what others have to say. We generally expect people to respond to our gaze and often become frustrated when they do not do so immediately.

The second important property of eye behavior is its extraordinary ability to *stimulate arousal*. It is virtually impossible not to experience some degree of arousal when we see another person. This arousal may be negative, as when we catch the glance of someone we would rather not interact with, or it may be positive, as when two lovers gaze at one another across a cozy table in a dimly lit restaurant.

The final important property of eye behavior is *involvement*. In our culture, it is difficult to establish eye contact with someone and not interact with her or him. Even with a stranger we meet for the briefest of moments while passing on the sidewalk, eye contact seems to oblige us to nod our heads and smile, if nothing else. Eye contact with another virtually commands involvement with that other. Given these properties, the eye engages in a variety of behaviors.

Kendon (1967), a notable writer in the area of visual behavior, first described the functions of the eye. Since then, other writers in nonverbal communication have expanded and elaborated on how our eyes serve to hinder, help, or otherwise influence interaction. Eye behavior appears to serve several primary functions. Let's consider each.

Scanning has and will continue to be one of the primary functions of our eyes. Our eyes scan, focus, and collect information about the world around us. Our prehistoric ancestors used scanning as a means to monitor the environment and to protect themselves from harm. People with poor vision were at a disadvantage and are unlikely to be our ancestors.

Establishing and defining relationships is another common function of eye behavior. Eye contact is often the first stage in the initial-encounter phase of a relationship. Eye-to-body or eye-to-eye contact can determine whether a relationship is established and can add definition to the relationship. When a person catches the eye of another person, and if the receiver looks at the source, a relationship begins. If the receiver looks away from the source, a relationship is not started.

Eye behavior can oblige us to interact with another person. Interpersonal encounters usually begin with the two participants looking at one another and establishing eye contact. A person can be perceived as "too fast" or "too forward" if he or she looks more than is deemed appropriate by society. In our culture, staring is considered unacceptable and rude unless it is used to control an unruly person (Argyle & Ingham, 1972; Dovidio & Ellyson, 1985).

Eye behavior functions to *express emotions*. The eyes have always been a valuable source of information about emotional states. While many areas of the face can be controlled, the eye area is considered one of the least controllable. As a result, the eyes and the area surrounding them probably reveal more accurate information about emotional states than other areas of the face. The eyes can provide much information about the emotions of fear, happiness, sadness, anger, surprise, contempt, and disgust than other facial areas. However, we should remember that our best judgments of another person's emotions are made when we have his or her entire face before us.

Another function of eye behavior is to *control and regulate our interactions* with others. The eyes, as well as nonverbal cues, are quite effective in regulating the back-and-forth interaction between speakers and listeners (e.g., teachers and students, managers and employees). The eyes assist in the synchrony of speech, conversation, and dialogue. Eyes tell us when to encode a message, when to decode a message, and when to respond to another person.

Research has shown that interactants look at one another more while listening than while speaking. *Gaze avoidance is increased by speakers who are using turn-maintaining cues.* Those who want to continue talking often signal their intention by dramatically reducing their eye gaze toward the listener. Furthermore, listeners who wish for the speaker to continue usually gaze toward the speaker. A primary turn-yielding cue used by speakers as they finish talking involves a head-turn in the direction of the listener, accompanied by increased eye contact. In contrast, a listener requests a turn by turning his or her head away from the speaker to reduce eye gaze.

Breaking eye contact and sustaining the break is a good indication that one is ready to end an interaction. For instance, if you are in an interview and feel that all is going well, check the eye behavior of the interviewer. He or she may be telling you, by breaking eye contact, that the time is up. Your failure to heed this signal may have a negative impact on the interviewer and negate all those wonderful qualities you have been espousing.

Bavelas, Coates, and Johnson (2002) have found that there is what they call a gaze "window" in a conversation. They claim that conversationalists have minor breaks in their narratives to allow for short responses prior to the other person's saying anything. At those points, there is a mutual gaze. This short gaze is then used by the listener to respond with "mmhm," a nod, a smile, or a similar expression to indicate microlevel understanding and/or agreement. The original speaker completes her narrative, and then the original listener responds.

Regulating and controlling interaction also involves *power displays*. The sustained gaze or stare is an effective means by which individuals can display power. Furthermore, these power gazes generally elicit one of two visual responses. Either the other person will stare back to communicate that your power display is being defied, or he or she will use gaze avoidance to escape. Surely you have played the childhood game of Stare-Down. What starts out as fun and games may quickly deteriorate into an out-and-out struggle for interpersonal supremacy. The one who stares the longest gains control of the other. Even between children and during harmless play, the result of a session of Stare-Down can have long-lasting interpersonal consequences, such as a feeling of powerlessness (Duncan, 1972; Ellsworth, 1975; Exline, 1963, 1971; Exline, Ellyson, & Long, 1975).

Eye contact can decrease *the physical distance* between people. With one steady look, a person can bring another person, who is physically distant, much closer. For example, speakers will scan and look at each person or groups of persons in an audience so that everyone in the audience feels closer to the speaker. With newer technology, it is possible for a celebrity, rock star, or evangelist to appear to be looking at each individual audience member. Projection technology takes the speaker to the audience.

Eye behavior can be used to *close others out* of a conversation. Simply looking intently and closely at a particular person or persons can function much like shutting a door in the face of any others present. By intently looking at one person, a source is telling others not to approach or enter the conversation. Last, eye behavior is a *sign that we are in communication* with another person. As Argyle and Dean said, "without eye contact, people do not feel that they are fully in communication" (1965, p. 289).

TYPES OF EYE BEHAVIORS

Eye behavior has been defined in many ways depending on the particular type of looking that is being studied. There are several types of eye behaviors (Argyle & Cook, 1976; Argyle & Ingham, 1972; Ellsworth, 1975; Exline & Fehr, 1982; Exline & Winters, 1965).

A mutual look or **mutual gaze** refers to two people looking in the direction of one another's faces. Eye contact is characterized by mutual gaze that is centered on the eyes.

A **one-sided look** or glance is a gaze of one individual in the direction of another person's face. Here, however, the gaze is not reciprocated. When someone avoids looking at another during an interpersonal encounter, even when the other is looking at him or her, gaze aversion has occurred.

Gaze aversion typically is an intentional act. A person who averts his or her eyes from another person normally does so consciously and is somehow motivated not to look. Gaze aversion may signal that you are not interested in what the other person has to say. One may be unsure of one's self and may not want him or her to read this in the eyes. Gaze aversion is also used as a regulator when wishing to stop communicating any further. For whatever reason it occurs, gaze aversion is normally intended as some kind of avoidance.

Gaze aversion should not be confused with **gaze omission**, which describes a situation where one person does not look at the other but is not intentionally avoiding eye contact. The confusion between aversion and omission may lead to interpersonal misunderstanding. Although the actual behavior may be similar, different messages are communicated. Analyze the following to determine whether aversion or omission is represented in each case below.

1. Brandy and Miguel are quarreling over what television program to watch. Finally, Brandy turns off the set and stares out the window while Miguel continues to argue.
2. Matt is a constant troublemaker in class. Mr. Baker has finally had enough of Matt's misbehavior and asks him to stay after class. As Mr. Baker scolds him, Matt looks toward the floor and smiles.
3. Denise sits at the end of the bar. Stephen enters the lounge and glances at her. Occasionally, Stephen looks toward her, hoping to catch her eye. Each time he looks toward her, she is happily engaged in conversation with someone else. He eventually becomes dismayed and concludes that Denise is not interested in him.

Well? What did you decide in each case? If you said that Brandy was engaged in gaze aversion, you are probably right. Her intention was to end the verbal dispute and conclude the interaction. She had had enough. What about Matt? He was also intentionally averting his gaze from Mr. Baker. By looking away, he may have intentionally transmitted a message to Mr. Baker that he was unconcerned, unshaken, and not a bit threatened by the dressing-down he was receiving. Denise, however, was more than likely unaware of Stephen. Although Stephen may have taken her lack of eye contact as a signal of rejection, chances are that she was completely oblivious to Stephen's apparent advances. Her eye behavior involved gaze omission rather than aversion.

A type of eye behavior called *civil inattention* can occur in many environments. This is the "elevator look." According to Goffman (1967), civil inattention is a behavioral ritual in which two people are mutually present but not involved in interaction. They exchange momentary glances, then avert their

Where Men and Women Look

The participants in this study were exposed to 30 photographs, 15 of men and 15 of women. All of the confederate models were casually dressed. When the participants looked at the photographs, their eye movements were recorded using an eye tracker. The results indicated that both men and women first look at the other person's face. Men look significantly earlier at women's breasts, and they look longer, but only after the original face-scan. Women looked at men's legs after looking at their faces.

Hewig, J., Trippe, R. H., Hecht, H., Straube, T., & Miltner, W. H. R. (2008). Gender differences for specific body regions when looking at men and women. Journal of Nonverbal Behavior, 32, 67–78.

gaze. There is a simple, brief acknowledgment of the other person's presence, but the gaze aversion guarantees the other person that he or she is not under scrutiny and that oral communication is not forthcoming. Quite simply, civil inattention is the glance, acknowledgment, and looking away—nothing more, nothing less. Civil inattention occurs frequently on busy streets, elevators, subways, and so on. Civil inattention allows each person to acknowledge the other, but there is no expectation of conversation.

Staring occurs when a person focuses in on another person and gives a long, hard, often invasive and uncomfortable-feeling look. Staring is considered impolite in this culture. In fact, the common retort in this culture to perceived staring is, "What are you staring at?"

CLEMs

Closely related to eye gazes are eye behaviors called **conjugate lateral eye movements (CLEMs)** or lateral eye movements (LEMs), from the theory called neurolinguistic programming (NLP) (Bandler & Grinder, 1979; Dilts, Grinder, Bandler, DeLozier, & Cameron-Bandler, 1979). These eye movements are involuntary lateral shifts of the eyes to the right or left (Theeuwes, Kramer, Hahn, & Irwin, 1998). CLEMs are thought to be closely associated with cognitive processing. That is, we look away to the left or to the right while we are thinking but look forward again when we stop processing information. Often one will look up and then to the right or left, then back to the receiver when he or she has finished information processing. Individuals can usually be categorized as either right- or left-lookers, because approximately 75 percent of an individual's CLEMs are in one direction. The suggestion is that when right-handed people look up and to the right, they may be trying to envision an event that has never been seen, and when right-handed people look up and to the left, they may be trying to recall an event. Since eye contact is needed for effective interaction, if a speaker is unaware of being a right- or left-looker, she or he might never fully communicate visually with a good portion of the audience. For example, teachers who look primarily left are visually neglecting a significant portion of their classrooms. Managers who look primarily right during meetings are visually excluding a significant portion of their employees from interaction. Therefore, once a person is aware of her or his tendency to look right or left, then adaptation must take place to visually include all persons whom the speaker is addressing.

In conclusion, CLEMs are usually quite prominent when someone is working on a task that requires thought or reflection. There is some speculation that when we call attention to someone's CLEMs and ask that person to control them, this may make it difficult for the person to concentrate and may distract from the cognitive processing.

PUPIL DILATION. The pupils of the eyes can *dilate* (increase in size) or *constrict* (decrease in size). This fact has been known for centuries. Whether pupil dilation and constriction are important to the communication process, however, is still open to question. The impact of pupil dilation and constriction on interpersonal interactions, and vice versa, is hardly clear-cut. Many factors influence this involuntary pupil response. Physical conditions such as the brightness or dimness of lighting invariably affect the size of one's pupils. Neurophysiological factors and chemical stimulants or depressants are known to affect pupil size as well. Nevertheless, research has provided some interesting findings that may have implications for social interactions (Bakan, 1971; Burkhardt, Weider-Hatfield, & Hocking, 1985; Exline & Winters, 1965; Exline, Gray, & Schuette, 1965; Hess, 1965; Hess & Polt, 1960; Hess, Seltzer, & Schlien, 1965; Hindmarch, 1970; Hood, Willen, & Driver, 1998; Scherwitz & Helmreich, 1973; Vlietstra & Manske, 1981; Richmond, 2002).

Researchers were interested in the effects of certain visual stimuli on pupil size. They found that men's pupils dilated when they viewed posters of women, and women's pupils dilated when they observed photographs of men. Another study found that the pupils of gay men dilated when they were shown photographs of men. Still another study found that women's pupils dilated when they were shown photographs of newborn infants.

These studies suggest that pupil dilation may be a good indication of positive emotional arousal and interest in what is being observed. Pupil constriction, on the other hand, seems to indicate an aversion to the thing or person being observed. Thus, it is not too great a leap to speculate that if we see that the eyes are dilated in the person with whom we are talking, it may be a sign that that person is interested in what we are saying or even in us.

When we are interested, we <u>look</u> interested.
Source: Photo by C. Price Walt

Indeed, one study found that dilated pupils in photographs of women enhanced perceptions of attractiveness. Long before this research, several hundred years ago, women used the drug belladonna to cause their pupils to dilate. (This is essentially the same drug eye doctors use during examinations today to dilate our pupils.) Dilated pupils, the women believed, made them more appealing to men. In the recent study just cited, two identical pictures of the same women were used, one picture with pupils retouched to appear dilated, and the other with pupils retouched to appear constricted. Men who evaluated the pictures attributed more positive characteristics to the one with dilated pupils and more negative characteristics to the one with constricted pupils.

An interesting phenomenon that has been discovered in the pupillometric research cited above is that there tends to be a reciprocal effect on individuals who observe dilated pupils. That is, in viewing the dilated pupils of someone, the viewer's pupils tend to dilate as well. This seems to suggest that dilated pupils enhance positive responses and create perceptions of attractiveness. Constricted pupils, on the other hand, do not generally elicit positive arousal and may reduce perceptions of attractiveness.

As to the importance of pupil dilation in human interaction, we leave the decision up to you. Clearly, it is easier to see dilation in blue-eyed people than in brown-eyed people. You usually cannot see the pupils of another person's eyes in a context in which emotional reaction is the primary determinant of pupil size; ambient lighting is always a factor. Under controlled conditions, however, it probably is possible to gain some emotional information from this aspect of human eye behavior. At least, that is what some poker players appear to believe. We are told that is why many professionals prefer to wear sunglasses to conceal their eyes, or eye shades or caps to cause their eyes to remain dilated regardless of the hand they draw. So can pupil dilation be important? We would not want to bet against it.

DECEPTION AND EYE BEHAVIOR. Characteristically, in our culture, it is common to assume that if someone does not look us in the eye about a critical issue, he or she is being insincere or deceptive. In America, at least, we should rarely rely solely on eye behavior (looking away or down) as a signal of deception or insincerity. Culturally, we have learned to control our facial and eye behaviors when giving deceptive, insincere, or bad information. In fact, most North Americans have learned skillfully to control the 12 inches of the upper body (upper chest, neck, and head). This has occurred because of the cultural norms established on detecting deceit. It seems that from an early age, we are taught (often unconsciously and unintentionally by a parent, teacher, friend, or sibling) to mask our deceit. For example, when we were younger and misbehaved or made a mistake, an adult would say, "Look me in the eye and tell me you did not do that." Therefore we would learn to mask and look the adult in the eye and inform her or him that we did not do that—even when we did do it! Because our culture relies so heavily on eye contact for communication, it is no wonder that we have learned to look another person in the eye and tell a big fat lie. Instinctively, we know that if we don't look other people in the eye or glance down or away, they will think that we are guilty of something. Hence, looking at the eyes or face is not a reliable indicator of when another person is being deceptive. People in this culture are better at controlling facial behaviors than any other aspect of their body. Slow-motion videos of people engaged in lying have shown that short bursts of facial activity interrupt their deceptive expressions. However, these last less than one-fifth of a second and are micro-momentary expressions. Because of the brief duration of these expressions, deception or dislike is more of a feeling that we sense than a conscious conclusive expression that we can see. If the person attempting to deceive us is not known well by us or is a skilled deceiver, it is unlikely that we can tell based on eye behavior when he or she is deceiving or being insincere. Deception is not easy to detect, no matter what cues are examined.

Feldman found that in 121 videotaped pairs of unacquainted college students during ten-minute introductory conversations, 60 percent of the students lied once. "Those who lied did so three times per conversation, on average, with one subject squeezing in twelve." Women lied to make "the people they were talking to feel better about themselves. Men tended to lie to make themselves look better" (Gravitz, 2002, p. 13). Both women and men lied at the same rate. It seems that in relationships, one should be skeptical of what another person has to say.

Levine, Asada, and Park (2006) have investigated eye behavior in relation to deception. However, their contention was that whether someone notices a particular behavior associated with deception may be based on whether they thought the person might be lying in the first place. The hypothesis certainly would support the notion that professionals (such as police) make errors in assuming that the person they arrest is guilty and therefore will lie. In fact, detecting deception is quite difficult. We amateurs tend to believe someone when they are lying, and police tend to believe a person is lying when they are telling the truth. All of us tend to make errors, just of a different type. Levine, Asada, and Park (2006) found that even amateurs (their subjects) "found" significantly less eye contact when the subjects had reason to think the person was lying in the first place.

EYE BEHAVIOR AND INDIVIDUAL DIFFERENCES

One researcher has reported that the normal gazing duration during interpersonal interaction ranges from 28 to 70 percent. Another reports that normal variation in looking ranges from 8 to 73 percent. What these findings suggest is that what is considered normal depends largely on the many individual differences among people. We must always keep in mind that normal behavior for some may be abnormal for others, depending on their gender, personality characteristics, and ethnic and cultural backgrounds, as well as the context in which the interaction occurs. Let's consider some of these individual differences as they affect the eye behavior of people during communication.

f Relationships

The type and amount of eye behavior can also reveal the nature of a relationship. Two conversants who differ in status usually engage in different visual behaviors toward one another. The higher-status individual generally receives more eye gazes from the lower-status person than the other way around. Both men and women look less at speakers who are lower in status than themselves. The relationship between status and eye behavior may indicate one of two things. First, it may suggest that lower-status individuals show their respect by gazing at their higher-status counterparts. Second, the higher-status person may simply feel less of a need to monitor the lower-status person; whereas, the lower-status person may feel it important to monitor the higher-status person.

The amount we look at others may also be a function of how much we like them. In a pair where interactants report liking one another, a mutual gaze tends to be more prominent. Eye contact is also greater between persons engaging in intimate relationships. You can be perceived as too fast or forward, however, if you look more than the other person deems appropriate. In such cases, you may be using eye contact to let the other person know you would like to become more intimate, and he or she may use substantially less eye contact to tell you to back off.

Increasing our gaze at a speaker also functions to signal the speaker that we are paying attention and are interested in what he or she has to say. This is a culture-specific visual activity, however; people in the United States equate looking with interest and attention, but this is not true in all other cultures. For example, one U.S. teacher became extremely frustrated with an Asian student and held him after class. While talking to the young student, the teacher became upset because the student constantly looked at the floor. Little did the teacher realize that the student was attending to her message but had been socialized to not look at higher-status individuals. To gaze at an authority figure while she lectures would, to the student, have been disrespectful. This unfortunate student was doing his best to behave appropriately but was being punished because the teacher was unfamiliar with the cultural differences in expected gaze behavior. It would be easy to criticize that teacher for her insensitivity to the student, but it must be recognized that very few teacher-education programs include instruction in nonverbal and/or intercultural communication.

Cultural Differences

A person's culture is the context in which he or she learns the social norms of appropriate or inappropriate behavior. The influence of one's ethnic and cultural environment on eye behavior has been observed by many scholars.

In an extensive investigation involving members of several different cultures, Watson (1970) found that Latin Americans, southern Europeans, and Arabs tended to focus their gaze directly on the eyes or face while talking and listening. However, northern Europeans, Indian-Pakistanis, and Asians tended more toward a peripheral gaze or no gaze at all. By peripheral gaze, Watson meant an orientation toward the other interactant without actually focusing on his or her face or eyes. When members of the latter cultures did not gaze at all, they either looked toward the floor or gazed into space.

Knapp and Hall (1992) suggest that many cultural differences are best seen in terms of duration rather than frequency of gaze. They noted, for instance, that Swedes do not look as frequently as the English during conversations, but when they do look they gaze for a longer period. Others suggest that some cultures, such as the Korean, place much more emphasis on the observance of the eyes than do others. That is, Koreans are highly aware of eye behavior because it is believed that real answers to questions they ask may be found there, even though the other's words say something else.

Contextual Differences

Often the context or topic of discussion affects the amount and duration of looking behavior during interaction. When we are attempting to persuade others, for instance, we tend to look more at our fellow interactants. Speakers who use more eye contact are judged by listeners to be more persuasive, credible, and sincere. Furthermore, when we find the situation comfortable, interesting, and happy, we tend to establish more eye contact with our partners. Conversely, eye gazes in the direction of the partner are found to decrease during moments of embarrassment, guilt, or sadness.

Personality Differences

It should not surprise you that the personality characteristics of individuals are closely related to the amount of eye contact they use during conversations. People who have a high need for affiliation, inclusion, or affection gaze more steadily at others. People who are dominant, authoritative, and extroverted have also been found to look more frequently.

Although there has been little research bearing directly on this question, what there is suggests that such characteristics as shyness, communication apprehension, or unwillingness to communicate may affect eye behavior. Individuals who have these negative orientations toward communication tend to establish less eye contact. Because eye contact, in our culture, almost obliges us to engage in interaction with others, those who experience anxiety about communicating use behaviors such as gaze aversion or gaze omission to avoid interaction when possible.

Gender Differences

If one finding seems clear concerning gender differences in eye behavior it is that, overall, women engage in more looking behavior than do men. Not only do they look more at their conversational partners while listening, they also look more while speaking. However, the amount of actual eye contact is greater in a male-male or female-female dyad than in a mixed-gender dyad. One study has suggested that women appear to use shifts in the gaze while speaking as a cue for liking, whereas men generally use the gaze for listening. Much of the difference in looking behavior between women and men may be

⟩ personality differences. Some studies, for example, indicate that females ౿-- ally report higher needs for inclusion, affiliation, and affection during interaction and may use more looking to fulfill those needs. It has also been suggested that females probably rely more heavily on visual stimuli than do males because they are more sensitive to the social impact of their eye behavior on interpersonal exchanges.

The female need for inclusion, affiliation, and affection noted earlier—needs that are commonly acknowledged to be at least partially culturally determined—probably are lower for today's females. Similarly, characteristics of dominance and assertiveness, which were considered appropriate only for males a quarter-century ago, are now considered less aversive for females. Because these personality factors have been found to be highly related to gaze behavior, it is entirely possible that the differences between male and female eye behavior observed are much reduced or even missing in today's society. We cannot be certain about such speculation. Additionally, more and more men and women are becoming androgynous (each sex possessing both masculine and feminine behaviors). Therefore the more assertive woman may gaze very much like a man, and the more responsive man may gaze very much like a woman.

To summarize, normal eye behavior includes a wide range of looking frequency and duration. It is generally necessary to consider personality, gender, culture, and contextual influences in evaluating the gazing activity of other people. Neglecting these influences may lead to interpersonal misunderstandings. Remember: Nonverbal cues do not occur in a vacuum. Often, their true significance is apparent only when we consider all the factors surrounding the nonverbal activity.

What do we know about eye behavior?

1. We know that we look at people and things we like.
2. We avoid looking at things and people we do not like.
3. Our eyes can express the basic SCADFISH emotions.
4. We look more at another person when seeking approval or wanting to be liked.
5. The type of gaze we use tells another person about our intentions.
6. Gaze aversion is an intentional act; gaze omission is not.
7. Deception can rarely be determined by looking solely at another person's eye behavior.
8. Our pupils dilate when we look at someone or something that is appealing or interesting to us.
9. Our pupils constrict when we look at someone or something that is not appealing or interesting to us.
10. Women will often look longer at their conversational partner than will men.

Glossary of Terminology

Conjugate lateral eye movements (CLEMs) are involuntary lateral shifts of the eyes to the right or left. CLEMs are thought to be closely associated with cognitive processing; that is, we look away to the left or right while we are thinking, but look forward again when we stop processing information. People can be categorized as either right-lookers or left-lookers because approximately 75 percent of an individual's CLEMs are in one direction.

Gaze aversion is when someone avoids looking at another person during an interpersonal encounter.

Gaze omission occurs when one person does not look at the other person but is not intentionally avoiding eye contact.

Mutual gaze refers to two people looking in the direction of one another's faces.

Oculesics is the study of eye behavior, eye contact, eye movement, and the functions of eye behavior.

One-sided look or glance is a gaze of one individual toward another person's face that is not reciprocated. When we are interested, we look interested.

CHAPTER 6

Vocal Behavior

Addington (1968, 1971), Archer and Akert (1977), McCroskey (2001), and Mulac and Giles (1996) have reinforced the notion that there is an enormous amount of information to be obtained from the human voice, including emotion, state of health, age, and gender. People are very astute at determining information about other people based on listening to the human voice. The actual verbal message is unclear to the receiver without the vocal cues that accompany it (Guerrero, DeVito, & Hecht, 1999). Many times the entire meaning is interpreted on the basis of how something is said. Gilbert (2006) has indicated that there are additional insights from the voice. She has reported that when subjects hear a voice, they can predict height, weight, and age just as well as if they viewed a photograph. In addition, men tend to lower their voices when they are speaking to someone they perceive as subordinate and raise their voices when talking with a superior. She found that people with attractive voices indicated that they had had more sexual partners during their lives. She reported that surgeons who had been sued for malpractice had dominant voices: "deep, loud, moderately fast, unaccented, and clearly articulated" (p. 15).

The study of the communicative value of vocal behavior, or **paralanguage,** is called **vocalics.** Paralanguage includes all oral cues in the stream of spoken utterances except the words themselves. The importance of vocal behavior as a type of nonverbal communication lies in the impact it has on perceptions of the verbal content of our messages.

Vocal cues can contradict the oral message. **Sarcasm** is saying one thing and communicating something else. We are sarcastic when our words say one thing and our vocal cues say the opposite. This brings up an important point about vocal behavior. Sarcasm is something we learn to communicate. It is also something we learn to understand; therefore, small children often do not understand sarcasm. Some studies have shown that small children tend to believe the verbal content of a message rather than the meaning signaled by the contradicting vocal cues. Furthermore, we usually cannot appreciate the sarcasm of people from other cultures. How we say something is influenced considerably by cultural factors (Berry, Hansen, Landry-Pester, & Meier, 1994; Davitz, 1964; Liggon, Weston, Ambady, Colloton, Rosenthal, & Reite, 1992; Mulac, Hanley, & Prigge, 1974; Newman & Smit, 1989; Plazewski & Allen, 1985).

Vocal behavior plays an extremely important role in regulating our interactions with others. We not only control the flow of conversations with our body movements and eye behavior but also signal to listeners with our voices. Regulative behaviors involved in turn-taking are rich with vocal information (Duncan, 1972, 1973, 1974; Wiemann & Knapp, 1975).

Vocal cues transmit many other messages as well. The way we speak can tell others about our status, background, gender, age, socioeconomic status, current emotional state, where we grew up, where we are from, and a variety of other demographic data (Johnson, 1985; Markel, 1965; McCroskey, 2001; Mulac & Giles, 1996; O'Hair, Cody, & Behnke, 1985; Siegman & Boyle, 1993; Starkweather, 1961; Semic, 1999). By listening to the vocal cues, receivers can glean accurate pieces of information and may use such information to stereotype the sender in several ways. For example, if we think a person sounds as though he or she were from New Jersey, we might have certain stereotypes that go along with our perceptions of New Jersey people.

CATEGORIES OF VOCAL BEHAVIOR

The study of what a person says is virtually meaningless without a study of the vocal cues that surround the words. The study of the text of a great speech tells one nothing about how the speaker actually presented that speech. The vocal atmosphere surrounding that speech is what paralanguage is all about. The primary difference between speaking and writing is the presence of paralanguage.

Although the verbal message (the text) may be the same, what is communicated can be and usually is very different. To study a speech is to study a text within its vocal atmosphere. The texts of long-deceased speakers, of course, may be studied by scholars today, but these texts cannot be studied as speeches unless a vocalic record is available for simultaneous study. Paralinguistic cues did not just emerge in recent years; they always have been critical. How you say something may stimulate more and different meanings than just the words you actually say. Vocal behavior, however, is more than just how something is said. It includes a variety of vocal activities that emanates from the oral cavity. Trager (1958) classified all paralinguistic activity as falling into one of several categories. Trager is widely credited for delineating the relationship between spoken language and paralanguage. It is useful to examine some of Trager's categories.

Voice Set

When we speak, we do so in what Trager describes as the "setting" of an act of speech. This vocal environment or contextual background is in some measure the result of the speaker's voice, which involves several of the speaker's personal characteristics. Included among these factors is age, gender, present condition of health, state of enthusiasm, fatigue, and sadness and/or other emotions. Even seemingly irrelevant factors such as social status, education level, and group identification may play an important role in contributing to the speaker's voice set.

Voice set is closely related to who the speaker is; such information helps us to interpret the speaker's words more accurately. We realize that the idea of voice set may be difficult to grasp. It becomes quite apparent to listeners, however, when different speakers say the same phrase with the same emphasis and express the same emotions. The remaining difference in their vocal activity can be attributed to their different voice sets. Consider several different individuals: a fragile older man, a truck driver, a minister, a schoolteacher, and a successful businesswoman. Think of how each of these individuals would sound while speaking the following phrases with the same amount of enthusiasm and emotion: "It is a very nice day." "Hello, Fernando." "That tastes great!"

You probably visualized differences in the vocal cues of these five individuals even before you considered the phrases. If you did, you were keying in on the phenomenon of voice set. For many successful performers, the key to playing any given role realistically is creating a voice set consistent with that character's identity.

Voice Qualities and Vocalizations

Trager distinguishes between two other categories of vocal behavior that he considers the actual objects of study in paralanguage. The first category is called **voice qualities**, and includes tempo, resonance, rhythm control, articulation control, pitch control, glottis control, vocal lip control, and pitch range. Voice qualities are modifications of the vocal cues that accompany spoken words. Changes in voice qualities can often signal important messages to others. Although they are considered content-free speech, one can surely see that a change in the tempo, such as speaking rapidly, may communicate a sense of urgency or excitement. Maria tells you she is angry; her extremely resonant vocal burst tells you exactly how angry she is.

Closely related to voice qualities are **vocalizations**. According to Trager, vocalizations are audible vocal cues that do not have the structure of language and may or may not be accompanied by spoken words. There are three different kinds of vocalizations. The first is the **vocal characterizer**, which refers to non-language sounds such as laughing, crying, whimpering, giggling, snickering, and sobbing. We might also consider many audible meditative chants to be vocal characterizers. Other characterizers include groaning, moaning, yawning, growling, muttering, whining, and sighing. Many people are well recognized by and closely associated with the characterizers they frequently use (Guerrero, DeVito, & Hecht, 1999).

Trager's second type of vocalization is called the **vocal qualifier**. Vocal qualifiers are similar to voice qualities but are considered separately for one main reason: Whereas voice qualities usually modify an entire stream of speech, vocal qualifiers qualify or regulate specific portions of the utterance. In other words, qualifiers provide variety within a spoken sentence. Vocal qualifiers include intensity, pitch height, and extent. Vocal cues that vary the rate, loudness, or softness during a given utterance are also qualifiers. The nonverbal function of accenting is effectively served by these vocal qualifiers. Janet emphasized the word *now* in her statement, "Put that pencil down . . . NOW," by pausing briefly before the last word, then increasing the loudness of her voice. This left no doubt in her son's mind as to when he should put the pencil down (Poyatos, 1991).

The last category of vocal behavior is the **vocal segregate**. Again, these vocal cues are audible but are not linguistic. Some segregates have been described as non-words that are used as words. These cues include vocalizations such as *shhh, uh-huh,* and *uh-uh*. Furthermore, vocal segregates include many common filler sounds such as *uh-uh-uh, er, ah,* and even seeming words such as *and-ah,* and *you know*. You probably can think of an acquaintance who uses more than her or his share of segregates.

See if you can identify the vocal segregates in the following conversation:

DICK: Uh, I think, you know, we ought to go to class, and, uh. . . .

BILL: Duh . . . What for? Ya know . . . we have better things to do, like, ah, ya know, smoking in the boys' room or terrorizing someone's kitten, ha, ha.

DICK: Uh-uh-uh, because we're having a test next week, ya know, we should go to class.

BILL: Uh-uh. I ain't going. No way. No chance. No how.

DICK: So, ah hum, like, ah, what you want to do?

Vocal segregates such as *uh-uh* and *uh-huh* function as substitutes for verbal utterances, but we also find them in the stream of speech of people who are thinking about what they are going to say next. While teaching a public-speaking course a few years ago, one speech professor counted sixty-seven *and-uhs* in one student's five-minute speech. The speech began with one of these vocal segregates and each sentence ended with one. Generally, when a person is in a novel situation, is the center of attention, or is anxious, the use of vocal segregates will increase. Think of communication situations when these vocal segregates are more likely to occur (Davitz & Davitz, 1959; Christenfeld, 1995).

Voice Printing

Voice printing is likely to become another means of identifying us in addition to the use of fingerprints and DNA analysis. The concept of voice printing is not new; it has been in existence for years. Voice printing is similar to finger-printing in that a person can be identified by unique characteristics and quali-ties in her or his voice. Weitz (1972) notes that voice printing (most notably recorded telephone conversations) has been used in some criminal cases. She also notes that there is a disagreement about the accuracy of voice printing. Some people advocate that voice printing is as much as 90 percent accurate, while others suggest only about 50 percent. Certainly, using vocal recognition and voice printing as a means of identifying a criminal can be considered one of the many facets pointing to innocence or guilt. Currently, however, more evidence is required than vocal recognition alone to declare guilt.

Silence and Pauses

Silence is an important aspect of communication, although it is not always considered a category of vocal behavior. You have no doubt heard the phrases, "Silence is golden" and "If you can't say anything nice, then don't say any-thing at all." Contrary to what many believe, silence is not the opposite of speech. Silence should not be equated with not communicating. It is an inte-gral part of our vocal behavior and, depending on the situation, can provide a great deal of information about our thoughts, emotions, attitudes, and rela-tionships with others (Braithwaite, 1999; Newman, 1982; Jaworski, 1999). Silence is generally discussed in terms of pauses in the stream of speech. These pauses can be identified as either unfilled pauses or filled pauses. **Unfilled pauses,** or **silence,** are periods when vocal activity stops during the spoken utterance. **Filled pauses,** on the other hand, are interruptions in the stream of speech content that are filled with audible sounds such as *uh, er, ah,* stuttering, and even slips of the tongue or repetitions.

Filled and unfilled pauses can be classified as three different silence phe-nomena: *hesitation silence, psycholinguistic silence,* and *interactive silence.* Hesitation silences are generally pauses during speech caused by anxiety or uncertainty about what to say next. Psycholinguistic silences, on the other hand, are pauses related to the encoding and decoding of speech. Pausing is most prevalent at the beginning of a grammatical stream of speech. It often is

A person's vocal quality can punctuate the message.

Source: Photo by C. Price Walt

necessary to pause while translating thoughts into words. Finally, interactive silences or pauses are products of the interaction itself and can communicate various messages about the relationship between two interactants. The silent moments two lovers share, the silence that signifies respect for an elder, the cold silence between individuals in conflict, and the silence that ignores are all examples of interactive pauses (Argyle, 1999; Lalljee & Cook, 1969; McCroskey, 2001; Richmond, 1996).

Pauses can also be classified as grammatical or nongrammatical. According to Goldman-Eisler (1968), pauses are grammatical when they occur at the following junctures: natural punctuation points such as the end of a sentence; just before a conjunction (*but, and, or*); just before relative and interrogative pronouns (*who, which, why*); in association with an indirect or implied question (*I'm not sure about that*); just before adverbial clauses of time, manner, and place (*I will leave when I'm ready*); or when complete parenthetical references are used (*I am sure my students, those in my nonverbal communication class, will vote for you*).

Pauses may also be nongrammatical. These pauses occur in the middle or at the end of a verbal phrase; as gaps or breaks between words and phrases that are repeated (*I think you will find /pause/ will find that /pause/ that I am right*); as gaps or breaks between verbal compounds (*I have /pause/ talked until I'm blue in the face*); and as a disruption or false start (*I am concerned /pause/ the problem is your attitude*).

Knapp and Hall (1992) have made an interesting observation regarding spontaneous speech: Only about 55 percent of all pauses in such speech are grammatical; whereas, well-prepared presentations, such as oral readings of texts, are generally characterized by a high consistency in grammatical pausing.

Uses of Silence in Communication

Silence can establish distance in interpersonal relationships. Although we may not physically remove ourselves, we can create a psychological distance by remaining silent (Jaworski, 1999; Braithwaite, 1999; McCroskey & Richmond, 1996; Mehrabian, 1968).

Silence is often needed for a person to put her or his thoughts together. As we suggested earlier, encoding messages is facilitated by silent moments during the process of putting thoughts into words. Silence is used to show respect to another person. Not only do we show respect through silence, but those in authority often use silent pauses to command the respect of others. Silence can be used to modify another's behavior. Parents throughout the ages have used the silent treatment on their children to get them to behave. Spouses and friends also have been known to use this approach.

Silence can be used to emphasize a point of content in the flow of speech or to make a piece of content more memorable. The silent pause before or after a startling statement in a speech can give significant meaning to the statement. Silence can be a means of displaying an emotional state. For example, some people will simply be silent as a way of supporting another person by not disagreeing with her or him, or as a sign of contentment.

VOCAL BEHAVIOR AND TURN-INTERACTION MANAGEMENT

In previous chapters, we introduced the concept of turn-taking during conversations. We suggested that many gestures and eye behaviors are used to regulate the back-and-forth interaction between speakers and listeners. Such behaviors are usually used with a variety of vocal cues that signal to others our speaking or listening intentions during conversations. Recall that there are four types of turn-taking behaviors: turn-maintaining, turn-yielding, turn-requesting, and turn-denying (Duncan, 1972, 1973, 1974).

Turn-Maintaining

There are times in our interactions with others when we wish to continue talking. That is, we wish to maintain our turn in the speaking process. Cues that speakers use to signal their listeners that they want to keep the floor are called **turn-maintaining cues.** These cues are most prominent in situations where the listener may be trying to interrupt. Vocal cues involved in turn-maintaining may include an increase in the loudness of speech. Such increases usually serve to drown out a listener who may be requesting a turn. Another turn-maintaining vocal cue is an increase in the rate of speech. It is generally difficult for others to break into a stream of speech that is moving quickly. It decreases the chances that a listener can get a word in edgewise.

Other effective vocal cues in turn-maintaining include the use of more filled pauses. Filling pauses with vocal segregates rather than leaving them unfilled can cue the listener that you may be at the end of a particular thought, but you are not finished talking. Mr. Jones, Jake's boss, scolds him for coming in to work late. As Jake tries to explain, Mr. Jones increases his speech rate and volume because he wants to add, "It should not happen again."

Turn-Yielding

When we are finished speaking and wish to signal our listening partner that he or she can now begin talking, we generally engage in **turn-yielding behavior**. Asking your listener a question is certainly a yielding cue. Questioning calls for us to raise the pitch of our voices at the end of the utterance. Another vocal cue that signals turn-yielding is an emphatic drop in voice pitch. Often the drop in pitch is used together with the trailing-off of the utterance. End phrases may be tacked on after the drop in pitch to make the comments trail off. Trailing-off phrases are usually more prevalent when the speaker is coaxing the listener to begin talking.

Intonation changes that deviate from the normal rising and falling of the voice during an utterance usually are signals of turn-yielding. Furthermore, your speaking rate can signal the listener that you are relinquishing the speaking turn. Of course, a long unfilled pause (silence) also serves the turn-yielding function. Long silences during a conversation can be uncomfortable for those involved. Although a listener may not have something important to say, he or she may begin speaking simply to break the silence. As an exercise, try this little experiment with silence. Get together with an acquaintance and strike up a conversation. Insert a few silent pauses after a few of your comments, and see how long your partner lets the silence remain unfilled. Chances are good that he or she will fill the silence with almost anything before too many seconds have ticked away.

The time that it takes a person to begin speaking after another person stops is called her or his **response latency**. People differ greatly in the length of their response latencies. People with very short response latencies often talk over their partners. That is, they start speaking before their partner is finished. They take the slightest pause as a sign to take over the conversation. In contrast, people with very long response latencies can cause their partners to be very uncomfortable. If we pause to let our partner take a turn, but our partner does not do so right away, we may feel forced to begin talking again. When a person with a short response latency interacts with a person with a long latency, the former usually dominates the interaction—even if he or she doesn't intend to do so (Newman & Smit, 1989; McCroskey, 2001).

Turn-Requesting

Think for a moment of a time when you were listening to someone speaking. As that person continued, you found yourself wanting to speak. You waited for the speaker to pause, if only for a brief second, so that you could begin. To your dismay and increasing frustration, the pause never came. You knew you had to speak soon, or you would forget what you were going to say. What did you do? If you are like most folks, you started to use **turn-requesting cues** in the hope that the speaker would wrap things up. In essence, you nonverbally helped them put on the speaking brakes. Such turn-requesting vocal cues include the stutter start (*BUT . . . but . . . but, I . . . I . . . I*), which may be inserted into the conversation even while the speaker is still talking. Stutter starts and other vocal cues such as vocal buffers ("*ER . . . ah*" or "*UH . . . well*") tend to encourage the speaker to finish in less time. Increasing the rate of responses such as *Mm-hmm* or *Yes . . . yes* also serves as an effective turn-requesting signal.

Turn-Denying

Finally, there are times when listeners transmit signals to speakers that they do not wish to take a speaking turn. **Turn-denying behavior**, or **back-channel cues**, occur most often when the listener has nothing to say when the speaker begins to yield the turn. Turn-denying includes a slower rate of responses and vocal cues that tend to reward the speaker for talking. Positive nonlanguage vocalizations such as *Mm-hmm* delivered at a slowed pace and accompanied by a positive head nod generally signal the speaker, "Please go on, I like what you're saying."

It should be noted that vocal behavior used in interaction management seldom occurs alone. Often, gestures and other body movements, as well as eye behavior, accompany the vocalizations. For instance, raising a finger along with the eyebrows, leaning forward, and inhaling audibly communicate a request to speak. Conversely, by accelerating your rate of speech, looking away, turning your body, increasing loudness, and exhibiting a halting gesture (putting up your hand to stop interruptions) toward the listener, you maintain your speaking turn. Similarly, verbal comments may function to decline turns. If listeners complete sentences for the speakers or request clarification on earlier comments, they may more easily maintain their position as listeners.

Interruptions

While there is a stereotype of women talking a lot and men interrupting them, Tannen (1990) has written that neither the amount of talk nor the concept of interruption is quite so simple. In regard to the amount of talk, Tannen has indicated that women talk more in private settings, and men talk more in public settings. Regarding interruptions to turn-taking, Tannen says that there are at least three different types of interruptions. First, there is the kind of interruption that most of us are used to. Here we see two commentators on television. They constantly interrupt one another before they even know what the other one is going to say. Essentially they are paid to create conflict. Generally they take extreme opposite ends of an issue, and probably few agree with either one of them. This argumentative type of an interruption Tannen calls a *negative interruption*. The second type of interruption is based on content irrelevant to the conversation. If you are talking about your trip to Europe with a friend while picking up a valuable artifact in her apartment, she may interrupt by saying, "Please let me hold that, and you can look at it." She is not interrupting your conversation per se but rather concerned about your talking and holding her vase at the same time. The third type of interruption is often in the form of a question (Hall, 1984; LaFrance & Carmen, 1980). Here let's assume that an instructor is explaining a nonverbal communication principle, and while she is talking, you ask, "Is that the same as body language?" Here there is no argument about the content of the subject, and the interruption is relevant. In this third type, too, one may be speaking about Washington. The other person interrupts with, "DC?" And the first person says, "yes, DC," and goes on talking. The third type is essentially a communicative interruption, a positive one. It is intended to keep the conversation moving while making certain the information is accurate. In some cases, people will agree as the conversation is going along, saying, "um-hum." Thus when we think about someone's interrupting, we should consider what the intent is as well as the interruption itself.

Accent and Dialect

Accent refers to the different ways words are said. **Dialect,** on the other hand, refers to the use of different words to reference similar meanings. Accent, then, is a paralinguistic concern; whereas, dialect is a concern of linguistics. People from different regions of the United States or from different cultural groups within a given region are likely to differ from each other in terms of accent, dialect, or both (Bradford, Farrar, & Bradford, 1974; McCroskey, 2001; Sayer, 1979).

If you are like most people, you do not think of yourself as having an accent or speaking in a dialect. We tend to see others, those who speak differently, as having an accent or dialect. Accent and dialect, then, can be viewed as perceptions one has of another's way of speaking. If you are from the New York borough of Brooklyn and speak with the stereotypical Brooklyn accent, you would probably not be considered to have a dialect by your Brooklyn neighbors. That is, you and a neighbor would characterize one another's speech as "normal." But both of you would say that the person down the block who moved in from the southeastern part of the United States talks "funny."

Similarly, a person who was born and raised in rural Kentucky, and who speaks with a southern Appalachian drawl, would not be perceived by her or his fellow Kentuckians as having an accent. Should the Brooklynite go to Kentucky, or the southern Appalachian travel to New York, each would have an accent and a dialect in relation to the local speakers. We never think of our own speech as different or funny; rather, it is the other person who talks funny; it is the other person who has the dialect. Essentially, perceptions of accent and dialect arise when one encounters speech patterns that are not consistent with how one has been socialized to speak. Factors that contribute to perceptions of accent include many vocal phenomena. First, vocal qualities are perceived as different. For instance, the southern accent is often characterized by a slower rate of vocal delivery, and the Texas drawl is even slower. Generally, northerners describe southerners' speech as containing more syllables. One southerner at a national communication conference recently commented in a humorous vein that the word *cowboy* does not have two syllables, it has four: "ca-o-bo-ah." Another southerner in the audience noted that such a word is very different from a true two-syllable word such as *fit* (pronounced "fee-it").

Another vocal phenomenon that contributes to perceptions of accent is difference in pronunciation of words. The name *Mary* is pronounced as "Merry" in some regions, "Marry" in others, and "Maury" in still others. Take the three words *I'll, all,* and *oil.* Say them aloud several times. Do you say each differently? People from most parts of the United States do. However, if you are from some parts of Texas, chances are you pronounce all three words the same way. Do you say "bird," "boid," or "bud" when referring to one of our feathered friends? When you point to a distant hillside, do you say "over yonder," "over yonda," or "ova yawner"?

Can perception of accent lead to other judgments as well? According to some research, it does. In the educational environment, teachers have been found to rate children with different patterns of speech as culturally disadvantaged and to judge those with foreign accents as lower on the social-status ladder. Still others have shown that English-speaking Hispanics are perceived by non-Hispanic Americans to be less successful, lower in intelligence, lower in social awareness, and lower in ability when they speak with a Hispanic accent. Some research suggests that the slower rate of southern speech can create perceptions of low intelligence and slowness of thought in other parts of the United States. The Brooklyn accent has been known to connote arrogance and other negative traits to people in the West and South (Argyle, 1999; Berry, 1990; Berry, Hansen, Landry-Pester, & Meier, 1994; Camras, Sullivan, & Michel, 1993; Kramer, 1963; Massaro & Egan, 1996; Sayer, 1979; Semic, 1999; Williams, 1970; Zuckerman & Driver, 1989).

You may be asking yourself, "Why does it seem so common to make such unfavorable judgments about people because of their accents?" It doesn't seem fair, does it? However, it does happen, and often negative consequences arise because of accent perceptions. Those consequences can range from relatively unimportant social disadvantages to not being considered for particular jobs. Particular regional vocal patterns and ethnic accents are often associated with individuals' ability to socialize, perform, and behave appropriately. No, it is not fair to discriminate against people because of how they speak. It is not fair to judge an individual's intelligence by her or his accent. Yet, it occurs every day. It is always wise to suspend judgment until you can validate your perceptions with sources of information other than accent. Know that everyone has a dialect and an accent. This becomes obvious only when you interact with people of other regions, cultures, or subcultures. As with most things, we tend to consider our own accent and dialect as the right, best, and normal one. That is part of what may make others refer to North Americans as *ethnocentric.* When they do, be assured that they do not intend it as a compliment.

Mulac (1976) indicates that we judge the accents of others according to three primary dimensions. His research demonstrated that accents are evaluated on

1. Sociointellectual status (status, occupation, income, literacy),
2. Aesthetic quality (how pleasing or displeasing the accent is), and
3. Dynamism (how aggressive, assertive, strong, loud, or active the voice is).

We hear these dimensions in our daily lives. For example, when we say someone has a "good voice," we could be saying that he or she sounds pleasant or that he or she sounds strong (Hecht & LaFrance, 1995; Semic, 1999; Zuckerman & Driver, 1989).

It is worthwhile to consider the words of Phillips, Kougl, and Kelly (1985) in their book on speaking:

> It is important to remember that people are entitled to choose how they wish to talk and what language communities they wish to seek membership in. . . . Learning language styles of various groups is not an easy task, but it is a mark of respect shown for one's origins and one's new affiliations (p. 241).

EFFECTS OF VOCAL BEHAVIOR

Vocal behavior can affect our interactions with others in several ways. The following pages present a discussion of the effects of vocal cues on the expression of emotion, judgments of personality, ability to learn, ability to persuade others, and effective delivery.

Vocal Behavior and Feelings

Choose a partner, classmate, or roommate to participate in this exercise. One of you should close your book while the other attempts to communicate the following list of emotions. Take turns as the communicator. There are a couple of rules.

1. Turn away from one another so that you are back to back.
2. The person with the job of communicating the emotion is allowed to use only one statement: "Onions taste great in the morning."

Speaking this sentence only, see if you can get your partner to guess each of these feelings:

anger	disgust	distrust	fear
concern	love	dejection	happiness
contempt	sadness	confusion	hate
sympathy	pleasure	frustration	surprise
guilt	betrayal	interest	boredom

Although your partner may not have guessed the exact feeling every time, you probably were quite successful with this activity. Given the restrictions of the rules, some people are surprised they can get any guesses right. Vocal behavior, apart from actual verbal content, carries much information about emotions (Bachorowski & Owren, 1995; Camras, Sullivan, & Michel, 1993; Davitz, 1964; Mehrabian & Ferris, 1967; Scherer, 1982; Scherer, Koivumaki, & Rosenthal, 1972; Starkweather, 1961). The vocal expression of emotion is found in the paralinguistic cues rather than the content of the spoken utterance. Research on the vocal expression of emotion often uses content-free speech techniques. That is, listeners are asked to judge which emotion is being expressed in the voices of others while the actual content of speech is made to be incomprehensible. This is similar to hearing your neighbors arguing without being able to discern what they are saying to one another. You certainly can tell they are angry, but you can't tell why.

Studies that use the content-free-speech approach have been quite helpful to our understanding of which vocal cues communicate a given emotion. Whether a speaker is excited or calm is associated with the extent and type of change in pitch and loudness. However, some emotions are more accurately judged than others.

Nervousness, anger, sadness, and happiness are the easiest feelings to interpret from vocal cues alone. On the other hand, surprise, fear, and love are often difficult to judge. Although their voices usually are different from one another, males and females use the same vocal activity to express the same feelings. For example, both sexes use increased volume while expressing anger, increased rate and pitch during impatience, and so on (Addington, 1968; Bachorowski, & Owren, 1995; Davitz, 1964; Kramer, 1963; Perlmutter, Paddock, & Duke, 1985; Scherer, Koivumaki, & Rosenthal, 1972). Most of the research on vocal cues and emotional expression appears to indicate five consistent findings:

1. Negative emotions are more accurately identified than positive feelings.
2. A listener's ability to identify emotions in the voice is affected by the speaker's ability to encode feelings into his or her voice.
3. Those who monitor and control their own feelings can more accurately identify the feelings of others through vocal cues.
4. When you are talking with another person from your own culture, it is easier to identify the various vocal expressions.
5. Subtle feelings are harder to detect.

The third generalization may need some explanation. People who are considered high self-monitors (unusually aware or attentive toward what they do) are much more sensitive to the vocal expressions of others. This probably is a result of having practiced observing how they express their own emotions and working to control the vocal cues. Knowing which vocal cues contribute to the expression of particular emotions has made them more competent judges of others' vocal expressions. High self-monitors not only surpass others in judging vocal expression but are also better at intentionally encoding certain emotions into the voice.

Scherer and Osinsky (1977) describe vocalic cues and the emotional state associated with them. Often these vocalic cues, not the content of the message, tell us what the other person truly means. Scherer and Osinsky and many other vocalic writers have suggested there are certain cues associated with particular vocalic emotional states. Based on the vocalic research, here are cues that are often associated with the emotions:

Sadness = slow tempos, low pitch, few harmonics, flat, little activity, bland, colorless

Anger = fast tempos, high pitch level, loudness, many harmonics, bitter, unpleasant, harsh

Disgust = slow tempos; many harmonics; flat, hard sound; little intonation; repulsive

Fear = pitch contour up, fast tempos, strident, discordant, inharmonious, piercing

Interest = even pitch, moderate tempos, moderate harmonics, lively, alert

Surprise = fast tempos, high pitch, up/down pitch, many harmonics, startled, stunned

Happiness = fast tempos, higher pitch variation, active, lively, animated, cheerful

Vocal Behavior and Personality

There has surely been a time when you formed impressions of others' personalities simply because of how their voices sound. You can probably think of someone who talks too fast or whines, or whose voice constantly trembles. What do you generally think of people who have tense voices, breathy voices, deep raspy voices, or throaty voices? Are there any stereotypical judgments we make about them? Consistent vocal quality of others' speech is often associated with particular personality characteristics. Let's consider the extensive work conducted by Addington (1968).

Addington was extremely interested in whether vocal cues consistently created stereotypical personality judgments about others. He identified nine qualities present in voices: breathiness, thinness, flatness, nasality, tenseness, throatiness, orotundity, increased rate, and increased pitch variety. Addington used in his research males and females considered to have these types of vocal qualities. The following is a brief, general summary of Addington's findings.

BREATHINESS.   A breathy voice is characterized by audible exhalation during speech. Although breathiness is not usually associated with males, there are males whose voices have this quality. Generally, men with breathy voices are perceived by others as younger and more artistic. Extreme breathiness in males may often be associated with perceptions of effeminacy and homosexuality.

Breathiness in females tends to elicit judgments of femininity and petiteness. Women with this vocal quality are perceived as prettier, more effervescent, more high-strung, and often more shallow.

THINNESS. For the most part, thinness of voice in males does not seem to be associated highly with any particular personality judgments. For females, however, a somewhat different picture emerges. Women with thin voices are more likely to be seen as socially and physically immature. They are also perceived as more immature emotionally and mentally. These perceptions of immaturity are generally considered to be negative judgments. However, two positive perceptions were also associated with thinness in female voices: a better sense of humor and greater sensitivity.

FLATNESS. A flat voice, whether in a male or female, tends to be associated with the same perceptions. Flatness of voice for both sexes is more likely to create perceptions of masculinity and sluggishness. Furthermore, persons with flatter voices are seen as colder and more withdrawn.

NASALITY. There is probably no vocal quality that is considered less desirable in our culture than nasality. People who "talk through their noses" often are seen as not much fun. However, this is a common voice problem among North Americans. According to Addington's research, nasality in both males and females provokes a wide array of socially negative perceptions, such as laziness, low intelligence, and boredom. This is not a good set of labels for anyone to be stuck with, unless, of course, you have no interest in having friends, a social life, or making a good impression during job interviews.

TENSENESS. If you tense the muscles in your throat and around your jaw, you will notice that as you speak, you are putting a strain on your voice. Vocal tenseness has also been found to relate to judgments others make of us. In Addington's work, men were generally seen as older if they had tense voices. Furthermore, they were perceived to be less yielding in conversations. On the other hand, women were seen much differently. Voice tenseness in females was more likely to provoke perceptions of the speaker being younger, more emotional, more feminine, and more high-strung. Women with tense voices were also perceived as less intelligent.

THROATINESS. The increased throatiness in the vocal quality of male voices tended to cause the judges in Addington's study to stereotype them as older, more mature, and sophisticated. They were also seen as more realistic in their outlook and better adjusted. What this seems to suggest is that throatiness in males is a positive and desirable characteristic. For females, the perceptions caused by this vocal quality are almost exactly the opposite. These speakers were characterized as unemotional, ugly, boorish, lazy, more masculine, less intelligent, careless, inartistic, naive, neurotic, apathetic, humble, and uninteresting.

OROTUNDITY. This quality refers to the robustness, clearness, and strength of the voice. Males with increased orotundity were perceived as energetic, more sophisticated, interesting, proud, enthusiastic, and artistic. The general perceptions of males are that they are more expressive, open, and aesthetically driven. Many similar personality characteristics were attributed to females. Women with robust and strong voices were seen as more gregarious, livelier, and aesthetically sensitive. According to Addington, however, they are also perceived as humorless and proud.

INCREASED RATE. Addington's research showed that increased vocal rate tended to create the same perceptions whether the speaker was male or female. Essentially, speakers with faster rates of speech were seen as more animated and extroverted than those who spoke at slower rates. That probably means that faster talkers are perceived as more socially oriented. Increased rate, then, is a socially desirable characteristic of vocal behavior because it seems related to positive perceptions. Others have noted that increased speaking rate is related to perceptions of competence or credibility of the speaker. People who can speak at quicker rates with few or no disfluencies in the stream of speech may seem more sure of what they are saying and therefore appear more confident (Kimble & Seidel, 1991; Markel, 1965).

INCREASED VARIETY IN PITCH. Judges in Addington's study commonly identified pitch variety as a feminine rather than a masculine behavior. Males generally do not see the advantages that may result from incorporating variety in their pitch. Addington's findings indicate that males who used more pitch variety were perceived as dynamic, effeminate, and aesthetically inclined. Females were seen as more dynamic and extroverted.

Vocal Behavior and Learning

A major concern of scholars who study communication in the classroom environment is the impact of vocal behavior on student learning, comprehension, and retention of material. There is probably no worse enemy to the classroom teacher than a monotone voice. Our own research shows that having a monotone voice is more closely related to negative evaluations of teachers by students than any other factor. The monotone voice incorporates little variety in vocal qualities during verbal utterances; monotone speakers have little or no inflectional variety or rate variety when speaking. Much like the dull moan of distant environmental sounds, monotonous speech tends to thwart the attention and interest of listeners. One thing is certainly clear: People cannot learn anything that does not capture their attention. Monotone contributes nothing to a speaker's presentation; in fact, it works against the presenter's efforts to stimulate student attention (McCroskey, 2001; Richmond, 1996).

Researchers and writers suggest that vocal variety, vocal clarity, and natural-sounding voices contribute to the comprehension and later recall of presented material. Seven decades ago, in one of the earliest empirical studies in the field of communication, Woolbert (1920) showed that vocal variety in tempo, force, and pitch contributed to higher retention of material. More recent studies have found that monotone actually reduces listeners' comprehension of orally delivered material (Markel, 1965). Others have even found that qualities such as nasality and breathiness hinder comprehension and retention. Being inarticulate or sounding unnatural can also hinder listeners' comprehension and recall (Addington, 1971; Kimble & Seidel, 1991; McCroskey, 2001; Sereno & Hawkins, 1967).

The impact of the rate of speech on learning has been studied extensively. It may surprise you to learn that, up to a point, increased rates tend to increase the amount that listeners comprehend and later recall of oral presentations. Many experts believe we can process and comprehend information much more quickly than we can speak. For this reason, we often let our minds wander between particular points the speaker is presenting. Should the speaker talk at a faster rate, there is less chance that we will turn our attention away from the speaker's presentation. Of course it is possible to talk too fast. Listeners may simply be unwilling to put in the effort to stay with the extremely fast talker. Excessive speed may also conjure up the stereotype of the used-car salesperson and lead to reductions in perceived credibility (Addington, 1971; Kimble & Seidel, 1991; Markel, 1965; McCroskey, 2001; Mehrabian & Williams, 1969; Miller & Hewgill, 1964; Miller, Maruyama, Beaber, & Valone, 1976; Richmond, 2002).

Warm, positive vocal behavior of teachers is also important to classroom learning. Positive vocal cues can serve to reinforce and encourage students to participate more actively in their own learning by talking more and seeking clarifications from their teachers. A teacher's positive vocal cues tend to create positive attitudes in the student toward the material and the teacher. Some research indicates that positive vocal behavior contributes even more to improved interest and learning for lower-class than for middle-class students, although improvement is generally seen in all social classes (Richmond, 1996, 2002).

Vocal behavior can enhance the clarity of verbal messages. The clarity of a verbal message directly contributes to listeners' abilities to understand oral presentations. Verbal utterances are clear to listeners in part because the speaker has used her or his vocal qualities to emphasize, accent, or point up certain parts of the message. Vocal cues can signal to the listener which portions may be most important, for example. Vocal cues highlight, underline, boldface, or italicize words or phrases and subsequently contribute to the listeners' abilities to retain the material (McCroskey, 2001).

Vocal Behavior and Persuasion

When we use the word *persuasion*, we are referring primarily to influencing the attitudes, values, and beliefs of others. Generally speaking, we can persuade by generating a new attitude in our listeners, reinforcing an attitude already held, or actually changing someone's attitude from one orientation to another. Can vocal behavior ease our ability to influence others? Can the qualities and vocalizations that surround what we say make the difference between changing and not changing an attitude, between someone believing us, or between selling or not selling a product? It should be obvious to you that many factors affect how we influence others and that these factors often interact to enhance persuasion. However, much research has shown that vocal behavior plays an extremely important role.

One study of vocal behavior and persuasion found that the speed with which we speak may influence our ability to persuade others. In short, the faster we talk (within reason, of course), the more likely we are to influence our listeners. Maybe there is something to the stereotype of the fast-talking salesperson. The probable explanation for this finding is that faster speech rates, as we noted before, are often associated with perceptions of competence, expertise, and intelligence. If we as listeners perceive those characteristics in speakers, we are more likely to consider them credible sources and consequently to believe their messages (Addington, 1971; McCroskey, 2001; McCroskey & Richmond, 1996; Mehrabian & Williams, 1969; Sereno & Hawkins, 1967). Often, the perception we hold of others greatly affects their ability to influence us. Although studies have failed to find any relationship between nonfluencies in a person's speech and the person's impact on attitude change, several studies have found that nonfluencies influence ratings of some speakers' credibility. According to these researchers, such vocal nonfluencies as tongue slips, stuttering, repetitions, and vocal buffers can harm perceptions of the competence and dynamism of the speaker. Although these studies have not demonstrated an immediate impact on persuasion, because they found the nonfluencies hurt a speaker's credibility, it is likely that these negative impressions of credibility would affect the speaker's persuasiveness (Addington, 1971; Kramer, 1963; Mehrabian & Williams, 1969; Miller, Maruyama, Beaber, & Valone, 1976).

Vocal Behavior and Attractiveness

Zuckerman and Driver (1989) conducted two studies that examined the impact of attractiveness of voice on listeners. Their assumption was "that individual differences in vocal attractiveness may elicit different impressions of personality" (p. 28). They found that listeners agreed on what the vocally attractive voice was. Zuckerman and Driver also found they agreed that speakers with more attractive voices were rated more favorably than speakers with less attractive voices. Attractive voices were perceived as dominant, likeable, and achievement-oriented (Semic, 1999).

Vocal Behavior and Confidence

It has been a given for years that if a speaker sounds confident, he or she will be perceived as confident. There are many ways in which a speaker can

Female Signals

The question for the researchers was whether human females send subconscious "signals" to their male counterparts that they are in the high-fertility phase of their ovulation cycle. The theoretical issue was that other mammals to do this through visual or olfactory means. The researchers collected two sets of vocal samples from 69 women. The two samples were from a low-fertility phase and a high-fertility phase. Bryant and Haselton found that the women's pitch was higher during the high-fertility phase. In related research, Jones, Feinberg, DeBruine, Little, and Vukovic (2008) found that males were more attracted to a higher pitch. From this research, it appears that women subconsciously heighten their pitch levels during high-fertility phases to attract males. Other subconscious signals may also do this. Durante, Li, and Haselton (2008) found that women dress more seductively during their high-fertility phase.

Bryant, G. A,., & Haselton, M. G. (2009). *Vocal cues of ovulation in human females.* Biology Letters, 5, 12–15.

demonstrate confidence in what he or she is saying. It is often done with verbal statements such as "I am positive of this," "I know this well," and "I am the expert in this area." It is also possible to display confidence through non-verbal means, such as by speaking faster, louder, more forcibly, and with dominance. Kimble and Seidel (1991) studied two paralinguistic variables, vocal loudness and response latency, to determine whether they were associated with perceived speaker confidence in answers to trivia questions. Their results showed the following: When people are confident in what they are saying, they exude confidence vocally and verbally. This confidence is shown by louder speech and faster response times. The more assertive a person is, the more likely he or she will respond with confidence. And confident responses were given more loudly, more enthusiastically, and more energetically. Therefore, to appear more confident, we should speak confidently.

Vocal Characteristics of Good Delivery

In another book, one directed toward presentational speaking, we summarized research and theory relating to the use of voice in such communication (McCroskey, 2001). We concluded there were six specific vocal qualities that may directly affect your ability to be a persuasive speaker. Because these qualities are valuable beyond the narrow confines of presentational speaking, we repeat them here.

1. First, *volume control* is essential, considering the audience for and circumstances of your speaking. It is important to realize that you should speak loudly enough to be heard but not so loudly that you will overpower your

audience. Loudness of voice is actually relative. What is too loud or too soft depends on where and to whom you are speaking. The point to remember is that talking too loudly can offend or turn off your listeners, and not speaking loudly enough can also irritate them. They will eventually give up trying to understand you, ending your chances for influencing them.

2. We have already discussed the rate of speech as a factor that affects your ability to persuade others. Although it does appear that *faster rates* enhance your persuasiveness, you can reach a point of diminishing returns. A good rate is characterized by speech that is rapid enough to hold attention and yet slow enough for the audience to digest one idea before the audience receives another idea. Most of us can speak at 140 to 160 words per minute. Most of us can successfully absorb content from those who speak within the 140 to 160 words-per-minute range. If someone speaks too slowly, we lose interest. If someone speaks too quickly—imagine a professional auctioneer as a manager or instructor, for example—we cannot retain the content because we get left behind in the rate of words.

3. A third important quality of voice is the *use of pitch* to clarify and accentuate the important points of the verbal message. To ensure that you are stimulating the desired meaning, you must incorporate appropriate variations of pitch in your messages. Remember that monotones are no fun. Monotonous speech is uninteresting and, according to some, difficult to listen to. Whether the pitch is too high, too low, or somewhere in the middle range, remaining at the same level with little or no inflectional change may require your listeners to exert too much effort to pay attention.

4. *Good articulation* is a fourth element of the voice to consider in your persuasive messages. Poor articulation or misarticulation can indirectly affect your ability to persuade others because it can work against listeners' perceptions of your competence, intelligence, and expertise. Our culture values good articulation and looks with disdain on those who do not appropriately articulate their words. What is good articulation? Such articulation merely includes all the sounds that normally should be in a word without stressing them too much. If you can speak a word without calling undue attention to how you say it, you are articulating appropriately. However, if you slur or butcher your words, you may cause others to conclude that you are careless with other aspects of your message as well.

5. Speech that persuades others should also be *fluent,* the fifth important vocal quality. Fluent speech is speech that flows smoothly. A nonfluent utterance, as you may recall, includes vocal activity such as hesitations, vocal buffers, repetitions, stutters, and conspicuous pauses. We have already suggested that these vocal cues can negatively affect your listener's perceptions of your credibility.

6. Finally, *effective pauses* can be used to call attention to particular ideas. A silent pause just before or after a statement can make that statement seem very important, a key element of your message. Unfilled pauses used in strategic locations can enhance a speech. However, filled pauses, those that interrupt the smooth flow of messages, serve no useful purpose but tend only to detract from fluency. They may signal that you are grasping for ideas that are not there and consequently may cause your listeners to conclude that you were not prepared to deliver the persuasive message.

Glossary of Terminology

Accent refers to the different ways words are said. An accent is thus a paralinguistic concern.

Dialect is the use of different words to reference similar meanings. Dialect is thus a concern of linguistics.

Filled pauses are interruptions in the stream of speech content that are filled with audible sounds such as *uh, er, ah,* stuttering, and even slips of the tongue or repetitions.

Response latency is the time that it takes a person to begin speaking after another stops.

Sarcasm is saying one thing and communicating something else.

Turn-denying behavior, or back-channel cues, are used by listeners to signal that they do not wish to speak. These cues occur most often when the listener has nothing to say when the speaker begins to yield the turn.

Turn-maintaining cues are used by speakers to signal listeners that they want to keep the floor.

Turn-requesting cues show others that it is our time to speak or that we want to enter the conversation.

Turn-taking in conversations involves the following four techniques:

turn-maintaining, turn-yielding, turn-requesting, and turn-denying.

Turn-yielding behavior is used to signal that we are finished speaking and wish to prompt our listening partner to speak.

Unfilled pauses, or **silence,** are periods when vocal activity stops during the spoken utterance.

Vocal characterizers are nonlanguage sounds such as laughing, crying, whimpering, giggling, snickering, and sobbing.

Vocal qualifiers are similar to voice qualities but are considered separately for one main reason: Whereas voice qualities usually modify an entire stream of speech, vocal qualifiers qualify or regulate specific portions of the utterance. In other words, qualifiers provide variety within a spoken sentence. Vocal qualifiers include intensity, pitch height, and extent.

Vocal segregates include many common filler sounds such as *uh-uh-uh, er, ah,* and even seeming words such as *and-ah,* and *you know.*

Vocalics or paralanguage is the study of the communicative value of vocal behavior. Paralanguage includes all oral cues in the stream of spoken utterances except the words themselves.

Vocalizations are audible vocal cues that do not have the structure of language and may or may not be accompanied by spoken words.

Voice printing is similar to fingerprinting in that a person can be identified by unique characteristics and qualities in her or his voice.

Voice qualities are characteristics including tempo, resonance, rhythm control, articulation control, pitch control, glottis control, vocal lip control, and pitch range. Voice qualities are modifications of the vocal cues that accompany spoken words.

Voice set is closely related to who the speaker is; such information helps us to interpret the speaker's words more accurately.

CHAPTER 7

Space and Territoriality

Red Shirt Supporters protesting throughout the streets of Bangkok.

Source: Photo by C. Price Walt

L ook around you. Are you in your space or in someone else's? If you are in your own, take note of how you have claimed it. What have you done to tell others, "this desk is mine"? Take a walk up and down your street. How do your neighbors communicate their claim to their space? Do they use fencing, hedges, signs, or unique little markers to enhance the dividing line between their territory and the rest of the world?

Human beings, much like other animals, seem to have a need to claim and stake out space to call our own. We defend territory, invade that of others, put distance between others and ourselves, and avoid using certain spaces. As a culture, we use our space differently from how other cultures use theirs. As individuals, we differ in how we use space depending on our age, gender, personality, and background. How we use space, claim it, defend it, or allow others to enter it has much to do with the nonverbal messages we transmit.

Whether we realize it or not, we spend a great deal of time negotiating the space we share with our fellow human beings. The difference between war and peace, success and failure, good relationships and bad, often involves how we use space. The way we interact spatially with others and the respect we show for others' sacred spots or space can be critical components in effective communication.

Furthermore, our ignorance of the spatial needs or behavior of others does not excuse our abuse or misuse of space. Effective interaction requires that we understand not only our own spatial behavior but also that of others. The study of how we use and communicate with space is called **proxemics.** Use of space and territory is highly related to culture. To a major degree, we cannot fully understand the use of space and territory without understanding culture, and we cannot fully understand culture without understanding use of space and territory. The way a person uses space, then, is determined by the dictates of that individual's cultural values. Although humans have an innate tendency to express territorial and spatial behavior, the specific ways they go about doing so are learned (Hall, 1963, 1966, 1968, 1973, 1983; Shuter, 1976; Watson, 1970).

The work of anthropologists like Edward Hall leads us to believe that a major way a culture can be distinguished is by its proxemic patterns. This work also shows that spatial norms are learned to such an extent that they become habitual and unconscious. That is, once we learn the appropriate distance between interactants, we do not have to continually remember to maintain this distance with every new conversation. However, when we go to a different culture, we may have to learn a new set of spatial norms.

This chapter discusses the concept of proxemics in three basic ways. First, the phenomenon of territoriality is presented. Second, the concept of personal space is discussed. Third, we consider the areas of proxemics called "crowding" and "density."

PHENOMENON OF TERRITORIALITY

Most of the research on territoriality, and conclusions subsequently drawn, has been based upon studies with different species. You are probably aware of the many accounts of territorial behavior in a variety of species, particularly those of dogs and cats. You may also have a pet that daily exhibits some form of territoriality in and around your home. Dogs, for example, are known to urinate on objects at the boundaries of their owner's property and defend those boundaries from invasion by other dogs. Wolves mark their territory as do dogs. Cats will do the same thing, but inside their owner's house. They also rub up against their owner's legs as a way of marking their owners. Bears will rub up against a tree or claw a tree as a sign of ownership.

In the animal kingdom, territory serves several functions. Two primary reasons animals claim and defend territory are to ensure a food supply and to provide an area for mating. Often female animals will only mate with those males who have marked certain prime territory. Because ownership of the better territory is a sign of the smartest and strongest of the animal world, only the best can breed. This selection process can help keep the population density of certain animals deemed undesirable to a minimum. Those who have studied intensively the territorial behavior of animals contend that territoriality is innate behavior that has been developed and fine-tuned through the process of evolution.

Humans also exhibit behaviors that are considered territorial in nature, though humans are called on to defend our territory much less frequently. We use different methods to mark our territories. Territory is such an important part of our lives that we have created numerous laws to protect all of our territories, from the physical space of our yards and homes to possessions we carry with us. In addition, laws about false imprisonment, assault, trespassing, and nuisances (barking dogs, loud parties) have been created (Hickson & Self, 2003).

Biological Foundations of Territoriality: Nonverbal Communication, Language, and the Law

While certainly much of our concept of territory is cultural, the authors of this article claim that there is still a significant part of it that is natural and inborn. The authors indicate that laws about territory have been created to support what is natural. Unlike some other animals, humans are somewhat restricted in movement when we are born. Therefore, our initial attempts to utilize territorial concepts (schemata) are vocalic. A cry may mean, "Come here, change my diaper!" or it may mean "Bring me some food!" With infants, the parents, then, are concerned about their children "learning" to talk, to go to the bathroom (in a certain place), and to walk. In essence, each of these abilities provides the infant with more independence. *Anchoring* themselves becomes a nonverbal equivalent to "I am not going to move" as a verbal statement. It may mean, simply "stop!" It means "do not feed me anymore" or "don't touch me." Thus, quite early in life, the infant understands the concepts of anchor versus move. For the infant, allowing another person into their territory becomes equivalent to allowing for immediacy because the infant likes the person or what the person is going to do. Eventually the child learns to *predict* what the parent intends to do. Thus, when it becomes time to go to bed and the parent comes toward the child, he or she may resist—anchoring himself or herself. In society, we have a more complex version because we cannot always wait until everyone becomes socialized to territorial claims. For that reason, *norms,* how most of us act, are transformed into laws. We learn that we cannot kidnap another person, we cannot lock them up, we cannot hold them against their will, nor can we break into their homes. The authors point out that the laws, though, are created out of norms, and many of the norms are biological and natural.

Hickson, M. III, & Self, W. R. (2003). Biological foundations of territoriality: Nonverbal communication, language, and the law. Journal of Intercultural Communication Research, 32, 265–283.

Whereas territoriality for animals is quite active and often necessary for survival, in humans this behavior is often primarily passive. **Human territoriality** is the presumptive claim by one or more persons of a geographic area with or without a formal legal basis for that claim. The claim is most commonly established through continuous occupation of that area (Ardrey, 1966; Baxter, 1970; Becker & Mayo, 1971; Edney, 1976; Hall, 1963, 1968, 1983; Lyman & Scott, 1967).

The **territory** of humans is semifixed or fixed space whose perceived owners can move in and out of it without giving up their claim to it. It is claimed, staked out in some way, and defended against encroachment. Furthermore, those claims are generally respected by other people.

Categories of Territory

Territories have been classified into several types by Altman (1975) and Lyman and Scott (1967). We will consider these six types: *primary, secondary, public, home, interactional,* and *body.*

1. *Primary territory.* Territory considered to be the exclusive domain of its owner is called **primary territory.** Your dormitory room, or at least your side of it, is your primary territory. Other examples include personal offices, Dad's chair, and Mom's study. If the territory is used by its owner virtually every day, then it would fall into this category. Primary territories are most often respected by others and most often are not violated by encroachers without the permission of the owner. There is little doubt about who the rightful claimant is.

2. *Secondary territory.* This type of territory usually is not central to the daily functioning of the owner. It is not under the owner's exclusive control. However, a **secondary territory** is generally associated with a particular person or group frequently seen in and around it. As an example, you can probably think of a popular meeting place, such as a bar or restaurant, that is frequented by a certain group. Possibly this group even sits at the same table every time it patronizes the establishment. In fact, the table is so closely associated with the group that it is perceived as its territory. Unlike primary territories, secondary territories are more vulnerable to invasion and takeover by others. They are more difficult to hold onto because the perceived owner does not generally use and control this space with the same frequency as he or she does primary space.

   Take, for example, the big-screen television in the family room. If Dad is disposed to sit in his chair and watch television every evening, the television may be seen as his secondary territory. However, it is more likely that there will be conflicts regarding who gets to use the remote control (secondary territory) than about who sits in Dad's chair (primary territory).

3. *Public territory.* The third type of territory identified is **public territory,** which is open to anyone and is seldom under the constant control of any one person or group. It is, however, subject to temporary ownership and is often protected with as much vigor as personal property. Spring break

may have found you among the many students at one of the beaches of Florida, Texas, California, or Mexico. If so, you may recall how individuals stake out and claim a small portion of the sand for themselves, if only for the day. CD players, towels, umbrellas, bottles of suntan oil, sunglasses, coolers with food and drink, and books are placed in strategic locations to tell other vacationers, "Find another place in the sun! This space is taken."

Other examples of public territory include parking spaces, theater seats, restaurant tables, library tables, park benches, bus stop shelters, and many other public properties that can be temporarily owned. It is with public territories that most disputes over ownership occur. They are the most difficult of all territories to maintain control. How often have you pulled into the parking lot at a shopping mall, spotted a parking space, and then, just before you reached it, seen someone else slip in ahead of you? Although this space is for anyone, you probably felt you had been wronged because some jerk took your space.

4. *Home territory.* When a group of people "colonizes" a public territory by taking it over and using it continuously, it becomes **home territory**. Regular patrons of a neighborhood bar, gangs operating on particular streets or in urban districts, and children who claim a huge elm tree for club meetings all represent groups who have taken a public place and made it their own. The major characteristic of home territory is that the claimants have a sense of freedom in terms of their behavior, and their control over the territory is somewhat continuous. Although the territory technically remains public, it functionally becomes secondary territory. It would be common for the owners to feel as comfortable and intimate in their home territories as they would in their own homes.

5. *Interactional territory.* Special places, called **interactional territories,** can develop wherever people congregate for social exchange. Although there may be no visible boundary markers for these conversational zones, they exist nonetheless. Consider two people standing in the middle of a hallway carrying on a conversation with one another. Have you ever noticed how passersby go to great lengths to avoid intruding? Rarely does someone pass between these interactants. To do so would constitute a gross violation of the interactional territory of those conversing. At social functions, such as parties or holiday open houses, one can usually observe pockets of four or five people engaged in communication. We refer to these spatial settings as communication clusters or cliques. These individuals have established an interactional territory. Newcomers to the interaction are expected to approach cautiously and often apologetically, realizing that they are guests of the owners of this arbitrary turf.

6. *Body territory.* Also known as *personal space,* **body territory,** unlike other types of territory, is portable; we carry it with us everywhere we go. Think of this personal space as an invisible bubble surrounding one's body. It is the individual's most inviolate form of territory. Strict control is maintained by the owner, and defense is usually not required because most people have

great respect for the personal space of others. We discuss personal space in more detail later in this chapter as a special topic of proxemics.

Territorial Defense and Encroachment

TERRITORIAL DEFENSE. Territorial defense can involve one of two primary methods. The first is preventive measures. The second method is reaction, which we will discuss shortly. Prevention is the action someone takes before encroachment occurs (Greenberg & Firestone, 1977; Scheflen, 1976; Scherer, 1974; Sommer, 1959, 1969; Watson, 1970). We will now consider the four preventive methods of territorial defense: *markers, labels, offensive display,* and *tenure.*

Markers are usually personal artifacts like backpacks, purses, umbrellas, overcoats, books, hats, and briefcases used to mark ownership of space. This method involves individuals staking out their territories by using markers to establish boundaries (Lyman & Scott, 1967). Sommer (1959) contends that for "markers to be effective in preventing encroachment, the object must be perceived as a marker and not as litter. This requires the item to have either symbolic meaning or some intrinsic value" (p. 53). That is, the potential encroacher must perceive the marker as an indication that someone, not just something, has laid claim to the space in question. The more personal the marker, the less likely it is to be moved (Becker, 1973; Fisher & Byrne, 1975; Guerrero, DeVito, & Hecht, 1999; Hughes & Goldman, 1978; McAndrew, Ryckman, Horr, & Soloman, 1978).

A bartender once showed one of the authors an effective method of reserving a table or place at a bar. He told him to buy a drink and place it at the table he wanted to reserve, with a napkin or drink stirrer placed over the top of the glass. Sure enough, just as he had suggested, the table with his or her marker was still empty when all of the other tables were occupied. Only then did a couple venture to sit there, and they carefully avoided sitting right where the drink was placed. We can't guarantee that this reservation method will always work (Schaffer & Sadowski, 1975). When we are possessing such a space as a restaurant table, we also sometimes feel that we have been "invaded" by the server. How often does a server need to ask whether we need anything? Many servers do not possess the nonverbal sensitivity to understand that the customers are having a serious conversation. Some restaurants have created a marker: a coaster with red on one side and green on the other. The red tells the server, "Don't bother us," and the green says "We need something."

Labels include signs saying Keep Out, Go Away, Attack Dogs on Premises, or Reserved, or even names placed on office doors, pens, computers, computer disks, and so on. What labels have you observed other people using?

Offensive displays include individuals' use prevention as a form of territorial defense is through a combination of assertive postures, stances, stares, and gestures. This method reflects the old adage that the best defense is a good offense. Offensive display simply calls for the owner to look aggressive and formidable to potential encroachers. One major drawback of this preventive measure is that the individual obviously must be present within the territory,

People mark and claim territory in a variety of ways. Vendors on the streets of Bangkok, Thailand, return to same place on the sidewalks each afternoon, selling items throughout the evening.

Source: Photo by C. Price Walt

whereas markers can hold spaces in the owner's absence. Another drawback, according to Sommer, is that in some situations offensive displays can backfire. Let's illustrate this point. Suppose you are one of the first passengers aboard an airplane, train, or bus with open seating. You settle into a window seat and hope that no one will decide to sit next to you. As the other passengers come aboard, you incorporate in your posture and position some behaviors that you hope others perceive as formidable. Sommer suggests that you will probably be quite successful at driving away the timid and introverted individuals, but this may leave you with a seat mate who is overbearing and highly aggressive because he or she perceived no potential threat in your offensive display. What offensive displays have you observed other people using?

Tenure indicates that people who have become associated with a particular territory over a long period can effectively lay claim to that territory. Sommer (1959) states:

> Their rights to this space will be supported by their neighbors even when they are not physically present. At a meeting it is not surprising to find a newcomer cautioned against sitting in a certain chair at the table (p. 52).

A new employee recently related an incident in which she unknowingly offended another, more veteran employee. She had just been transferred from another part of the company and, being the new person in the employee's lounge, had no knowledge of the unspoken rules and norms the more experienced employees had established long before. After a long morning, she retired to the lounge for a brief respite. Upon entering, she spotted a large cushioned chair in the corner, unoccupied. She could not imagine why none of the other employees present had taken this inviting place to relax. She gladly crossed over to the chair and sat. A coworker quickly warned her to find another seat in case Mrs. Jones entered. Before she could ask who Mrs. Jones was, an older woman appeared at the door. Mrs. Jones had arrived. The new employee quickly learned that she had taken the wrong chair. Later, her coworker told her that Mrs. Jones had claimed that chair since before anyone could remember. The new employee noted that it took three months before Mrs. Jones would speak to her and stop giving her the evil eye.

Having reviewed the four preventive techniques of territorial defense, consider the second primary method, reaction. This method of defense is important if prevention has failed. When our territories are encroached on by others, we become physiologically aroused. When we become aroused because of encroachment, we label that arousal as either positive or negative. That is, not all encroachment is interpreted as a bad thing. Sometimes it makes us feel good, relieved, or comfortable, as often happens with two close companions. At other times, however, encroachment is interpreted negatively because it creates stress, anxiety, or even embarrassment.

Depending on whether we decide that the arousal caused by encroachment is positive or negative, our reaction will take one of two forms. If we see the encroachment as positive, we will *reciprocate.* This means essentially that we encroach on the person who encroached on us, also in some positive way. For example, John finally gets up the nerve to put his arm around Heather while watching a movie. Heather interprets this encroachment positively and reciprocates by resting her head on John's shoulder. Often, however, we perceive the encroachment negatively. There are three general types of encroachment that we usually perceive negatively: *violation, invasion,* and *contamination* (VIC) (Lyman & Scott, 1967).

Types of Negative Encroachment

Violation is the unwarranted use of someone's territory. Unlike invasion, violation usually is temporary in nature. The encroacher uses someone's sacred spot without permission. While Dad is out, little Sonya feels free to sit in his chair. A major complaint of many college students about their roommates is that the roommates use their car, DVD player, hair dryer, clothes, or television without first getting permission. Newlywed couples often have difficulty adjusting to married life because, for the first time in their lives, someone encroaches on their possessions regularly.

Invasion is a drastic and permanent encroachment in which the invader actually crosses the territorial boundaries of another with the intention of taking over and keeping the territory. When an invasion occurs, the encroacher imposes her or his physical presence on the territory of the owner and usually wants to propel that owner out. Of course, an invasion can occur on a large or small scale. One country invading another to expand its own territorial boundaries represents a large-scale invasion. On the other hand, the school bully who invades the area of the playground claimed by others illustrates a small-scale invasion (Fisher & Byrne, 1975; Hughes & Goldman, 1978).

Invasions may take on rather subtle forms as well. Two people sharing a table in a restaurant usually claim parts of that table as their own. It is common in instances such as this for one person to slowly move an object—the water glass, for example, or salad plate—into the space of the other to increase the share of space.

Contamination is rendering the territory of another person impure with respect to its definition and usage. As one student so aptly put it, "This means going into someone's territory and stinking up the place." It is not so much encroaching with your physical presence as it is leaving something of yours in the territory.

Blocking involves another person occupying the territory you need in order to move from one place to another. Whether they are acting intentionally or not, we feel that these people are standing or sitting in our way. This is what happens when we are in a traffic jam. Others are blocking our path to get where we want to be. Long lines at the grocery serve the same function. Some of us, especially those of us with type A personalities, become quite irritated about blocking. "Road rage" has even been used as an excuse for murder.

Encroachment Reactions

When our territory has been encroached on either through invasion, violation, contamination, or blocking, and we interpret that encroachment negatively, we may compensate or adjust our behavior in several different ways. Negative encroachment prompts classic flight-or-fight responses. These responses can be classified as *withdrawal, insulation, turf defense,* or *linguistic collusion* (Lyman & Scott, 1967).

Withdrawal means that we compensate by moving away from the encroacher and letting her or him take over. In short, we flee without a fight. This is the classic flight response, a normal reaction to something frightening. Although most encroachment does not actually create fear, what we may fear is what will happen if we make a fuss (in other words, fight). We are most likely to find withdrawal the best form of reaction when someone invades a public territory that we have occupied temporarily. If someone sits too close to us on a park bench, we will likely move over or get up and walk away rather than ask the encroacher to move. One study conducted in a library showed that when invaders encroached on the tables of students who were studying, every student moved to another location rather than actively defend the territory (Greenberg & Firestone, 1977; Hall, 1983).

Insulation is a second type of reaction of owners whose territory is invaded. This response can be thought of as sophisticated fighting. When we perceive others encroaching on our territory, we may build formidable boundaries to stop them. These may take the form of markers, as discussed earlier, or body movements and gestures that block the invaders' advances. While attending a conference in Chicago, one of the authors boarded a city bus to see the sights. The behavior of the other bus riders became more fascinating, however. Sitting across the aisle was an elderly woman with a package and an overcoat resting in her lap. The seats on each side of her were vacant. At the next stop, several passengers came aboard. Noticing that they were looking for places to sit, the woman placed her package on the one side and her coat on the other. The unfortunate newcomers stood while the elderly woman sat quite contented that she had insulated herself from potential encroachers.

Insulation often is accomplished by use of markers. Some markers are more effective than others. A study was conducted in which personal and nonpersonal markers were used to protect areas of a study hall in a school. Personal markers such as sports jackets and combinations of pens, notebooks, and textbooks seemed to signal potential invaders that someone would return. On the other hand, nonpersonal markers such as magazines and newspapers

Good fences make very good neighbors.

often were ignored. The personal marker could hold off encroachers for as long as two hours, whereas randomly scattered magazines worked for only thirty-two minutes (Bell & Barnard, 1984; Conigliaro, Cullerton, Flynn, & Rueder, 1989; Greenberg & Firestone, 1977; Hughes & Goldman, 1978; McAndrew, Ryckman, Horr, & Soloman, 1978).

The gender associated with markers may also be important. Some research has found that feminine markers are not as effective at discouraging encroachment as are masculine markers. In one study, tables in barrooms marked with women's sweaters, purses, and jackets were taken over more frequently and in less time by arriving customers than were tables marked with masculine objects. This outcome, of course, may be the simple result of the assumption that males would be more likely to react in an assertive or aggressive manner when their territory is invaded.

Turf defense is the third type of reaction to a territorial invasion and is closest to the classic fight response. This is the most active form of defense available. Turf defense calls for the owner to expel the invader from her or his territory. Children often play a game called King of the Mountain. This usually involves one individual claiming a piece of high ground, such as a mound or small hill, and protecting it from approaching invaders from all directions. The object of the game is to keep control of the mountain by fighting off intruders. One wins the game by taking the high territory and keeping it. Turf defense is an adult version of King of the Mountain.

Turf defense is also seen among other animal species. It is represented by a dog fight, for example. For humans, however, this reaction to encroachment generally is used as a last resort. Fighting back, repelling, and standing one's ground are most common in situations where the invasion is intense and persistent or the territory is unusually highly valued. Highly desirable territories may cause many of us to forgo social etiquette and, instead, give in to a more selfish disposition to obtain or retain the best territories. Less desirable territory may be seen as not worth the fight.

In addition to the physical space itself, Goffman (1971) has indicated that there are secondary issues involved with our turf. For example, we may find staring to be an invasion of our space. Auditory interference, too, is considered a violation of our space. For example, when a person is at a restaurant, and another customer receives a cell phone call with a loud ring and begins a loud conversation, we consider that a violation. Most teachers strongly object to cell phones and other electronic devices ringing in their classrooms. Certain olfactory elements (smells) may also be considered an invasion of one's territory.

Linguistic collusion involves a complex set of processes by which the territorial integrity of the group is reaffirmed, and the intruder is labeled as an outsider (Lyman & Scott, 1967, p. 249). The people defending the space may engage the intruders or outsiders in a conversation, with gestures and movements that are designed to confuse or make invaders feel as if they were outsiders (or do not belong). Defending interactants will often speak in language that is unfamiliar or foreign to the intruder. Often defending interactants will speak louder, longer, and more harshly, using outrageous gestures that tell the intruder that he or she does not belong. Many times the intruder will simply leave the space because the linguistic collusion is too much to deal with.

Factors Influencing Territorial Defense

Several factors influence the defense of territory. These determine the defensive methods we use and the success or failure of those methods. Knapp and Hall (1992) suggest that the intensity of our reactions to encroachment depends mostly on seven considerations:

1. Who violated our territory?
2. Why did he or she violate our territory?
3. What type of territory was it?
4. How was the violation accomplished?
5. How long did the encroachment last?
6. Do we expect further violations in the future?
7. Where did the violation occur?

You would probably react more forcefully if the invader were a lower-status person. On the other hand, at work you might tolerate and endure intrusions of your manager, for example. You are also less likely to react aggressively

In Bangkok, glass shards cemented in the top of a wall keep the unwanted visitors away.
Source: Photo by C. Price Walt

with a friend than with a stranger. Furthermore, you may choose to withdraw from a public space when encroached on but insulate or actively defend a primary, more private territory. You may realize that the encroachment was unintentional or could not be helped, in which case you would react less forcefully or decide to tolerate it. Small children, for example, do not understand the idea of territoriality as it applies to others (however, they react when others invade their territory).

The intensity with which someone invades a territory usually affects how the owner reacts. One investigation showed that if invaders intrude and simply move the belongings of the occupant of a public space, the occupant will usually withdraw. The study also indicated that when invaders approached and sat across from an occupant, withdrawal rarely occurred. It is more common to resort to withdrawal if one is encroached on quickly and aggressively in public settings. A quick response is called for, and retreat is simpler than any other response. Only people with strong aggressive and defensive tendencies are likely to react differently. Gradual intrusion is less likely to be seen as threatening because it is not so startling. Therefore a more reasoned response is likely.

Another factor influencing territorial invasion and defense is density conditions. Under high-density conditions, territorial defense is less effective than in low-density conditions. The reason for this is simple. The more people there are, the less space there is available per person, and therefore the less likely it is that any individual can hold on to a larger amount of space. We consider density in more detail later in this chapter.

PERSONAL SPACE

Although territoriality is seen as a fixed area of space, **personal space** is an invisible bubble that surrounds us and expands or contracts depending on personalities, situations, and types of relationships. Furthermore, personal space is portable; we take it everywhere we go.

The two major considerations about the variability of personal space are as follows: (1) appropriate use of space is socially learned though communication with other people in our culture; and (2) our choices of space distancing communicate information about ourselves, our relationships, and our needs. With these considerations in mind, let's consider the many factors that influence the invisible bubbles or space cushions we carry with us constantly (Becker & Mayo, 1971; Hall, 1983; Sommer, 1959, 1969; Watson, 1970).

Interpersonal Distance

The work of Hall (1963, 1966, 1968, 1973, 1983) suggests that the type of interpersonal relationship in which we are involved affects the distance we place between ourselves and others. Our comfort level during interaction depends on our spatial orientation with others and their relationships to us. Hall describes four interpersonal distance zones that are characterized by the type of communication relationship involved. It should be noted that Hall's distance zones represent U.S. norms and are still in use today. Other cultures differ considerably regarding their distance norms. The four interpersonal distance zones are *intimate, casual-personal, socio-consultive,* and *public.*

The **intimate zone** of our personal space bubble represents the innermost interaction region. It ranges from touching to a distance of 18 inches. This zone usually is reserved for the few special people in our lives. Lovers, very close friends, and intimate family members are the only ones we voluntarily allow into this zone for any length of time. We often find ourselves in public places and situations, such as crowded elevators or long waiting lines, where complete strangers or children with no awareness of appropriate interpersonal distances encroach on the intimate zone. Although these generally are brief encounters, they can be very stressful. Our desire may be to push those people away, but the situation demands that we tolerate the intrusion. You might, then, follow Hall's standard of 18 inches and add six more inches. In this way you will rarely if ever be accused of invading another person's intimate zone.

The **casual-personal zone** is the next region of our personal space bubble. It ranges from 18 inches to about four feet. The casual-personal distance is used during conversations with close friends and interactions with relatives. Longtime business associates often are permitted into this range because we see them as friends.

Most of the people we encounter are expected to remain in the **socio-consultive zone.** Ranging from four to eight feet, this region of personal space is often the distance at which we transact business. Salespeople are often trained to keep within the socio-consultive area in dealing with potential buyers. A stroll through a corporate office complex reveals that, when business is the topic of discussion, the socio-consultive distance usually is strictly observed. When the topic turns to casual or personal matters, it is quite common to see the interactants move closer to one another.

The socio-consultive distance is also used when teachers communicate with older students, with other teachers, and parents or principals. Teachers of young children, however, learn quickly that little children have no sense of these interaction zones (Fry & Willis, 1971).

The **public zone** represents the outer region of our interaction space bubble. This zone begins at eight feet and extends to the outer limits of interaction potential. The outer limit can vary depending on the situation. At a public speech, for example, it is quite possible to have several thousand people present, and because of state-of-the-art technology, they are all within the public zone.

Gender Differences

Gender is a major factor influencing personal space. Females, for instance, tend to interact with others more closely than do males. However, male-to-female dyads interact more closely than either male-to-male or female-to-female dyads. Other studies have shown that the relationship between gender and personal space is dependent on other factors. Females allow others to approach them from the sides more closely than from the front, whereas males allow the opposite. At least one study, however, has found the results reversed. It would also appear that the degree of the acquaintance and the social setting also affect gender and personal space. Females approach their best friends very closely; males approach people they consider to be just friends.

Other nonverbal behavior has been found to affect the relationship between gender and personal space. Several studies have shown that males and females approach another person differently depending on whether that person is looking at them. Males, for instance, are more likely to stand closer to nonlookers; whereas, for females the degree of personal space depends on the other person's gender. When approaching males, females stand closer to nonlookers. When approaching females, they are more likely to stand closer to lookers than to nonlookers.

Cultural Differences

The differences in how other cultures use space is a major reason we often experience culture shock when traveling abroad. In short, many problems two people from different cultures experience in communicating can be attributed to differences in personal-space norms. Hall (1973) describes one situation in particular:

> In Latin America the interaction distance is much less than it is in the United States. Indeed, people cannot talk comfortably unless they are very close to the distance that evokes either sexual or hostile feelings in North Americans. The result is that when they move close, we withdraw and back away. As a consequence, they think we are distant and cold. . . .We, on the other hand, are constantly accusing them of breathing down our necks, crowding us, and spraying our faces (p. 164).

Research has shown that North Americans feel more comfortable when interacting at greater distances. For this reason, our culture is commonly referred to as a noncontact culture. Other noncontact cultures include those of northern Europe, Asia, Pakistan, and India. On the other hand, many cultures interact at much closer distances and are referred to as *contact cultures*. Among the contact cultures are those of Latin America, southern Europe, and Arab countries.

Several investigations have shown that the above classifications into noncontact and contact cultures do not always hold true. To assume, for instance, that people in all Latin American countries prefer close distances when interacting is a mistake. For example, Shuter's (1976) research suggests that Panamanian and Colombian Latin Americans interact at greater distances than do Costa Ricans. Moore, Hickson, and Stacks (2010) suggest that the stereotypes associated with Italians and Germans hold only for males in these cultures. Generalizations, therefore, probably should not be made beyond the single-country level, and often there are substantial differences between groups within a single country.

Age Differences

Younger children are the real "space invaders." Spatial orientations are culturally learned, but that learning does not occur quickly. It is therefore no surprise that small children in our culture would just as soon crawl up into the lap of Mrs. Witherspoon from down the street as that of Grandma. After all, both laps are soft and warm. By the age 12, however, most children have reached adulthood concerning personal space orientations. This is probably a result of differing expectations adults have about twelve-year-olds in relation to younger children (Fry & Willis, 1971).

One study used five-, eight-, and ten-year-old children to investigate adult reactions to the invasion behavior of children. That study revealed that the older children who invaded adults' personal space in a line at a movie were perceived in a negative manner. On the other hand, the five-year-old children were actually received positively. Essentially, the older children were treated as adults would have been and were expected to know better than to invade the space of others. Although age differences have received little research attention, we can offer two generalizations. First, Knapp and Hall (1992) contend that it is reasonable to assume that we would interact closer to people in our own general age range. This may be a simple function of people of the same age being more likely to have more things in common than people of substantially different ages. Second, Baxter (1970) suggests that, up to a point, there appears to be a direct relationship between age and distance when comparing personal space orientations of children, adolescents, and adults during conversations. Children converse more closely, and adults converse at greater distances. Thus, the observed differences in the usage of interpersonal space sometimes attributed to age may just be a function of interpersonal similarity. Whether this is indeed the case must be tested in future research.

Personality Differences

In their comprehensive books on nonverbal communication, Harper, Wiens, and Matarazzo (1978) and Richmond and McCroskey (1998) have summarized research that suggests that extroverts require less space than introverts during conversations. Introverts are particularly likely to stand farther away if the situation is an intimate one.

Those with general anxiety predispositions have also been reported to require greater distances while interacting. An interesting study showed that highly anxious individuals tended to recall previous interactions as occurring significantly closer than did relaxed individuals. Others have also found high social anxiety scores to be positively related to interaction distance. The closer a person stands to another, the more the situation demands communication, so it is not surprising that shy people have been found to prefer greater interpersonal distances.

Some studies indicate that individuals with a high need for affiliations are likely to move closer to their interaction partners. It also appears that persons with an internal locus of control establish closer spatial orientations to strangers than do those with an external locus of control. Requiring less distance has also been associated with self-directed people, low authoritarians, and individuals with high self-concepts (Gifford & O'Connor, 1986; Moore, Hickson & Stacks, 2010; Mehrabian & Diamond, 1971).

Stigmas

Hickson, Stacks, and Moore (2010) suggest that "an area that has received less attention is the finding that people maintain greater distances from others who have stigmas." These stigmas can be of two basic types: *physical* and *social.* Physical stigmas include being in a wheelchair; using crutches, a cane, or a walker; being blind; being an amputee; or having a burned, scarred face or body. Conigliaro, Cullerton, Flynn, and Rueder (1989) found that pedestrians gave a legally blind person with a white cane 33.8 inches of space as opposed to 5.6 inches when the person had no cane. A social stigma includes such things as a reputation of being an ex-convict, an ex-stripper, or having sexually transmitted diseases such as herpes or AIDS. In this culture at least, we seem to maintain greater distances between ourselves and those with physical or social stigmas.

Psychiatric and Deviant Groups

Malandro, Barker, and Barker (1989) identified deviant populations as including "those with histories of mental illness such as schizophrenia, prisoners, other individuals with criminal records, and disruptive high school students" (p. 192). One major commonality among these populations is that their members generally require more space than "normal" members of society. It appears that deviants, whether criminal, schizophrenic, disruptive, or violent, depend on their spatial distancing to provide a means of protection and require larger body-buffer zones between themselves and others than do nondeviant members of society (Hickson & Roebuck, 2009). Hickson and Roebuck found that faculty members who have deviant tendencies tend to keep their office doors closed and locked.

CROWDING AND DENSITY

Density refers to the number of people in space. High density, therefore, is a large number of people in a given area. Because there is less personal space available for each individual, high-density conditions often create much involuntary encroachment.

Density should not be confused with *crowding.* **Crowding** is a person's perception of spatial restrictions. High density does not always cause people to feel crowded. Living and working in high-density conditions, these people have learned to cope with constant invasion and spatial restriction. Density may or may not lead to crowding. This perception may depend more on what

Territorial closeness can make a person feel crowded.

we find acceptable in our day-to-day encounters with others than how dense the physical conditions actually are (Carey, 1972; Galle, Grove, & McPherson, 1972; Sommer, 1969; Watson, 1970).

Three factors can cause people to feel the discomfort associated with crowding. **Surveillance**, the first factor, is the degree to which you sense that strangers are watching you. When you perceive that surveillance is high, you may become uneasy and seek to escape that condition.

Behavioral constraint, the second factor, refers to a reduction in one's freedom of movement. The more constrained one's activity becomes, the more likely one is to experience crowding.

The third factor that leads to crowding, **stimulus overload**, refers to the plethora of noises, sounds, sights, and other stimuli that bombard the senses simultaneously. If the individual is unable to cope with the myriad of stimuli in a given context, her or his reaction may be to withdraw and find refuge in quieter places.

Any one of these factors, or a combination of them, can lead to crowding. The major point is that individuals differ in the amount of surveillance, stimulus overload, or behavioral constraint they can experience before feelings of crowding set in. An individual has to perceive the factors of surveillance, constraint, or stimulus overload as present, whether they are or not, for high density to cause feelings of crowding.

The Impact of High Density

It probably is not surprising that crime is more prevalent in large urban areas, where density is high, than in low-density rural regions of the country. One study has shown that urban dwellers more frequently commit vandalism. The same study also showed that people in cities are less willing to help others than are people who live in rural areas. Results such as these have led many experts to conclude that high density causes antisocial behavior. Although there may be some truth to that assertion, other researchers suggest that negative activity such as crime and delinquency in urban areas may be attributable to education, social status, and income level rather than density.

Some have maintained that a higher death rate, increased health problems, and greater fertility rates are closely related to high density (summarized in Knapp and Hall, 1992). Overall, the research literature seems consistent in one major respect: High-density areas are generally plagued with a greater number of human woes per capita than low-density areas. Furthermore, people who dwell in large urban centers spend much of their day coping with the stimulus overload, surveillance, and behavioral constraints caused by density conditions. The behaviors those city dwellers use to cope with crowding can lead others to feel that they are uncaring. According to Knapp and Hall (1992), coping methods used by such people include the following:

1. Spending less time with each other (i.e., shorter conversations)
2. Disregarding low-priority interactions (i.e., ignoring other people on the street, subway, elevator, or commuter train)
3. Shifting the responsibility for some transactions to others (i.e., not requiring bus drivers to make change)
4. Blocking others out (i.e., having guards protect apartments and limiting access)

It is unfair for those who live in smaller communities to label people from large cities as "not friendly, cold, and distant." The negative-seeming behaviors we observe when we visit cities are quite probably the very methods city residents use to survive the continuous conditions of high density. If Frank learns to act "cool and distant," he might enjoy his next trip to the city much more than his last one.

Glossary of Terminology

Behavioral constraint is a reduction in one's freedom of movement. The more constrained one's activity becomes, the more likely one is to experience crowding.

Body territory also is known as personal space, the individual's most inviolate form of territory. Unlike other types of territories, it is portable and can be thought of as an invisible bubble surrounding one's body.

Casual-personal zone is the region of personal space that ranges from 18 inches to about four feet.

Contamination is rendering the territory of another person impure with respect to its definition and usage.

Crowding is a person's perception of spatial restrictions.

Density refers to the number of people in a space. High density, therefore, is a large number of people in a given area. High density does not always cause people to feel crowded. Because there is less personal space for each individual, high-density conditions often create much involuntary encroachment.

Home territory is a public territory colonized by a group that takes it over and uses it continuously.

Human territoriality is the presumptive claim by one or more persons of a geographic area with or without a formal, legal basis for that claim.

Insulation is a reaction to an invasion of territory that includes building formidable boundaries. This response can be thought of as sophisticated fighting.

Interactional territories are special places that develop wherever people congregate for social exchange.

Intimate zone of our personal space represents the innermost interaction region. It ranges from touching to a distance of 18 inches.

Invasion is a drastic and permanent encroachment in which the invader actually crosses the territorial boundaries of others with the intention of taking over and keeping the territory.

Labels or markers with symbolic meaning are a type of prevention. Labels include signs or name plates that are used to prevent takeovers of space.

Linguistic collusion is when a group of people defending their territory, verbally and nonverbally, makes the intruder feel like an outsider.

Markers are usually personal artifacts used to mark ownership of space.

Offensive displays are assertive or aggressive postures, stances, stares, and gestures that are meant to prevent encroachment.

Personal space is an invisible bubble that surrounds us and expands or contracts depending on personalities, situations, and types of relationships. Personal space is portable; we take it everywhere we go.

Primary territory is territory that is considered to be the exclusive domain of its owner.

Proxemics is the study of the ways in which humans use and communicate with space.

Public territory is open to anyone and is seldom under the constant control of any one person or group. It is, however, subject to temporary ownership and is often protected with as much vigor as personal property.

Public zone is the outer region of the personal space bubble. This zone begins at eight feet and extends to the outer limits of interaction potential.

Secondary territory is generally associated with a particular person or group, who is frequently seen in and around the territory. Secondary territories are more vulnerable to invasion and takeover than primary territory.

Socio-consultive zone is the region of personal space that ranges from four feet to eight feet. This region is often called "the distance at which Americans transact business."

Stimulus overload is a reaction to the plethora of noises, sounds, sights, and other stimuli that bombard the senses simultaneously.

Surveillance is the degree to which you sense that strangers are watching you.

Tenure is a form of prevention from encroachment; when people have become associated with a particular territory over a long period, they can effectively lay claim to that territory.

Territory of humans is a semifixed or fixed space whose perceived owners can move in and out of it without giving up their claim to it. It is claimed, staked out in some way, and defended against encroachment.

Turf defense calls for the owner to repel the invader from her or his territory.

Violation is the unwarranted use of someone's territory. Unlike an invasion, violation usually is temporary in nature. The encroacher uses someone's sacred spot without permission.

Withdrawal refers to compensating by moving away from an enroacher and letting her or him take over.

CHAPTER 8

Environment and Physical Surroundings

What does environment have to do with human communication? What is so important about the physical surroundings of individuals when they come together for social interaction? Do environmental factors such as spatial arrangement, design, color, lighting, temperature, and scent affect how people feel, what they discuss, how they perceive messages, how they behave? Can the ways individuals use and manipulate environments transmit messages about their personalities, intentions, moods, and other characteristics? The research suggests that the answer to all of these questions is a resounding yes.

Hall (1966) referred to **fixed-feature space,** which is space that is fixed or immovable, such as the physical features in our homes, offices, rooms, schools, and even the layout of our cities and towns. Fixed-feature space is difficult to change, move, or alter, whereas **semifixed-feature space,** the movable objects in our environments, are much easier to change, move, or alter. Among these objects are tables, chairs, desks, and other furniture and accessories that adorn, accent, highlight, and personalize the physical areas in our world.

Consider for a moment the layout of your home, your dorm room, or your apartment. Think of what your furnishings, color choices, and arrangement say about you. Are you comfortable in your environment? Do others feel at ease, or have you set up your surroundings so that visitors conform to your wishes? Do you find that one room is your favorite and another is seldom used?

Clearly some environments, even different rooms in the same house, are used more than others. Psychologists have found that our environmental surroundings affect our emotional states. Environments can create arousal in us, and depending on how we interpret that arousal, this can make us feel stimulated, alert, frenzied, or active. We may experience pleasure or displeasure because of the influence of physical surroundings. Some surroundings evoke feelings of happiness, joy, and contentment, and others produce discomfort, uneasiness, and dissatisfaction (Buslig, 1999; Carr & Dabbs, 1974; Cook, 1970; Gifford & O'Connor, 1986; Hanson & Hillier, 1982; Hayduk, 1994; Moore, Hickson, & Stacks, 2010; Howard, 2002/2003; Knapp, 1978, 1980; Koneya & Barbour, 1976; Korda, 1975; Krupat & Kubzansky, 1999; Lanagan, 1999; Mehrabian, 1976; Miller & Schlitt, 1985; Molloy, 1983; Richmond, 1997; Sommer, 1965, 1969, 1970; Sutton, 1985; Zweigenhaft, 1976).

In this chapter, we look at environment in several ways. First, we discuss the perceptual characteristics of environment. Second, we consider the relationship between architectural design and the impact of environment. Third, we deal with spatial arrangements and individual differences associated with them. Fourth, we present a discussion of the impact on human interaction of environmental factors such as attractiveness, color, lighting, temperature, and scent.

PERCEPTUAL CHARACTERISTICS OF ENVIRONMENT

Our physical surroundings can be perceived in a variety of ways. Perceptions of the environments in which we interact affect our communicative behavior. Often we create our environments in ways so as to intentionally manipulate certain perceptions in the people who use them. Knapp (1980) described six **perceptual characteristics of environments:** *formality, warmth, privacy, familiarity, constraint,* and *distance.*

Perception of Formality

Think for a moment about the church buildings and sanctuaries with which you are familiar. Are there common characteristics of these particular environments? Generally, churches, synagogues, and temples are constructed and furnished in a way that creates a perception of formality. As with many other environments, the more formal a church looks, the more formal the communication behavior in it will be. That is, if we perceive the environment to be formal, our communication behavior is likely to be less relaxed and more superficial, hesitant, and stylized.

It is no accident that some environments produce a more formal atmosphere. We would expect that the more one wishes to have individuals conform to rules and norms, the more likely one will strive to make the environment more formal. Surely you have seen such formal rooms as the "un-living" room in someone's home. It more realistically resembles a showcase than a place to relax and interact with others. This is the room where guests are ushered during more ritualistic or formal, and sometimes unpleasant, occasions such as meeting with angry neighbors, talking to an unfamiliar salesperson, waiting with acquaintances to attend a funeral, and the like.

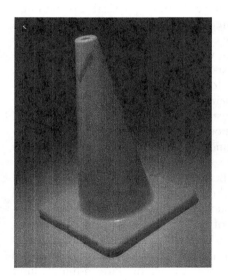

What do the above objects/structures communicate?

Many American males know the feelings that arise when sitting in the un-living room waiting for their date to come downstairs for their first evening out. Later, if the dating continues, the young woman's parents get to know the young man better and may eventually invite him to share the more relaxed and less formal family den. The more informal we perceive the physical surroundings to be, the more we expect the interaction to be relaxed, open, and inviting.

Perception of Warmth

Environments can also create perceptions of warmth or coldness. Consider the cold, hard marble walls of a bank building or courthouse. In contrast, think of the warmth associated with the family den or the kitchen. The degree to which environments create a psychological feeling of warmth is the degree to which we feel comfortable and relaxed and want to linger in those physical surroundings. Warm environments tend to encourage interaction among individuals. Through color, lighting, and textures in rooms, one can ease interaction and keep people from taking their leave. On the other hand, we can move people along by "cooling off" the physical surroundings. Fast-food chains such as McDonald's, Wendy's, Burger King, and Taco Bell have found a winning combination by manipulating the warmth or coldness of their restaurant environments. Because these businesses rely on a rapid rate of customer turnover, their establishments must display enough warmth to invite the customer in but include enough coldness to discourage them from staying around and taking up seats after they have finished that jumbo burger or burrito.

Of course, not all fast-food restaurants are alike. While visiting a fast-food restaurant in a large city, we noticed that the decor was unusually attractive and the seats more comfortable than in most such restaurants. It is likely that the increased display of warmth was their way of dealing with the heavy competition in the area. However, the management still wanted customers to move through quickly (and the warmer environment certainly was not helping). The problem was solved by displaying a large sign on the wall that read: "Fifteen-minute limit for consuming food on the premises." It may be hard to get colder than that.

Perception of Privacy

The degree to which an environment is enclosed and small (allowing few people to enter) is the extent to which it may be perceived as private. Privacy is enhanced when individuals feel that there is less opportunity for their conversations to be overheard by others. An eating establishment can lose its regular customers by changing the dining room from a smaller and more private area into a large expansive one, a realization many formerly busy restaurants come to after expanding to meet high demand that suddenly disappears. Some restaurants prefer to keep customers within their establishments, unlike fast-food chains. The finer places enhance their profits, not so much by rapid turnover but by attracting an affluent clientele that lingers and continues to spend money. The longer the customers remain, the more drinks they will buy. Getting the clientele to linger often means providing an environment that allows them to talk privately in an intimate atmosphere. People often select restaurants and lounges to patronize because their environments encourage and permit intimate interactions. Bringing in a loud band can put such an intimate setting and its owners out of business very quickly.

Perception of Familiarity

A fourth perceptual characteristic of environments is the degree of familiarity or unfamiliarity. Physical surroundings that are unfamiliar to us often create feelings of uneasiness. Because we do not know what to expect in such unfamiliar situations, we tend to be rather cautious, deliberate, and conventional in our communication behavior. Unfamiliarity often generates high levels of arousal as a function of our trying to figure out how we should behave. We are unsure of the norms and rituals of unfamiliar places. We are apt to engage in many adaptor behaviors.

Imagine getting in your car to take a long trip. You drive onto the interstate highway and set your cruise control. After a few hours, you become hungry and begin to look for places to stop. If you are like many individuals, you will pass by several restaurants because they are unfamiliar to you. You want to relax, not worry about how to behave. After a while, you see a welcome and familiar sight. Beckoning you to approach are the two golden arches. You can already taste that Big Mac and fries. You know what to expect. You probably can even guess where the restrooms are located.

Most chain restaurants, hotels, convenience stores, and gas stations count on your making this kind of decision. They know that most people want to avoid hassles when they travel. They go out of their way to make you feel at home when you enter their establishment. If you have learned that you can count on a chain to be reliable, even if their food, room, or other amenities are not the best, you are much more likely to stop there than to go to their competitor across the street. Have you ever stopped at what you thought was a familiar chain operation only to learn that it was not what you had come to expect? If you have, you know the frustration, even anger, of unexpectedly encountering an unfamiliar environment. Holiday Inn conducted an advertising campaign that appealed to this concern. This was their "No Surprises" campaign. They would show people finding unusual environments in other hotels, then would show the consistency of the facilities at Holiday Inns, and would conclude with their "No Surprises at Holiday Inn" slogan.

Perception of Constraint

Constraint is the opposite of feeling free to easily enter or leave an environment. Perceptions of constraint can become intense if there is a realization that little space is available to us. If we are granted a small portion of the space and simultaneously find it difficult to leave (along with finding that it offers no privacy), we feel extremely constrained. Riding in a crowded subway car with the knowledge that your stop is forty-five minutes down the line may influence you to take your leave sooner if you can get to the door before it closes at the upcoming station.

Many have commented that we can more easily tolerate temporary constraint (as in the subway ride) if we are aware that it is only temporary. Sometimes constraint is of a more permanent nature, such as sitting in a plane awaiting takeoff for hours. Crowded classrooms sometimes give students a similar feeling, particularly if they are required to take the class. They feel that there is little or no hope of escaping soon, much like the person confined in the plane. In Chapter 7, we discussed the idea of crowding. Essentially, environments that are constraining tend to produce the factors that lead to this feeling of psychological discomfort: stimulus overload, behavior restriction, and increased surveillance.

Perception of Distance

Finally, environmental factors can create perceptions of distance. Distance perceptions can influence the type of response we make to others because of how close or far away we are from them. Actually, perceptions of distance in environments depend on other nonverbal cues. We can establish physical distance by placing ourselves far away from others. In large environments with several other people, this may require that we speak more loudly (which, of course, causes our interactions to be less personal or private). We can also create psychological distance, although we may be physically near another person. In the crowded subway or elevator, we may turn away from others or engage in gaze avoidance to establish a distance that otherwise would not be possible. This turning away, though, may be a cultural phenomenon. The authors have found, for example, in Thai culture elevator behavior mimicks other behavior in a crowded society. In Bangkok, people think nothing of being crowded. They allow other cars to pull out in front of them, without yelling or blowing their horns. They walk through crowded streets without bumping into one another and without chastising one another.

Our proximity to the center of power in an organization affects other people's perceptions of our power. That is, the closer we are to power, the more powerful we are perceived to be. The person whose office is next to the president's office, even if he or she is an administrative assistant, is perceived as powerful, and even more powerful if there is a private door between the two offices.

ARCHITECTURE AND ENVIRONMENT

Buildings, landscaping, and the positions of walls, partitions, rooms, and stairways all influence human interaction in one way or another. Often, the perceptual characteristics are considered before the architect and building engineer even start to design a new shopping mall, office building, or even a home.

Take a few minutes to try this activity: If you could design your own home, what environmental characteristics would you incorporate? Where would the living room be located? What about the bedrooms? What colors would you choose to decorate your home? Is the exterior going to be brick, wood, aluminum siding, or stone? Will the interior walls be paneled, wallpapered, or

We use and manipulate environments to transmit messages.

Source: Photo by C. Price Walt

painted? Will the inside be open and airy or closed and private? What will the windows be like? Now think of your choices and explain why you made each.

Buildings are designed to express feelings and impressions to those who see them as well as to those who enter them. Is it any wonder, then, that banks of the past were built of stone, with marble walls and floors, and often incorporated tall granite pillars on the facades? What were the bank owners attempting to communicate to the public? They wanted to create the impression of endurance, stability, and security. Can you imagine a family in the early 1930s selling their farm, loading the truck with all their belongings, and driving into the big city to look for a new way of life? Can you imagine them pulling up to a flimsy-looking, drive-through bank such as we see today? After all, the truck could just about knock the thing over, exposing all that money. If you were in that family's place, would you feel safe depositing your life's savings into a vacuum-powered air chute?

Now turn to the Architecture Attractiveness Measure (Figure 8.1). Complete the measure and see how your score reflects your preferences. Building designs can have a great impact not only on people's behavior but also on their impressions of the owners of those buildings (Hall, 1966; Hanson &

Directions: Complete the following measure about environment and communication. Please write one of the following beside each item: (5) Strongly agree; (4) Agree; (3) Neutral or undecided; (2) Disagree; (1) Strongly disagree.

_____ 1. I really dislike dull, dark, heavy-looking buildings.

_____ 2. I like clear, open, airy buildings.

_____ 3. I prefer old, dark, heavy buildings with a history.

_____ 4. I perform at my best when there is a lot of sunlight coming into my-work area.

_____ 5. I really dislike open, airy, sunny architecture.

_____ 6. I dislike new, modern architecture.

_____ 7. I am very irritable when I have to work in a dark building.

_____ 8. I am very alert in clean, clear, open buildings.

_____ 9. I am very irritable when I have to work in new modern buildings with lots of windows.

_____10. I am very alert when I am working in a building where there is little light.

_____11. I rarely do well on assignments when I work in a setting where the environment is ugly.

_____12. I usually do very well on assignments when I work in attractive buildings.

_____13. Working in unattractive environments does not affect the outcome of my work.

_____14. I do well on assignments when working where there are a lot of distractions.

_____15. I like to do my assignments in attractive buildings.

_____16. Doing my assignments in unattractive buildings does not impact my productivity.

Scoring: Step 1: Add responses to the items underlined
Step 2: Add responses to the items *not* underlined
Step 3: Complete the formula:

$$AAM = 48 - \text{Total step 1} + \text{Total step 2}$$

Score should be between 16 and 80
>50 is a person who prefers high AA
<40 is a person who prefers low AA

FIGURE 8.1

Architecture Attractiveness Measure

Hillier, 1982; Hickson & Stacks, 1993; Krupat & Kubzansky, 1999; Lanagan, 1999; Maslow & Mintz, 1956; Mehrabian, 1976; Miller & Schlitt, 1985; Mintz, 1956; Remland, Jones, & Brinkman, 1991).

Have you ever wondered why almost any courtroom you have ever seen tends to command from you and all who enter a sense of respect? It is by design that we are made aware of the seriousness and importance of the decisions that are made in our halls of justice. Status and power messages speak loudly in the courtroom. The elevated bench gives the judge a clear and visible position of dominance and control over all transactions. Even the opposing lawyers and their clients have carefully placed territorial boundaries that are respected by all. Only within the confines of the counselor's table can an attorney talk freely and openly with his or her client without intrusion by the opponent.

Bruneau (1972) studied the architectural design of office spaces in educational organizations. He was primarily interested in how the office designs controlled the communication of both owners and nonowners of the spaces. As the status of the owner of the office increased, the more control the design placed on the nonowner's behavior. The higher the status of the owner, the greater the number of outer offices nonowners had to pass through to reach the owner. In the study, students moving too rapidly through offices of teachers and administrators appeared to be in gross violation of norms, and most office areas had prescribed routes for movement.

From Bruneau's work and that of many others, it is clear that people use architectural design to control the movement and the communication of visitors who enter their environment. When we enter an environment where we find it difficult to decide where we are and are not supposed to go, it may be because the architect slipped up, or it may be that we have never been in that type of environment previously. Recall, if you can, the first time you entered a dormitory,

Architectural View

The researcher investigated what architects think is important about communication. She indicates that the architecture of a building "conveys feeling and gives an impression of the occupants" (p. 36). For example, we tend to make judgments about people based on whether they live in a mobile home or a mansion. Jackson asks three questions from an architect's viewpoint. First, what kind of building is this? Second, what does the architecture "mean"? Banks, in particular are designed to illustrate that one's money is safe and secure there. Whereas, a prison is intended to show that the prisoners cannot get out. Thirdly, Jackson discusses how buildings' appearances are changed for rhetorical purposes. For example, if an old office building is rented out, with the lower floor for restaurants, often awnings are added to demonstrate that it is no longer "just" an office building, but also a place where customers can feel comfortable eating.

Jackson, N. (2006). The architectural view: Perspectives on communication. Visual Communication Quarterly, 13, 32–45.

a post office, a police station, a hospital, a church, a synagogue, or the lobby of a large hotel. Was it easier to know what to do in subsequent encounters with these types of environments?

SPATIAL ARRANGEMENT

How we arrange our environments for purposes of interaction can transmit a variety of signals. In this section, we discuss spatial arrangement in three ways. First, the impact of the shapes of tables is discussed. Second, we present the topic of seating arrangement and its relationship to task situations and personality differences. Third, the topic of office arrangement and how it is related to professional and social interaction is reviewed.

The Shapes of Tables

Consider for a moment the three different table structures in Figure 8.2. The round table is characterized by a circle. There are no distinct and visible sides. As a result, the round table often is taken as a symbol of equality and unity among the individuals occupying it. The round table has taken on particular meaning concerning power and dominance. Although King Arthur used the round table to express unity and equality among his knights, there nonetheless developed a power message depending on where the knights were seated. The closer they were to the king, the more powerful they were seen to be. Do not be misled by the apparent equality projected by a round table. A powerful person at a round table, even in a democratic society, is still a powerful person and unlikely to be treated as an equal by others sitting at the same table, or to expect such treatment.

The square table is just that: square, or nearly so. Because it has four equal sides, it communicates equality of status and power. However, its distinct sides and prominent corners also suggest a separation among the interactants. The square shape facilitates perceptions of equality but not of unity. Square tables are excellent for interactions involving competition and negotiation.

The rectangular table is often found in corporate and business settings. The impact of this type of table resembles that of the square table. That is, there are four separate sides that suggest a lack of unity to the interactants. However,

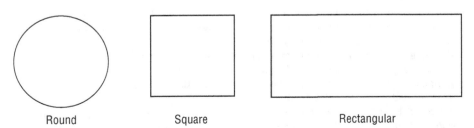

Round   Square   Rectangular

FIGURE 8.2
Three Table Structures

two of the sides are short, and the other two usually are twice as long or longer. One of the short sides is generally perceived as the head of the table, especially in instances where the other short side is left vacant. At the rectangular table, the center of power is at the head and gradually diminishes as the position gets farther and farther away. The person at the head usually controls the interaction at the table and normally is looked to for leadership by the group. A longer oval table can have many of the same effects as the rectangular table.

Seating Arrangement

Do our seating choices say anything about us? Research in this area suggests that one's choice of a place to sit may be determined by several things. Even in the classroom, where it may appear that seating is little more than random behavior, researchers have determined that students choose their seats with considerable care. Factors such as the task before us, the kind of communicative relationship in which we are engaged, and even our personality characteristics contribute to where we decide to sit in relation to other people. The research cited below is provided by Sommer (1965, 1969, 1970).

THE TASK SITUATION. Sommer was interested in the seating behavior of young people. In his investigation, Sommer asked his subjects to imagine that they were sitting at a table with a same-sex friend. He then asked them to consider four task situations. These were described as follows:

Conversation means sitting and talking for a few minutes before class.

Cooperation means sitting together and studying together for the same test.

Co-action means sitting together and studying for different tests.

Competition means competing to see who is the first to solve a series of puzzles.

All of Sommer's subjects were shown diagrams of two different types of tables, rectangular and round. Figure 8.3 displays the rectangular table arrangement, and Figure 8.4 displays the round-table arrangement. Subjects were to indicate which seating represented conversation, cooperation, co-action, or competition. In the conversation task situation, the rectangular table appeared to elicit either corner seating (table 1B) or opposite seating across the short distance (table 1A). At the round table during conversation, table 1 was chosen by 63 percent of the people in the study.

For the cooperation task situation, table 2 was chosen in the rectangular arrangement, and table 1 was chosen by 83 percent of the respondents in the round table arrangement. Evidently, working in cooperation with another person requires us to sit side by side, despite the table's shape.

The co-action situation, studying at the same table but for different tests, seemed to require a considerable amount of room for both parties. In the rectangular arrangement, table 3A was chosen by 43 percent, and table 3B was

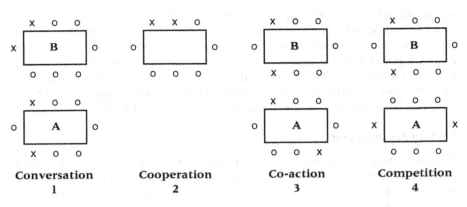

FIGURE 8.3
Rectangular Seating Arrangements

chosen by 32 percent. In the round table arrangement in Figure 8.4, tables 2 and 3 with opposite seating allow the most room for both parties. This table was chosen by 51 percent of the respondents.

During competition situations, one arrangement was the predominant choice. Whether at a rectangular or round table, most respondents chose opposite seating. Forty-one percent chose table 4A in Figure 8.3, and 63 percent chose table 3 in Figure 8.4. It may be that during situations where two persons are competing against one another, they feel it necessary to keep their "opponent" in full view. Sitting at closer distances, as at rectangular table 4B, rather than at greater distances, as at rectangular table 4A, may allow for greater control and dominance over the opponent. At least one study has shown, however, that this may be true only for American students. Cook (1970) replicated Sommer's study with a group of students and nonstudents in the United Kingdom. His respondents chose to have the greater distance allowed by rectangular table 4A during competitive task situations. Knapp (1980) has sug-

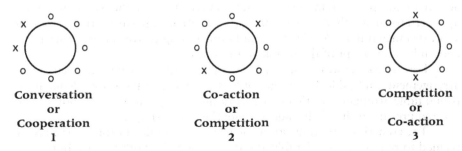

FIGURE 8.4
Round Seating Arrangements

gested that for Sommer's respondents, the closer opposite arrangement "would afford them an opportunity not only to see how the other person is progressing but would also allow them to use various gestures, body movements, and eye contact to upset their opponent" (p. 89).

INTIMACY LEVEL. The intimate nature of the relationship also seems to have an impact on our choice of seating, or intimacy may be implied by our seating choice. In his study, Cook found that side-by-side seating was most preferred by very intimate friends while sitting in a restaurant or in a bar. However, corner seating is selected for same-sex friends and casual friends of the opposite sex when seated in a bar. Sommer found that the intimate level of the relationship may be the primary determinant of where we choose to sit. He concluded, on the other hand, that the topic of discussion of the individuals probably has little impact. According to Sommer (1970), "Apparently it is the nature of the relationship between individuals rather than the topic that characterizes a discussion as personal or impersonal. Two lovers discussing the weather can have an intimate conversation, but a zoology professor discussing sex in a lecture hall containing 300 students would be having an impersonal session despite [the] topic" (p. 65). Therefore greater intimacy is implied by closer seating.

PERSONALITY DIFFERENCES. Personality characteristics and other individual differences have an impact on our seating preferences. Research has shown that people with different personalities prefer different seating positions if they are free to select where they want to sit. For example, students who choose to sit in the front of the class have been found to be more enthusiastic about school and learning. They also are more enthusiastic about reading, place more value on creativity and imagination, are more focused on their life goals, and desire to be alone more often than others (Richmond, 1997; Walberg, 1969).

In contrast, students who prefer to sit in the back of the room are less likely to become leaders and organizers, see little value in being popular with other students, are less interested in making good grades, and generally are unhappy with school. A third group of students, those who choose to sit near a window, are more likely to dislike school and studying. Of course, there are some students who care little about where they sit.

Dominance has also been related to seating choices. Researchers have observed that people who score high on measures of dominance tend to select one of two seats at tables: the seat at the head of the table, or the seat at the center of one of the sides of the table. In either case, the position chosen by the dominant individual is central to the interaction and allows for high visibility and eye contact with other seated interactants. People who are highly willing to communicate, those who find communicating to be a pleasant experience in itself, have been found to behave much like people with dominant personalities. No doubt many of these people are both dominant and highly willing to communicate, but some are simply gregarious individuals who like to be in the center of communication activities.

Closely related to dominance is the quality of leadership. Research has revealed that leaders choose seating that is similar to that of dominant people. Leaders are more likely to sit at the end of a rectangular table; whereas, individuals who sit at the corners contribute very little to the group. While an individual's personality will largely determine whether he or she chooses to be a leader, a person may emerge as a leader of a group in part because of where he or she is sitting. Seating position can and does determine communication flow. The flow of communication, furthermore, affects who can emerge as a leader (Hall, 1966; Hare & Bales, 1963; Howells & Becker, 1962; Korda, 1975; Russo, 1967; Sommer, 1965).

In one study of five-person decision-making groups, three of the individuals were assigned to sit on one side of a rectangular table, while two sat on the opposite side. The results showed that the side with the two people could influence the others more often, and those two people talked more than the other three. As a result, leadership emerged from the two-person side in most cases (Howells & Becker, 1962).

The work of Russo (1967) has revealed several variables that are influenced by environmental arrangement. Russo was particularly interested in the seating preferences of friendly and talkative individuals. Figure 8.5 displays Russo's five different seating arrangements. Not surprisingly, she found that the friendliest people preferred the seating arrangement in table A. The most hostile individuals tended to choose arrangement E. In comparing all five arrangements on friendliness, level of acquaintance, and talkativeness, arrangement B was seen as more friendly, intimate, and talkative than arrangement C; C was seen as more so than D; and D more than E.

Introverts and extroverts also tend to display their differences from one another in a variety of ways. One major difference that has been found involves their seating preferences. Introverts are far more likely to choose seating with reduced visibility and greater physical distance from others. We suspect that the extreme introvert would prefer arrangement D in Figure 8.5 over any of the others. Table D provides for the greatest possible distance while simultaneously preventing the straightforward eye contact present at table E. Extroverts, conversely, tend to choose a seat opposite the other individual, as in tables C and E. Extreme extroverts also prefer to sit near others, which suggests that they would prefer table C as the most desirable arrangement.

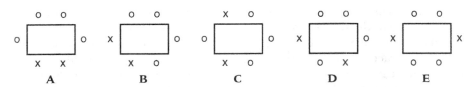

FIGURE 8.5
Russo's Seating Arrangements

Arrangement of Office Space

In recent years, much has been written to advise the owners of office space how best to arrange the office for greater success and control. Back in 1979, the editors of *Consumer Reports* magazine compiled a book for the sole purpose of instructing upwardly mobile businesspeople on how to decorate their work areas to achieve greater success. The editors emphasized that the size and placement of furniture in an office is usually the prime factor in communicating the occupant's personality. These writers suggest that improving one's office requires great care and planning. They present a planning process that involves two steps:

1. Develop a specific plan for projecting your personality and style.
2. Review how the various aspects of an office can project character. Then plan the physical changes that express the qualities you wish (p. 17).

Since the *Consumer Reports* publication, Korda (1975) and others (Buslig, 1999; and Richmond, 1997) have contended that a person can communicate power by how he or she arranges the office. In fact, Korda places more importance on arrangement and use of office space than on the quality or size of things in the space:

> Power lies in how you use what you have, not in the accoutrements per se. All the leather, chrome, glass, and expensive artwork in the world will not replace a truly well-thought-out power scheme. A large office is pointless unless it is arranged so a visitor has to walk the length of it before getting to the power desk, and it is valuable to put as many objects as possible in his path. (pp. 231–232)

Korda and others have suggested that it is quite common to see large offices divided into two distinct areas: the pressure area and the semisocial area. According to Korda, different communication rules, although unwritten, apply to each area.

The **pressure area,** or the business transaction area, is centered on the desk of the office's occupant. It is here that firm decisions, hard negotiations, and tough bargaining take place. Korda contends that if the occupant of the office escorts the visitor away from this area and into the **semisocial area,** he or she is probably not very interested in discussing business on a serious level. The semisocial area is used primarily to "delay or placate a visitor" (p. 235).

Similarly, Zweigenhaft (1976) investigated the office arrangements of faculty members in an academic setting. He was interested in how faculty of differing rank positioned the furniture in their offices to manage interaction with students. Zweigenhaft asked the teachers to make sketches of how their offices were currently arranged. The results of this study showed that most senior faculty members (associate and full professors) placed their desks between themselves and the visiting student. However, less than half of the assistant professors and lecturers put their desks in the same "blocking" position. A more interesting result of this study involved students' perceptions of the faculty members. Student perceptions were more positive for teachers who did not place their desks in the "blocking" position. Students rated them as more willing to encourage different points of view, more willing to give students individual attention, and less likely to show undue favoritism.

Our interactions with colleagues on several campuses suggest that the students' perceptions quite likely are accurate. Young colleagues tend to see students as more like them and as individuals with whom it is pleasant to interact. More senior colleagues suggest more negative experiences in their office interactions with students, often feeling that students usually come to their offices to complain. It is quite likely that as professors age, they are seen by their students as having less in common with students and therefore as being less desirable targets for interaction. Thus it is less likely that the students would visit the older professor's office for informal interaction. Student-professor office interactions, therefore, would more likely be related to problems the student was confronting. A cycle probably develops. The student interactions involve pleasant interactions less frequently, so structures are placed between the student and the professor. As these barriers go up, the likelihood of pleasant interactions decreases further, and so on.

OTHER ENVIRONMENTAL FACTORS

Besides spatial arrangement, other aspects the environment have been found to influence communication behavior. In this section, we discuss the impact of environmental attractiveness, color, lighting, temperature, and scent on interaction among individuals.

Environmental Attractiveness

The decor of rooms, whether attractive or ugly, tends to influence human behavior in several ways. One of the most widely cited, classic studies investigating the effects of room attractiveness was conducted by Maslow and Mintz (1956) and Mintz (1956). In this study, the researchers selected three rooms in which to carry out an experiment. The first room represented a beautiful condition. There were two large windows, draperies, and carpeting, and the walls were a beige color. There also was indirect overhead lighting, and the room was attractively furnished. The second room represented an ugly condition, including dingy gray walls and a single lightbulb overhead with a soiled lampshade. The furnishings gave an impression that the room was a storage area. The third room, considered to represent the neutral or average condition, was a professor's office. Subjects were placed in each of the three conditions and asked to rate photographs of people's faces. The researchers carefully controlled for noise, odor, seating, time of day, and experimenter.

The results of this investigation showed that subjects in the "beautiful" condition gave substantially more positive ratings to the pictures than those in the other two conditions. These findings are interesting, but they were expected. What was not expected, however, was that both subjects and experimenters in

Environment creates the ambiance.

Source: Photo by C. Price Walt

the ugly room engaged in a variety of escape activities. The ugly room produced perceptions of monotony, headaches, hostility, and other negative reactions. The beautiful room, on the other hand, tended to elicit myriad positive reactions, including a desire to continue the exercise and perceptions of comfort, importance, and enjoyment.

Other studies over the last three decades have indicated that the results of this classic study were not an accident. People react strongly to the attractiveness level of the environment in which they must reside, even if only temporarily. People spend more time in their offices, given free choice, if the office is attractive. People are willing to wait longer without complaining if asked to wait in attractive places. People find others more attractive if they communicate with them in attractive places. Students even learn more in attractive classrooms than in unattractive ones.

Color in the Environment

Is environmental color important to human interaction? Research into color suggests that if one is feeling depressed, down, or hurried, the color of the surrounding walls may be the reason. For example, red is the most arousing color, followed by orange, yellow, violet, blue, and green. According to many specialists in nonverbal behavior, colors have had symbolic meaning throughout history.

The Pantone Color Institute reinforces the idea that color can affect a person's responses. Institute representatives note that **chromadynamics** (the study of the physiological effects caused when people observe color) research by many scientists has proven that certain colors affect vision, hearing, respiration, and circulation. Table 8.1 shows an outline of colors and the symbolic meanings that have come to be assigned to them.

Clearly, the mood and tone of an environment can be controlled to a major extent by manipulating the colors present in that environment (Baker, 1985; Birren, 1950; Williams, 1954; Richmond, 1997). For over half a century, doctors have used colors to relax mentally disturbed patients. Similarly, restaurant and bar owners use color to stimulate or control the emotions of

TABLE 8.1

Colors and Meaning*

Red	Excitement, happiness, vitality, vivaciousness, anger, rage, hostility, defiance, sin, blood, lust, energy, royalty, fun
Blue	Coolness, calmness, pleasantness, tenderness, dependability, dignity, truth, royalty, businesslike attitude, softness, tranquility, acceptance
Yellow	Excitement, fun, boldness, glory, cheerfulness, light, clarity, brilliance, softness
Orange	Activity, perhaps unpleasantness, excitement, disturbing stimulation, distress
Purple	Royalty, control, demandingness, coolness, calmness, thoughtfulness, wisdom
Mauve	Calmness, respect, coolness, serenity, peace, acceptance
Green	Coolness, pleasantness, spring or summer, freshness, appeal, security, peace, tranquillity, softness, crispness, cleanness, vegetables to consume
Gray	Dependability, coolness, calmness, businesslike attitude, reliability, standards, faithfulness, sturdiness, stability, somewhat boring
Black	Sadness, intensity, control, power, unhappiness, death, potency, strength, command, domination, masculinity, decay
Brown	Disappointment, sadness, down feelings, neutrality, humility, protection, acceptance
White	Purity, cleanliness, virtue, crystal, babyhood, innocence, joy, femininity, perhaps coldness or neutrality depending on shade, lightness

*Many of these standard colors have a variety of shades that can change the meaning. Here we are speaking only about the standard colors and associated meanings.

their patrons. In one of the more interesting classic studies on the impact of color, Ketcham (1958) examined the relationship between color and student achievement in the classroom. Using kindergarten children as subjects, Ketcham selected three schools in which to conduct his experiments. The first school needed painting but was left unpainted. The second school was painted in standard institutional fashion—light buff walls and white ceilings. The third school was painted using the principles of color dynamics as a guideline. The hallways were painted a bright, cheerful yellow hue. Classrooms facing north were painted a pale rose color, and those facing south in cool shades such as blue and green. The front walls in the classrooms were painted a darker shade than the side walls, and the art room was done in a neutral gray so as not to interfere with the colorful work within it. Ketcham's observations of the behavior in each school spanned a period of two years. According to Ketcham, the results were clear. The students in the colorful school showed the greatest improvement in social habits, health and safety habits, language skills, arithmetic, social studies, science, and music. Those in the first school (the one left unpainted) showed the least improvement, and those in the second school only slightly more. When we first discussed this research with a large class of public school teachers, one of them asked, "After all this time, why are so many schools in the United States still painted like the ugly room?" Good question.

Lighting in the Environment

Closely associated with color in the environment is the factor of lighting (Williams, 1954). Obviously, color would be immaterial without some form of illumination. Additionally, lighting may be colored itself. Certain colored lights have been found to be associated with particular emotional responses. Red lights are often related to danger, pale yellow lights to contentment, pale green with kindness, green with death, peacock blue with sinister things, orange with warmth and excitement, blue with quiet, violet with delicacy, and lavender with wistfulness.

Behavior is affected not only by the color of lighting, but also by its intensity. High illuminations of gold and pink lighting produce a festive atmosphere, whereas subdued lighting, particularly blue, tends to elicit a somber mood. Lighting that is too blue and subdued can actually create drowsiness.

Some studies have explored the effects of bright and dim lighting. One study placed subjects into a room with either bright lighting or dim lighting for a period of one hour. Subjects were allowed to do whatever they pleased. Each room contained four females and four males, and both rooms were the same size: 10 feet by 12 feet. The results showed that verbal output was strikingly different in the two rooms. In the brightly lit room, a continuous stream of speech was maintained; whereas in the dimly lit room, almost all talking had stopped after about thirty minutes.

Some have suggested that bright lighting and dim lighting differentially influence perceptions of intimacy and relaxation (Carr & Dabbs, 1974; Gergen,

Gergen, & Barton, 1973). Low lighting makes people want to linger because the environment is more relaxing; whereas, extremely bright lighting may produce fatigue or create a desire to escape. Dim lighting, coupled with intimate questions among nonintimates, has been found to produce hesitancy during responses, reduced eye contact, and a significant decrease in the duration of gaze (Carr & Dabbs, 1974).

Temperature and the Environment

Based on the research on environmental temperature, researchers have concluded that 62 to 68 degrees Fahrenheit may be the optimal temperature for indoor environments. Knapp (1980) has provided an excellent summary of the research that has been conducted. He reports that Huntington (1915) advanced a seemingly bizarre theory in the early twentieth century that an average outdoor temperature of 50 to 60 degrees Fahrenheit is better than one above 70 degrees (p. 58). According to Knapp, the experts have suggested the following effects of weather on human behavior:

1. Monotonous weather is more apt to affect your spirits.
2. Seasonally, you do your best mental work in late winter, early spring, and fall.
3. A prolonged blue sky reduces your productivity.
4. The ideal temperature should average about 64 degrees Fahrenheit (p. 58).

In his book *The Achieving Society,* McClelland (1976) reported that achievement motivation appears greatest in societies where the average yearly temperature is between 40 and 60 degrees Fahrenheit. McClelland also suggested that a variation of at least 15 degrees, either daily or seasonally, produced high achievement motivation. Other studies have suggested that temperature and aggression are related. We may be more likely to act aggressively in higher temperatures than in lower ones. Aggressive acts, for example, rarely occur in cold weather.

All of this appears to suggest that lower temperatures may affect human behavior in more positive ways than higher ones. Higher temperatures may also cause us to react more negatively toward other people. Although many of us who live in northern climates complain about cold weather and long for summer, we may not know what is best for us. Our desire for warm room temperatures may have just as negative an impact on our behavior.

Griffitt and Veitch (1971), in a classic study, explored such a possibility by looking at the effects of room temperature and room density. In the low-density conditions, there were an average of four subjects per room; whereas, in the high-density conditions, the average was fourteen subjects. Two temperature conditions for both high- and low-density conditions were used (93.4 and 73.4 degrees Fahrenheit). The subjects in all conditions were asked to complete several questionnaires including a measure of attitude toward a hypothetical stranger. The results of the study indicated that the subjects in the high-temperature, high-density room reported less liking, less positive personal reactions, and less positive social affective reactions toward strangers than in any of the other conditions (Baron & Bell, 1976).

Scent and Smell

The air around us is filled with scents and smells that express a variety of messages to us. Scents can communicate memories, fear, love, dominance, and excitement—and may even arouse powerful feelings about another person. If someone smells offensive or emits offensive odors (such as flatulent air) while we are interacting with them, we will probably end the conversation and think very negative thoughts about them (Burton, 1976; Cain, 1981; "Heaven Scents," 2002; Luka, Berner, & Kanakis, 1977; Ponte, 1982; Wiener, 1979; Winter, 1976).

Within the past twenty years, researchers and scholars have started to acknowledge the powerful nature of scents in the communication process. The study of scents and smells and how we perceive and process them is referred to as **olfactics.** Our olfactory senses often help us, unconsciously, to form opinions of others.

IMPORTANCE OF SCENTS

Scents are important in this culture: It is estimated that in 1998, the American public spent more than $3 billion on deodorants. This is an incredible amount of money to spend just to smell good! No other culture in the world spends near that amount to smell good. In fact, many other cultures prefer natural body scents to the artificial ones. In this culture, Winter (1976) notes: "We know that in society we can't have bad breath, sweaty underarms, or noticeable genital odor. You can tell people they need a haircut or to wash their faces, but if you tell them they smell, you are really insulting" (p. 16). Our sense of smell affects how we communicate with others and how we perceive them.

Research has clearly shown that animals have scents of their own and that they can smell other animals. Dogs and cats have distinctive scents and even mark their territory with their scents to keep other animals out. Cats' scent glands are near the base of the whiskers; when they rub their cheeks against a person's leg, they leave their scent behind. Other animals mark their territory by urinating on or around it. Wolves, bears, and many other animals leave their scents around their territories to keep others out. Elephants defecate to mark their territory—with a very powerful scent.

We all have an individualized scent, which some call an **olfactory signature.** Like animals, humans use scents. It is a means of making ourselves unique. We try to wear different perfumes or colognes that set us apart from others.

Most living creatures have **pheromones,** chemical secretions that attract other animals for mates. However, no pheromones have been isolated in humans. This term originated from the Greek *pherein* (to carry) and *horman* (to excite or stimulate). Whereas animals exude scents when they are attracted to another, humans become more sensitive to scents when they are in a state of arousal.

The average person can recognize at least four thousand distinct scents. Some can recognize as many as ten thousand. People differ not only in their sensitivity to scents but also in their evaluation of a given scent. It is not uncommon, for example, for one person to find a scent pleasant, another to find it extremely unpleasant, and still another to not notice the scent at all. Nor, unfortunately, is it uncommon for a person who finds a scent pleasant to expect that everyone else should find it pleasant also.

Not only do individuals differ in their responses to scents, but there is also evidence that scent is influenced to some extent by gender. Women and men may perceive odors differently.

Scents are invisible messages. What they communicate, as with other verbal and nonverbal messages, depends on the way the receiver perceives them. Scents are powerful messages and often determine whether communication will be initiated, continued, or terminated. Our reactions to others may be triggered by our conscious or unconscious awareness of the scents around us. The following sections review scent and smell in relation to attractiveness, touch, and environment.

SCENT AND ATTRACTION. Some popular writings today suggest that there is a link between smell and attraction between sexual partners. Dr. Robert Henkin at Georgetown University's Taste and Smell Clinic found that 25 percent of people with olfactory disorders lose interest in sex. He isn't sure why but suggests that a similar thing happens when the olfactory sense of animals and insects is impaired. Alex Comfort, who wrote *The Joy of Sex,* suggests that the combined natural scents of a woman— such as her hair, breasts, skin, armpits, and genital region—may be a greater asset than her beauty.

Some researchers are trying to figure out whether males and females excrete something like animal pheromones that attract them to one another. Some people believe that alpha androstenol, a chemical found in male urine and sweat, might affect attraction. Androsterone, a male sex hormone that also is found in male urine, might also have an effect. Others are looking at the possibility that women exude scents from their genitals that attract men. The research here is sparse and inconclusive. At this point, the search for human pheromones has yet to find anything even remotely similar to animal hormones in communicative power.

The desire to find such an element, however, appears strong. As an example, Burton (1976) suggests that there is evidence supporting the idea that male pheromones might attract females. He cites the following apocryphal tale as evidence: "A young man was reputed to have great success with girls. After a dance he would wipe the perspiring brow of his partner with a handkerchief that had been carried in his armpit. Apparently his body odor acted as an aphrodisiac, and the young man claimed that his technique was highly successful" (p. 113). This is obviously weak evidence that human male pheromones can attract females. Until we have far better evidence than this, we should presume that pheromones are one thing that separate us from other animal life.

As suggested earlier, we use a variety of artificial scents to attract others or to make ourselves appealing. We are the most scent-conscious culture in the world. However, olfaction also is a very important means of communication in other cultures. As Hall (1966) notes:

> Olfaction occupies a prominent place in Arab life. Not only is it one of the distance-setting mechanisms, but it is a vital part of a complex system of behavior. Arabs consistently breathe on people when they talk. However, this habit is more than a matter of different manners. To the Arab good smells are pleasing and a way of being involved with each other. To smell one's friend is not only nice but desirable, for to deny him your breath is to act ashamed. Americans, on the other hand, trained as they are not to breathe in people's faces, automatically communicate shame in trying to be polite. (pp. 159–160)

We spend billions of dollars trying to smell appealing to others. The perfume industry employs people to be smell testers in order to pinpoint the smell that will sell. These people are sensitive to more odors than the normal person and can sense odors that are appealing or unappealing. In the perfume business, "the nose has it." All fragrance companies have one goal in mind: to convey some message that sells their product. Check out your bathroom or makeup kit, and you will find various messages given by colognes and perfumes. The perfume and cologne industry definitely knows how to communicate with the American public. These industries often relate scent to sexiness, sexual arousal, attraction, and life.

Some researchers suggest that perfume and attraction are related. However, the relationship, if it exists, must be very complex. For example, to be perceived as attractive, the woman who dresses elaborately may not require as much perfume as the woman who dresses down. Does Miss America need to wear perfume to be seen as attractive? Will a homeless person be attractive if he or she wears cologne? The research in this area is insufficient to be sure, but we are reasonably certain that the impact of perfume and cologne is less than the advertisers would have us believe.

The norm of our culture is that if someone doesn't smell appealing, we are not attracted to them. However, what attracts one person might offend another person. Overpowering perfumes and colognes offend some people's senses; whereas, others are turned on to the scent. We need to remember to stay within the norms of our culture and try to have a scent that is attractive to others. People can react very negatively to bad scents. A professor at a southwestern university rarely took a bath and insisted on wearing wool jackets year-round. He seldom if ever took the jackets to the cleaners. He hung them outside a few times a year and stated that "wool cleans itself." Finally, students started to complain, and faculty members became offended. Some faculty members refused to sit near him in faculty meetings. They felt that they could not say anything about his odor. A colleague started placing cans of deodorant in the professor's mailbox. It helped. The professor started bathing more and using the deodorant. Do not expect that the "subtle" approach will always work. Most people who smell very bad to others do not think they smell bad, and often it is hard to change their minds.

SCENT AND TOUCH. Consider the following: An older man is lying in the hospital bed looking worn, shallow, and weak. His eyes are closed and his breathing is shallow. As you reach out to touch his arm, he inhales deeply and exhales breath into your face and simultaneously flatulates. Will you touch him? Will you unintentionally draw away? You may run.

People approach things and persons who are attractive. Therefore if someone looks unpleasant or has bad breath or body odor, it is unlikely that we will want to touch them. Some parents refuse to touch their babies when they have vomited or messed their diapers, because of the odor. In nursing homes and hospitals, the attractive patients get more and better care from the staff. Attractive people in society receive more touch. Attractiveness is related to scent. Those who smell attractive, pleasing, and good are much more likely to receive more touch than those who smell unattractive, unpleasant, and foul.

Hospitals are notorious for their distinctive scents and odors. Often, the staff and doctors are insensitive to them. The odors in hospitals can make patients feel bad and visitors feel frightened. Many hospitals are trying to improve their atmospheres by using scents that cover up the "hospital odor." They have to be cautious, however, so that the scents they use do not trigger people's allergies.

SCENT AND THE ENVIRONMENT. Our environment is flooded with a variety of odors that assault our olfactory senses. We have pollution in the air, cigarette smoke, strong perfumes, scented toilet tissue, scented underwear, scented yard sprays, and scented house and carpet cleaners.

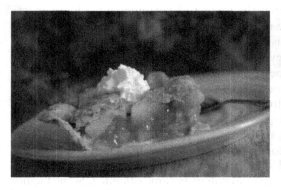

Some things smell better (or worse) than other things!

All environments in this culture are flooded with a variety of scents. Some scents are worse than the original odors. It is difficult to purchase an unscented product on the market, and when they are available they are usually 10 to 15 percent more expensive. We must pay to keep the manufacturer from putting in the perfume. Oddly enough, some unscented products actually have a natural scent, but they contain scents to make them seem unscented.

Many people suffer from scent-related allergies or breathing maladies. Because we have so many scents in the environment, it can take an allergist days and several types of tests to determine what someone is allergic to and where the scent is. In this culture, we are very sensitive to odors and may even react to them violently. In 1979 (before the federal ban on smoking on domestic flights), a smoking war took place on Eastern Airlines flight 1410. Smoking and nonsmoking passengers got into an argument over the contamination of the air on the plane by the smoking passengers. Both wanted their rights to the air. The nonsmokers did not want their air contaminated by smoke, and the smokers wanted to smoke. The plane had to make a forced landing because of the confrontation that followed. This might seem amusing, but in a sense it isn't. Each of us feels that we should have a right to control the air in our space; when that air is invaded by undesirable scents, we are willing to fight to get clean air. There are many stories of people becoming angered and enraged at others for flooding the environment with undesirable odors. Recall that one form of territorial invasion is contamination. When our air is fouled, our territory is fouled. We are likely to respond with the fight response.

What we need to remember is that all people do not prefer the same scents. A scent that smells good to one may smell foul to another. We must be sensitive to others around us and how our scents and the way we use environmental scents can affect others. Some people spray their homes with disinfectants and use strong carpet cleaners to hide pet odors. Their visitors think the place just plain stinks.

We are flooded with environmental odors that communicate things to us about others. We react to environmental scents. We may even make judgments about others based on the scents they allow in their environments.

EFFECTS OF SCENT AND SMELL. Scent clearly is a means of interacting with others. We can use our scents to increase our communication with one another. We can also use our scents to guarantee that others do not communicate with us. Therefore, scent is a powerful although invisible component of the nonverbal communication process.

First, scent can be used to increase perceived attraction between two people. People are attracted to others who exude pleasant odors. Heightening one's positive scent may entice or repel others. Be careful what you do.

Second, scent can also influence the attractiveness of food. Often, smell is primarily responsible for creating flavor. Sometimes taste actually takes on a secondary role. Therefore much of our taste experience depends on how good or bad, pleasant or unpleasant something smells. Unpleasant-smelling foods may never be tasted, much less eaten. We may know something will taste bad because it smells awful.

Taste sensations tend to be intense and acute when we are young; as we age, our taste sensations tend to decline. This is why many older people lose their appetite for foods they previously enjoyed, and why many children hate pungent cheeses and spicy foods.

Although smell plays a dramatic role in what we taste, there are other factors that must be considered. Other things that influence our preference for foods beside smell are our expectations, our personality, the color of the food, the texture of the food, and the frequency of ingestion.

Third, scent and smell can evoke meanings and memories of things, people, and environments from the past. Smell is one of the best senses for helping us form meanings and to recall past events. People who have **smell blindness** cannot detect certain odors and scents, may be unaware of the scents around them, and cannot form certain meanings and memories of things and people.

Fourth, we daily use what is called **smell adaptation.** This means that we adapt our sense of smell every time we enter a new environment. For example, when we enter a chocolate store, we instantly inhale the pleasant aroma of chocolate. Smell adaptation permits us to have pleasant scents linger longer and to keep unpleasant scents from lingering.

Fifth, we experience what is called **smell memory,** the phenomenon by which scents and smells trigger spontaneous recall of events that are associated with them. We may recall the smells in our parents' home and the pleasant memories they evoke. Smell blindness, smell adaptation, and smell memories are very important in finding our meanings and evoking memories.

Sixth, scent and smell can be used to educate students about the world around them and to stimulate the learning processes of deaf and mute students. Winter (1976) reported that when researchers paired long lists of words with odors that matched the words, students could retain the words for a long period. The Braille Institute of America and the Perkins School for the Blind use scratch-and-sniff labels with learning tools that are written in braille.

Seventh, smell and scent have recently become of scientific concern in many medical communities. The diagnosis of disease by smell is not a new technique but one long practiced. Several patient odors have been associated with particular diseases. Yellow fever smelled like the butcher shop. Scurvy and smallpox had putrid odors. Typhoid fever smelled like freshly baked bread. Diphtheria had a very sweet odor, and the plague had the odor of apples. Many of these diseases do not exist in the United States now, but people should still be aware of the power of scent in diagnosing an illness. As a function of more recent research, for example, doctors can determine what type of alcoholism a patient is suffering from, what type of poison a patient swallowed, and whether a patient is in a diabetic coma (by the odor of acetone). All of the above can help a physician in making a diagnosis.

In summary, environmental factors are important in human communication. Whether it is attractiveness, color, lighting, temperature, or scent and smell, these factors can affect our reactions to others, our emotional states, and our perceptions. If we understand the environmental factors present in a given situation, we may be better able to understand the communication that occurs in that situation.

Glossary of Terminology

Chromadynamics is the study of the physiological effects caused by observing color.

Fixed-feature space is space that is fixed or immovable, such as the physical features in our homes, offices, rooms, schools, and even the layout of our cities and towns.

Olfactics is the study of scents and smells and how people perceive and process information about them.

Olfactory signature is the individualized, unique scent that each person has.

Perceptual characteristics of environment are *formality, warmth, privacy, familiarity, constraint,* and *distance.*

Pheromones are chemicals that animals excrete to attract other animals for mates. The term originated from the Greek *pherein* (to carry) and *horman* (to excite or stimulate).

Pressure area, or the business-transaction area of an office, is centered on the desk of the office's occupant. It is here that firm decisions, hard negotiations, and tough bargaining take place.

Semifixed-feature space includes the movable objects in our environments, such as furniture and accessories that adorn, accent, highlight, and personalize the physical areas in our world.

Semisocial area is used primarily to delay or placate an office visitor, to socialize, or to conduct less demanding talks, decisions, and bargaining.

Smell adaptation is the ability to adapt from one smell to the other, particularly from one strong scent to a stronger scent or to a weaker scent.

Smell blindness is an anatomical defect of the nose that impairs a person's ability to detect or distinguish certain scents.

Smell memory is the phenomenon by which scents and smells can trigger spontaneous recall of events that are associated with them.

CHAPTER 9

Touch and Communication

Tactile communication is the earliest and probably the most basic form of communication. The most primitive life forms rely almost exclusively on touch to interact with the environment around them. Humans depend on tactile sensitivity as their first and possibly most important form of contact with other human beings (Argyle, 1975; Dolin & Booth-Butterfield, 1993; Fromme, Jaynes, Taylor, Hanold, Daniell, Rountree, & Fromme, 1989; Glausiusz, 2002; Jones & Yarbrough, 1985; Mehrabian, 1971; Montagu, 1978; Richmond, 1997, 2002). Even before the infant is born, it is nurtured, caressed, and usually held secure in the mother's womb. The omnipresent heartbeat of the mother provides a comforting life rhythm that soothes and satisfies the infant (Clay, 1966; Maurer & Maurer, 1988).

The five senses are sight, hearing, smell, taste, and touch. But while sight, hearing, smell, and taste are located in specific parts of the human body, the sense of touch is found all over the body. Our sense of touch originates in the bottom layer of our skin, called the dermis. The dermis is filled with tiny nerve endings that send information to the brain about things that our skin contacts. The nerve endings communicate if we are hot, cold, or in pain. Some parts of our body are more sensitive to touch than others. For example, the least sensitive part is the middle of the back. The most sensitive parts are the hands, lips, face, neck, tongue, fingertips, and feet. Since these parts of the body are touched most often by other people, we are continually receiving signals about how others feel about us from their touch.

In the previous chapter, we discussed the idea that human beings use spatial orientations to communicate various messages. Proxemic behavior in humans tells us a great deal about relationships, attitudes, and feelings. The proxemic phenomenon that we have reserved for this chapter is probably one of the most important and controversial of all nonverbal codes associated with the process of communication. Called **haptics,** it is the study of the type, amount, uses of, and results of tactile behavior. Touch and body contact provide rich and powerful tools for communication and are vital to the survival and normal development of animals and human beings.

Furthermore, touch is important because it is the most effective means to communicate our feelings and emotions. Body contact is a signal of liking and acceptance. The withholding of touch, on the other hand, may communicate an assortment of negative feelings such as resentment, hostility, anger, or distrust. Touching others can help fulfill our need for closeness. Can you imagine having a romantic relationship with someone without the assistance of a good dose of touching?

In their book on interpersonal communication, Adler and Towne (1975) stressed that touch was essential to life itself:

> Besides being the earliest means we have of making contact with others, touching is essential to our healthy development. During the nineteenth and early twentieth centuries many children born every year died of a disease then called "marasmus," which translated from the Greek means "wasting away." In some orphanages the mortality rate was nearly 100 percent, but even children in the most "progressive" homes, hospitals, and other institutions died regularly from the ailment. . . .They hadn't enough touch, and as a result they died. (pp. 225–226)

Other writers have emphasized the extraordinary function of touch in the relationship between parents and children. Even the unconscious feelings of parents are received by children through touch and can sometimes create confusion and conflict. Many experts contend that touch deprivation may eventually lead to a myriad of problems related to communication, such as reduced learning of speech and symbol recognition (Boderman, Freed, & Kinnucan, 1972; Davis, 1978; Despert, 1941; Johnson & Edwards, 1991; Morris, 1971, 1976; Thayer, 1986).

Hall (1966) contends that the study of touch is an integral part of keeping people within the context of their culture. He laments that much of the research "has failed to grasp the significance of touch, particularly active touch. They have not understood 'how important it is to keep the person related to the world in which he (she) lives'" (p. 57). The point Hall was making is important. How we touch, the amount we touch, and what we use touch for are largely a consequence of our culture's norms.

In this chapter, we discuss the impact of touch on the process of communication in several ways. First, we discuss a section on life-span development and touch. Second, we present the functions of touch and touch norms, particularly in our society.

LIFE-SPAN DEVELOPMENT AND TOUCH

Tactile stimulation is a highly necessary form of interaction throughout the life spans of animals and humans. In this section, we discuss the nature of touch during human development. Much of the early research on touch was done with animal populations. It provided considerable insight into the effects of touch on growth and development.

Touch in Animals

We suggested earlier that tactile communication is the primary if not the only means of interaction for many basic forms of animal life. Consider the communication among social insects such as bees and ants, which is highly dependent on touch. Through their antennae, these insects transmit the messages that ensure the smooth operation of their microsocieties. Touch signals in most animal species generally are coupled with chemical signals detected through smell.

Two important tactile phenomena that occur among various species are *gentling* and *licking*. These are kinds of touch adult animals use with their offspring just after birth. **Gentling** behavior is the stroking and touching of animal newborns. **Licking** is used in the animal world to clean the offspring. Licking also plays an important role in stimulating the physiological functions of newborn animals and therefore contributes dramatically to their survival.

Some of the most notable research concerning the effects of touch on animals was conducted by psychologist Harry Harlow and his associates using monkeys (Harlow & Zimmerman, 1958; Harlow, Harlow & Hansen, 1963). Harlow was interested in the bodily contact between mother monkeys and their offspring. Under tightly controlled laboratory conditions, the investigators observed that infant monkeys separated from their mothers grew fond of gauze pads attached to their cages and essentially attached themselves to them. Upon removing the pads, Harlow and his colleagues noticed that the infant monkeys became violent. They also found that infants reared in bare wire-mesh enclosures had considerable difficulty surviving during the first several days after birth.

In a later study, the researchers placed two surrogate mothers in the cages with the infant monkeys. One surrogate mother was made of terry cloth with a light bulb behind the head to give off heat. The second surrogate mother was constructed out of wire-mesh material. The cloth mother "lactated" through a bottle in half the conditions, and the wire mother "lactated" in the other half. The baby monkeys had equal access to both mothers and were allowed to spend any amount of time they wanted with either. The results were somewhat surprising. Even when the wire mother lactated, the infant monkeys preferred the cloth mother. The researchers concluded that the attraction to the cloth mother was due to the tactile comfort she provided. Harlow and his colleagues were surprised to observe that the affection and love stemming from the tactile comfort seemed to far exceed the need for the infant monkeys to nurse. At least in some circumstances, touch may be more important than food.

Human Development

CHILDREN. Just as touch is crucial for animals, it is also important for human growth and development. Knapp and Hall (1992) have commented on the vital role touch plays in human communication:

> Tactile communication is probably the most basic or primitive form of communication. In fact, tactile sensitivity may be the first sensory process to become functional. In fetal life, the child begins to respond to vibrations of mother's pulsating heartbeat, which impinge on the child's entire body and are magnified by the amniotic fluid. . . . In one sense, our first input about what "life" is going to be like comes from the sense of touch. (p. 231)

The implication of these remarks, and those of other experts, is that tactile communication in the early stages of life may establish the foundation of all other forms of communication that humans later develop. As we suggested at the beginning of this chapter, touch in the infant years is necessary for the subsequent development of the abilities to learn speech and recognize symbols.

Around the turn of the century, **marasmus**, the "wasting-away disease" (often referred to today as "failure to thrive") among infants, was determined to be the result of a lack of tactile stimulation. However, it was not until years later that the medical community accepted touch as a treatment. A dramatic illustration of how important touch was to the survival of infants occurred shortly after the end of World War II in Europe. The death rate among babies in orphanages was extremely high, although they were well fed and technically were well cared for. (The babies had received a lot of instrumental touch but little expressive/caring touch because of the large number of infants and few staff persons.) When older women, many of whom were widowed or childless, were hired to hold, rock, and feed the babies, however, the infant death rate dropped to almost zero. Touching, holding, rocking, and caring for the babies literally saved their lives. Additionally, the older women, many of whom had lost their entire families to the war, survived and thrived much better than they had prior to coming to care for the infants.

As infants, we receive more touch from other human beings than at any other time of our lives. Both the frequency of touch and the duration of touch between mothers and their infants are at their peak between the ages of fourteen months and two years. Touch decreases consistently after this period. Although male infants actually receive more touch than females in the first six months, females receive more touch after this time and are encouraged to engage in greater amounts of touch than are their male counterparts. This suggests that as early as the first year of life, parents are socializing their children's tactile behavior to conform to the expectations of adult gender roles. Boys are encouraged to play away from parents; whereas, girls are often rewarded for doing the opposite (Clay, 1966; Glausiusz, 2002; Harrison-Speake & Willis, 1995; Montagu, 1978; Morris, 1976; Nguyen, Heslin & Nguyen, 1975, 1976; Patterson, Powell, & Lenihan, 1986; Thayer, 1986; Willis & Briggs, 1992; Willis & Hofman, 1975).

As the child moves from infancy into later childhood, the frequency with which he or she gives and receives touch appears to decline steadily. Willis and Hofman (1975) found this trend among children from kindergarten to sixth grade. Once adolescence is reached, the amount of physical contact falls to about half that observed in the early elementary grades. These writers note, however, that even adolescents touch each other more frequently than adults do. In short, children experience less touch as they grow older, but they also experience more of it than they will for the rest of their lives. Some writers suggest, however, that adolescence brings with it a latency period during which touch is greatly reduced. Once sex becomes significant, physical contact

One interesting notion about touch sensitivity is that women are more sensitive to touch than are men. The researchers in this study hypothesized that the reason that this is so is because the women generally have smaller fingertips. They first measured the size of the fingertips of 50 men and 50 women. They were all tested on a "tactile grating orientation task." They found that tactile perception (at least in the fingers) improves with the decreasing size of the fingertips. They concluded that their study explains the sex difference because most women have smaller fingertips than do men.

Peters, R. M., Hackeman, E., & Goldreich, D. (2009). Diminutive digits discern delicate details: Fingertip size and the sex differences in tactile space acuity. Journal of Neuroscience, 29, 15756-15761.

increases sharply (Fromme, Jaynes, Taylor, Hanold, Daniell, Rountree, & Fromme, 1989; Johnson & Edwards, 1991; Morris, 1971, 1976; Nguyen, Heslin, & Nguyen, 1975; Pines, 1984; Pisano, Wall, & Foster, 1985; Sigelman & Adams, 1990; Thayer, 1986; Willis & Briggs, 1992; Willis & Hofman, 1975).

ADULTS.   When humans reach adulthood, tactile behavior becomes considerably more restricted. Much of the adult's touch is restricted to greetings and goodbyes. Furthermore, it appears that touching becomes more rule-governed. Most or all societies hold adults accountable for the amount and type of touch they use. As a result, our culture requires that grownups exercise caution in engaging in physical contact with others. It is during adulthood that cultures enforce their touch norms. Violation of these norms can have extensive social consequences (Boderman, Freed, & Kinnucan, 1972; Jones & Yarbrough, 1985; Schutz, 1971; Willis & Hofman, 1975). It is also during this stage that the cultural differences become prominent (Remland, Jones, & Brinkman, 1991; Shuter, 1976). A particular restriction on physical contact, according to many writers on nonverbal communication, is placed on touch between two adult males in our society (Roses, Olson, Borenstein, Martin, & Shores, 1992).

Many more women than men today are involved with the physical care of children and others in their surroundings; they are less likely to have negative feelings about touch. Unlike most men, many women perform touch behaviors such as bathing, drying, powdering, kissing, dressing, undressing, lifting, carrying, combing, grooming, feeding, holding, smoothing, caressing, and comforting on a routine basis. Men who share equally in such touching routines may be less fearful or anxious about touch.

As adolescents move into adulthood, tactile communication gradually gives way to other forms of communication. Because adults may experience a great deal of frustration from lack of physical contact with others, it is common to see them resort to a variety of substitutes. According to Morris (1971), adults often use the services of **licensed touchers** to fulfill the body contact needs that result from decreased adult contact in our society. We hire masseuses and masseurs, barbers, and beauty specialists, and may sometimes even increase our visits to the doctor merely to get a good dose of tactile medicine.

Many American adults are so touch-starved that they may resort to a variety of different forms of substitute touch. Some use substitutes such as dogs or cats. In addition, some of us "suck our thumbs or smoke cigarettes; we drink out of bottles that are the same size as baby bottles, we will hug ourselves when we're in distress . . . attempting to get back some kind of infantile comfort" (Rosenfeld & Civikly, 1976, p. 130). This touch-starved orientation still holds true for our culture.

Substitute touch is how many adults meet their touch needs. Your family's pet may be more important to the daily comfort of the grownups than it is for the pleasure of the children. It is not uncommon for pets originally purchased for a child to become more Mom's or Dad's. Usually it is explained that the child is negligent in caring for the pet, so the adult is forced to step in. One may wonder which came first, the child's negligence or the adult's caring.

As humans grow older, the decline in touch continues. Senior citizens, for the most part, have begun to decrease even the sexual contact that gained full strength during early adulthood. One study investigating touch among senior citizens found that the rules governing touch may be more restrictive at this age than at any other. Results of a study of older persons in senior housing led to the following conclusions: When the elderly are touched, it is far away from the genital area; touch is highly restricted between residents and staff members of the other sex; the initiator of any touch is usually of high status; and residents who are physically impaired received less touch. The researcher noted that extremely impaired males in such institutions are the least touched of all because most staff members are female. One might question whether the impairment presaged the lack of touch, or the reverse. Without a doubt, our senior citizens are the most touch-deprived of any age group in our culture. This acute lack of touch in the later years is a major contributor to seniors' growing feelings of isolation (Watson, 1975; Willis & Hofman, 1975; Harrison-Speake & Willis, 1995).

CATEGORIES OF TOUCH

Morris (1971) distinguished between touching others and touching one's self. He concluded from field observation that there are "457 types of body contact" (p. 92). He also suggests that there are 14 major types of public contact that could occur between two people. He refers to these as *tie signs,* because this contact signals that some type of relationship is present between the two persons. Table 9.1 lists Morris's major categories of touching.

Our touch behavior functions in a variety of ways. Depending on our interpersonal relationships with others, how we touch and the amount we touch serve different functions. The following discussion centers on five categories of touch, each of which serves different functions: *professional-functional, social-polite, friendship-warmth, love-intimacy,* and *sexual-arousal* (Heslin, 1974).

Professional-Functional Touch

We have all experienced being examined by a physician, chiropractor, or dentist, or having a haircut. In such professional interactions, the professional must touch the patient to provide a thorough examination. Often, these encounters involve body contact that in any other situation might appear extremely intimate and inappropriate. However, we generally accept physicians' probing and jabbing as necessary; likewise, hair stylists' handling our head and hair. In situations such as these, touch is used on an impersonal level.

Professional-functional touch is impersonal, business-like touch used to accomplish or perform some task or service. It is not only in medical contexts that professional touch occurs. It may occur when you are trying on shoes, when you visit your hair stylist, or when you are exchanging money with others. Touch is also used in sport. Kneidinger, Maple, and Tross (2001) studied touching among players of college sports during their games and found that females

TABLE 9.1

Morris's Major Categories of Touch

Category	Description
1. The Handshake	The strength of the tie or desired tie between the participants often can be observed by watching the nonshaking hand.
2. The Body Guide	Here, touching is a substitute for pointing. The person guiding the other's body is frequently in charge during the encounter.
3. The Pat	Morris says when adults pat other adults it is often a condescending gesture or a sexual one. The well-known exception is the congratulatory pat (often on the buttocks) following a successful performance in team sports.
4. The Arm-Link	This form of touching may be used for support when one person is infirm, but it is also frequently used to indicate a close relationship. The person in charge, says Morris, is less likely to be the person grasping the other's arm.
5. The Shoulder Embrace	This half embrace is used in romantic relationships as well as to signify buddies in male-male relationships.
6. The Full Embrace	This gesture, sometimes called a hug, frequently occurs during moments of intense emotion, sporting events, romance, greetings, and farewells. It is also used ritualistically to show a relationship closer than a handshake would indicate.
7. The Hand-in-Hand	When adults hold hands with children it is designed for support, to keep the child close, or to protect the child. As adults, hand-holding (because both parties are performing the same act) suggests an equality within the relationship. It is often thought of in opposite-sex relationships, but same-sex hand-holding is not uncommon, particularly in groups.
8. The Waist Embrace	This, according to Morris, is frequently substituted for the full embrace when the participants wish to signal more intimacy than hand-holding or a shoulder embrace yet still remain mobile.
9. The Kiss	The location, pressure, duration, and openness of a kiss help to signal the closeness or desired closeness of a relationship at a particular moment.
10. The Hand-to-Head	Given the highly vulnerable nature of the head area, letting someone touch you on the head shows a trusting and often intimate relationship.

(continued)

TABLE 9.1 (continued)	
Category	Description
11. The Head-to-Head	Two people touching heads renders them incapable of regarding other ongoing activities in a normal manner, so this form of touching is usually thought of as an agreement by both parties to shut out the rest of the world, a condition common to lovers especially.
12. The Caress	This is a signal associated with romantic feelings for one's partner; although, like any signal, it can be used by nonintimates who are trying to deceive others about the depth of their relationship.
13. The Body Support	As children, our parents often support us by carrying, lifting, or letting us sit in their lap. As adults, such support may be sought in playful situations or when one person feels physically helpless.
14. The Mock Attack	These are aggressive-looking behaviors performed in a nonaggressive manner, e.g., arm punches, hair ruffling, pushes, pinches, ear nibbles, etc. We sometimes allow or even encourage such gestures with friends to show the range of behavioral understanding between us. And sometimes these mock-attack touches are substitutes for more loving touches that, in the case of some fathers wishing to show love for their sons, may be too embarrassing.

Adapted from D. Morris (1977), *Manwatching*. New York: Abrams.

touched one another more, males touched more at away games, females touched more at home games, and females performed more touching after negative events. All these situations have in common the fact that the touch is incidental to the purpose of the transaction between you and the other person.

Social-Polite Touch

The type of touch known as **social-polite touch** serves to communicate a limited form of interpersonal involvement. When this form of touch is used, we touch another person as more than a mere object. Rather, our body contact serves to acknowledge the other in a social role, as during a greeting. Social touch, however, follows strict cultural rules. As a result, we find that cultures may differ widely about what is considered proper social touch. In U.S. culture, the handshake is a largely accepted way to acknowledge another person; however, the length of time one holds another person's hand can signal more than politeness. Therefore it is critical that the handshake say only, "Hello, nice to meet you." In other cultures, we see shoulder clasps, kisses on each cheek, and perhaps kisses on the cheek or mouth serving the same function. Social touch is a form of tactile behavior that neutralizes the status differential between two persons.

Friendship-Warmth Touch

Friendship-warmth touch lets another person know that we care for, value, and have an interest in her or him. This form of touch is probably the most difficult to interpret, both for the receiver of the touch and for an outside observer. One reason is that relationships in which friendship touch occurs are often so close as to be confused with intimacy and sexual attraction. Another reason is that this type of touch often is unique to the relationship itself. Interpersonal involvement at this level sees interactants touching for more than professional or social reasons. Here, two people touch one another as people, not objects, and as people who know each other, not as strangers passing in the night.

More cross-cultural variability occurs with friendship touch than any other type. In our culture, for example, touch that signals friendship-warmth is handled with great care. Because we are members of a noncontact-oriented society, we appear to have many unwritten rules that dictate when it is appropriate to use touch in this fashion. In this culture, when close friends are alone together, there is substantially less friendship touch between them than in other cultures. This is because in our culture we tend to associate touching in private with intimacy and sexuality. In an open public area, as with two friends meeting at an airport after months or years apart, this type of touch is more appropriate. Later, when the two are alone, it seems less appropriate. In some other cultures, men touch men much more in public and in private settings than do many North Americans, male or female.

Love-Intimacy Touch

In relationships between intimate lovers and spouses, touch takes on more important characteristics. Love-intimacy touch may include caressing the cheek, holding another person around the waist, hugging, embracing, kissing, and many other gestures that signal a particularly close and involved association between individuals. Intimate touch is highly communicative, expressing caring, love, and emotional and affective attachment. Intimate touch is accompanied by many other nonverbal cues to make sure its intent is clear. We also use love-intimacy touch to satisfy the touch needs of our loved ones, even if we ourselves are inconvenienced in doing so.

Intimate touch can convey some of our most important interpersonal messages. Through this kind of touch we complement and validate our verbal messages that say, "I love you," "You are very special to me," and "You are a very important part of my life." An important point to remember is that intimate touching does not necessarily involve sexual activity. The sex is not what makes two people intimate. This confusion has led many couples to become

Close, very close.

dissatisfied with their special relationships. One of them may not understand that frequent sexual contact does not fulfill the needs of the other.

Sexual-Arousal Touch

As implied above, sexual arousal is often equated with intimate touch. Think about it for a moment. Can you have sexual intercourse with someone without being intimate? How about the prostitute and her or his client? The client may be satisfying an intense personal drive; whereas, the prostitute views the entire experience purely as a business transaction. Furthermore, the prostitute most likely will see the touch involved as professional in nature. We could hardly describe this encounter as loving and intimate. How about another purely sexual phenomenon called the one-night stand? Although it is possible for a one-night stand to involve a temporary form of "instant intimacy," most are strictly pleasurable experiences. The relationship between the participants can barely be described as friendship, much less intimacy. **Sexual-arousal touch** is the most intense form of touch. It may also be the most communicative. Many therapists believe that effective sexual intercourse is the ultimate in communication. We feel that many of these therapists may be correct if they are looking to the ideal (Sloan, 2002).

TOUCH NORMS AND COMMUNICATION

What is normal touch? The answer depends on many factors. Your concept of normal may not be mine, especially if we are not from the same culture, are not approximately the same age, are not of the same gender, and so on. Normal touch is highly individualized, which has made research in this area so difficult.

One of the most widely cited researchers in this area is Sidney Jourard (1966a). In his first study on the touch behavior of humans, he devised a body-accessibility survey and administered it to unmarried American college students. This survey instrument included figures of human beings that were divided into several areas. The subjects were asked to indicate the amount of touch they received from significant others, such as parents and close friends, in each of the body areas, and the extent to which they touched others in those areas. Jourard's investigation revealed, not surprisingly, that the hands, arms, shoulders, back, and head were most frequently involved in touch. Other interesting results included the following: Males in the study touched their mothers less than they were touched by their mothers; people (both male and female) who considered themselves unattractive indicated that they were touched less in all body areas; and Jewish females reported less touch with their boyfriends than did Protestant and Catholic females (Jourard, 1966a, 1966b, 1968, 1971; Jourard & Friedman, 1970; Rosenfeld, Kartus & Ray, 1976).

To ascertain whether the touch norms had changed over the years, a group of researchers conducted a study similar to Jourard's much later (Jones, 1999). They found much the same results concerning touching between subjects and their mothers, fathers, and same-sex friends. However, two major differences in the results of this study did emerge: Males had increased the amount of touch they initiated with female friends in the body areas ranging from chest to knees; and females touched their male friends more frequently about the chest, stomach, and hips. It is speculated that these differences are a reflection of changes in our culture and are reflected in the behavior of young people.

Jones (1999) notes that there can be a blueprint for touching. His research revealed 18 different meanings of touch, which are grouped into seven types: *positive affect (emotion), playfulness, control, ritual, hybrid (mixed), task-related,* and *accidental touches.* Last, he and other researchers have made it clear that there are *nonvulnerable body parts* (NVBP) in our culture. These NVBPs are the hand, arm, shoulder, and upper back. He suggests there are also *vulnerable body parts* (VBP). These VBPs are all other body regions. When in doubt, touch only on the hand, arm, shoulder, and upper back (Richmond, 1997).

Touch norms depend on the type of situation in which interpersonal interactions take place. Touching is likely to be more frequent in some situations than in others. The contexts in which touching is more likely and more frequent include the following:

- Attempting to persuade rather than being persuaded
- Getting "worry" or "concern" messages from others rather than sending them
- Engaging in involved and deep conversation rather than superficial and casual conversation
- Signaling excitement and enthusiasm rather than receiving such messages

- Giving rather than asking for advice
- Giving rather than taking orders
- At social gatherings (as at parties) rather than in professional settings such as the office

If these situational constraints seem normal to you, it is a sign that you have assimilated the norms of the culture around you. If they do not, you may find your touching behavior (or lack of it) communicating something very negative to others (Goldberg & Rosenthal, 1986; Henley, 1973, 1977; Patterson, Powell, & Lenihan, 1986; Pines, 1984).

Cultural Differences

What is considered normal in the amount and type of touch an individual gives or receives depends not only on the situation but also on the culture in which he or she lives. According to Argyle (1975), several types of tactile behaviors are common to western culture. Table 9.2 summarizes the types of touch and the areas of the body usually touched, as shown in Argyle's work.

Studies have shown that body contact is less frequent among North Americans, British, Germans, Finns, and Japanese than among individuals in other cultures. North Americans are often called noncontact oriented. A study

---

TABLE 9.2

Type of Touch

Type	Body Region
Patting	Head, back
Slapping	Bottom, hand, face
Punching	Chest, face
Pinching	Cheek
Stroking	Hair, face, upper body, knee, genitals
Shaking	Hands, shoulders
Kissing	Mouth, cheeks, breast, hand, foot, genitals
Licking	Face, genitals
Holding	Hand, arm, knee, genitals
Guiding	Hand, arm
Embracing	Shoulder, body
Linking	Arms
Laying-on	Hands
Kicking	Legs, bottom
Grooming	Hair, face
Tickling	Almost anywhere

Adapted from M. Argyle (1975). *Bodily Communication*. New York: International Universities Press.

by Jourard (1966a) found that the rates of touch per hour among adults in several cultures differed considerably. His results showed that, while observed in coffee shops, adult couples in San Juan touched 180 times per hour; in Paris, 110 times per hour; in London, 0 times per hour; and in Gainesville, Florida, 2 times per hour.

Although North Americans are not frequent touchers compared to most other cultures, at least one study has shown that we engage in body contact more often than do the Japanese. Barnlund (1975) conducted a study using a similar technique to that used by Jourard. He asked both Americans and Japanese to indicate the amount and frequency of touch they give and receive in various body areas. The results showed that for nearly all areas, Americans touched their partners more.

We stereotypically view macrocultures as either contact or noncontact oriented. One such stereotype is that all Latin Americans touch frequently. Research has shown, however, that even within the culture of Latin America, subcultural differences for touch are evident. Shuter (1976), for example, observed the three Latin American cultures of Panama, Costa Rica, and Colombia. According to this study, the amount of touching and holding behavior decreases the farther south the culture is. Before this research, there were some who argued that there was a worldwide pattern of touch. The belief was that the closer a culture is located to the equator, the more its people touch. Although this was an interesting speculation and many cultures conform to this pattern, the Shuter study indicates that touch patterns are more complex than that.

Gender Differences

In general, if the person touching one is a close friend or lover, then there are usually no "no-go areas." However, touch behavior differs between males and females in our culture. Not surprisingly, women usually are seen as more touch oriented than men. This has been a general and consistent observation (Andersen & Leibowitz, 1978; Larsen & LeRoux, 1984; Fromme, Jaynes, Taylor, Hanold, Daniell, Rountree, & Fromme, 1989; Richmond, 1997). What is more interesting, however, is that the two sexes perceive touch differently. Women discriminate among their body parts in terms of touchability more than men do. Females feel that hand-squeezing is a sign of love and friendliness, and they do not see the squeezing of their chests as playful. Males, on the other hand, are not as concerned about specific parts of their bodies. Males are not as likely to apply specific meaning to specific kinds of touch but are more concerned about the type of touch they receive than about the areas of the body that receive the touch. Women may engage in more self-touching to fulfill their need for touch. Women who marry touch-resistant men will often engage in sexual relations to be held and cuddled. Some conclusions about men, women, and touch follow.

Relationship	Conclusion about Being Touched
Close friend of opposite sex:	Women: all over Men: anywhere between head and just below the knees
Close friend of same sex:	Women: head, neck, arms, hands, upper back Men: back of head, arms, hands, below the knees, upper back
Stranger of the opposite sex:	Women: no part of the body Men: back of head, shoulders, arms, hands, chest, back, upper thighs, knees
Stranger of the same sex:	Women: arms and hands Men: back of head, upper shoulders, upper back, arms, hands

Touch Apprehension

In this section, we review the concept of *touch apprehension*. Andersen and colleagues speak of a similar construct referred to as *touch avoidance*. Much of the touch apprehension review is based on the early works of these investigators (Andersen & Leibowitz, 1978; Andersen & Sull, 1985; Guerrero & Andersen, 1994, 1999).

Do you have some friends who touch you and others constantly, without regard for personal space or touch norms? We shall call this group the *touchers*. The touchers constantly touch and sometimes are told by others, "Stop touching!" Despite the situation or the person, these touchers touch others. They do not seem to be aware of the touch norms of others around them, nor do they seem to realize that their constant touching can be annoying to those they touch.

On the other extreme, do you have some friends who rarely touch and do not appreciate it when others touch them? We shall call this group *the untouchables*. They are very conscious about whom, when, and where they touch or receive touch. Again, it matters little with whom they interact or what the situation is; these people generally avoid touching. They are called **touch avoiders.**

Are you a high toucher or touch apprehensive? Does it depend on the people and situation? Please complete the measure of touch apprehension (Figure 9.1), and you will know how your score categorizes you. Remember this is your perception, not another person's perception of you.

A certain pattern of behaviors is referred to as *touch apprehensive*. When a person seldom or never initiates touch and prefers that others not initiate touch with her or him that person, most likely, is **touch apprehensive.** Research on touch apprehension is sparse. However, what is available shows that males typically are more touch apprehensive than females with members

Directions: Complete the measure based upon how you feel about touching others and being touched. Please indicate the degree to which each statement applies to you by marking in the blank beside the item: (5) Strongly agree; (4) Agree; (3) Are undecided or neutral; (2) Disagree; (1) Strongly disagree.

_____ **1.** I don't mind if I am hugged as a sign of friendship.

_____ **2.** I enjoy touching others.

_____ **3.** I seldom put my arms around others.

_____ **4.** When I see people hugging, it bothers me.

_____ **5.** People should not be uncomfortable about being touched.

_____ **6.** I really like being touched by others.

_____ **7.** I wish I were free to show my emotions by touching others.

_____ **8.** I do not like touching other people.

_____ **9.** I do not like being touched by others.

_____**10.** I find it enjoyable to be touched by others.

_____**11.** I dislike having to hug others.

_____**12.** Hugging and touching should be outlawed.

_____**13.** Touching others is a very important part of my personality.

_____**14.** Being touched by others makes me uncomfortable.

Scoring: **Step 1:** Add responses to the items underlined
Step 2: Add responses to the items *not* underlined
Step 3: Complete the following formula:

TA = 42 + Total of step 1 − Total of step 2

Score should be between 14 and 70
>53 Approach Oriented (Approacher)
<31 Avoidance Oriented (Avoider)

FIGURE 9.1
Touch Apprehension

of the same sex. Females, on the other hand, are more touch apprehensive than males with individuals of the other sex. Religious affiliation and age are also related to touching behavior. Protestants, for example, are more touch-avoidant than non-Protestants. Also, individuals who are older and married tend to be highly avoidant of members of the opposite sex. Approximately 20 percent of the North American population is touch apprehensive.

Individuals who are not touch apprehensive are more likely to initiate touch with other people and are more comfortable when receiving touch from other people. These persons are also more talkative, outgoing, cheerful, social, and less bound by societal norms on touching. Touch avoiders (highly touch-apprehensive) people are more likely to reject touch from others and are less likely to touch others than the normal person. These highly touch-apprehensive persons are likely to be less talkative, more shy, emotionally fragile, and socially withdrawn.

Sorensen and Beatty (1988) had research assistants approach and touch subjects to study the perceptions that these subjects then developed. Using the Touch Avoidance Measure developed by Andersen and Leibowitz (1978) to identify touch avoiders and high touchers, they found that the high toucher consistently rated the research assistants who touched them more positively, and touch avoiders consistently rated them negatively. Sex differences were also found. In general, touch from females was seen as more acceptable than touch from males.

WHAT DOES TOUCH COMMUNICATE?

Touch and Emotion

Tactile communication is an effective means by which we communicate emotion. Immediacy is closely related to touch. As with other immediacy cues, we see more touch occurring between individuals who like one another and a greater amount of avoidance behavior between persons who dislike one another. Touching, like other immediacy cues, tends to increase interpersonal attraction (Richmond, 1997, 2002).

Touch also tends to increase between persons when the situation becomes more emotional. Observations of people in airports found that when it came to greetings and goodbyes, 60 percent of those observed engaged in touch (Knapp, 1978). Other studies have shown that touch enables us to better discriminate among the emotions of others.

A variety of interpersonal attitudes can be communicated through physical contact. Touch can signal sexual interest, affiliation, friendliness, and even negative attitudes such as aggression, disrespect, or disgust. It should be noted, however, that the specific emotional messages communicated may depend to a large extent on the individual. Recall the earlier discussion on gender differences. What may be perceived as playfulness, friendliness, love, or sexuality depends on the gender of the individual as well as the area touched and the kinds of touch (pat, stroke, or squeeze, for example). Generally, however, we tend to associate stroking with love, warmth, and sexual desire; whereas, the pat is usually perceived as playful (Boderman, Freed, & Kinnucan, 1972; Goldberg & Rosenthal, 1986; Henley, 1973, 1977; Johnson & Edwards, 1991; Jones & Yarbrough, 1985; Montagu, 1978; Morris, 1971, 1976; Nguyen, Heslin, & Nguyen, 1975, 1976; Patterson, Powell, & Lenihan, 1986; Pines, 1984; Pisano, Wall, & Foster, 1985; Watson, 1975; Willis & Briggs, 1992; Willis & Hofman, 1975).

Touch and Status

Henley has advanced three general conclusions concerning the literature on touch and status:

1. Individuals have certain expectations about touching and being touched in particular role relationships. For example, individuals expect to touch

subordinates more than they touch superiors, and to be touched more by superiors than by subordinates.

2. Touching depends on the situational context.

3. Touching and dominance are related. Specifically, dominant persons are more likely to initiate touch.

Consistent with Henley's conclusions, it has been observed that people who initiate touch are more likely to be attributed higher status. We would then expect the professor rather than the student and the manager rather than the assembly-line worker to be the initiator of touch (Storrs & Kleinke, 1990).

Touch and Self-Intimacy

Have you ever found yourself in a traumatic situation and realized that you were in some way attempting to comfort or reassure yourself by self-touching? Morris (1971) suggests that these self-intimacy behaviors represent a psychological need whereby people soothe themselves during moments of crisis. These behaviors are quite similar to the self-adaptor behaviors discussed earlier. They generally are most prevalent when we feel nervous, lonely, frightened, or depressed. According to Morris and other writers, self-touching includes shielding actions (covering ears or mouth), cleaning actions (wiping, rubbing, picking, scratching), and self-intimacy (hugging yourself, holding your own hand, masturbating).

Intimate self-touching may indicate a need or wish to be held by someone. Touch is such a strong need of humans. If that need is not satisfied by others, we may be driven to satisfy it ourselves.

EFFECTS OF TOUCH DEPRIVATION

We conclude this chapter by summarizing what we believe may be one of the most acute problems of human beings and their interactions. Throughout this chapter, we have referenced a variety of ways in which physical contact influences communication. The effects of touch deprivation, however, go far beyond social exchange itself. Lack of touch can negatively affect the ability to develop normal speech, reading skills, and symbol recognition; furthermore, many have claimed that touch deprivation in early life can result in a variety of health problems, including skin diseases and allergies.

Skin hunger is a strongly felt need for touch, just as regular hunger is a strongly felt need for food. It results from insufficient body contact for psychological and possibly physical well-being. Touch deprivation can not only lead to psychological problems, but may also negatively influence the ability to withstand stress. Hite (1977) reports the work of Seymour Levine, who studied the effects of three conditions of touch on a sample of newborn rats. In the first condition, the infant rats were allowed physical contact with their mothers. In the second, the rodents were completely deprived of touch. In the third condition, electric shocks were administered to the infant rats. After a period of time had elapsed, the touch-deprived group was found to be weak and suffering from illness. The rats allowed to have physical contact with their mothers, on the other hand, were healthy and vital.

What most surprised Levine was the condition of the rats that had been shocked. They were as lively and healthy as those in the mother-contact group! These findings may suggest a rather startling effect. Could it be that "bad" touch is better for normal biological development than no touch at all? That may be a bit farfetched, but these dramatic results illustrate that touch deprivation certainly is not good.

Glossary of Terminology

Friendship-warmth touch lets another person know that we care for, value, and have an interest in her or him.

Gentling behavior is the stroking and touching of animal newborns.

Haptics is the study of the type, amount, uses of, and the results of tactile behavior.

Licensed touchers are professionals we hire to fulfill the body-contact needs that result from decreased adult contact. They include masseuses and masseurs, barbers, beauty specialists, and even doctors.

Licking is used in the animal world to clean newborn offspring.

Love-intimacy touch is touch that expresses emotional and affective attachment and caring. It is usually a hug, caress, or stroke.

Marasmus is the wasting-away disease among infants that was determined to result from a lack of tactile stimulation.

Professional-functional touch is impersonal, businesslike touch used to accomplish or perform some task or service.

Sexual-arousal touch can be a part of love-intimacy, but it can also be distinct. Sexual-arousal touch can include the use of a person as an object of attraction or lust, or even monetary gain.

Skin hunger is a strongly felt need for touch, just as regular hunger is a strongly felt need for food. It results from insufficient body contact for psychological and possibly physical well-being.

Social-polite touch affirms or acknowledges the other person's identity. This type of touch follows strict cultural codes. In North America, social-polite touch is exemplified by the classic handshake.

Touch apprehensive is when a person seldom or never initiates touch and prefers not to be touched.

Touch avoiders are people who do not like to receive touch or be expected to reciprocate touch in most situations.

Time

Chronemics refers to how we perceive, use, study, structure, interpret, and react to messages of time. Moore, Hickson, and Stacks (2010) say that the study of chronemics is a "significant area of nonverbal communication because we generally perceive our actions and reactions as a time sequence" (p. 284). The North American concern with time is evidenced in everything a person says and does. We have nonverbal elements of time everywhere.

Americans are schedule-driven people. Much of our communication, both verbal and nonverbal, is a result of a time schedule. We can see our scheduling mania in a variety of ways. For example, our schools, classrooms, and businesses are on schedules; it is the rare institution that is not. Our workplaces have schedules. We schedule appointments with others and for ourselves. We eat at a certain time. We sleep at a certain time. We vacation at a certain time. If we miss that time, we miss our vacations because the other time factors have priority. We set priorities based on how much time a person or element in the work environment deserves.

Our oral language clearly makes time an overriding force. Let's look at a few of the things we say on a daily basis that reference time. "Time is running out." "How much longer will this take?" "What time is lunch?" "I don't have time for that." "I will make time for that." "Time got away from me." "Where has the time gone?" "I need more time." "Where did the time go?" "The time was well spent." "I sure wasted a lot of time today." "I wish I had more time." "Can I get the deadline extended?" "You do it this time, and I'll do it the next time." "Time is money." "I simply can't afford the time."

Time has become a part of nonverbal and verbal communication to such an extent that it rules what we do and when we do it. We are subordinates to time (Bloomfield & Felder, 1985; Brophy, 1985; Fine, 1990; Gonzalez & Zimbardo, 1999; Lakein, 1973; Levine, 1989; *Office Hours,* 1999; Potter, 1980; Richmond, 1997).

TIME ORIENTATIONS

Hall (1959) has written that we should examine the kinds of time we have. He states, "As people do quite different things (write books, play, schedule activities, travel, get hungry, sleep, dream, mediate, and perform ceremonies), they unconsciously and sometimes consciously express and participate in different categories of time" (p. 206). This section reviews the three time orientations to which Hall (1959, 1972, 1973, 1976, 1984) refers, *psychological, biological,* and *cultural,* and their impacts on communication.

Psychological Time Orientation

The **psychological time orientation** is how people feel, think, or perceive time and how it influences their daily communication and lives. Individuals and cultures have different orientations in terms of psychological time. Throughout the study of psychological time, three orientations have emerged: *past, present,* and *future.* We discuss each orientation here.

1. *Past-oriented people place high regard on the past, the reliving of past events, and cherishing past happenings.* Their motto could be "Remember the past," or "Use your hindsight." Cultures that have a past-oriented philosophy tend to view new situations in the context of past events. They use the past to shape the present. These societies have respect for older persons and listen to what their seniors have to say regarding the past. The

traditional Chinese culture is very much a past-oriented society. They use the words of the elders to guide them. Native American tribes also place great value on the past and tradition. They exert great effort to transmit the wisdom of the ages to the young. In general, one develops more of a past orientation as one ages, regardless of the general culture in which one lives. It seems that it is normal for people to value the learning they have gained from their own experiences.

2. *Present-oriented people live for today.* Their motto could be "Eat, drink, and be merry, for tomorrow we may die." They live for the present. They work for the present. They go to school for the present. They invest for the present. It is easy to understand why people in some impoverished nations would adopt such an orientation. It makes little sense to ponder the distant future if you are not sure where your next meal is coming from. In cultures with a strong present orientation, seniors may receive less respect than they do in past-oriented societies. In fact, some younger persons say things like, "What do they know? They lived back in the dark ages." Some students feel this way about their teachers. Some children feel this way about their parents. American industry is coming under increasing criticism for its often overly present-oriented organizational culture. Critics claim that too many business decisions are made to enhance immediate profits at the expense of the company's long-term well-being.

3. *Future-oriented people base today's behavior on what they believe will occur in the future.* The future-oriented motto could be "Tomorrow is just around the corner: be prepared." Future-oriented people believe that tomorrow is what we should work and strive toward. For example, they work so that their children can have a better place to live, play, and work. Future-oriented people tend to rely on what they think the future will bring. Many claim that this is the orientation with which most immigrants identified when they came to this country. It represents a save-and-build approach to life, which many cite as the explanation for the country's success.

Differences in time orientation can create many differences in communication. Let's look at a fictitious example of past-, present-, and future-oriented executives trying to decide together how to sell a new product called "Moments." Moments is a fragrance that is supposed to put one's significant other in the mood for love and affection. The discussion might go something like this:

PAST-ORIENTED EXECUTIVE: Let's look at the past advertising campaigns and see what we can use. Perhaps we should talk with Mrs. Gwinn, who was with the company when it started thirty years ago. Some of those old campaigns were real classics. They made the company what it is today.

FUTURE-ORIENTED EXECUTIVE: I don't think we need to confer with Mrs. Gwinn. Let's determine what people will want in the future. The Internet is is the wave of the future. Let's have ads that are similar to the most popular sites. This is the trend of future advertising.

PRESENT-ORIENTED EXECUTIVE: Wait a minute, you two. What we need is something that will sell today. Who cares about next year? If we don't sell Moments now (this moment!), we won't have a job next year! Let's have a current, up-to-date, cool person be our spokesperson. We need someone who is hot to sell our ideas.

With these diverse time orientations, our fictitious executives might never agree, and the product might never be marketed. Because of their different psychological time orientations, they are making completely different assumptions based on different values. They cannot communicate to make good decisions because their differing views of time place their definitions of good decisions in different points in time. People need to be aware of these differences and their impact on communication. The psychological time orientation of a person or a culture can determine the potential success of a communication transaction (Moskowitz, Brown, & Cote, 1997).

Biological Time Orientation

The **biological time orientation** is how people feel and react physically to time and the effects of time on physical well-being. A popular biologically based time orientation is *biorhythms*. These come in three cycles: the *physical cycle, the sensitivity cycle,* and the *intellectual cycle*. Biorhythms vary in length. The physical cycle of an individual averages twenty-three days; the sensitivity cycle averages twenty-eight days; and the intellectual cycle averages about thirty-three days. It is suggested that biorhythms begin at birth and are with us monthly until our deaths. According to biorhythm theory, a person's energy is high in the first half of all three cycles and low in the second half.

During the first phase of the physical cycle, we are at our strongest; our energy is at its height. We can accomplish more in less time. We work hard and feel good about working hard. We can expend a lot of energy and not feel exhausted. During the second phase of the physical cycle, we are at a low. We

---

This study incorporated the relationship between one's perception of time and how one transmits that concept to others. Temporal (time) gestures illustrate past and future as well as such notions as "hurry up." Such gestures are usually co-speech gestures—when we speak and gesture at the same time. The authors discuss what they call transversal temporal gestures "in which time is conceptualized as moving from left to right across the body" (p. 181). Five types of these gestures are analyzed: placing, pointing, duration-marking, bridging, and animating. The authors suggest that these gestures are culture specific.

Cooperrider, K., and Nunez, R. (2009). Across time, across the body: Transversal temporal gestures. Gesture, 9, 181-206.

do not have much energy and spend a lot of time trying to get up the energy to do something.

During the first phase of the sensitivity cycle, we experience positive emotions and have a positive outlook on things. We get along with people better during this phase. During the second phase of the sensitivity cycle, we are less positive, less cheerful, less happy, and have a less-than-positive outlook about others. We may even be grumpy and short-tempered with others. We spend a lot of time bolstering our emotional energies.

During the first phase of the intellectual cycle, we are more alert, attentive, and responsive to information. We process information better, retrieve it better, and apply it better. During the second phase of the intellectual cycle, we are slower at processing information, have difficulty retrieving it, and are less alert and less attentive. We may even have to force ourselves to concentrate. Our mental capacities are at a low ebb. In this phase, we spend time trying to recharge our mental capacities.

Advocates of biorhythm theory suggest that people can have critical days. These critical times are the days on which a cycle shifts. When a person's sensitivity cycle is shifting, he or she may be moody. When a person's intellectual day is shifting, he or she may have difficulty processing information. When a person's physical cycle is shifting, he or she may have less energy or seem tired.

Some people go to great lengths to chart their biorhythms so they can plan their lives to avoid making mistakes on critical days. Although it is a scientific fact that humans do have biological cycles, the evidence that such charting enables a person to plan communication better is less than solid.

We think there is a much more important distinction to be made about biologically based time orientations. This is the difference between people who are biologically more active in the evening and those who are biologically more active in the morning. This difference has been euphemistically called the difference between "owls" and "sparrows."

Our own orientation in this regard is quite easily determined by most of us, in contrast to the difficulty most people have in figuring out their own biorhythms. Additionally, the orientations of our acquaintances can be judged fairly accurately by most of us. This distinction has been the subject of some social scientific research. The self-report measure we use to determine this orientation, measure of time orientations (MTO), is presented in Figure 10.1. Circle your responses to the items on this scale and compute your score, using the instructions. An average score on the MTO is 48. If your score is much higher than 48, you probably exhibit more owl than sparrow tendencies. In contrast, if your score is much lower than 48, you probably exhibit more sparrow than owl tendencies. Owls are at their best in the late afternoon and evening. Sparrows are at their best in the morning. This simple distinction has extensive implications for businesses and schools.

Owls are often punished by the 8-to-5 or 9-to-5 time schedule most of us are expected to follow. Owls have great difficulty functioning in the morning. They are just starting to be truly functional by noon. In other words, they do

Directions: Below are a series of questions concerning your time orientations. Please answer honestly. There are no right or wrong answers. Use the following to determine the time orientation that most closely approximates your feelings.

SA = Strongly Agree
A = Agree
N = Neutral or Undecided
D = Disagree
SD = Strongly Disagree

S	D	N	A	SA	
1	2	3	4	5	**1.** I really dislike getting up in the mornings.
1	2	3	4	5	**2.** I like taking afternoon classes.
1	2	3	4	5	**3.** I prefer morning classes.
1	2	3	4	5	**4.** I am at my worst in the mornings.
1	2	3	4	5	**5.** I really like getting up in the mornings.
1	2	3	4	5	**6.** I dislike taking afternoon classes.
1	2	3	4	5	**7.** I am very irritable in the mornings.
1	2	3	4	5	**8.** I am very alert in the afternoons.
1	2	3	4	5	**9.** I am very irritable in the afternoons.
1	2	3	4	5	**10.** I am very alert in the mornings.
1	2	3	4	5	**11.** I rarely do well on tests in morning classes.
1	2	3	4	5	**12.** I usually do very well on tests in afternoon classes.
1	2	3	4	5	**13.** I usually do very well on tests in morning classes.
1	2	3	4	5	**14.** I rarely do well on tests in afternoon classes.
1	2	3	4	5	**15.** I like to do my studying late at night.
1	2	3	4	5	**16.** I like to do my studying early in the day.

Scoring: **Step 1:** Add the numbers you circled for items 1, 2, 4, 7, 8, 11, 12, and 15. (Your score must be between 8 and 40, or you have made a mistake.)
Step 2: Add the numbers you circled for items 3, 5, 6, 9, 10, 13, 14, and 16. (Again, your score must be between 8 and 40.)
Step 3: Add 48 to your score from Step 1.
Step 4: Subtract your score in Step 2 from your total in Step 3. This is your MTO score. (It must be between 16 and 80, or you have made a mistake.)

FIGURE 10.1
Measure of Time Orientations

not do their best work between 8 and 11 a.m. Owls are the workers who want to work late and the students who like evening classes. Owls try not to do anything important early. They have learned that they do not function well in the morning. This is a biological fact. Even with the help of several cups of coffee, an owl's heart just does not beat strongly until later. What does the dominant time orientation in this culture do to owls? We force them to be in school and at work by 7 or 8 a.m. We force a heavy workload on them in the early hours when their eyes are just beginning to open and their ears are just barely able to recognize sounds. It is no wonder that many owls do poorly in school and have a hard time holding a regular job.

We have had the opportunity to observe and talk with hundreds of owl schoolchildren and employees. The overwhelming majority say that they do much better work in the afternoon. The schoolchildren suggest that their concentration and retention skills improve. They say that they do better on assignments and tests in the afternoon, and they express a preference for their afternoon teachers. They also say that their afternoon teachers like them better. We think this is simply because teachers do not like or respond well to children who sleep or appear to be asleep in class. Owl children often fall asleep in morning classes; if they manage to stay awake, they do not function well. Therefore their morning teachers do not respond to them as well as do their afternoon teachers. By afternoon, the young owls are ready to answer questions and be responsive.

Sparrows, in contrast, do their best work in the mornings. Whereas owls are just waking up in the morning, sparrows are at their peak. Sparrows come into work or school at 6, 7, or 8 a.m., chirping loud and clear, while owls are barely functional. However, sparrow children do not do as well in afternoon as they do in morning classes. They are less attentive, more tired, and do not do as well on tests and assignments in the afternoons. Evening classes are difficult for these sparrows.

As we can see, this can have a broad impact on communication. The owl teacher has difficulty responding to the chirpy sparrow; whereas, the sparrow teacher has difficulty responding to the attentive owl in the afternoon. The owl supervisor has difficulty responding to the chirpy sparrow employee; whereas, the sparrow supervisor has difficulty responding to the attentive owl employee in the afternoon. Our time orientations determine how effective a communicator we can be at various times of the day. Most people have learned to function fairly well between 9 a.m. and 5 p.m. We call these people *sprowls*. They are neither sparrows nor owls. Much of the population fits into this sprowl time category, but at least 20 percent are owls and 20 percent are sparrows. This means that two in five persons is either an owl or a sparrow. Businesses are just starting to recognize the impact of time scheduling. Many corporations are using flextime, which allows the individual employee to establish her or his hours within certain parameters. Organizations doing this have found that production increases and employee morale improves. In other words, owls can work owl shifts, and sparrows can work sparrow shifts, and there are still lots of sprowls to hold down the fort. Many of our schools are attempting to let children enroll in classes that correlate with their body times. This should improve student production and teacher morale. College students have the advantage in that they can generally, after their first year, choose a schedule that fits their biological time orientation.

Our biological time orientation influences our communication with others. It affects how we perceive others and how they perceive us. If we are aware of when we function best, we can make modifications in our schedule to capitalize on those times. We may also make strategic choices of when to talk with others if we can figure out their biological time orientations. It is the wise student who avoids asking owl parents for money at the breakfast table.

Biological influences on time orientations not only affect people on a day-to-day basis but can also determine how people react to the various times of the year. Persons with **seasonal affective disorder** (SAD) often do better in the spring, summer, and fall but do not cope well or respond well to the dark, longer months of winter because of the shorter days and lack of daylight time. They do their best work when days are longer and lighter (Howard, 2002/2003).

Cultural Time Orientation

Cultural time orientation deals with how cultures perceive and use time. Understanding the time orientations of various cultures is not an easy task. Hall (1959) suggested there are three different cultural time systems: *technical, formal,* and *informal time.* We address the first two now and the third later.

Technical time has the least correlation with interpersonal communication. It refers to precise, scientific measurements of time counted in precise, logical sequences. An example of technical time is the means of tracking time used by NASA. Technical time is a very ordered, scientific method of keeping time. It is noninterpersonal and nonemotional.

Formal time is the way in which a culture keeps track of time. For example, we keep track of days, months, years, and so on. This is not scientific like technical time, but it is somewhat precise in that cultures have traditional means of keeping track of time. Farmers use formal time when planting crops and go by the seasons. People who live near the beach might go by the tide time. Therefore each culture has a means of tracking time, and because cultures vary so much, their use of time varies.

Hall identified seven components that distinguish formal time from other types. He suggested that the way one uses *ordering, cycling, valuation, tangibility, synthesisity, duration,* and *depth* all contribute to distinguishing formal time.

Ordering deals with the nature of time as fixed concerning the ordering of events. For example, "a week is a week not only because it has seven days but because they are in a fixed order" (Hall, 1973, p. 145). Hall notes that ordering of events can vary from culture to culture. Therefore communication about the ordering of events can lead to some misunderstandings. For example, some people say that Monday is the first day of the week; others say that Sunday is. Still others claim that it is Saturday.

Cycling focuses on the North American need to have time flowing in cycles. We group days into weeks, months, years, and so on. These units of time are cyclical; they are limited, and eventually the cycle starts over. Some other cultures do not believe in cycling. For example, Pueblo Indians are taught that things occur only when the time is right, so they wait until the time is right. They do not do things on a cyclical basis. While the Pueblo understand when the time is right, visitors can rarely understand why this is so.

People in the United States place great emphasis on the next three components: *valuation, tangibility,* and *synthesisity* of time. *Valuation* is the value the culture places on time. *Tangibility* is the culture's consideration of time as a commodity. *Synthesisity* is the culture's desire or need to synthesize or add up time. For example, sixty minutes make an hour, twenty-four hours make a day, and so on. Hall suggests that U.S. culture places great value on time and how it is used and spent. We also consider time a valuable commodity that should be used wisely. Lastly, we synthesize time and use time to decide how we synthesize other elements in our culture. Hall wrote, "We are driven by our own way of looking at things to synthesize almost everything" (p. 147). Therefore we have great difficulty communicating with people who don't place the same value on time as we do. We have great difficulty communicating with people who do not feel that time is a commodity and do not synthesize time and events the way we do. We often have misunderstandings about time and synthesis because of our inability to adapt to others.

Duration is usually measured by a clock in this culture. Duration may be relevant in other cultures, and it may not. For example, the European tradition says that time is something that occurs between two points. The Hopi defines *duration* as follows: It is what happens when the corn matures or a sheep grows up, a characteristic sequence of events (Hall, 1973, p. 146). In other words, the duration of length of time is considered differently by different cultures. Small children certainly have different meanings for duration from adults in any culture.

Last, Hall reviews the *depth* of time. He suggests that depth is when the present emerges from some past. Even people in the United States feel that the present is heavily influenced by the past. Every time we have a presidential election, politicians and pollsters draw on the past to predict the outcome. Stockbrokers try to predict future financial trends based on past trends. Sports fans try to predict outcomes of present and future games based on past games. In most cases these predictions based on past events are less than perfect predictors of what happens later.

To sum up, components of formal time determine how we use and perceive formal time. They also determine how we communicate with others around us. We cannot assume that others around us place the same value on time that we do. If we often presume this, we may find that it is not so. We must also remember that children usually do not have a good grasp of the aspects of formal time in their culture until they are about twelve years old. By the age of twelve, they usually develop or are developing the norms of their culture concerning time.

Now we turn to the third time system found in cultures: **Informal time** is the most difficult cultural time orientation to understand and learn to use. This type of time can vary greatly from culture to culture. It is the casual time employed by a culture. It is often unconscious and determined by the situation or context in which it is used. For example, when we say, "we will arrive in a minute," we might mean "in a while" or "in a little bit." These informal, unwritten time orientations are the most difficult for people, particularly children, to learn and understand. There is no precision or logic to them. To a person from another culture, when we say "in a minute," it could mean in a day. Take a few moments and list many of the informal casual time statements that you have used or heard others use.

Eight levels of duration exist in our informal time system. They are *immediate, very short, short, neutral, long, very long, terribly long,* and *forever.* Exactly how can we communicate these durations precisely? A supervisor communicated with her secretary on several different occasions that she needed a letter sent as soon as possible. The secretary who performed this duty knew precisely what the supervisor meant because they had worked together for five years. Immediately meant "yesterday" to this supervisor. Immediately to others could mean "in a while," "shortly," or "tomorrow."

The term *forever* has a very imprecise meaning. When students say, "I thought that class would never end. I felt like I was in there forever," what do they mean? Terribly long? Or terribly boring? Probably both. Their way of expressing it was by saying "forever." What does the phrase "I'll love you forever" mean? To some people, it means "until death do us part." To others, it means "for tonight!" Our use of informal time is not only confusing to us in this culture but also confuses others outside the culture. We need to remember that informal time is also very confusing for small children, so we need to have patience in dealing with others who do not understand our use of this concept.

Punctuality

Punctuality (or the lack of punctuality) has long created communication problems in our culture. When we say we want someone to be punctual, we mean on time if not a little before. Punctuality is not a form of informal time, but it is often used in the informal sense. People seem confused about what *punctual* means. Little children do not understand the importance of being on time or punctual. After they are late several times and told by adults to start being on time or punctual, they learn what punctual is. Watch small children as they leave home to go to school or are on their way home from school. Most of them meander along without a care in the world. Their mothers or fathers are at home anxiously waiting for them to arrive. The child is late, and the mother cannot understand why. Time has little meaning for small children. By age six, most American children know the days of the week. If they do not know them by six, they will learn when they enter school. By age eight, children usually can tell time by a watch or clock and have learned the seasons and what they mean. All of you can probably remember when you were small and your parents or brothers or sisters helped you get ready for school. One of the biggest concerns was that you would be late. They probably said things like, "Hurry up and eat"; "Don't miss the school bus"; "Please hurry—teachers don't like it when you're late." This is how the idea of punctuality is learned.

Hall suggests that there are two ways of viewing punctuality: as a "displaced point pattern" and as a "diffused point pattern." The point is the time a person expects others to arrive for a social event. Presume the point here is 8 p.m. People who view time as "displaced" will arrive before the appointed time. In other words, they will arrive between 7:30 and 7:57, with the majority arriving about 7:55. People who view time as "diffused" will arrive between 7:55 and 8:15. These people do not consider time to be as fixed as do the others, so they arrive in a somewhat diffused pattern. This can be disconcerting for people who expect others to arrive "on time." Sometimes, to arrive past the appointed time can be perceived as an insult or lack of respect. Variables that influence people's use of the time point are the type of social occasion, what food or drink is being served, the status of the individuals involved, and the individual's personal way of handling time. It is the rare person who would arrive late for a meeting with the president of the United States. However, the president might arrive late and no one would think much about it.

Trying to beat the informal time rules can lead people into mistakes that are somewhat amusing, although not immediately so. The authors of this book were once invited to what was announced as a two-hour, get-acquainted social gathering. They did not want to be the first to arrive, so they intentionally set out to be late, assuming that they would miss the formal aspects of the gathering but could talk with friends on their arrival. Approximately two hundred people were invited, so they knew they would probably not stand out if they arrived thirty minutes after the appointed hour. When they arrived thirty minutes late, no one appeared surprised or upset. However, they quickly learned that they had missed the cocktails, shrimp, lobster, and crab hors d'oeuvres. But they were there "on time" to listen to the thirty-minute welcoming speech.

People make judgments about one another based on their use of time and punctuality. For most Americans, it is almost unforgivable to be more than fifteen minutes late for any appointment without a good excuse. Many teachers respond to this. If the student's excuse for being late was not a life-threatening issue, the teacher will be uncompromising about allowing the student to make up work. Businesses often deduct money from an employee's paycheck for lateness or tardiness. To be perceived in a positive manner in this culture, one must always be on time, if not a little early (Bloomfield & Felder, 1985; Brophy, 1985; Fine, 1990; Lakein, 1973; Levine, 1989; Richmond, 1997).

Monochronic and Polychronic Time

Even if we are on time, there are two aspects of informal time that characterize how we use our time. Hall and Hall (1990) refer to these aspects as *monochronic time* and *polychronic time*. **Monochronic time** (M-time) is the norm in our culture. M-time emphasizes the scheduling of activities one at a time, the segmentation of work, and the promptness of work. Monochronic time means doing one thing at one time. Therefore, people in the general U.S. culture believe that things should have order, scheduling, and organization so that one thing is being worked on at a time. There is little room for flexibility.

Polychronic time (P-time) is the norm for many Latin American cultures. P-time emphasizes the involvement of many people and is less rigid about the ordering of events and scheduling. People functioning on P-time believe in handling several transactions at once. In parts of Latin America, it is usual to find several business meetings taking place simultaneously in the same room with many people involved. The person in charge is often walking from group to group and transacting business.

In our culture today, many people are beginning to engage in what has come to be called *multitasking*. This has arisen out of use of personal computers that allow numerous connections to be "open" at the same time. Young people who have grown up with this technology appear to have little difficulty transferring this capability in their use of computers to other facets of their lives—they can operate in the polychronic world. Older people in this culture, however, have great difficulty even coping with the multitasking on the computer, much less transferring it to other parts of their lives. Once a person is acculturated to be monochronic or polychronic, it is difficult to adjust to the other orientation. Also, one tends to become quite intolerant of the behavior of people from the "other" culture.

This difference in time orientations can create some serious communication problems. American business executives are insulted when they are expected to meet with several other groups simultaneously in the same room to transact business. They find the situation confusing, irritating, and insulting. Latinos, or Latin Americans, find monochronic business practices too rigid. They cannot understand the one-meeting, one-time, one-room mentality of the U.S. business executive. They like to involve lots of people. Some Arab cultures have similar time norms for business meetings. Often North Americans, Arabs, and Latin Americans have very unsettling and stressful business transactions because of the differing time orientations.

Clearly time talks, as Hall suggested. In fact, it talks so loudly that people misperceive others because of their differing uses of time. We expect others to conform to our time ideals. Often they do not. We must learn to understand the time orientations of others around us to become more effective communicators.

EFFECTS OF THE USE OF TIME

It is clear from the above discussions that time can influence our communication and perception of others. How we use time, or let it use us, determines numerous things.

First, time communicates our status to others. Higher-status persons are granted more time deviancies. They can be early or late for functions; whereas, the rest of us cannot. For example, teachers can make students wait for them, but students do not have the luxury of being late to class.

Second, time expresses liking. Studies reveal that the amount of time we spend with a person is an indication of the amount of liking we have for that person. Of course, this is referring to time we choose to spend, not time we are assigned to spend with them. People can tell from the time we give them how we feel about them. If we consistently tell someone, "I have only a few minutes," they eventually will get the message. Parents must be careful not to do this with children. Children need to know that they are important enough to warrant time with the parent.

Third, studies suggest that time may be an important variable, although not the only one, in the physician-patient relationship. The amount of time a physician spends with a patient is related to the patient's willingness to continue the physician-patient relationship. The amount of time the patient is given to talk to the physician may determine the patient's feeling about whether the physician is concerned or cares about him or her. The actual amount of time in an interaction is less relevant than whether the patient feels that the amount of time taken is enough. Being rushed in and out of the physician's office will probably lead to the perception that the physician did not spend enough time. Improving physicians' encoding and decoding of nonverbal behavior is critical to an effective physician-patient relationship. Time is one variable that can be used to improve that relationship.

Fourth, the use of time communicates our cultural orientations. It is easy to tell the cultural upbringing of others by their use of time and how they value time. We can also learn to understand others if we learn more about their time orientations.

Fifth, time communicates our personality and background orientations. For example, Perry, Kane, Bernesser, and Spicker (1990) and Cinelli and Ziegler (1990) found some interesting results concerning type A and B personalities. The student with a type A personality (aggressive, impatient, hostile, achievement-oriented, and time-urgent) was more likely to cheat on an exam than the student with a type B personality. In addition, type A students were more likely to have more daily problems than type B students. It seems that type B people are time-conscious but not time-driven; whereas, type A people are time-driven and often drive others, too.

Sixth, Levine (1989) found that the 36 fastest-paced cities also reported the highest rates of heart disease. Levine defined pace based on the walking speed of pedestrians; how long it took bank tellers to give change; how long it took postal clerks to explain the differences among regular mail, certified mail, and insured mail; and whether people wore watches. The following cities (presented from 1 to 36) had faster speeds, more watches worn, and higher coronary heart-disease rates: Boston, MA; Buffalo, NY; New York, NY; Salt Lake City, UT; Columbus, OH; Worcester, MA; Providence, RI; Springfield, MA; Rochester, NY; Kansas City, MO; St. Louis, MO; Houston, TX; Paterson, NJ; Bakersfield, CA; Atlanta, GA; Detroit, MI; Youngstown, OH; Indianapolis, IN; Chicago, IL; Philadelphia, PA; Louisville, KY; Canton, OH; Knoxville, TN; San Francisco, CA; Chattanooga, TN; Dallas, TX; Oxnard, CA; Nashville, TN; San Diego, CA; East Lansing, MI; Fresno, CA; Memphis, TN; San Jose, CA; Shreveport, LA;

Eventually time runs out for all of us.

Sacramento, CA; and Los Angeles, CA. Of course, many of these cities have several things in common: major highway and freeway systems, large and diverse populations, major businesses, major mass-transit systems, and stimulus overload on a daily basis.

Last, we can teach and learn timing. This can help us to become better communicators. When is it a good time to ask for a day off from work? Get to know your boss's time orientation, and decide what is the best time of the day to ask. Timing is a most critical component of the communication process. If you don't know how to time your communication, you might be perceived as an ineffective communicator.

Glossary of Terminology

Biological time orientation is how people feel and react physically to time and the effects of time on physical well-being.

Chronemics is the study of how a culture perceives, uses, studies, structures, interprets, and reacts to messages of time.

Cultural time orientation refers to the ways in which different cultures perceive and use time.

Formal time is the way in which a culture keeps track of time.

Informal time is the most difficult cultural time orientation to understand and learn; it varies greatly from culture to culture. It is the casual time employed by a culture. It is often unconscious and determined by the situation or context in which it is used.

Monochronic time (M-time) is the norm in the North American culture.

M-time emphasizes the scheduling of activities one at a time, the segmentation of work, and the promptness of work.

Polychronic time (P-time) is the norm for many Latin American cultures. P-time emphasizes the involvement of many people and is less rigid about the ordering of events and scheduling. People functioning on P-time believe in handling several transactions at once.

Psychological time orientation is how people feel, think, or perceive time and how it affects their daily communication and lives. Both individuals and cultures vary concerning psychological time orientations.

Seasonal affective disorder (SAD) is a negative psychological reaction to short days and lack of sunlight.

Technical time refers to precise, scientific measurements of time. It has the least correlation with interpersonal communication.

CHAPTER 11

Female-Male Nonverbal Communication

From a nonverbal perspective, the communication that females and males share with same- and opposite-sex friends has a wealth of information for both researchers and practitioners. "The ways that males and females characteristically use nonverbal cues helps them develop their distinct gendered identities (Gamble & Gamble, 2003, p. 96).

Two children, both four years old, are walking down a street. Both are about the same height, both are wearing similar clothing, and each has the same length hair. Their faces are not visible, only their backs. Child A moves with a swagger down the street, with arms swinging, and takes long strides. Child B sways down the street, with the whole body engaging in one smooth, swaying motion. Can you tell the sex of each child? If you said child A is male and child B is female, you are tuned in to common differences in the nonverbal walking behavior of most males and females. As early as age three or even sooner, there are distinct nonverbal differences in the behavior of males and females. Males tend to exhibit a typical male walk, and females tend to exhibit a typical female walk, as in the four-year-olds described here.

Males and females differ with regard to these and many other nonverbal behaviors. Given that such differences occur, our concern in this chapter is threefold. First, what is the difference between sex and gender? Second, how do males and females develop different nonverbal behaviors? Third, how do these different behaviors affect communication?

DEFINITION ISSUES: SEX AND GENDER

Sex is the biological and genetic difference between girls and boys, men and women. In other words, this is the biological sex we are born with. Anatomically, sex is expressed in the distinct sexual organs of men and women (Bate & Bowker, 1997; Bem, 1974; Canary & Dindia, 1998; Eakins & Eakins, 1978; Gamble & Gamble, 2003; Hall, 1984; Hickson & Stacks, 1993; Knapp & Hall, 1992; LaFrance & Mayo, 1978; McCroskey & Richmond, 1996; Tannen, 1994).

Gender is the psychological, social, and cultural manifestations of what people perceive to be the appropriate behaviors of females and males. These manifestations may or may not be representative of a person's biological sex. In other words, not all men exhibit the stereotypical cues of the masculine man. Not all women exhibit the stereotypical cues of the feminine woman. Some men will have a feminine or responsive side, and some women will have a masculine or assertive side (Bate & Bowker, 1997; Bem, 1974; Canary & Dindia, 1998; Eakins & Eakins, 1978; Gamble & Gamble, 2003; Hall, 1984; Hickson & Stacks, 1993; Knapp & Hall, 1992; LaFrance & Mayo, 1978; McCroskey & Richmond, 1996; Tannen, 1994). Therefore this chapter focuses on the nonverbal—possibly biological—sex differences between females and males. It also examines the nonverbal gender differences between feminine and masculine behaviors.

DEVELOPMENT OF NONVERBAL BEHAVIOR IN FEMALES AND MALES

Research suggests three theoretical explanations for why males and females generally develop different nonverbal behaviors (Bate & Bowker, 1997; Birdwhistell, 1970; Canary & Dindia; 1998; Eakins & Eakins, 1978; Gamble & Gamble, 2003; Henley, 1977; Kalbfleisch & Cody, 1995; Mehrabian, 1971, 1972). The causal factors are believed to be *genetics,* modeling of older males and females, and *conditioning* or *reinforcement* provided for certain behaviors within a given culture.

GENETICS. Some scholars suggest that genetics plays no role in the development of differing male and female nonverbal behavior, but we disagree. Biological research has shown that males and females inherit different bone structures and body types. It is even possible to identify the sex of a person whose skeleton has been buried for hundreds of years. These skeletal differences are critical in the performance of some nonverbal behaviors. Inherited traits such as body type and structure usually cannot be significantly altered. They tend to determine our walk, gestures, and posture and can influence other nonverbal behaviors such as our smile. The shape of our bodies determines many of our nonverbal behaviors. For example, the average woman typically has larger breasts than the average man. This influences a woman's posture. A man usually has a larger shoulder span than a woman. This is a contributing factor in determining the man's posture. Genetics provides a full explanation for some differential development of nonverbal behavior in males and females. This fact, of course, does not deny the existence of other causal factors.

MODELING. If you ask parents how their children develop nonverbal behavior, many will give the explanation of *modeling*. We learn many of our behaviors by observing others and imitating their behavior. This is modeling. Children are very careful observers of their parents, siblings, teachers, and peers. Little boys and girls learn how to act like "big" boys and girls by observing others in their environment and modeling their behaviors. A little girl may try to model her mother, and a little boy may try to be like his dad.

This modeling explanation of differences in nonverbal behavior of females and males suggests that children observe the behavior of others and attempt to emulate it. This theory certainly helps to explain why children in one culture grow up with behavior typical of the adults in that culture; whereas, children in another culture grow up with different behavior typical of their culture. This also explains, at least in part, why females and males differ in their nonverbal behavior within a single culture. Research has not confirmed that modeling is the primary reason for the development of female and male nonverbal behavior. However, it is probable that modeling makes a significant contribution.

REINFORCEMENT OR CONDITIONING. Another popular explanation for the development of different nonverbal behavior by males and females is *reinforcement* or *conditioning*. The basic premise of reinforcement theory is that behavior that is reinforced or conditioned will increase, but behavior that is not reinforced will decrease. If a role model reinforces a child for walking like a man or woman or for wearing clothing suitable for his or her sex, the child is likely to continue the behavior. If a child is not reinforced for the walk or clothing, the behavior might not continue. The culture in which we live reinforces or punishes children for appropriate or inappropriate behavior. Little boys often are punished for playing with dolls, but little girls usually are not. Little girls often are punished for playing with trucks, but little boys usually are not.

Although reinforcement plays a large role in the development of nonverbal behavior of females and males, it is not the definitive explanation. As much as many people wish it were otherwise, there is no single definitive explanation for these differences. All three explanations outlined above—genetics, modeling, and reinforcement or conditioning—are credible explanations, and no one explanation precludes the validity of the others. Most likely these factors all contribute to the development of nonverbal behavior of females and males. The degree to which each contributes is unknown and, for the present at least, unknowable.

DISTINCTIVE AND SIMILAR CHARACTERISTICS: THE DILEMMA

Simply to distinguish female nonverbal behavior from male nonverbal behavior is no easy task. One must first look at the characteristics of females and males that determine why each sex employs certain nonverbal behavior.

Many writers believe that we must understand the different gender-role expectations that cultures have for men and women before we can understand their different nonverbal behaviors. Such role expectations are primarily a function of culture, and as such can change only as a culture changes. Writers describing U.S. culture say that expectations for women in the United States are characterized by *reactivity;* whereas, expectations for men are characterized by *proactivity.* This means that women in our culture are expected to be sensitive, responsive to others, emotionally expressive, and supportive. In contrast, men are expected to be assertive, independent, self-assured, confident, and decisive.

Mehrabian (1981) suggests that the male in this culture is expected to have a dominant social style; whereas, the female is expected to have a submissive social style. He concludes that women generally have more pleasant, less dominating, and more affiliative social styles than men. Males are more aggressive and dominant in their social styles. In a similar vein, Henley (1977) and Eakins and Eakins (1978) suggest that nonverbal behaviors differ between women and men because men in this culture generally have been in superior positions and women have been in subordinate positions. Society expects subordinates (women) to behave submissively (to perform the subordinate role) and supervisors (males) to behave in a dominant manner (to perform the superior or assertive role). Other writers are quick to note that the study of how sex differences might affect the way that people communicate presents a difficult research undertaking (Canary & Dindia, 1998). They note that many authors suggest that the differences between men and women are not as strong or definite as once thought (Canary & Dindia, 1998). We hasten to note that we are not advocating the desirability of such stereotypical gender-role identifications (after all, the senior author of this book is female). Rather, we are

It is not unusual for men and women to display different seating behaviors.

Source: Photo by C. Price Walt

presenting this information in the hope of identifying where these stereotypes come from. Many people, both female and male, may wish that such stereotypical norms would just go away, but they will do so only if the culture changes sufficiently to make such stereotypical behavior dysfunctional in everyday life. That has yet to happen.

The distinctive differences between male and female communication behavior seem to be based on what are deemed the appropriate societal roles of women and men. Men tend to be more assertive and women to be more responsive. Years ago, Bernard (1968) said: "Women are expected to stroke others and give reassuring smiles and silent applause." Currently, there is still, whether we like it or not, a strong cultural, societal bias for women to be the supportive persons and men to be the assertive persons in this culture. Therefore the stereotypical gender roles (assertive or responsive) may explain the gender differences in nonverbal behavior. The remainder of this chapter reviews the differences in nonverbal behavior of men and women that result from these culturally defined assertive and responsive functions.

Appearance and Attractiveness

In this society, the person who is perceived to be physically attractive and has an attractive appearance is more highly rated than one who is not attractive, despite the sex of the person. This society does not value unattractiveness. Although beauty is in the eye of the beholder, there are still several conclusions that can be drawn from the research on general attractiveness of females and males (Widgery & Webster, 1969). As said earlier, attractive people are perceived by others as more sociable, more outgoing, more likeable, more intelligent, and happier. Less attractive people, on the other hand, are perceived as less sociable, less extroverted, less likeable, less intelligent, and not very happy.

Culturally, females may have to meet higher attractiveness standards to be perceived as credible than do males. Eakins and Eakins (1978) found significant differences as a function of attractiveness of males and females presenting a well-reasoned talk. They had two women and two men give persuasive speeches about the merits of debate. Each gave her or his speech twice. Once, the speaker was made to appear attractive; the next time, the speaker was made to appear unattractive. Clothing was held constant. The talks were set up as follows: The first speech favoring debate was cogent and well reasoned; the first speech opposing debate was poorly reasoned and dogmatic; the second "pro" debate speech was poorly reasoned and dogmatic; and the second "con" debate speech was cogent and well reasoned. The raters were college students who had already completed a pretest on their attitudes on the speakers and would complete the posttest on the speakers.

The results revealed that differences in the attractiveness of each speaker did affect the receivers' acceptance of the speaker's arguments. The results further revealed the following:

> Both speakers of the well-reasoned talks had a greater persuasive effect when made up in their attractive state, as was anticipated. An interesting result was a difference in persuasiveness that occurred between the females and males in their unattractive states, whether they gave the poorly reasoned or well-reasoned talk. The males made up unattractively were only slightly less effective than in their attractive state. However, there was considerable difference in the influence of the females, depending on physical state. Unattractiveness in the female caused a decidedly more negative reception of her views. In fact, in one of the videotaped versions, the unattractiveness of the female who delivered the cogent pro talk weighed so heavily that the attractive female who answered with the poorly reasoned and ill-constructed con speech had the greater impact on the listeners. Both

females and males seemed more accepting of arguments or views from an unattractive male than from an unattractive female. Males were most negative toward the unattractive female's stand. (Eakins & Eakins, 1978, p. 166)

Notice that unattractiveness did have a negative impact on male speakers. The difference between male and female speakers was one of degree: both were hindered by unattractiveness, but the female more so. In other research, which involved ratings of the credibility of individuals based on their photos alone, it was found that despite the gender of a speaker, attractive people are rated higher on the character dimension of credibility than unattractive people. Although the research in this arena is still sparse and does not permit precise conclusions, in their classic study, Eakins and Eakins suggest that "the views of unattractively made-up males were accepted more readily than those of unattractively made-up females" (p. 167). Are such judgments still being made today? The answer is a definitive *yes*. Not only are women judged more harshly by society (by both women and men), but the first conversational observation about a female might concern her appearance or dress, not her competence. Again, this orientation that women have to be attractive to be acceptable or credible is alive and well. Yet interestingly, an overly attractive woman may suffer even more than an unattractive woman at the hands of society. For example, the overly attractive woman may be perceived by both women and men as a "sexual object" rather than a "credible human being." For women, then, there is a constant nonverbal dilemma of "what to wear, how to look, and what does appearance communicate to others." It is then safe to conclude that regardless of sex, one should always try to present a good first impression, but even more so if one is female. The culture has not changed much in this regard over the last forty years.

Clothing styles change quickly, often before any conclusions can be drawn about how one particular style affects communication, but it is safe to conclude that one should dress for the occasion. If the occasion demands a business suit, then wear whatever is appropriate for your sex. If the occasion demands formal wear, then wear what your sex is expected to wear. If one chooses not to follow the norms on dress for one's sex, one can expect to encounter ridicule and even expulsion from certain groups. To be perceived as credible and sociable, one must wear the cultural garb expected for one's sex role.

Gesture and Movement

As early as preschool, small children exhibit the body movements and gestures of their biological sex. In preschool, little girls have more pronounced body movements when paired with little girls than when paired with little boys. When with little boys, they tend to act shy and to be more reserved in their movements. Gender differences in behavior are evident in preschool children. Children exhibit the behavior expected of young men and young women early (Birdwhistell, 1970).

In the classic writings of Birdwhistell (1970), some of his studies of young children concluded that sex-role differentiation begins at a very early age. He cites the following example:

> One female infant . . . by the age of 15 months had learned portions of the diakinesic system . . . of the Southern upper-middle-class female. She had already incorporated the anterior roll of the pelvis and the intra femoral contact stance which contrasts sharply with the spread-legged and posteriorly rolled pelvis of the 22-month-old boy filmed with her. (p. 49)

Males tend to use more dominant or commanding gestures and movements when communicating with females. Similarly, as compared to their male partners, females tend to use more compliant or acquiescent gestures. The results of several studies reveal that females may be predisposed to do the following when communicating with males: take up less space, shrink or pull in their bodies, tilt their heads while talking or listening, arrange or play with their hair more often than males, put hands in lap or on hips, tap hands, cross legs, cross ankles, yield space, lower eyes, blink more, and keep legs and feet together while sitting. Males may be predisposed to do the following when communicating with females: stare more, point, take up more space, keep head straight, stretch hands, stand with legs apart, or sit with legs stretched out with ankles apart, knees spread while sitting, stroke chin more, use larger and more sweeping gestures, more leg and foot movement, and hold arms away from body more.

In female-male interaction there is a greater display of dominant gestures by males and a greater display of acquiescing gestures by females. These behavioral patterns do not seem to be simply each sex's reaction to the other, because these same patterns are seen in both sexes while interacting with another member of their own sex, but on somewhat a less extreme scale. This observed pattern in male and female gesture and movement is probably due in part to genetic tendencies and in large part to the role each sex plays in society, cultural stereotypes, and perceptions of what is appropriate for males and females. Essentially, members of each sex are predisposed toward and learn the appropriate survival skills for the culture in which they live.

Face and Eye Behavior

Men tend to mask or hide their emotions more than women. It seems that our culture allows the female to be facially expressive but punishes the male for the same behavior. In one study, males and females were shown slides deliberately selected to arouse emotions and strong facial expressions. Included among the slides were images of burn victims, happy children, scenic views, and sexual displays. The study's coders watched the subject's facial expressions and then judged the emotion displayed. Coders found it much easier to code the accurate emotion based on the women's facial expressions. The men seemed to internalize or hide their emotions. In other words, they did not display their emotions on their faces. Researchers suggest that this is because our culture tells boys that it is not appropriate for them to cry or show emotion in public (Buck, Miller, & Caul, 1974). Therefore males learn to internalize their emotional responses; whereas, females remain free to externalize their emotions through facial expressions.

Most of us have heard the song lyrics, "When you're smilin' . . . the whole world smiles with you" (Louis Armstrong, "When You're Smiling"). Well, this is partially true. Women have learned that in this culture they should smile whether they are happy or not. Research suggests that women smile more often than men in general, although both genders smile more when seeking approval. Women smile more than men when a woman and a man greet each other and when the two interactants are moderately acquainted. Women smile and laugh more than men, and women smile to mask or hide anxiety or nervousness. Research also suggests that women smile more than men even when the women are alone (Berman & Smith, 1984; Bugental, Love, & Gianetto, 1971; Dittmann, 1972; Duck, 1998; Hall & Halberstadt, 1986; Henley, 1995; Trees & Manusov, 1998). Perhaps the best explanation for why women smile more often is that it is a means of being responsive and acculturating oneself. Our culture expects women to be sensitive and responsive. The smile is the international sign of friendship and understanding. Therefore women are conditioned to smile more often because it is the communication expected of them.

Children respond differently to male and female smiles. The reason for this is that males smile primarily when amused or happy; whereas, females smile even while sending negative messages. Therefore children can interpret

Men often mask their emotions more than women.

Source: Photo by C. Price Walt

the male's smile as one of friendliness, but they may have to completely understand the situation to interpret the female's smile correctly. Why do women smile more even when sending a negative message? Society has socialized women to send negative messages with the public/social smile. Society has socialized women to send the public/social smile often, regardless of the communication situation. Simply watch visual clips of various presidents and their wives when receiving information. There are differences between the reactions of two sexes. This is not to suggest that these couples are the representations for all female and male communication behaviors. They are simply easier to view than many other couples. Their lives are very much in the public eye. In conclusion, women are conditioned to look pleasant and sensitive, not harsh and demanding. The smile is the form of socially ingratiating behavior that women have learned to use even when delivering negative messages. Therefore women smile more often than men when they are scolding their children.

The old saying "the eyes tell all" is somewhat true. The authors of this book have a friend who rarely makes eye contact with her friends and acquaintances. In this culture, people find it frustrating to communicate with someone who is looking everywhere but in one's eyes. Our friend rarely looks at her students when teaching. They also find it equally frustrating and feel that she is an unresponsive teacher. Her behavior is not typical for females or males in general. When someone is not looking at you while conversing, you feel as if you are not really a part of the conversation. Males and females have similar functions for eye behavior; however, their use of eye behavior differs. It usually differs in terms of amount, frequency, and duration.

Research reveals that women look more at the other person in a conversation than men do. They also look more at one another than men do and hold eye contact longer with another woman than men do with another man. In general, women look at their conversational partner more and longer than men do. As with facial expression, the primary explanation for this behavior is that women feel this is a method of establishing and maintaining interpersonal relationships (Bate & Bowker, 1997; Gamble & Gamble, 2003; Hall & Halberstadt, 1986; Henley, 1977; McAndrew & Warner, 1986; Mulac, Studley, Wiemann, & Bradac, 1987).

Society expects women to be affiliative, and eye contact and gaze show affiliative tendencies. Another explanation is that women are stereotyped as holding the subordinate position, and men are stereotyped as holding the superior position. The person in the subordinate position is expected to give the superior position more attention, but the person in the superior position is not expected to follow suit. An exception to this pattern occurs when the female and male are positioned at a considerable distance from one another. Both males and females look more when distance increases between them. This is simply an attempt to reduce the physical distance, but it tends to overpower the affiliative situational demands that exist in closer proximity.

In interpersonal relationships, women gaze more and men stare more. Women lower their eyes when conversing with a male who is staring at them.

This seems contradictory to the above. If women look more and hold gazes longer, then why do they lower their eyes more than males? The answer is quite simple. Most of a woman's eye behavior consists of a mutual gaze. The women break the mutual gaze but also engage in mutual eye contact more than males. Women also tend to engage in fleeting glances at another person's face while the other is gazing elsewhere. Because women are more often listeners than speakers in female-male interaction, they watch the other person more because eye contact is closely associated with attentiveness. In the acquaintance stage of a relationship, the male is usually the one who establishes eye contact with the female first. Rarely is it the other way around. Again, the male is seen as the asserter, the female as the responder.

Because males expect affiliative behaviors from females, ambivalence is seen as a negative. Heisel and Mongrain (2004) found that in conflict situations, women who were ambivalent about an issue expressed more negative nonverbal facial expressions. When such negative facial expressions were made, men countered with similar expressions of dislike and anxiety. In another study, Lee and Wagner (2002) had women talk about a positive or negative experience. When an experimenter was present, the women talked less about their emotions, and they exaggerated those positive emotions that they did show and reduced their negative expressions. Thus, again, women appear to have a self-concept that supports the idea of expressing only positive feelings publicly.

Of course one primary purpose of interacting is to determine whether you like another person and whether that person likes you. Ray and Floyd (2006) investigated that question using an eight-minute interaction (similar to speed dating). Researchers were looking for nonverbal expressions (kinesic and vocalic). Outside observers also made evaluations of their liking for one another. They found that their confederates, their partners, and observers had similar findings of liking and disliking. Thus, although most people are not "trained" to determine who likes them, they are pretty good at it.

Sternglanz and De Paulo (2004) attempted to determine whether strangers (as in the case above), close friends, or less close friends could analyze the emotional expressions of another. They found that friends were better than strangers, but interestingly, they found that less close friends could better analyze expressions than could close friends. While our abilities to analyze the expressions of others is good, as we get to know someone very well we tend to cover up our emotions more (Smith, Cottrell, Gosselin, & Schyns, 2005).

Consistent with theories that females select the male, Reninger, Wade, and Grammer (2004) investigated male behavior at a bar. They found successful males had different body behavior than their less successful counterparts. The successful males exhibited more glances that were short and direct, more "space maximization movements, more location changes, more nonreciprocated touches of surrounding males, and a smaller number of closed-body movements" (p. 421).

McAndrew and Warner (1986) studied male and female undergraduates who were randomly paired in same-sex (male-male, female-female) or mixed-sex (female-male) dyads and were asked to maintain a silent mutual gaze for as long as possible over two or three trials. The students first completed the Mehrabian Arousal-Seeking Scale. Then they were asked to engage in a staring contest. They were to look or stare into a partner's eyes for as long as they could without breaking the gaze. The length of visual engagement was timed with a stopwatch. When one of the two subjects had "won" two out of three staring encounters, the experiment was ended and the subjects debriefed.

The results yielded the following. When subjects were divided into "winners" and "losers" on their performance in the gazing encounter, it was discovered that in the "male-male dyads the person with the higher score on the arousal-seeking scale won the encounter 100% of the time, and that in the female-female dyads the high arousal seeker won 90% of the time." Only in 1 out of 20 dyads did the individual with the low arousal-seeking score come out the winner. Therefore, high arousal-seeking persons in same-sex dyads can hold gazes longer than low arousal-seeking persons. This type of nonverbal gaze behavior can give them a certain amount of power in a relationship.

In mixed-sex dyads (female-male), "this advantage of high arousal seekers over low arousal seekers did not hold up as well" (p. 170). In these dyads, high arousal seekers dominated only four of the ten dyads while low arousal seekers won six times. The influence of the arousal-seeking tendency may have been moderated in these dyads by an apparent advantage of females over males in these encounters, as females were the winners in seven out of the ten pairs.

McAndrew and Warner (1986) concluded that "individual differences in arousal seeking do in fact predict how well a person can maintain mutual gazes when no one is speaking, especially in same-sex dyads." High arousal seekers can hold the gaze longer in same-sex dyads. However, there seems to be a strong influence of gender on this behavior.

Females look more than males on all measures of a gaze, especially mutual gaze. This would serve as an explanation for the mutual gaze situations being "less novel and unsettling" for females than males in the mixed-sex dyads, leading to the females' greater willingness to maintain eye contact. In same-sex dyads where this gender difference is absent, arousal seeking would become a more salient variable (p. 171).

Women and men differ in their use of eye behavior. The differences in large part are due to the cultural stereotypes of how males and females should behave.

Vocal Behavior

If we like the sound of a person's voice, we are more attentive, more open to listening, and more likely to engage in an extended conversation with that person. Some voices are more pleasant than others. Some accents are more pleasant than others. Some people find the Bronx accent (New York) to be strident and offensive, and others find the southern drawl to be slow and dumb-sounding. We read people's voices as indicators of their personalities, and—as we noted earlier—to some extent at least, the voice is an accurate projection of personality. However, the primary differences between female and male voices are hormonal in origin, not personality-induced, as noted earlier concerning vocal changes during females' fertility phases.

Children learn that their voices should sound as society says a male or female voice should sound. For example, our culture does not respond well to the female with a deep bass voice. In a similar vein, our culture does not respond well to the male with a high-pitched, feminine-sounding voice. Our society does not respond well to someone who uses incorrect grammar, informal speech, or a regional accent. However, our society is less critical of the male who uses incorrect grammar, informal speech, or a regional accent than it is of females who exhibit these characteristics. Females begin talking earlier than boys and acquire mature articulatory skills before boys. What then are the acceptable vocal qualities for males and females?

In a classic and impressive study, Addington (1968) completed a most comprehensive examination of voice judgments. Two males and two females simulated nine vocal characteristics and listeners rated the personalities of the speakers. Addington found that certain voice qualities were acceptable for both males and females.

- Both females and males could use increased rate and still be perceived in a positive fashion.
- Nasality was perceived by listeners as having a wide array of socially undesirable characteristics for both males and females.
- The male who had a high-pitched voice was seen as dynamic, feminine, and aesthetically inclined. In contrast, the female with a high-pitched voice was seen as more dynamic and extroverted.
- The female with the orotund vocal characteristic was perceived as humorless yet lively. The male with the orotund vocal characteristic was seen as energetic, proud, and interesting.
- The female with the throaty vocal characteristic was seen as ugly, boorish, and uninteresting; whereas, the male with the throaty vocal characteristic was seen as older, mature, and well adjusted.
- The female with the tense vocal characteristic was seen as young and emotional. The male with the tense vocal characteristic was seen as older and more unyielding.
- Males and females with flat vocal characteristics were not seen in a very positive light.
- Females with a thin voice were seen as emotionally and socially immature while simultaneously getting ratings of increased sense of humor. There were no significant correlations for the male with the thin voice.
- Females with the breathy voice were seen as feminine and shallow; whereas, males with the breathy voice were seen as younger and more artistic.

It is difficult to suggest any definite conclusions based on the above results. These vocal differences exist whether a person is communicating with their own or the opposite sex and therefore are not a function of cross-sex communication. Clearly very different perceptions of females and males can be based on the same vocal characteristics.

A few differences have been noted specifically within the context of female-male interaction. These differences are, again, consistent with the distinction in stereotypical sex and gender roles. Males tend to use greater intensity and talk louder than do females. Females tend to raise their pitch and speak in quieter tones when talking to men.

Space

As early as the second grade, children are using the space norms of their culture. Elementary school children sit farther away from others and touch others less than preschool children. Lomranz, Shapira, Choresh, and Gilat (1975) had three-, five-, and seven-year-olds sit next to an unknown peer and perform a task. The three-year-olds sat closer than the other two groups and even touched the unknown peer. When children enter school, they start becoming more aware of the adult space norms. They find out it is no longer appropriate to sit in one another's lap and that the teacher wants space of her or his own. Although children usually learn the space norms of their culture by third or fourth grade, males and females still use space differently.

Young boys seem to need more space than young girls. This may be genetically produced, because it occurs before the boys become physically larger than the girls. However, most parents and other adults in society reinforce boys for playing with toys that require more space (trucks) than those girls play with (dolls). The type of toy often determines the amount of space needed for play. Therefore, boys may learn the need for more space than girls do. However, the possibility of a biological impact should not be totally rejected. Boys prefer to spend more time outside than do girls, play in more areas than do girls, and require as much as 50 percent more space than do girls. As boys and girls mature, these noticeable spatial differences do not disappear.

In a classic statement, Piercy (1973) may have described the spatial differences of males and females best when describing movement in a theater:

> Men expanded into available space. They sprawled, or they sat with spread legs. They put their arms on the arms of chairs. They crossed their legs by putting a foot on the other knee. They dominated space expansively. Women condensed. Women crossed their legs by putting one leg over the other and alongside. Women kept their elbows to their sides, taking up as little space as possible. They behaved as if it were their duty not to rub against, not to touch, not to bump a man. If contact occurred, the woman shrank back. If a woman

bumped a man, he might choose to interpret it as a come-on. Women sat protectively using elbows not to dominate space, not to mark territory, but to protect their soft tissues. (p. 438)

These observations suggest that women require less space, protect their bodies by using less space, and are more likely to have their space invaded. The rest of this section examines these behaviors.

Research on sex differences concerning space has revealed several interesting distinctions. The personal space bubble surrounding women appears to be smaller than the personal space bubble for men. In public settings, female dyads stand closer together than male dyads do. Male-female dyads, however, stand closest of all. The reactions of men and women placed in crowded versus uncrowded rooms for periods of one hour were found to be very different. Women felt the experience was pleasant, liked the others more, and found them to be friendlier than the men. Men found the situation to be an unpleasant experience, liked the others less, and found them to be less friendly. In waiting rooms, females in a pair sit closer to each other than males in a pair. Women are approached more closely than men by both males and females in initial interaction situations.

It seems that women require less space than men do and do not become as upset if less space is awarded to them. This might be because women are more used to having their space invaded or having to share their space. In the typical household, it is the mother who gives up space to the children and her husband. Rarely is it the man who gives up space. When a new child is born, it usually is the mother who gives up her space and time to spend time with the child. Another reason for women requiring less space could be that of the difference in the male-female status roles. By virtue of having been granted higher status in the society, the male may have been granted the right to more space in the perceptions of men and women alike.

Given the abundance of research evidence showing major differences in the use of space by males and females, it should come as no surprise that females and males use space differently when encountering one another. In a classic study, Silveira (1972) found that when male-female pairs approach one another on the street, the female is expected to yield the space. In observing 19 mixed-sex pairs, it was found that in 12 of the 19 cases, the woman moved out of the man's way. In 4 of the 7 remaining cases, both sexes moved to make way for the other. In only 3 of the cases did the man move to make way for the woman.

So what does this body of research suggest? In typical female-male interactions, men command the bulk of the available space. The woman may not contest for more of the space. Although in spatial-invasion studies involving strangers it is usually the woman who flees the scene, in female-male interactions the female is unlikely to perceive her loss of space during an interaction as an invasion. Perhaps women feel that to be perceived as affiliative they must not fight over space. Perhaps they feel it is easier to give in than to either fight or flee. Perhaps they simply need less space, so they do not even notice that the male takes more. In any event, the negotiation of space in female-male interaction usually is a smooth process, requiring the conscious attention of neither person.

To the extent that occupation of more space reflects dominance, we again find the male exerting a dominant position in interaction with the female (Grady, Miransky, & Mulvey, 1976). However, much of this spatial dominance is changing as more and more women move into equivalent work positions of men, and men move into equivalent work positions of women. For example, the female executive can command the best space and more of it than the male subordinate; and the male nurse may still give up space to the higher-status person, the physician. Therefore it may be the societal or work role the person holds, not her or his sex role, that determines the use of space.

Touch

It is sad but true that in this society human touch diminishes from infancy on. Think of all the songs associated with touch. Our culture sings a lot about touch, but people rarely engage in the act itself. This society is very selective about whom, when, and where we touch. In the eyes of many, it is an invasion for two males to touch each other except in the context of a sports event. If two males touch in this society, people immediately read something negative into it. As early as infancy, differences are noted in female-male touch. Female babies receive more touch than male babies do, but that difference starts to diminish around two years of age. In this culture, boys are encouraged to touch less and learn to need touch less.

Women seem to be more concerned about the type of touch they give or receive than men are. In a classic study, Nguyen, Heslin, and Nguyen (1975) asked unmarried college students what a pat, a squeeze, a brush, and a stroke meant when directed to different body parts by someone of the opposite sex. The differences between the two sexes were striking. Males understood the differences among patting, stroking, and squeezing but were not concerned with the body part being touched. Men felt that warmth, love, sexual desire, and pleasantness all had the same meaning. However, women were very concerned about the body part involved. They felt that touch directed to the hands, head, face, arms, and back meant love and friendliness but that touch in the genital areas or breasts was a sign of sexual desire. Hence, women interpreted the type of touch and part of body being touched to mean either friendship or sexual desire. In contrast, men associated friendship and sexual desire with similar touch regardless of the body part. Such perceptual difference in the meaning of touch portends problems within female-male interactions.

In male-female relationships, it is often the man who initiates the touch. Women are taught that for them to initiate the touch could mislead the man into thinking that the woman was promiscuous. Society is quite clear on this. Men should be allowed to initiate touch, not women. In fact, when women are approaching others, they often stop out of the touching range. In the male-female relationship, the man usually moves in on the woman and touches first. It is rarely the other way around.

In conclusion, until our society eliminates some of its cultural taboos on touching behavior (male touching male, female initiating touch with male) we will remain a very noncontact-oriented society. We have been conditioned from childhood not to "reach out and touch someone" (although a very long-running ad for a long-distance telephone company implored us to do so). Touch between males and females in this society is reserved mostly for intimate relationships, and the touch is seen most often as sexual in nature. What little occurs outside this narrow range generally is initiated by the male and accepted by the female. Unlike many nonverbal behaviors we have discussed in this chapter, however, touch is much more likely to occur at the conscious than the subconscious level. Touch between members of the opposite sex in this society carries such strong sexual overtones that it is virtually impossible for touch to occur without being noticed by one or both of the interactants (Jones, 1986; Jourard, 1966, 1968; Jourard & Rubin, 1968).

In this section we have enumerated many distinctions between females and males in nonverbal communication behavior. Table 11.1 provides a brief summary of some of the more important distinctions. You may find it a useful review of this material.

TABLE 11.1

Nonverbal Behaviors in Female-Male Communication

Performed Primarily by the Female	Performed Primarily by the Male
Lowers eyes	Stares
Smiles	Frowns
Tilts head	Holds head erect
Does not point	Points
More positive gesturing	Less positive gesturing
Takes up less space	Takes up more space
Moves out of the way of his space/yields space	Moves in on her space
Accepts touch	Initiates touch
Pulls body in	Has erect posture
Stands/sits with legs together	Stands/sits with legs apart
Bats eyelashes	Initiates looks
Hands at sides or in the lap	Hands on hips
Cuddles	Strokes
Leans into	Leans over
Talks more softly	Talks more loudly
Less likely to interrupt	More likely to interrupt

LIKING AND COURTSHIP OF THE AMERICAN
FEMALE AND MALE

Scheflen (1965) studied American courtship rituals and how they related to liking and disliking. He did a content analysis of films of various interpersonal encounters and found some similar behavioral patterns across encounters that related to dating or courtship. He called these nonverbal behaviors **quasi-courtship cues** and classified them into four categories.

The first category Scheflen called *courtship-readiness cues*. He included such things as reduced eye bagginess, higher muscle tone, reduced jowl sag, little slouching, no shoulder hunching, and decreased belly sag. He concluded that both males and females engage in courtship-readiness behavior. After all, no one is attracted by a saggy belly in either a male or a female.

The second category is *preening behavior,* characterized by behavior such as stroking one's hair, fixing makeup, fixing clothes, looking in a mirror, leaving buttons open on shirts or blouses, adjusting suit coats, pulling up socks, and adjusting a tie. Obviously both males and females engage in some of the above, depending on the situation.

The third category Scheflen called *positional cues*. These cues are reflected in seating arrangements. A person positions herself or himself to indicate to others that he or she is not open to conversation with anyone other than whomever he or she is already talking to. For example, the person arranges his or her arms, legs, and body so that others cannot enter the conversation without great difficulty.

The fourth category Scheflen called *actions of appeal or invitation*. These are cues such as rolling the pelvis, casting flirtatious glances, holding another's gaze, crossing a leg to expose one's thigh, showing one's wrist or palm, and flexing muscles.

Obviously all of the above categories are related to male-female quasi-courtship behavior. Both sexes use cues from each category to attract the other sex.

In a similar vein, Birdwhistell (1970) suggested that there are 24 steps from initial male-female contact to a fully intimate sexual relationship, and that there is a sequence to the steps. For example, if a female does not reciprocate a male's eye contact, then he should not progress to the next step. Both females and males are labeled as "fast" or "slow" depending on whether they follow the steps. If steps are ignored or skipped, then someone is labeled as fast. If someone does not respond to steps or chooses to ignore steps, then he or she is labeled as slow. However, at certain steps it is expected that the female will slow the process. For example, a man expects the woman to block him, at least for a while, when he makes a move for her breast.

Perhaps Morris (1971) gave us the most popular view of the courtship ritual. He suggests there are twelve steps that couples in western culture go through, from initial contact through intimacy. He indicates that the steps have an order and that this order usually is followed in female-male relationships. These connective steps are as follows:

1. eye to body
2. eye to eye
3. voice to voice
4. hand to hand
5. arm to shoulder
6. arm to waist
7. mouth to mouth
8. hand to head
9. hand to body
10. mouth to breast
11. hand to genitals
12. genitals to genitals

The person who skips steps or fails to respond to a step may be seen as fast or slow by another person. The first five of the twelve steps can be classified as immediacy behaviors. The sixth may also fit in this group.

However, the last six are definitely intimate behaviors. Therefore, because immediate behaviors often foreshadow subsequent intimate ones, immediacy often can be mistaken for an overture to intimacy. Recognize that although we see the first six steps as within the immediacy range, another individual may see everything from step three on as intimate. However, according to Tieffer (1978) step seven is often the defining step. She has written:

Deep kissing causes other physiological changes. The presence of a lover's tongue in one's mouth induces the secretion of saliva, which is under neural control (seventh and ninth cranial nerves) and thus appears in response to any stimulus in the mouth. Most societies find juicy kisses more desirable than dry ones, but they seek a balance. Excessively wet kisses are unpopular (as the Danes say: "He's nice to kiss—when one is thirsty.") but a dry, tight kiss is usually regarded as either immature or inhibited. (p. 23)

We have taken the time to outline the Scheflen, Birdwhistell, and Morris examinations of male and female behavior not because of a particular interest in courtship behaviors but because many of these same behaviors frequently are used in female-male interactions that are not intended as courtship. Certainly the first few of Morris's steps and nearly all of the behavior Scheflen identified occur in noncourtship encounters between females and males. They are common behaviors exhibited every day in offices, stores, classrooms, libraries, hospitals, and virtually everywhere else where females and males come in contact. Clearly these behaviors are an invitation to communicate, even if they are not intended as an initiation of courtship. Rejection of such an invitation, if made quietly, by simply turning away, for example, usually terminates the invasive behavior if it is unwelcome. Sometimes, however, the outcome is not so easy or positive. People differ greatly in their sensitivity to the nonverbal behavior of others. Some, as an extreme example, see sexual harassment in what others see as a flirtatious glance. People are also sometimes insensitive to their own non-verbal behavior and cannot understand when someone else takes offense.

Avoiding Problems

How can verbal and nonverbal communication problems be avoided in female-male communication? It is not likely that they can be avoided completely. However, becoming aware that these behaviors exist and can be subject to multiple interpretations goes a long way toward keeping the number of problems down.

- Remember that meaning is in people's minds. It is not in words, and it is not in nonverbal behavior.
- When we find a person's words offensive, we can tell the person so he or she can try to avoid the problem in the future, we can ignore the offense and go on to something else, or we can avoid that person so that we don't have future interactions with him or her.
- We have similar options with offensive nonverbal behavior, whether of others or our own. If we or the person we offended chooses the confrontation route, serious conflict is most likely to occur. The relationship will be damaged, possibly very severely, and friends of the parties most likely will become involved.
- Obviously prevention is better than cure, and appropriate instruction in nonverbal behavior and communication is the best preventive system found to date.

Nonverbal Sensitivity

We alluded to the fact that some people are more sensitive to nonverbal cues than others. Is it possible that one sex is more sensitive than the other?

- Some observers claim that females are more sensitive to nonverbal cues than males. On at least one measure of nonverbal sensitivity, the Profile of Nonverbal Sensitivity test (PONS), females do score higher (Rosenthal, Hall, DiMatteo, Rogers, & Archer, 1979).
- Various studies have indicated that women have been found to be more accurate in judging various emotional states than men.
- Much of the literature suggests that women are more responsive nonverbally than men. For example, they look at others more, give up space to others, allow others to touch them more, and can interpret facial expressions more easily than men.
- Are females more nonverbally sensitive than males? It seems that they may be, but the reason for any difference is not clear. Perhaps males are less sensitive because they have not been encouraged in this culture to be responsive. If men were encouraged to be more responsive, they might be as sensitive to nonverbal cues as women. Responsiveness in large part is

cued to the nonverbal behavior of others, so it is hard to be responsive without developing nonverbal sensitivity.

■ Women tend to show emotions more than men do in this society. It is acceptable for women to externalize their emotions but not for men to do so. Men are taught that to show emotions or to be expressive is a sign of weakness or failure. Therefore men have learned not to be too expressive. Perhaps this is why men have more difficulty recognizing the implications of the nonverbal behavior of others. They may simply see such behavior as meaningless and not in need of interpretation.

Throughout this chapter, we have alluded to the commanding male as the initiator of more of the interaction between females and males. Could it be that the true initiator is the female? Mehrabian's early landmark research on affiliative tendencies and approach behavior indicates that women definitely have more affiliative tendencies and approachable behavior than men. Affiliative tendencies are behaviors that show others how friendly we are. Women definitely display more affiliative, responsive tendencies than men. Men display more dominating tendencies than women. But who really initiates and controls female-male interactions?

ADVANTAGES OF IMMEDIACY

Because males and females who appear to be more immediate are perceived as more pleasant and friendly than males or females who appear to be nonimmediate, they are perceived as more approachable. Males and females who appear to be more immediate are also perceived as more likeable than males or females who appear to be nonimmediate. Others want to be closer to likeable people, talk to them more often, and even spend more time with them.

More immediate-seeming males and females are perceived as more popular than are males or females who appear to be nonimmediate. Popular people usually appear to be more approachable and friendly, so immediacy increases popularity.

Males and females who appear to be more immediate receive more communication from others than nonimmediate males or females. People approach and want to communicate more with people who give off cues that say they are approachable. The immediate person, through her or his nonverbal behavior, says that he or she is open to communication and welcomes it. The nonimmediate person discourages communication through her or his nonverbal cues. For example, are you more likely to approach someone who has an open body position to ask the time or someone who has her or his arms folded across the chest and is looking at the ground? Obviously, most of us would approach the open-looking person and ask the time.

Notice that all of these advantages are common to all kinds of relationships. They are not unique to female-male relationships. We reemphasize them here, however, because immediacy is critical to the development of relationships between females and males. Immediacy in these relationships may also have certain disadvantages.

DISADVANTAGES OF IMMEDIACY

Immediacy leads to more verbal and nonverbal communication. This is something that many people do not want, however. Increased communication means increased interaction with someone, regardless of sex. Therefore, if one wants to decrease communication in a female-male relationship, he or she should be nonimmediate.

Immediacy can lead to misperception. The nonverbal behavior of immediacy can be misjudged as cues suggesting an intimate relationship. For example, the female who smiles constantly at many males might be perceived as an easy target; whereas, she may simply be immediate in her behavior. Think of some immediate behavior to see how such misunderstandings can happen. Imagine you are in a restaurant, and the person two tables away smiles at you and has direct eye contact. You might misperceive that behavior.

Immediate behavior can lead to negative perceptions for both males and females. For example, the immediate male might be perceived by other males as effeminate or girlish; whereas, the immediate female might be perceived as easy or friendly but dumb. One must be cautious not to be too immediate and decide what situations dictate immediacy and what situations do not. Clearly, not all female-male relationships call for increased immediacy.

THE ANDROGYNOUS PERSON

The term **androgyny** is a combination of the Greek words *andros,* meaning man, and *gyne,* meaning woman. An androgynous person is one who can associate with both masculine and feminine characteristics. In terms of psychological gender orientation, this type of individual can adapt to a variety of roles by engaging in either responsive or assertive behavior, depending on the situation. At present, the responsive role in this society is primarily defined as the female's role, and the assertive role is primarily defined as the male's role. Androgyny is the answer for those who want to be more assertive while still being responsive and for those who want to be more responsive while still being assertive. The androgynous person can be warm, compassionate, sincere, helpful, sympathetic, and acquiescent in one situation and in another situation be competitive, risk-taking, assertive, independent, and dominant. An androgynous male might be a weight lifter (stereotypical male) who works in a home for underprivileged children on weekends. An androgynous female might be a home economics teacher (stereotypical female) who enjoys watching professional football and playing pool.

Typically, the androgynous person is highly flexible in her or his behavior. The individual does not feel limited in her or his verbal or nonverbal communication with others. He or she is fully aware of and adaptable to the affiliative and control needs of others. Thus, the androgynous person can sense another's needs and adapt to them. This type of person recognizes when an interaction partner requires affiliative behavior and can provide it. He or she also recognizes when someone needs to be assertive and can adapt to that situation. People who are gender-role stereotyped (can only perform typical female or typical male behavior) are not as flexible in their verbal and nonverbal communication. They respond in the stereotypical ways. They are also less responsive to the needs of others. In sum, the androgynous individual is likely to be more sensitive nonverbally than the stereotypical male or female.

Many have researched the area of androgyny, including Bem (1974); Richmond, Beatty, and Dyba (1988); Richmond and McCroskey (1989); Richmond and McCroskey (1990); Richmond and Martin (1998); and others. They have found that the androgynous male and the androgynous female are more flexible and adaptive to situations than males and females who follow the traditional roles assigned by society. Societal norms dictate that the female must usually react in a responsive manner in some situations and do not allow for assertiveness on her part. Similar norms dictate that the male must react in an assertive or dominant way in some situations and do not allow for responsiveness on his part. People who follow these societal norms are sex-typed. Their communication behavior corresponds closely to the normative descriptions we have provided in this chapter.

Some individuals, however, find these norms to be an impediment to their full development as men or women. They see each of the stereotyped gender roles as representing only half a person. Unfortunately, the solution advanced sometimes is as bad as the problem. Females sometimes attempt to assume the

❙ Immediate or intimate?

behavior role of males, or males that of females. All that is accomplished in such attempts is to exchange one half a person for the other half, and the new half usually does not work as well as the old one did.

There are situations that call for the male to be responsive and situations that call for the female to be assertive. One should remember that the traditional roles developed because they were functional in some ways. There will remain situations where males should be assertive and females should be responsive. Therefore individuals should strive to develop some nonverbal skills that help increase responsiveness in males and assertiveness in females, whichever is needed, without sacrificing the alternate skills that already have been developed. The androgynous person is much more likely to be able to respond appropriately across contexts than the gender-role-stereotyped individual. To respond appropriately, one must be able to assess the situation. If the situation calls for assertive behavior, then be assertive. If the situation calls for responsive behavior, then be responsive. Competent communicators are capable of both types of behavior and smart enough to know which is appropriate.

Glossary of Terminology

Androgyny is a combination of the Greek words *andros,* meaning man, and *gyne,* meaning woman. An androgynous person is one who can associate with both masculine and feminine characteristics. Such individuals can adapt to a variety of roles by engaging in either responsive or assertive behavior, depending on the situation.

Gender is the psychological, social, and cultural manifestation of what people perceive to be the appropriate behaviors of females and males. These manifestations may or may not be representative of a person's biological sex.

Quasi-courtship cues are nonverbal cues used to show interest in courtship. They are classified into four categories: courtship-readiness cues, preening behavior, positional cues, and actions of appeal or invitation.

Sex is the biological and genetic difference between girls and boys, men and women. In other words, this is the biological sex we are born with. Anatomically, sex is expressed in the sexual organs of men and women, which are distinct for each.

CHAPTER 12

Supervisor and Employee Relationships

The relationship between supervisors and employees is best characterized by the dominant-submissive continuum. This refers to the degree to which a person feels in power, in control, or influential versus feeling submissive, controlled, or dominated. In this culture and others, we can learn much about the relationship between two people by watching their approach or avoidance behavior. In many relationships, it is clear who is the supervisor and who is the subordinate. The person of higher status is given more space, allowed to touch the person of lower status more, and is considered the more dominant person in the relationship.

Status is a person's rank or position in a group. Therefore, in most relationships, someone is usually of higher status and someone is of lower status by virtue of age, experience, training, education, or other factors (Richmond & McCroskey, 2001). Mehrabian (1971), citing Lott and Sommer (1967), suggests that it is easy to identify high- and low-status persons in a visitor situation:

> The clue to status and dominance differences is the degree of hesitation and discomfort shown by the visitor at each stage as he or she is about to approach the other person. If the status differential is significant, the visitor must wait for permission before making any major move in coming closer, or risk offending the higher status other. The visitor will be hesitant to presume familiarity by casually dropping into a seat, as this implies relaxation and an intention to stay on. Indeed, even when invited to sit, the visitor will still behave in a way that is consistent with her or his status in the situation as he or she sees it. If there is more than one visitor's chair, the visitor will tend to sit at a distance from the host. If the two are intimate or are peers, however, the visitor will feel free to take a seat without being invited to do so, one close to the person being visited. (pp. 58–59)

Although we like to think all people are equal, we know better. There are high-status persons and low-status persons in almost any relationship. For example, in the teacher-student relationship, the teacher is generally perceived as the higher-status person. In the work environment, the **supervisor** is generally the higher-status person; the **subordinate** the lower-status person. This chapter discusses supervisor-employee relationships in the work environment. It looks at the distinctive characteristics of the supervisor-subordinate relationship and reviews the nonverbal characteristics in such relationships.

DISTINCTIVE CHARACTERISTICS

Let's look at the distinctive characteristics of the supervisor-employee relationship. First, a supervisor in the work environment has the legitimate right to request that certain job responsibilities be carried out by the subordinate. A legitimate authority is often assigned a subordinate or subordinates as soon as he or she achieves the role of supervisor. Legitimate or higher authority then gives the supervisor the right to request certain behaviors, even compliance, from subordinates. Most organizations have certain job responsibilities that are delegated to each person, and each person must carry them out. Therefore the supervisor in an organization can ask, will ask, and will expect his or her subordinates to carry out certain tasks.

Second, the supervisor-subordinate relationship demands that a certain amount of respect be given to the supervisor because of her or his higher position, title, and expertise.

Third, in supervisor-subordinate relationships, the supervisor can bestow rewards or punishments on the subordinate. Most organizations grant a supervisor certain rewards (e.g., bonus money) and punishments to use as motivators for employees. For example, many organizations allow supervisors to reduce an employee's pay if he or she does not complete a job. Many organizations allow supervisors to rate employees on the quality of their work. If the quality is rated low, the subordinate might be asked to leave. Thus, the higher-status person in an organization generally has control over the rewards and punishments distributed to lower-status persons. The higher-status person may not be directly in control of rewards and punishments. However, he or she may be asked to participate in assessing what types of rewards and punishments should be given.

Fourth, in supervisor-subordinate relationships, the supervisor is the person who has the most informational power. That is, the supervisor knows not only her or his primary job but also commands information about other units, changes, policies, and so on, which often the subordinate needs to know to do her or his job well. Therefore, the supervisor once more can maintain control and status by either sharing or not sharing needed information with the subordinate. Without the needed information, often jobs can be difficult, tedious, and time-consuming. Therefore, when a supervisor has informational power, it is best to stay on her or his good side.

In many instances you can determine who is the subordinate and who is the superior simply by observing nonverbal cues.

In summary, the four main distinctive characteristics in the supervisor-employee relationship in the work environment are as follows:

- The supervisor has the legitimate right to ask subordinates to perform certain job responsibilities.
- The supervisor has a right to higher status.
- The supervisor can often bestow rewards or punishments on the subordinate.
- The supervisor can share or not share needed information with subordinates (Richmond & McCroskey, 2001).

These unique relational characteristics establish the power (control-acquiescence) feelings in a supervisor-employee relationship.

ROLE OF NONVERBAL MESSAGES

Nonverbal messages primarily help in defining the work relationship. Nonverbal messages such as gesture, touch, seating, tone of voice, use of time, and use of space, artifacts, and objects, all contribute to defining who's the boss and who's the employee. They also help define how "big" the boss is and how low the status of the employee is. Korda (1975) described the power metaphor in the supervisor-subordinate relationship. He states:

> It isn't necessary to be six feet tall and built like a football tackle, but there are some physical signs that hint at power: certain immobility, steady eyes, quiet hands, broad fingers, above all a solid presence which suggests that one belongs where one is, even if it's somebody else's office or bed. (p. 19)

A visitor who understands status hierarchies when entering an organization can determine who is of higher status and who is of lower status by looking at the various symbols in use. Common status symbols are found in many organizations: job titles, levels of pay, clothing, size and location of desk or office, type of car assigned (if cars are assigned), secretaries, privacy, furnishings, privileges (flextime, not having to punch a time clock), and ceremonies of induction.

The role of nonverbal messages in organizations is to define the status of the individuals in an organization. This helps a newcomer to know how to communicate with others in the workplace. It is critical that status is somewhat clear so that people can adapt their messages accordingly. When a higher-status person is offended by the communication of a lower-status person, it can have dire consequences both for the lower-status person and the organization. Flippo (1974) has illustrated how important nonverbal messages of status are in organizations:

> With the company, however, many of the symbols are within the control of the management, and constitute the basis for many bloody

battles. Executives have gotten down on hands and knees to measure and compare sizes of offices. Windows are counted, steps from the president's offices are paced off, secretaries are sought, parking space is fought for, and company cars are wrangled. (p. 219)

Although we joke about status symbols, we are still uneasy about our own status. Everybody wants some status. Those who say they want none are kidding themselves. Through nonverbal messages, we establish or communicate our status to others. The rest of this section reviews each type of nonverbal message and how that message communicates status or power (control-acquiescence) in the supervisor-employee relationship.

Physical Appearance

First impressions may be lasting impressions. Often we are judged more by our clothing than any other nonverbal factor. Cash and Kilcullen (1985) and Kaiser (1997) support the idea that people judge others based on their clothing and general physical appearance in interviewing and hiring situations.

Two women enter the executive vice president's waiting room. Both are there to be interviewed for the same position: assistant to the executive vice president. They approach the secretary simultaneously. Applicant A is wearing a solid-colored gray suit with a pale-blue shirt and matching stockings and shoes. Applicant B is wearing a black and red plaid suit coat with a solid black shirt and red stockings and shoes to match. The secretary says to applicant A, in a pleasant but professional tone, "Ms. Smith will be with you in a few minutes. Please be seated." The secretary says to applicant B, in a very sneering tone, "Ms. Smith is very busy and will see you in a little while. You'll have to wait over there."

Which applicant is likely to get the job? Applicant A has the edge over applicant B because her dress and appearance fit the expectations of the organization. Applicant B may be more qualified, but her flashy appearance is going to hurt her chances. According to Korda, the "overriding essential of all corporate business clothing is that it establishes power and authority" (p. 230). Plaids do not establish power and authority. Solid colors do.

Clothing often determines how the receiver reacts to the wearer. Korda (1975) suggests that "people who look successful and well educated receive preferential treatment in almost all of their social or business encounters" (p. 12). The employee who dresses for success is more likely to be successful. Bixler and Nix-Rice (1997) note that appearance can count not only in promotions but "often in cold hard cash" (p. 6). They suggest that, based on our appearance, our salary offers could range from 8 to 20 percent higher, as a "result of upgrading a mediocre business appearance to one that is polished and effective" (p. 6).

Companies are willing to pay for employees who look the part. These "look-the-part employees" do not need training in appropriate business attire; thus, other, more critical job issues can be introduced to them earlier than to employees who need training in "looking the part." Because business clothing establishes power and status, people who dress accordingly are much more likely to be considered for better jobs, to get promotions, and to receive preferential treatment. We know that in the supervisor-subordinate relationship, the type of dress worn by each party is often determined by the organization, the job in the organization, and the status of the person. For example, a machinist will almost always be seen in a pair of jeans. However, if he or she appears at a company party or function dressed in an outfit that denotes power and status, he or she might be the next job boss in the machinist unit.

Granted, styles for men and women are not always the same, and styles for different organizations vary. For example, a college professor can dress more casually than an IBM executive. The professor also can dress more casually than can her or his chairperson or a dean or president of the university. Employees must remember to dress for their role if they want to receive the proper respect. Clothing serves as a symbol of status. If people fail to dress as expected, their occupational mobility may be hindered (Henley, 1977; Moore, Hickson, & Stacks, 2010; Molloy, 1975, 1977, 1988, 1996; Richmond & McCroskey, 2001). People dress according to their jobs to impress others.

Others associate our clothing with socioeconomic status, achievement of goals, and satisfaction. In the 1970s, Molloy (1975, 1977) suggested that what you wear to the office suggests whether you are there for business or monkey business. Molloy suggests that women who want to move up the executive ladder should not wear sweaters, because sweaters denote lower status. Sweaters that are soft and tight are also seen as sexy; few women want to get ahead by being seen as sexy. A sexy image will not get them the respect they might have earned. Molloy suggests that for women in business, the matching skirt and jacket are the looks that say, "I am a professional and want to be treated as one." Women, perhaps more than men, must be cautious about what they wear to the office. Primarily this is because the work world is just becoming used to the higher-status female executive. Therefore, unless they own the businesses in which they work, women should strive to adapt to clothing norms of the professional businesswoman. Last, women and men should strive to dress similarly to the *next-highest-ranking person* in the organization, unless that person has unusual or idiosyncratic dress. The more we look like the person above us, the better our chances of being the person above us. When our supervisor moves up or out, we may have a chance at her or his job.

Men should also wear the clothing dictated by the organization. Every organization has an image to uphold. People who do not fit the image will not move ahead unless they are unusually bright and irreplaceable. For example, the authors of this book have an eccentric friend who dresses rather casually: His shirt is always coming out of his slacks, usually unbuttoned too far, and has food stains from lunch. This person is employed by a large organization as a computer expert and analyst. They put up with his idiosyncratic attire because he is so good at his job. He is such an expert that they are not interested in what he wears. This is an unusual case. His wife, on the other hand, is also very good at her job. She always wears a professional business outfit to work. This is because she is in an upper-level management position that few women ever have a chance to attain. Therefore, to command respect and liking from her subordinates, she must dress in the professional style dictated by the organization.

The color one chooses for clothing often denotes certain traits or moods. People who wear brighter colors typically want to be perceived as active. Timid or shy people often wear more drab colors so as not to call attention to themselves. However, research suggests that men and women should avoid unusually bright colors in the work environment. Bixler and Nix-Rice (1997) suggest the following guidelines on appropriate wardrobe colors: Warm colors are brown/black (black is a wardrobe classic for everyone), camel, cream, teal, plum, olive, deep rust, coral, and tomato red. Cool colors are black, gray, white, navy/royal blue, royal purple, hunter green, burgundy, pink, and ruby red.

We suggest that when in doubt about what to wear, stay with the basics: solid colors or pinstripes in classic black, navy, or gray and basic styles and accessories. We suggest that the following should be avoided: unusually bright, neon, or garish colors; busy patterns such as plaids; unusual styles; too many accessories; clothing that is too tight; and short skirts or slacks. Short skirts are acceptable on many television shows but not in the real world. Short slacks look tacky and often show too much sock.

In a survey, Bovee and Thill (1983) noted the top ten negative factors perceived by an interviewer that may lead to rejection in an employment interview. Six of the ten are nonverbal factors. Below is their list:

1. Has poor personal appearance*
2. Is overbearing, overaggressive, conceited, has a superiority complex, seems to know it all*
3. Is unable to express self clearly—poor voice, diction, grammar*
4. Lacks planning for career—no purpose or goals*
5. Lacks interest and enthusiasm—passive, indifferent*
6. Lacks confidence and poise—nervous, ill at ease*
7. Has failed to participate in extracurricular activities
8. Overemphasizes money—interested only in the best-paying job
9. Has poor scholastic record—just got by
10. Is unwilling to start at the bottom—expects too much too soon

The factors marked by * deal with various facets of nonverbal behavior, including physical appearance, kinesics, paralanguage and vocalics, chronemics, facial expressions, and eye behavior. These nonverbal behaviors are crucial for competing in the job market. The greatest faux pas that an interviewee can make is to be late for a job interview. If one is late for the interview, one might as well not go. Organizations usually rate interviewees who are late as uninterested and not time-conscious. Additionally, organizations usually rate interviewees who do not know how to dress as careless, uninterested, and more difficult to train.

Hickson, Stacks, & Padgett-Greely (1998) have suggested that the interviewee should not appear nervous. Biting one's fingernails, tugging on clothing, scratching or shaking one's legs or feet all tend to make one appear nervous. While nonverbal communication is usually unintentional, we need to learn to be aware of the impressions that we make. There may even be other factors that we have not considered. The interviewee should wear comfortable, well-fitting clothing. All efforts should be made to avoid sweating during the interview. A candidate should take a handkerchief in the event that he or she should feel the need to sneeze. If the interviewee has a cold, he or she may want to seriously consider rescheduling the interview. While annual reviews may not be as important as the job interview, employees should consider all of these factors during those interviews as well.

One's body type might determine how one is treated in the work environment. Endomorphs are often not hired because they are judged by their body type as lazy or unqualified. The ectomorph is usually perceived as intelligent and might have a better chance at a job. Being an ectomorph can have its drawbacks, however. People might perceive an ectomorph as high-strung and anxious. Mesomorphs are the most likely to be hired, promoted, and retained. They are perceived by employers as dependable and confident.

Artifacts such as briefcases, watches, eyeglasses, and jewelry also denote a person's status or power in an organization. Higher-status persons usually have more expensive briefcases and watches than do lower-status persons. Eyeglasses denote intelligence; if a person wants to look more serious and intelligent, he or she could wear glasses. As for jewelry, one must be careful not to overdo it. Too much jewelry detracts from one's overall appearance. Although jewelry can be a sign of wealth, it can also be a sign that someone is insecure about her or his position. Jewelry should be kept to a minimum for both males and females in the work world. Higher status people are less likely to carry numerous electronic devices, such as laptops and cell phones, because they have a person to handle other communications while they are in meetings.

The employee who is generally attractive is more likely to get the better positions and opportunities. There have been instances where people have not received jobs because they were viewed as physically unattractive. Employees who are unattractive should strive to make themselves more attractive so that they can reap the same benefits as their attractive counterparts.

The following are conclusions that we can safely draw about appearance and dress in the supervisor-employee relationship.

- The higher people are in an organization, the more status their clothing denotes.
- The higher people are in an organization, the more idiosyncratic they can be about their clothing styles and appearance.
- Lower-status people must conform to the clothing and appearance norms of the organization more than higher-status people must.
- The dress for males and females varies from one organization to another.
- More attractive personnel are more likely to receive preferential treatment.

- Less attractive personnel are more likely to receive negative treatment.
- The person who adapts to the image and appearance norms of the organization is likely to be accepted more readily, liked more, given better opportunities, and given more preferential treatment.

Gesture and Movement

Types of gesture and movement can indicate the relationship between boss and subordinate. When two strangers meet, it is relatively easy to figure out which one is of higher status by looking at the posture of each. The person with the relaxed body position is perceived as having higher status by both interactants. In ongoing relationships, similar postural cues suggesting relative status often are present also. The higher-status person in an organization (the supervisor) can assume a relaxed stance or posture. The lower-status person assumes a watchful, tense, cautious posture. The higher-status person is already in control; the lower-status person is trying to get some control over her or his own world.

When speaking with a higher-status person, a lower-status person is likely to exhibit more adaptive nonverbal behavior. This is primarily because he or she is anxious about communicating with a higher-status person. As the higher-status and lower-status persons become more familiar with each other, the lower-status person may exhibit fewer adaptors. People who exhibit too many adaptors are perceived by others as anxious and tense. Therefore, whether one is of higher or lower status, one should try not to exhibit adaptive behavior. Chewing on one's nails does not convey confidence or competence.

In sitting positions, the higher-status person is allowed to assume the more relaxed posture. For example, the higher-status person can slide back and relax in her or his chair; whereas, the lower-status person almost sits at attention. If the lower-status person is familiar with the higher-status person, he or she may sit in a more relaxed position. When in doubt, always assume the more rigid, upright posture when communicating with someone of higher status. Relaxation by the subordinate can be perceived by the higher-status person as a sign of disrespect or apathy. Relaxed posture can also be a sign of defiance or arrogance. However, if an employee assumes the relaxed posture without knowing her or his supervisor well, it usually is simply a sign that the subordinate does not know what is acceptable and what is not.

People with higher status usually keep their heads raised and shoulders straight when conversing with people of lower status. People with lower status lower their shoulders and may keep their heads lowered during the interaction. In other words, the higher-status person projects the image of the more dominant person, and the lower-status person projects the image of the less dominant person. The higher-status person might lean over the lower-status person if he or she is seated. If both are seated, the higher-status person might lean backward in the chair while the lower-status person leans toward the higher-status person. This does not mean that the lower-status person looks cowed or belittled. It only means that one assumes the role of dominance and one assumes the nonverbal behavior of submissiveness. LaFrance and Mayo (1978) suggest that while sitting or standing, the higher-status person will exhibit arm positions different from those of the lower-status person. The higher-status person will have one arm in his or her lap and the other over the back of the chair. Lower-status people sit with their hands together or their arms at their sides. LaFrance and Mayo conclude:

> The posture of the person with the higher status is marked by a sideward and backward tilt of the torso, crossed legs, loosely extended fingers, and the head resting on the back of a chair or couch. The lower-status member of the encounter sits upright, with both feet flat on the floor and hands clasping some object or clenched together. (p. 99)

Think carefully: When was the last time you interviewed for a job? Did you sit or stand casually, or did you sit or stand as if you were interested and attentive? Think of when you had to see a teacher about a problem you were having in her or his class. How did you sit or stand? Probably in a tentative, rigid pose, waiting for the teacher to set the pace of the interaction.

Persons of higher status are afforded the right to have a more relaxed body position. Persons of lower status usually have a more tense body position when interacting with someone of higher status and usually exhibit more adaptive behavior. Lower-status persons who assume a relaxed or casual body position in the presence of a person of higher status might be perceived as disrespectful, uninterested, or defiant. Therefore, in the organizational environment, until one is sure he or she knows what is acceptable with the supervisor and what is not, one should assume the nonverbal behavior that denotes respect, interest, attention, and submissiveness.

Face and Eye Behavior

The face plays just as important a role in the supervisor-employee relationship as it does in any other interaction. For example, the person who is considered the supervisor can express facial expressions more freely than the subordinate can. The subordinate learns to mask or disguise certain expressions when talking with a supervisor. For example, the subordinate learns not to look sad, bored, disgusted, or uninterested when the supervisor is introducing a new way of doing things in the work environment. If the subordinate looks interested, he or she might be asked for information and can influence the supervisor about the decision. Someone who looks bored or uninterested is much less likely to be asked for ideas. Therefore facial expression can be used to the subordinate's advantage.

Higher-status people usually receive more direct and prolonged eye contact from persons of lower status than vice versa. Persons of high status look at persons of lower status less and often avert their eyes in speaking with a lower-status individual. The higher-status person controls the eye behavior in an interaction with a person of lower status. They control when it is the lower-status person's turn to talk, to stop talking, to continue talking, or to remain silent. A higher-status person also might use a steady gaze or stare to make the lower-status person uncomfortable or unsure. A higher-status person might stare to reinforce the oral communication. Looking at a high-status person while he or she is communicating can be a means for the low-status person to show respect and interest. Looking away can also be a means for the low-status person to show respect. However, if the low-status person looks away too long, he or she might be perceived as uninterested in what the higher-status person is saying. Thus, higher-status persons can control the supervisor-subordinate relationship by using eye contact. They feel less compelled to look directly and longer at some low-status persons; whereas, low-status persons feel more compelled to look directly and longer at high-status persons.

Vocal Behavior

One can use her or his voice to sound more authoritative and in control. For example, a lower-status person using a self-assured, confident voice is more likely to be promoted and given preferential treatment than one who has a thin, squeaky, mousy-sounding voice. Whether you are male or female, vocal qualities such as self-assurance, confidence, maturity, animation, and extroverted tones denote authority. Shallow, nasal, whiny, and unhealthy-sounding voices denote powerlessness. The voices that denote authority also denote higher credibility and status; voices that denote powerlessness also denote lower credibility and status. People have been known not to be hired in certain professions because their voices did not fit the job. A man with a high-pitched, thin voice would not make a credible sports announcer. A woman with a throaty, deep voice might not make a good receptionist.

In communicating with a higher-status person, the lower-status person is likely to sound anxious and to have more filled and unfilled pauses than normal. A higher-status person communicating with a lower-status person will sound more self-assured and authoritative. As anxiety decreases, the lower-status person will display fewer is disfluencies and fewer filled and unfilled pauses.

In discussing vocal behavior, the use of silence must always be considered. Silence can mean many different things in a supervisor-employee relationship. Generally, silence on the part of the subordinate suggests he or she is paying attention to what the supervisor is saying. Silence can also mean that the subordinate knows better than to interrupt the supervisor. In most supervisor-subordinate relationships, the subordinate is generally silent more often than the supervisor, but there are exceptions. For example, if the subordinate presents a new idea to the supervisor, he or she might be talking more than the supervisor. Silence from the supervisor might indicate that he or she is processing the subordinate's ideas.

In the work relationship, the supervisor is rarely judged on her or his voice qualities. However, the subordinate might be. The subordinate who sounds bored and lazy might be perceived negatively. Last, silence can be used to improve the supervisor-subordinate relationship. Silence on the subordinate's part might show respect or interest. Too much silence on the subordinate's part, however, might show that he or she is timid or shy.

Space

Perhaps more than other nonverbal behaviors, the use of space defines who is in the dominant role and who is in the submissive role. Studies reveal that higher-status persons within organizations are more likely to invade lower-status persons' interpersonal space than vice versa. The organizational structure informally says it is acceptable for the supervisor to invade or enter the employees' work area or personal space zone (Hall, 1966, 1973; Hickson, Grierson, & Linder, 1991; Hunsaker, 1980; Jorgenson, 1975; McCaskey, 1979; Mehrabian, 1971; Remland, 1984; Richmond & McCroskey, 2001; Robinson, 1998).

In organizations, supervisors are responsible for and supposed to know how well their subordinates are doing their jobs. Therefore they are given the power to invade the subordinates' domain and privacy. They may even invade their interpersonal space by standing closer to them.

Jorgenson (1975) found in one company that although pairs of employees with equal or unequal status did not stand closer or farther apart, they did display different body orientations. People of equal status faced each other more and at a more direct angle; whereas, people of unequal status did not. Mehrabian (1971) notes that the "prerogative to approach the other belongs to the one with higher status" (p. 63). He cites several studies in support of this conclusion. Sommer (1969) concluded that "higher-ups have more and better space, as well as greater freedom to move about" (p. 25). He suggests that this is obvious not only in our interpersonal relations but in the physical layout of businesses and corporations. This layout aspect is reviewed further in the section on environment later in this chapter.

Touch

The boss enters the employees' work area and stops to chat with a few subordinates about how things are going. As the boss is leaving, he or she pats each subordinate on the shoulder or squeezes his or her arm. Is this sexual harassment or is it simply a boss being a boss? Most people would agree that it is the latter. This supervisor is trying to let her or his employees know that he or she is pleased with their work, and touch is one major means of doing so.

Recently it has become increasingly difficult for a higher-status person to touch a lower-status person of either sex (Cohen, 1983; Hickson, Grierson, & Linder, 1991). Touch has always been a means of letting subordinates know that you are pleased with them. Many supervisors complain that they are afraid to use touch as a means to communicate with their subordinates. Sexual harassment laws and policies have made touch a touchy issue in the work environment.

How do you know sexual harassment when you receive it? Well, it's like pornography; you think you know it when you see it, but there is no universal agreement on what it is. Let's look at an example. Supervisor John walks into Jane's office and saunters behind her desk and asks her how things are going. As she is answering, he puts his hand on her neck and caresses it. He then goes on to tell her she could do better in his organization "if you know what I mean."

Jane says "no," while moving away from his touch. This is a case of sexual harassment. If Supervisor John had entered Jane's office and sat across from her and asked how things were going and touched her on the arm when she answered, this would probably not be sexual harassment. This is probably the case of a higher-status person trying to encourage a lower-status person by touch.

That, of course, does not mean that Jane will see it that way. Consequently, our advice to supervisors is to keep hands off unless a very well-established, positive, but nonintimate relationship exists between you and your subordinate. Although research from a couple of decades ago showed that higher-status persons were freer to touch lower-status persons, times have changed. There are many other immediacy cues that can be used to indicate reassurance and friendship. Touch is not required to accomplish this objective, and in today's organizational environment, its use invites needless risk of misperceptions.

Environment

This section views two major aspects of the workplace environment: how much space or territory is granted to people in organizations, and how furnishings convey status. Higher-status persons find positions from which to observe or view what is going on around them, and higher-status persons who seek such "head positions" or central positions are assumed by others to be of higher status or more dominant. In almost any organization in this country, you can enter any unit and distinguish the higher- from the lower-status positions. One organization has a supervisor who has her office right in the middle of all the subordinates, and her office has glass walls. She can see every transaction that takes place and is considered by all to have the highest-status position. Many of us wouldn't want to be in the center of things, but she does. Many other supervisors have their territory protected by barriers such as surrounding offices and secretaries to guarantee their privacy.

The higher-status person is more likely to move in on a subordinate's space than vice versa. It is assumed that the higher-status person has the legitimate right to invade the space or privacy of a subordinate. Therefore the higher-status person often moves in on the subordinate's space, and the subordinate thinks nothing of it. The higher-status person also has territorial rights to more space than lower-status persons have. Those with more space are viewed by others as being of higher status. The higher up one is in an organization, the more space one is granted (Hall, 1966, 1973; Heckel, 1973; Hunsaker, 1980; Jorgenson, 1975; Korda, 1975; Lott & Sommer, 1967; Mehrabian, 1971; Oldham & Rotchford, 1983; Richmond & McCroskey, 2001; Sommer, 1969).

Korda (1975) suggested that "office furnishings have strong symbolic value. . . . Power lies in how you use what you have, not in the accouterments per se" (pp. 230–231). We suggest that one can design an office or environment to reflect power and status, immediacy, or both. The office that reflects both power and immediacy is the optimal environment. It allows one to assume a power or status position when needed, and yet it allows one to assume an immediate, responsive position when needed. Most successful organizational leaders have both qualities in one office.

In a large office, writers suggest, furnishings should be arranged so that a person has to walk by several objects and walk the length of the office to reach the supervisor. Additionally, Korda (1975) notes the following guidelines for small offices where people want to convey power:

> However small the office, it is important to have the visitor's chair facing toward you, so that you are separated by the width of your desk. This is a much better power position than one in which the visitor sits next to the desk, even though it may make access to your desk inconvenient to you. When a small office is very narrow (and most are) it is often useful to have the desk placed well forward in the room, thus minimizing the space available for the visitor, and increasing the area in which it is possible for you to retreat, at least psychologically. (p. 232)

Earlier, we suggested that the optimal office allows one to assume a power position or an immediate position. Korda (1975) has designed office space that he refers to as having semisocial space and pressure space. This is similar to our concept of the office that allows for status and immediacy. In the pressure area, people are focused strictly on business. In the semisocial area, people can be more at ease and relaxed. Figure 12.1 gives an example of an office that includes both an area of power or status and an area of immediacy. Note that the higher-status person can stay behind the desk or come out from behind the desk and assume a more immediate role. This office is optimal for a higher-status person: it allows her or him to break down the status barrier or to establish the status barrier as needed when communicating with others. Other furnishings, such as the type of desk, the objects on the desk, the accompanying furnishings (such as chairs), windows, and color all enhance or inhibit status. People with large, imposing desks are usually perceived as having higher status. The objects on the desk also denote status, as do the pictures on the wall. The offices with windows in most organizations are considered the higher-status offices. The color, lighting, and carpeting in an office all denote the rank of its occupant in an organization. The higher-status persons in organizations generally have more and better space than do the lower-status persons. American organizations use this as incentive to strive to do better or as a reward when one has done a job well. As an example, in our department, the full professors get their choice of the offices before associates and assistants. They also get their choice of furniture. When our department became computerized, the full professors received the computers and word processors before the associates and assistants got theirs.

Not surprisingly, then, higher-status persons usually have better territory than lower-status persons. Higher-status persons are usually given more space and better furnishings than lower-status persons. American organizations use office space and territory to reward employees for jobs well done.

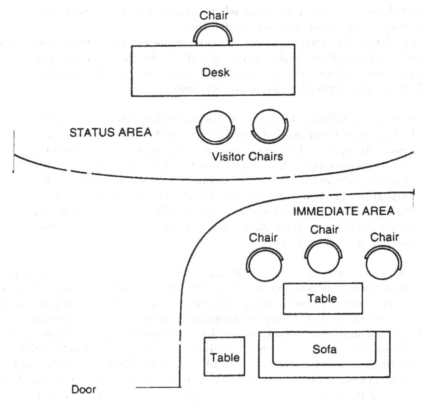

FIGURE 12.1
Status Area Versus Immediate Area

Time

Use of time communicates a person's feelings and attitudes toward an organization. Often, subordinates are judged by supervisors on how they manage their time. Several years ago in our department, at the first faculty meeting of the year, the newest member of the department showed up a half-hour late and informed the rest of us that he couldn't stay more than an hour because his wife was picking him up and he had to leave. No one said a word, but his career in the department was decided from that point on.

Gordon (1975) noted that during an interview, time can be a relevant factor in judging the interviewee. If an interviewee is late for the interview, this can suggest a lack of interest on her or his part. Gordon also notes that an interviewer can use time to her or his advantage. The interviewer can use a chronemic technique to control the length of pauses and rate of speech of her or his own remarks. He or she can also control the length of time to wait before responding to the interviewee's comments. Gordon calls the first technique *pacing* and the second technique *silent probe*. Both techniques might encourage the interviewee to talk more and thus give more information for the interviewer to use in evaluating the interviewee.

Time is a respected element in most organizations. It is a means of judging others. Those who are prompt are respected and rewarded. Those who are late are not respected, are often considered lazy and unreliable, and are sometimes ejected from the organization. The time clock (whether real or imaginary) is part of an everyday American's work life. In business, time is money, and an employee who is casual about his or her use of time can cost an organization a fortune. Therefore it is easier to fire and replace a time-waster than to try to train the person to use time wisely.

Time and status are related. Higher-status people are allowed to abuse time (be late or demand that others be on time) more than lower-status persons. Lower-status persons are expected to wait for higher-status persons. If a lower-status person leaves before the higher-status person arrives (although he or she is already late), the lower-status person is more likely to be in trouble than the higher-status person. Hall suggests that Americans of equal status allow a person five minutes of tardiness before an apology is expected. This culture demands that people be on time. Higher-status people are the only ones allowed to deviate from the norm.

Higher-status people can also demand more time from lower-status people. For example, the supervisor can ask her or his employees to put in extra time on a project, but the employees cannot ask a supervisor to do the same.

In organizations that use flextime, which allows employees to organize their schedules around their daily lives, higher-status persons more than lower-status persons are allowed to choose the time schedules that fit them. For example, if a higher-status executive is a night owl, he or she will be allowed to choose a later schedule; whereas, lower-status employees might still get the nine-to-five routine until they have earned the right to ask for a better schedule. This is common in hospitals, post offices, and similar organizations where night shifts are used. Most people do not want to work the schedule 11 p.m. to 7 a.m., so the newest employees usually are assigned to those times.

Time communicates many messages about status in supervisor-subordinate relationships. Higher-status persons are given more control over their time and their subordinates' time and can choose better time schedules. Lower-status persons must adapt to the higher-status person's schedule and are expected to devote more of their time to the higher-status person's assignments if asked.

CONCLUSIONS ABOUT SUPERVISOR-EMPLOYEE RELATIONSHIPS

Table 12.1 illustrates the supervisor's use of nonverbal codes that we have discussed in relation to the employees' use of them. The superior role belongs to the higher-status person or the one who is dominant or more powerful. The subordinate role belongs to the lower-status person or the one who is submissive or less powerful. It is clear from Table 12.1 that the dominant or higher-status person can control the nonverbal codes to assure they remain the more

TABLE 12.1

Superior and Subordinate Nonverbal Relationships

Nonverbal Code	Superior (Higher Position)	Subordinate (Lower Position)
Appearance	Solid colors communicate power. Looks successful. Clothing should establish higher status. Can have idiosyncratic dress.	Looks less successful. Clothing states rank. Dress matches organizational standards. Must dress for respect.
Gesture and Movement	Relaxed body position. Calm, relaxed stance/pose. Relaxed posture. Fewer adaptors. Relaxed when seated. Head held high. Straight shoulders. Leans over others.	Tense body position. Watchful stance/pose. Tense posture. More adaptors. Sits at attention. Slightly bowed head. Lowered/slumped shoulders. Folds into self.
Face and Eye	Allowed to express facial expressions more freely. Looks at others more and longer. Controls turn-taking with eyes. Allowed to stare.	Learns to mask facial expressions (e.g., boredom). Gives more eye contact, but will also look away/down first. Watches superior for turn-taking cues. Does not stare.
Vocal Behavior	Sounds authoritative. Tries to sound like one with higher status and more credibility. Less anxious tones. Fewer disfluencies. Uses silence to communicate authority.	Sounds submissive. Tries to sound interested in what superior is saying. More anxious tones. More disfluencies. More filled and unfilled pauses. Uses silence to appear to be listening.
Space	Invades subordinate's space and privacy. Prerogative to approach. More and better space. More freedom to move about organization.	Cautious about entering superior's space or invading privacy. Lets superior approach. Less and inferior space. Less freedom to move about organization.
Touch	Initiates touch more. Controls relational touch. Freer to touch.	Receives touch from superior. Accepts touch. Never initiates touch. Reciprocates touch when appropriate.
Environment	Territorial rights on space. Central positions. Head positions. Erects barriers to keep others out of territory. Given more space. Better furnishings. Large desk.	Takes what space is assigned. Assumes low status space. Space is invaded by superiors. Given less space. Leftover furnishings. Smaller desk.
Scent	More freedom granted them on scents.	Less freedom granted them on scents.

(continued)

TABLE 12.1 (continued)		
Nonverbal Code	Superior (Higher Position)	Subordinate (Lower Position)
Time	Abuse and use time more casually. Can arrive late or leave early. Freedom to deviate from time norm. Allowed to select optimal time work schedule. Can call unscheduled meetings.	Must be prompt. Not allowed to abuse time. Must follow time norms of organization. Follows time work schedule assigned. Must attend unscheduled meetings.

powerful. This has one big drawback: communication between supervisor and subordinate will be influenced in a negative manner.

The greater the status differential between persons in an organization, the less effective the communication between supervisor and subordinate. The smaller the status differential, the more effective the communication between supervisor and subordinate. Status differentials are always needed, but they don't need to be so large as to create major communication barriers. Status differentials can be reduced to a manageable level through interpersonal solidarity between supervisor and subordinate.

Solidarity is interpersonal closeness that forms favorable perceptions of the other person and includes mutual trust. Higher solidarity exists when there is a high level of trust and mutual liking between persons. Therefore, as solidarity increases, effective communication increases between supervisor and subordinate. As solidarity increases, status decreases. We do not mean that one has to be buddy-buddy with one's subordinates, but a closer, more communicative relationship will improve the information flow between supervisor and subordinate. How does one increase solidarity? By increasing liking and trust. A good method is the use of nonverbal immediacy. The supervisor who is immediate with her or his subordinates is perceived by them as caring, responsive, and trying to build solidarity while still maintaining her or his status. Let's look at the advantages and disadvantages of immediacy in the supervisor-subordinate relationship (Powell & Hickson, 2000).

IMMEDIACY IN THE WORKPLACE

Advantages of Immediacy

Research shows that employees want a supervisor to be sensitive, warm, accepting, responsive, and immediate. Subordinates feel they can work better for that kind of supervisor. The supervisor who is immediate is more likely to gain cooperation from her or his subordinates without using coercive power. Cooperation is key to any organization's success. Immediate supervisors generate more cooperation (Hickson, Powell, Turner, Neiva, & Adams, 2002; Richmond, 2002; Richmond & Martin, 1998; Richmond & McCroskey,

1998, 2000, 2001; Richmond, McCroskey, & Davis, 1986; Richmond, Wagner, & McCroskey, 1983; Richmond, Davis, Saylor, & McCroskey, 1984; Richmond, Smith, Heisel, & McCroskey, 1998, 2001, 2002; Robinson, 1998).

- The immediate supervisor is perceived as more accepting, responsive, assertive, and sensitive.
- A supervisor's use of immediacy suggests an interest in and concern for the employee. Subordinates usually respond similarly. Immediacy promotes immediacy. Most subordinates will never be as immediate with their supervisors as their supervisors are with them, because the status barrier still exists. Immediacy from the supervisor opens the channels for immediacy from the subordinate.
- Immediacy improves communication between supervisor and subordinate. The relaxed subordinate feels freer to express her or his feelings to a supervisor than does the anxious subordinate. Immediacy helps subordinates relax and feel more comfortable with the supervisor.
- Immediacy will promote a more positive relationship between supervisor and subordinate. Additionally, subordinates of supervisors perceived as exhibiting higher immediacy will evaluate their communication more positively.
- Supervisors perceived as exhibiting higher immediacy will be perceived by their subordinates as more competent and credible and interpersonally attractive.
- Last, supervisors perceived as exhibiting higher immediacy will have subordinates who report higher job satisfaction and motivation.

Disadvantages of Immediacy

A supervisor who is immediate might be perceived by her or his boss as not being in control or being too easy with subordinates. This creates a double bind for the supervisor. How can one be immediate without being perceived as not being in control or too friendly with one's subordinates? Simply put, do not be too immediate when the boss is near. Keep the status roles distinct between you and your subordinates. Resume immediacy when the boss is gone.

Some subordinates try to use the boss who is immediate to their advantage. They think that the immediate supervisor is a pushover and can be manipulated. Remember, just because a supervisor is immediate does not mean that he or she cannot carry out orders and reprimand others.

Last, immediacy opens the lines of communication. Therefore the supervisor might receive more communication than he or she can handle effectively. An effective supervisor has to learn what communication to handle and what to delegate to others.

On balance, immediacy has more advantages for both the supervisor and the subordinate than it has disadvantages. It is only when immediacy is taken to excess that real problems are likely to arise.

Glossary of Terminology

Status is a person's position or rank in a group or organizational structure.

Subordinate is the employee.

Supervisor is the manager or boss, the one who monitors, controls, and supervises others.

CHAPTER 13

Teacher-Student Nonverbal Relationships

E arly research on communication in the classroom was primarily focused on the verbal interaction between student and teacher. Within the past thirty years, however, researchers, scholars, and practitioners have realized the relevance of nonverbal communication in the classroom environment. The nonverbal component of the communication process normally is as important to the teacher-student relationship as the verbal component is, and often is much more important (Ambady & Rosenthal, 1993; Andersen, 1986; Andersen & Andersen, 1982; Buhr, Clifton, & Pryor, 1994; Frymier, 1993; Kearney, Plax,

Richmond, & McCroskey, 1984, 1985; McCroskey, 1992; Kougl, 1997; McCroskey & Richmond, 1983, 1992; McCroskey, Richmond, Plax, & Kearney, 1985; Mottet & Richmond, 1998, 2002; Plax, Kearney, McCroskey, & Richmond, 1986; Richmond, 1990, 1997, 1999, 2002a, 2002b; Richmond & Martin, 1998; Richmond & McCroskey, 1984, 1998; Richmond, Gorham, & McCroskey, 1986; Richmond, Wrench, & Gorham, 1998; Richmond, McCroskey, Kearney, & Plax, 1987; Richmond, McCroskey, Plax & Kearney, 1986; Richmond, Smith, Heisel, & McCroskey, 1998, 2001, 2002; Sidelinger & McCroskey, 1997; Smith, 1979; Thompson, 1973; Thweatt & McCroskey, 1996; Wiemann & Wiemann, 1975).

TEACHER ROLES

The Teacher as Speaker

When we think of lecturing as a method of instruction, we often think first of our college classes in which we frequently experienced lectures. Any time a teacher assumes the role of information giver, speaking with a structured agenda, he or she becomes a lecturer. In this situation, the speaker holds the floor. It is her or his responsibility to hold the attention of the listeners.

Lectures are an efficient use of instructional time. They can communicate a large amount of information to a maximum number of students without requiring much (if any) equipment. They allow teachers to present material not available in textbooks or other easily accessible resources and, if presented well, can motivate and excite students. Research has indicated that students taught by lecture do as well as or better on tests of factual recall than those taught by discussion methods. Some students, such as those with a high level of communication apprehension, prefer the relative anonymity of a lecture format, in which the fear of being called upon to speak does not interfere with their ability to concentrate on the material being presented.

On the downside, lectures are not as effective as other methods in fostering higher levels of learning (application, analysis, synthesis, and evaluation) or in developing psychomotor skills. Students tend to be passive; according to various studies, their attention frequently wanes in fifteen to twenty-five minutes, and their retention decreases by as much as 80 percent within about eight weeks. Lectures are a whole-group method of instruction, a form of mass communication, and must be structured with an assumption that all the students are at about the same level of initial understanding and have approximately the same ability to learn. Feedback is limited. Students who do not learn well by listening are at a disadvantage.

Lectures demand that teachers practice the verbal and nonverbal skills of effective presentational lecturing and speaking. Students expect that:

1. The instructor will be knowledgeable enough to explain the topic in understandable terms.
2. The lecture will be organized.
3. The instructor will secure and hold their attention.

4. The lecture material will be selected with attention to its interest value.
5. The instructor will be competent, caring, and enthusiastic.
6. The instructor will demonstrate a sense of humor.
7. The instructor will demonstrate effective instructional communication skills.
8. The instructor will be assertive and responsive to their needs.
9. The instructor will be a professional role model.
10. The instructor will demonstrate the principle of immediate communication.

Violation of these expectations will diminish the students' affect, for the speaker, the course, and the subject area.

One way to maximize a lecture's effectiveness is to abide by the general rule (supported by research) that a speaker should plan to cover material for only half of the allotted lecture time, and use the rest of the time to buttress and repeat information with pointed examples and illustrations that relate the concepts to the students' own experiences. Teachers should take the time to introduce humor, either as a clarifying device or simply to break up the serious presentation and reawaken attentiveness—students like teachers who have a sense of humor, and that liking rubs off on the material. Where possible, teachers should also develop visual aids to enhance the lecture's appeal. Students learn better if they know what they are about to learn. An effective lecturer will provide advance organizers throughout the presentation to help students sort the information into meaningful units. Students perform better on tests when they have been given notes of some sort to refer to during lectures. When the teacher provides an extensive outline of key points with diagrams, tables, and a place for students to record explanatory notes during the lecture, students learn more than when left to their own note taking. This technique also gives the students a sense not only of where the teacher is going but also of how far he or she has to go before reaching closure. Anyone who has ever been caught in a traffic jam and experienced the anxiety associated with not knowing how long he or she will be stuck will understand the benefits of being able to predict likely progress.

An alternative strategy for helping students organize their notes is the *guided lecture procedure*. Students are encouraged to simply listen and refrain from taking notes during the teacher's lecture, which is planned for approximately the first half of the period. They are then asked to write down what they recall from the lecture. The instructor takes five minutes or so to review main points and answer questions, after which the students move into small groups to cooperatively prepare a set of notes that are shared among group members. This procedure has the benefit of allowing students to see the big picture before trying to decide which of its components need to be recorded for future reference, and it is a means of personalizing the class atmosphere by encouraging supportive interaction within smaller groups. The downside is that only half as much material may be covered in a lecture. This is of less concern if we keep in mind that it is *not* the amount of material that the teacher covers that is important—it is the amount of material that the students learn.

Finally, effective lecturers must be careful not to allow the potentially impersonal strategy of lecturing to interfere with their attempts to establish an immediate teacher-student relationship. Using student names, incorporating personal anecdotes and other means of self-disclosure, asking questions and encouraging students to talk, referring to the class as "our" class and to what "we" are doing, and using humor all contribute to immediacy, as do maintaining eye contact with the students, smiling, having a relaxed body position and using animated gestures, moving about the classroom during the lecture, and—this point is very important to remember—using a dynamic, vocally expressive style of delivery. These strategies have been shown to have both cognitive and affective learning payoffs. They help to personalize the instruction, to highlight important points, and to maintain interest by presenting continually shifting visual and oral cues.

The Teacher as Moderator

Several studies of instructional strategies and classroom interaction have concluded that students develop a greater affect for subjects taught through class discussion than those taught strictly by lecture. Discussion allows students to formulate principles and applications in their own words, giving a sense of ownership of course concepts. Discussion also provides teachers with prompt feedback on how students are processing information. Richmond, Wrench, and Gorham (1998) have demonstrated effective teaching instructional skills that were related to classroom interaction: fluency in asking questions, reinforcing student participation, using probing questions, using questions that address higher-level cognitive objectives, facility with divergent questions, appropriate use of nonverbal communication cues to reduce reliance on teacher talk, and using interaction techniques to reduce boredom and inattention.

As common as claims of desiring and encouraging class discussion are, many teachers find that getting students to talk is a difficult and frustrating task. One of the problems teachers have in generating class discussion is their assumption that the students should be the initiators. Most students, however, do not come to class with questions or observations, at least those they wish to share. One of the keys to successful whole-class discussion is the teacher's ability to ask questions, not just to ask for them. Furthermore, the kind of question the teacher asks is central to her or his success in the role of moderator.

Closed questions, which have only one or a limited number of correct responses, are a good way of keeping students on their toes but rarely foster discussion. "What year did World War II begin?" "Can anyone explain how a rainbow is made?" or "How would knowledge of immediacy cues be useful in a sales position?" address knowledge, comprehension, and application objectives and invite students to become active participants in class, but require specific, correct answers.

Educators need to be careful not to make answering such questions a threatening experience. Students with a high level of communication apprehension will often answer, "I don't know," just to avoid being called on again, and any student will suffer some degree of embarrassment if put on the spot with a question he or she can't answer. For that reason, teachers should avoid calling on individual students who do not signal their willingness to participate. While calling only on those students who volunteer may limit interaction to the more extroverted students, the teacher should question her or his motives for insisting students answer questions when they do not want to. Is this important to the instructional objectives for that unit? Or is this just another instance of the "Gotcha" game played by so many teachers?

Systems of questioning around a circle or down the rows are viewed with increasing terror by many students as their time to look bad approaches. All that such systems are certain to accomplish is to reduce the cognitive learning of some students while generating negative affective learning. In any case, the teacher's response to wrong answers and her or his sensitive use of appropriate, helpful prompts (rather than just "I'm waiting" or "Go on") will improve a nonthreatening environment in using closed questions.

With closed questions, the teacher remains the primary focus of the educator-student interaction. It is the use of open questions that is most effective at shifting that focus to a genuine discussion atmosphere in which the teacher steps back into a moderator's role. Open questions are particularly appropriate for getting at analysis, synthesis, and application objectives. At their best, open questions motivate discussions among students when the teacher steps in only to draw closure or redirect the discussion's focus. A classroom adaptation might be: "What if Romeo and Juliet had not been successful in killing themselves when they attempted suicide, but pulled through? What do you think would have happened to them?" Posing this question to a class not only asks them to draw on what they know about Romeo and Juliet, their families, and other insights from the play they have read; it also invites them to draw on their own experiences with and attitudes about parent-child relationships, love, early marriage, suicide, and so forth.

Participation in classroom discussion can often be maximized by the use of buzz groups—small groups of students who put their heads together to briefly discuss a question among themselves and then report their responses to the class as a whole. With open questions, this technique gives more students an opportunity to express their ideas in a finite amount of time. With closed questions, it takes the spotlight off individual students and encourages peer teaching. Most students are less apprehensive about communicating in a buzz group than they are in front of the class as a whole. A final recommendation regarding the teacher's role as a moderator concerns wait time. It is extremely common to observe teachers answering their own questions, usually because a student response is not immediately forthcoming. Students quickly learn this pattern and absolve themselves of any responsibility for participation. Questions are not perceived as real questions. Many of us have heard at one time or another a teacher monologue that goes something like this: "OK, who read the chapter? Anyone? What was it about? World War II. Anyway, what was that war about? It was about power, wasn't it? Was it worth fighting a war over? I think it was. Does anyone disagree with me? Nobody does? Well, then, what was the first battle in World War II?" Most students enter classes having had little experience with participatory classroom norms and with teachers whose questions were primarily rhetorical. We have to spend some time changing students' expectations, and we have to give them time to think. It is estimated that as many as 70 percent of the students at the college level never participate in class discussion. Is it because they were taught not to ask questions by teachers who did not wait long enough for responses?

The Teacher as Trainer

Teaching psychomotor skills require that students have an opportunity to practice skills until they master them. Sometimes, as in learning to drive a car, students are highly motivated to repeat the same task over and over until they learn how to do it. Sometimes students are not as highly motivated to continue practicing and become bored with repetition. When faced with such a situation, the effectiveness of skill lessons is enhanced by the teacher's offering ways to vary the performance of the skill. For example, children who are learning to write the alphabet may lose interest in writing letters over and over on lined paper, but remain excited about painting an alphabet mural, drawing letters in pudding with their fingers, creating alphabet people, being given the opportunity to write on the chalkboard or whiteboard, and so forth.

For teachers to effectively coach students until they master a skill, it is essential that they be able to break the performance of the skill into separate components so that they can offer corrective instruction. One of the authors clearly remembers years of physical education classes in elementary school where the teacher rewarded students for being able to do things and punished them for not being able to do them but never offered coaching. Having moved on to high school, the author was amazed that one didn't have to simply *be* a good baseball player; one could become a better one by following some

Teachers and students can have productive communication.

corrective instruction in how to bat. Some students got better and better at baseball just by getting more playing experience, but others simply repeated ineffective moves until they were pulled out of the game and allowed to concentrate only on one aspect of play until they got the hang of it.

Teachers or trainers of highly skilled students are characteristically masters of isolating and working on specific components of performance in their training programs: the competitive golfer's trainer will work on eliminating a small twist of the wrist that compromises control; the violin prodigy's teacher will note that additional finger dexterity might enable the young musician to reach new heights, and therefore will assign dexterity exercises. Teachers who can help students figure out why they are not mastering a skill have themselves mastered a primary coaching skill.

The Teacher as Manager

Small-group projects typically involve two to six students working together on a common task. They provide an opportunity to maximize students' active involvement in class, to develop their interpersonal communication and cooperation skills, and to reinforce their knowledge through peer teaching. Research provides evidence that students retain information longer when they have an opportunity to verbalize it, especially to their peers. Working in small groups tends to increase students' motivation, partly because they enjoy the opportunity to interact with their peers and partly because they care about being regarded positively by their peers and don't want to let their classmates down by failing to do their part.

Some teachers are uncomfortable with small-group activities, because they cannot monitor what is going on with all students at all times and feel loss of control over what is going on in the classroom. Some have observed that students spend too much of the time off task, that one or two group members tend to carry the others, and that grading individual contributions to group projects is difficult. Some teachers are not exactly sure what they are supposed to do while students are working in groups and feel like they are abdicating their responsibility to be teaching. The concern of these teachers is well founded, for if the teacher is not a good manager, group activities may be worse than useless.

The teacher's role in small-group instruction is that of a manager of resources and of personnel. As a manager, the teacher should clearly define the task at hand and provide guidance as to time lines and the organization of various steps needed to complete the assignment. Some group tasks are designed to be completed within a single class period, while others may continue for several weeks or even months. In the latter case, it is particularly helpful to guide the groups in determining short-term goals within the longer-term objectives. Giving students a list of resources and telling them "Do a report on effective communication; see you in six weeks" is an ineffective management practice. Two of the primary reasons that groups flounder and spend time off task are that they don't know what they are supposed to be doing, or they don't know how to go about doing it.

As managers, teachers consider the composition of task groups and make strategic decisions on how they will be formed. There are valid reasons to form home groups that remain together throughout various projects: students get to know one another and their individual strengths and limitations, and they tend to work more efficiently as time goes on, becoming a sort of interdependent minicorporation. And there are equally valid reasons to create a new mix each time groups are assigned: students develop broader sociological ties, and cliques are less likely to develop. There are valid reasons to mix motivated with less motivated students and equally valid reasons to let the motivated students work together and let the unmotivated ones work things out on their own. At best, new leaders are discovered; at worst, the usual leaders don't feel put upon. The choice of a grouping strategy will often relate to the educator's affective objectives for a particular class. Once the groups are formed, the teacher-as-manager should monitor working relationships and intervene if conflict is undermining the group's ability to function.

As resource managers, teachers should be able to provide groups with access to the information and materials they require to accomplish their tasks. The teacher will monitor the groups' progress and suggest means of following up on ideas, checking information, and presenting their products. It is often wise not to overmanage up front. If students are given all the resources needed at the outset and a very specific model of what they are to come up with, much of the incidental learning from the group's process will be lost. The groups are then the educator's staff, working on the teacher's project rather than on their own.

The Teacher as a Coordinator

The use of resources to supplement instruction can serve many purposes. Computer-aided instruction and other programmed instruction packages can be created or purchased to be used as either a primary instructional strategy or a supplemental tool. Films, videotapes, audiotapes, instructional television, books, magazines, newspapers, demonstrations, guest speakers, simulations, PowerPoint presentations, and so forth can be used to complement other instructional strategies or as the cornerstone of instruction.

Most of the time, resource-based instruction is supplementary. Resources are used within a traditional teacher-directed classroom to stimulate various senses, present information in alternative formats, and enhance text and lecture material. Sometimes they are used as a break for the teacher or as a reward for the students.

The key to using resource-based instruction effectively is to know exactly how the resource will be used to enhance instructional objectives. Whatever the type of resource, the teacher should experience it in its entirety before using it in the classroom, and should coordinate the logistics for its effective use.

Few instructional resources are so powerful that they work alone without some sort of setup and follow-up activities. Resource-based instruction is the most effective when teachers use resources rather than defer to them. Maximizing their effectiveness requires considerable logistical coordination on the teacher's part; however, it is usually worth the effort.

Employing a variety of instructional strategies appeals to various learning styles and tends to keep both teachers and students from getting into a rut. The teacher's preferences and individual strengths will influence strategic decisions, although the instructional objectives at hand should always be central to selecting the most appropriate teaching role at a given point in a course of study. In this section, we have suggested that a teacher might wear many hats: speaker, moderator, trainer, manager, and coordinator. Most teachers look good in all of them, and most students get tired of looking at the same hat every day. The hat most students prefer on their teacher—whether the teacher is in speaker, moderator, trainer, manager, or coordinator mode—is the nonverbally receptive, expressive, supportive teacher.

The Teacher as Controller, Supervisor, and Helper

The teacher acts as a controller by getting students to acquire certain behavior and knowledge. Teachers act as supervisors by selecting student activities and deciding what is the student's responsibility and what is the educator's responsibility. Last, the teacher acts as helper by encouraging student understanding and expression of emotions and feelings. We would add to this list one other teacher role: entertainer. Teachers must know how to present material in an interesting and entertaining fashion. Students will then attend to it and retain it longer.

Educators have a bigger responsibility to be effective and affective communicators than any other group we discuss in this book. They have control over children who have not yet formed their attitudes and ideas. If teachers are not effective and affective communicators, they cannot control, supervise, help, or entertain their students. In fact, they will turn many students off to school. This turnoff can happen at any level. Teachers can either motivate or fail to motivate students by their communication.

It is no wonder that so many students become alienated from school. In no other context within a free society are individuals required to spend more than six hours a day, five days a week, for months at a time listening to one other person. We expect one person to hold the attention and maintain the interest of all those captive listeners. He or she must ensure that those captives learn all they need to know to become contributing adults in our society. An easy task? Society must think so, for in many areas we pay our teachers less than we do sanitation workers. Unfortunately, effective communication in the classroom may be the most difficult communicative task in society. Surprisingly, few teachers receive intensive training in communication. Most receive nothing more than an introductory class in public speaking if they receive even that much. Only a small fraction receives any instruction in nonverbal communication.

ROLE OF NONVERBAL COMMUNICATION

As we learned in Chapter 1, nonverbal communication can function to repeat, contradict, substitute, complement, accent, or regulate the verbal. This is especially true of nonverbal communication in the classroom. In a survey of more than ten thousand teachers, we found that most teachers feel that nonverbal behavior is a more effective communicative tool for improving student-teacher relationships than verbal communication. They feel this way because nonverbal communication permeates every facet of the classroom environment. In addition, many teachers are finding that nonverbal communication is more effective than verbal communication at helping them be better speakers, controllers, managers, helpers, and entertainers. Nonverbal communication is subtler and can be used more often. Students get bored with instructor talk and eventually ignore it. Teachers can use nonverbal behavior to communicate to students without making a big point of it.

Ambady and Rosenthal (1993) completed a landmark study titled "Half a Minute: Predicting Teacher Evaluations from Thin Slices of Nonverbal Behavior and Physical Attractiveness." These researchers conducted three studies. In studies one and two, subjects were asked to rate college teachers' and high school teachers' nonverbal behavior and physical attractiveness based on ten-second silent video clips. In study three, the researchers investigated whether strangers' ratings of teachers would predict nonverbal behavior and physical attractiveness from study one and two if even "more thinned slices of the video" were shown. The clips were reduced from ten seconds to five and two seconds. The results were astonishing; they revealed the following:

> There were no significant differences in the accuracy of judgments based on video clips 10s, 5s, and 2s in length. In addition, there were no significant differences in the accuracy of judgments for the two samples of teachers. . . . Moreover, judgments based on 30s exposures (three 10s clips of each teacher) were not significantly more accurate than judgments based on 6s exposures (three 2s clips of each teacher). (pp. 437–438)

Ambady and Rosenthal suggest that the human ability to form impressions is strongly supported by their studies. In fact, as has always been suggested in the nonverbal literature, impression formation takes place very early in a relationship. Often, these initial impressions determine the communication that follows. Ambady and Rosenthal conclude that, based on nonverbal behaviors shown in very brief (less than thirty-second), silent video clips, we evaluate our teachers as accepting, active, attentive, competent, confident, dominant, empathic, enthusiastic, honest, likeable, calm, optimistic, professional, supportive, and warm. Subjects observed specific nonverbal behavior such as symmetric arms, frowning, head nodding, head shaking, pointing, sitting, smiling, standing, strong gestures, head touching, upper torso touching, walking, and weak gestures. Ambady and Rosenthal conclude the following:

> Teachers with higher ratings tended to be more nonverbally active and expressive. They were more likely to walk around, touch their upper torsos, and smile. Less effective teachers were more likely to sit, touch their heads, and shake rather than nod their heads. These results suggest that teachers with higher ratings showed more nonverbal expressiveness and involvement than less effective teachers. (pp. 436–437)

They also suggest that teachers "should be made aware of the possible impact of their nonverbal behavior and perhaps even trained in nonverbal skills" (p. 440). The researchers caution, however, that these judgments are most accurate for the affective side of teaching.

We have stated for years that the **primary function of teachers' verbal behavior** in the classroom is to give content to improve students' cognitive learning. The **primary function of teachers' nonverbal behavior** in the classroom is to improve students' affect or liking for the subject matter, teacher, and class, and to instill in them the desire to learn more about the subject matter. One step toward that is the development of a positive affective relationship between the student and teacher. When the teacher improves affect through effective nonverbal behavior, then the student is likely to listen more, learn more, and have a more positive attitude about school. Effective classroom communication between teacher and student is the key to positive affect toward learning. As communication improves between teacher and student, so does affect. When teachers are trained to use verbal and nonverbal communication in the classroom more effectively, student-teacher relationships improve and so do students' affective and cognitive learning. When positive affect is present, cognitive learning increases.

The nonverbal behavior of the teacher communicates meanings to students. For example, the teacher who rarely looks at a student when talking is communicating that he or she is not very interested in that student. Students' nonverbal behavior likewise communicates meanings to teachers. The student who is always yawning might be bored, tired, or both. The teacher should review the context and determine whether the student simply is tired or whether the teacher is so boring that he or she is putting the student to sleep.

The remainder of this chapter focuses on discussion of the various types of nonverbal behaviors and how each affects the student-instructor relationship. We direct primary attention to the teacher's behavior and how this might influence communication with the student. The reason we take this approach is that it is the student's perceptions of what the teacher does that determine how effective the communication is. If a student perceives that a teacher is using coercive power, then he or she will respond in a negative fashion. If a student perceives that a teacher is using immediacy, then he or she will be more responsive to the teacher.

When a student perceives that a teacher does not like her or him, the student most likely will learn to dislike the teacher (Richmond, Wrench, & Gorham, 1998). The remainder of this chapter centers on how teachers and students can use nonverbal behavior to express affect and liking. All the examples discussed can be applied to the typical classroom setting. The concept of immediacy is critical to communication in the classroom.

IMMEDIACY

Immediacy is the degree of perceived physical or psychological closeness between two people. The concept may be best understood in terms of the immediacy principle outlined by Mehrabian (1966, 1971, 1981), who introduced this concept. He stated that "People are drawn toward persons and things they like, evaluate highly, and prefer; they avoid or move away from things they dislike, evaluate negatively, or do not prefer" (Mehrabian, 1971, p. 1). This social-psychological perspective suggests that positive affect causes people to become more immediate, while negative affect reduces immediacy.

While immediacy has received some attention from communication scholars interested in interpersonal, organizational, and health communication, it has been researched primarily in the context of the college classroom (Andersen, 1979, 1985; Barringer & McCroskey, 2000; Chesebro & McCroskey, 1998, 2001; Christophel, 1990; Frymier, 1994; Gorham, Cohen, & Morris, 1999; McCroskey & Richmond, 1992, 1996; McCroskey, Richmond, & Stewart, 1986; McCroskey, Sallinen, Fayer, Richmond, & Barraclough, 1996; Moore, Masterson, Christophel, & Shea, 1996; Mottet & Richmond, 2002; Plax, Kearney, McCroskey, & Richmond, 1986; Richmond, 1990, 1997, 1999, 2002a, 2002b; Richmond & Hickson, 2002; Richmond & McCroskey, 1990, 1998, 2000, 2001; Richmond, Gorham, & McCroskey, 1986; Richmond, Wrench, & Gorham, 2001; Richmond, Smith, Heisel, & McCroskey, 2001; Rocca & McCroskey, 1999; Thomas, Richmond, & McCroskey, 1994; Thweatt & McCroskey, 1998). Several studies have been conducted looking at immediacy behaviors of teachers during instructional communication with their students. These studies have found immediacy behaviors to be associated with more positive affect as well as increased cognitive learning and more positive student evaluations of teachers. This research has suggested the appropriateness of a communication principle that is the reverse of Mehrabian's social-psychological principle: "The more communicators employ immediate behaviors, the more others will like, evaluate highly, and prefer such communicators; and the less communicators employ immediate behaviors, the more others will dislike, evaluate negatively, and reject such communicators." We prefer to call this idea the *principle of immediate communication*. There are two primary forms of immediacy: *verbal* and *nonverbal immediacy*. Each is discussed below.

Verbal Immediacy

What people say can cause us to feel either closer to or more distant from them. **Verbal immediacy** is the use of language that increases immediacy between interactants. Increased immediacy is produced by verbally immediate or verbally effective messages that show openness, friendship, or empathy with the other person. Such simple things as the use of the pronouns *we* or *us* rather than *you* or *you and I* can increase the feeling of immediacy. For example, in trying to denote verbal immediacy to a peer, say "we can do this together" rather than "you should try this."

One of the most important ways to increase immediacy in a relationship is to send verbal messages that encourage the other person to communicate. Such comments as "I see what you mean," "Tell me more," "Please continue," "That is a good idea," "This is a team effort," and "Let's talk more about this" create increased immediacy. Contrast these statements with the following comments: "Oh, shut up," "You've got to be kidding," "No way, I thought of that," and "That is just dumb." If you were to hear any of the latter, would you want to communicate more? Probably not. You would not feel very close to people who made such comments unless it was clear they were joking.

Nonverbal Immediacy

Most categories of nonverbal behavior can be used to increase or decrease nonverbal immediacy. Let's consider each one.

Physical Appearance

As we have stated, one's general physical appearance is a means of communication. What is communicated varies depending on the attractiveness of the person as well as his or her body, scent, hair, dress, and use of artifacts.

ATTRACTIVENESS. We know that attractive people are perceived by others as more likeable, sociable, outgoing, friendly, popular, persuasive, successful, and happy than unattractive people. Research clearly shows that in most situations attractive people are more likely to be responded to more favorably than unattractive people. For example, the attractive male is more likely to get the high-powered sales job than the unattractive male, particularly if their qualifications are equal. There have even been reports of people being refused employment because they were too unattractive. Being perceived as attractive might produce two nonverbal immediacy–related results.

1. Because attractive people are perceived by others as more likeable and sociable, they may also be perceived as more approachable. If they are responded to in an immediate fashion by others, they will most likely respond in kind.
2. Because attractive people have been treated as if they were more responsive and sociable, they are likely to exhibit more immediate behavior. For most of their lives, attractive people have been approached by others, often

simply because of their looks. Therefore they have learned to be immediate with others, which makes them even more attractive. This is not to suggest that unattractive people are not immediate. Many unattractive people have learned that immediacy is one means of increasing their attractiveness.

Instructor Appearance

Appearance sends important messages in the classroom setting. An instructor's attire influences the way students perceive that instructor. Teachers who dress very formally are seen by students as competent, organized, prepared, and knowledgeable. Teachers who dress casually or informally (not sloppily) are seen as friendly, outgoing, receptive, flexible, and fair.

We have found that when teachers dress very formally, it makes students feel as if the teacher is not receptive to their needs and not likely to communicate with them. The teacher is perceived as competent but not as receptive. The teacher who dresses casually is perceived as open, friendly, and more immediate but perhaps not as competent as the teacher who dresses more formally. Therefore our advice is to dress formally for a week or two or until credibility is established. Then dress more casually to project the image that one is open to student interaction. The teacher who always dresses formally may communicate that he or she does not want much student interaction, even though the dressing behavior may simply reflect the teacher's clothing preferences. Whatever the teacher's motivation, the students' perceptions are what counts (Gorham, Cohen, & Morris, 1997, 1999; Morris, Gorham, Cohen, & Huffman, 1996; Roach, 1997).

Unattractive instructors also have a more difficult time in the classroom than attractive instructors. Students are more immediate and receptive to the attractive teacher and less immediate and receptive to the unattractive teacher. Therefore, the unattractive teacher must work harder at establishing credibility, similarity, and liking than the attractive teacher.

Teachers who are ectomorphic are usually perceived by students as anxious and less composed but perhaps intelligent. The endomorphic teacher is generally perceived by students as slow, lazy, underprepared, and not dynamic in the classroom. The mesomorphic teacher is perceived as credible, dependable, likable, and competent but possibly also tough and dominant.

Student Appearance

Because instructors' dress affects how students perceive them, how does students' dress influence teachers' perceptions? Teachers make very definite judgments about students based on their dress. The student who is always sloppily dressed, never put together well, and does not seem to take any pride in her or his personal appearance is likely to be perceived by teachers as lazy, slow, and not very interested in school. One teacher told us about a sixth-grade student who always dressed in a sloppy, disheveled manner. After several years of being treated as if he were lazy and slow, he began to meet those expectations. The teacher found that he had above-average intelligence and exceptionally good reading skills. She started to reach him by letting him read whatever he wanted to read. Then she started getting him to pay more attention to his schoolwork. By the end of the sixth grade, the student was a strong B student. She even managed to get him to take more care of his appearance and dress. Other teachers commented on how "something has really changed him" when they noticed his change of dress.

Students who dress in an unusual or weird manner might also be perceived in a negative manner by teachers. Teachers often punish or criticize the student who does not fit the norm of school dress. Sometimes they criticize the student's dress so much that it impairs the student's learning and the communication between teacher and student. In the early sixties, many schools had very strict dress codes. These codes did not allow young women to wear slacks, and young men had to keep their hair short. We know of one situation where a boy was persecuted so often and so much by his teachers, peers, and principals that he never finished high school. His great sin was that his hair touched his ears. He was suspended from school because the teachers and the principal felt he was a disturbance to the other students. Similar cases were reported across the United States, and many students were persecuted because of their appearance. Although appearance factors that are considered distracting today may differ from those of twenty years ago, the response of teachers and school administrators often does not.

Students who have a neat, clean, acceptable appearance are generally accepted by instructors, peers, and administrators. They are often given more latitude than the sloppy or unusually dressed student. For example, students who dress as the teacher thinks they should dress are more attractive to the teacher and are likely to be helped more. The teacher will spend more time interacting with them and helping them with their assignments.

It is sad but true that attractive children are often given better treatment than unattractive children in the school environment. Unattractive children are discriminated against in the classroom and the social environment of the school. The attractive child is communicated with more often by teachers than the unattractive child. Both teachers and peers interact more positively with the attractive child. The unattractive child does not receive the amount or type of teacher-student interaction that the attractive child does. He or she is also perceived more negatively by peers than is the attractive child (Richmond, 1997).

Often without realizing it, the teacher will avoid the unattractive child and display nonimmediate cues with the unattractive child while being immediate with the attractive child. Unattractive children are commonly ignored by teachers, given less time to answer questions than their attractive counterparts, encouraged less to talk, given less eye contact, given more distance, and touched less by their teachers. This type of nonverbal behavior communicates to the unattractive child that he or she is not as good as the other students. Unattractive children often receive lower grades than the other students. Much of this is because of the different nonverbal treatment given them by the teacher. They feel that they are not liked or not as good as the other students and eventually tune out the classroom environment and learn less. We have heard teachers tell us hundreds of stories about this type of situation in their schools. We have also heard students say things like, "Mrs. Jones doesn't like me." When asked how they can tell, the student says, "I can tell—it's the way she behaves" or "it's the way she treats me."

Body type determines, at least in part, how a person is perceived by others. The ectomorphic student is likely to be perceived by the teacher as high-strung, anxious, and nervous but probably competent. He or she might be perceived by peers as nerdy and generally not as a star athlete. The endomorphic student might be perceived by the teacher as slow, lazy, and not too bright but really nice and funny. Such students are not perceived as star athletes either. The mesomorphic student is usually perceived as being dependable, intelligent, competent, dominant, and appealing by the teacher. They are also often perceived as the best athletes.

The general appearance and attractiveness of a teacher or student can have a major impact on student-educator communication. Generally, the more attractive student or teacher is given preferential treatment. The unattractive student or teacher must work harder to be perceived as competent and likeable. Parents should be encouraged to help their children present a reasonably attractive appearance in school. Many cannot accomplish this alone, and it does make a difference in student achievement.

HAIR. The length, style, and color of hair can be used to foster immediacy or nonimmediacy. For example, the person with the currently acceptable hair length, style, and color is much more approachable than the person with the unusual length, style, and color. Many rock stars may be perceived by one segment of the population as very approachable or immediate, but another segment of the population may perceive them as outlandish and unapproachable. Much of it has to do with hair length, style, and color.

DRESS AND ARTIFACTS. Dress and the artifacts one chooses can communicate immediacy or nonimmediacy. Informal but not sloppy dress usually communicates that one is approachable. People are often intimidated by very formal dress. Formal dress is one method of denoting higher status, and heightened status decreases immediacy. In some situations, people want to be perceived as having higher status and want decreased immediacy. For example, during job interviews, interviewers want to establish who is the interviewee and who is the interviewer. This is often accomplished by the interviewer's style and quality of dress.

Artifacts are items that adorn the body, such as jewelry, clothing, glasses, makeup, pipes, briefcases, books, and so on. There are instances when a person's use of an artifact suggests that he or she is immediate or nonimmediate. For example, the person who wears a T-shirt that says "Take me, I'm cute and cuddly" is probably communicating something different from the person whose T-shirt reads "Get outta my face." Reflective sunglasses that do not allow you to see the wearer's eyes also generally denote nonimmediacy.

Gesture and Movement

Small children often use gestures and movements to explain what they cannot say verbally. As they grow older, they tend to use fewer simple hand gestures and increase their use of complex hand movements. In this culture, we tend to use more gestures when we are excited or giving complex messages. On the other hand, we use fewer gestures when we are bored or transmitting a simple message. Therefore, in the early grades, children are likely to use more gestures and movements than verbal messages to communicate. However, about the time children reach age 12 they should be acquiring the adult norms and using more complex gestures and a wider variety of verbal messages.

In the classroom, adaptors are probably the most common gestures used by students. The classroom is an anxiety-producing situation for many children. Observe a typical classroom, and you will find students chewing pencils, biting their nails, picking at their desks or notebooks, pulling at their hair, smoothing their clothing, and clicking their pens. A classroom that has an inordinate amount of student adaptive behavior is one in which the anxiety level is high or the teacher is boring. Students use more adaptors in classes where they feel anxious or bored. These behaviors are often perceived as a form of misbehavior and are punished. The student who is constantly clicking her or his pen is perceived by the teacher as disruptive. Students may not even realize they are engaging in such behavior until they are reprimanded for it.

Adaptors are more prevalent during the first few days of school, near holidays, and near the end of school. Students unintentionally use more adaptive behavior at these times. Teachers also tend to use more adaptive behavior during the first few days of a new school year. It is anxiety-producing for most teachers when they are meeting new classes for the first time. Teachers who use more adaptors are perceived as nervous and anxious.

There are also people (both students and teachers) who gesture very little in the classroom. Students and teachers who gesture very little might be perceived as boring and unanimated. Teachers should use illustrators and affect displays more with their verbal messages to keep the classroom lively and interesting. The teacher's delivery style should be animated and dynamic, and gesturing is one method of achieving this. The animated and dynamic teacher can keep the class interested in the subject for longer periods of time. Nonanimated, boring teachers put their classes to sleep.

Instructors who assume an open body position communicate to their students that they are receptive and immediate, whereas teachers who fold in or keep a closed body position are perceived as nonimmediate and unreceptive. Students using similar positions are perceived in similar ways by their teachers. Students who slouch in their seats when talking to the teacher are perceived as bored, rude, or even arrogant. Teachers expect students to look interested. One of the best indications of interest is body position.

Both students and teachers use adaptive gestures, but they should strive to decrease their reliance on them. Teachers should consciously work to be more animated and dynamic. This will improve student-teacher interaction and make the classroom a more exciting environment (Richmond, 1997).

Facial Behavior

The student or teacher with a glum, dour facial expression is perceived as less animated and less immediate than the student or teacher with a pleasing facial expression. The use of facial expressions communicates a lot in the classroom environment. People cannot always hide their real feelings. The teacher can unintentionally express her or his real feelings about a student through facial expression. Smaller children do not understand many facial expressions and sometimes perceive any expression that is less than positive as a negative one. The frown is often associated with negative facial affect. Children usually do not learn the range of facial expressions until around age 12. Before then, they have difficulty discriminating among the facial expressions of their teachers. Therefore, a small child might react to a teacher's thoughtful expression as if he or she had done something wrong. Teachers need to be very careful in controlling their facial expressions with young children.

Students' facial expressions also influence how teachers react to them. The student who is staring out the window and has a totally bored expression on her or his face is not likely to be called on by the teacher, except as punishment. This student also is not likely to receive any preferential treatment from the teacher. One of the authors had a student who literally slept through several sessions of his evening class. There were 146 students in the class, and this student was the only one who looked bored. This bothered the teacher, until one day the student approached the instructor and apologized for sleeping in class and looking bored. He explained that he worked at the post office from 11 a.m. to 7 p.m. and had difficulty staying awake in all of his evening classes.

Teachers' facial expressions can affect how students feel about the classroom environment. The teacher who has a dull, boring facial expression when talking is perceived by the students as uninterested in them and the subject matter. This type of teacher is likely to have more classroom disruptions because students become bored with the teaching style. Teachers must have pleasing facial expressions that show that they are interested not only in the subject matter but also in their students. Pleasing facial expressions are often accompanied by positive head movements.

The teacher who uses positive head nods in response to a student's comments is perceived as friendly, concerned about the communication between teacher and student, and immediate. An instructor who rarely nods, or uses more negative head movements than positive ones quickly stifles teacher-student communication. Not many students volunteer to talk when they realize that their educator will not respond in a positive or at least encouraging fashion. Positive head nods are a means of stimulating classroom interaction and student responses. Students who use similar head nods help promote student-teacher interaction and help the teacher to know whether the students have understood the class content.

Smiling has long been associated with liking, affiliation, and immediacy. The teacher who smiles and has positive facial affect is perceived as more immediate and likeable than the one who does not. Students react more favorably to the teacher who smiles than to the teacher who frowns a lot or does not smile much. Similarly, teachers react more favorably to the student who smiles than to the student who frowns or does not smile much. They each perceive the other as more open to communication. Therefore, the student-teacher relationship is improved by smiling. Students from kindergarten through graduate school respond better to teachers who smile.

Both instructors and students must use pleasing facial expressions. It improves the perceptions and the communication between teacher and student. The teacher or student with the pleasing facial expression is perceived as more immediate and approachable than the teacher or student who is dour or sour-looking (Richmond, 1997).

Eye Behavior

The instructor's and student's eye behavior can affect the interaction between the two. Students who look away, avoid teacher eye contact, or look down when the teacher calls on them are perceived as uninterested, shy, or unwilling to communicate. None of these are very positive perceptions. We know that people like to have eye contact in communicating with one another. Eye contact might be one of the biggest indicators of student interest in the classroom environment. Students who do not make eye contact with the teacher are perceived as uninterested. Teachers are the same as other people. They want those to whom they are talking to look at them and to make eye contact with them. If that does not occur, it is taken as rejection of their teaching content and as a personal rejection as well.

Some instructors seldom make eye contact with their students. This usually suggests to the student that the teacher is not interested in her or him and that the teacher is not approachable. Teachers who make little eye contact with students often are very shy and probably should not be in the classroom at all. When there is little eye contact between students and teachers, students do not know when to talk, when to ask questions, or how to approach the teacher. This is a common complaint on college campuses. It often is directed toward some foreign-born instructors. The students complain that the instructor never looks at them when lecturing. This behavior may be the result of the instructor's cultural upbringing. In some cultures, it is considered inappropriate for instructors and students to make direct eye contact.

There is one situation in the classroom that can cause deviant eye behavior. This is test-taking time. Often teachers assume that students' wandering eyes are a sign of cheating. This is not always the case. Test time is a very anxious time for most students. Teachers need to be cautious about accusing a student of cheating because he or she looks around during a test. When processing information on a test, students have many conjugate lateral eye movements (CLEMs), which we discussed in Chapter 5. If a student is consistently and constantly looking at another's paper, we can safely assume that he or she is cheating. When a student is glancing left or right or looking up, he or she most likely is just processing information.

Eye behavior is a significant indicator of the relationship between student and teacher. Students who make eye contact with their teachers are perceived as more interested and better students. Teachers who look at their students are perceived as more animated, more interested, and more immediate (Richmond, 1997).

Vocal Behavior

Recently we surveyed students to determine the vocal qualities that students liked or disliked most in teachers. Overwhelmingly, students felt that the monotone voice was a teacher's most objectionable vocal behavior. They felt that the monotone voice projected the image of boredom, noncaring, and nonimmediacy. They also said they learned less when the teacher had a dull or monotone voice, were less interested in the subject matter, and liked the class less. Students want the teacher to have a lively, animated voice (Richmond, 1997).

Of all voice qualities, the monotone voice seems to draw the most negative criticism from both teachers and students. Both say that they perceive the person with the monotone voice as boring and dull. Students who use the monotone voice in class are not helping themselves at all. Instructors want to teach students who sound interested in the class.

An author of this book had a professor who taught the philosophy of education. He droned on and on in a monotone voice for every class period. The class had more than a hundred people in it, and most dozed off. This teacher was the worst model that an education department could employ to teach prospective teachers about how to be an effective and affective teacher. The most significant criticism the students had about him was not his competence but his monotone voice.

There should be a sign placed in all classrooms that says "Laughter is encouraged in this class." No one ever said learning had to be boring. A really good teacher laughs with the students and encourages and allows laughter when something occurs that all can enjoy. For example, one of the authors was lecturing one day, and during the lecture she moved backwards to reach for her notes. She tripped over the garbage can behind her, fell in, and got stuck. The class was stunned and then broke up laughing. She also laughed and finally some students helped her out of the garbage can. Had she not laughed or had she criticized them for laughing, the class would have suffered. Laughing also allows students to release tension and to relax. In research completed as early as 1929, Barr studied good and poor social science teachers and found that good teachers laughed more and allowed laughter in the classroom; whereas, poor teachers did not. Many things have changed since then, but it is certain that the role of laughter in the classroom has not. Teachers who laugh and encourage laughter from their students are still more immediate than those who do not.

Space

How a teacher or student uses interpersonal space with another interactant communicates how he or she perceives that person. The teacher who stands behind the desk or podium and rarely approaches students or allows them to approach her or him is perceived by students as unfriendly, unreceptive, unapproachable, and nonimmediate. This does not help to improve student-teacher relationships.

The student who backs away when the teacher approaches or will not allow a teacher to stand or sit close to him or her will be perceived in a similar manner by the teacher. The student might even be perceived as uninterested in learning and hostile to the classroom environment. Some people simply do not like being approached by others. These people are touch-avoidants. When someone approaches them, they move away or back to avoid contact. We must be cautious to not judge the person who draws away from interaction too harshly. He or she might simply be a touch-avoidant (Andersen & Leibowitz, 1978).

There is also some research that suggests students who are abused at home have greater space needs than those who are not abused, and they may behave like a touch-avoidant. Some research also shows that disruptive students have greater spatial needs than students who are not disruptive. Their disruptiveness may stem from their feeling closed in and under pressure.

Differences in size might make a big difference in how students and teachers feel about their space. For example, elementary school teachers tend, even if they are rather short, to tower over their students. Hence, we suggest that a simple means of getting closer without intimidating the student is to let him or her stand close while the teacher is seated. The teacher could also occasionally sit or kneel on the floor so that he or she is closer to the students. Likewise, students in college and high school often tower over their teachers and should strive not to do this. Teachers do not like to feel as if a student were trying to intimidate them. The tall student is probably unaware of this. The easiest solution is for the student to stand farther away from the teacher. This reduces the towering-over effect and makes communication easier for both.

In summary, space communicates in the classroom environment. The teacher who withdraws from students is perceived as nonimmediate and noncaring. The student who withdraws from the teacher might be perceived as uninterested or hostile. We need to look beyond these perceptions to find out whether another problem is present (Richmond, 1997).

Touch

It is unfortunate that there is very little expressive touch in our classrooms today. Teachers are reluctant to touch students because of the insinuations that others might make. Students above the lowest grade levels have always been reluctant to touch teachers because of the status differential.

Studies reveal that human touch helps people grow and adapt better in society. However, our schools have adopted the noncontact philosophy that our society perpetuates. If you survey most schoolchildren from kindergarten through the twelfth grade about the kind and amount of touch they receive from their teachers, most will say that they get less touch as they get older and much of what they receive is associated with a reprimand. Some students cannot recall the last time a teacher touched them in an expressive fashion. Touch is a form of communication that can be very useful in establishing and maintaining an effective teacher-student relationship. Touch can be used by the instructor to reinforce a student for a job well done. It can be used by the teacher to substitute for the verbal reprimand or control without ever saying a word. For example, the teacher who walks up and touches on the shoulder the child who is misbehaving has gotten her or his attention. The child knows that he or she should stop what he or she is doing. Touch should be an acceptable form of communication in the educator-student relationship. Touching a student on the arm, hand, shoulder, or upper back should be acceptable. This type of touch can be a very effective means of communicating a message without ever uttering a word.

In the early grades, touch is an essential component to establishing an effective student-teacher relationship. Most small children are used to receiving much touch at home. They expect the same at school. The elementary school teacher is often seen as the surrogate parent, and the children expect touch from that teacher. There is nothing wrong in giving it. If a teacher does not touch them, often the children feel as if there were something wrong with them, or they feel unloved. A teacher must be cautious not to touch one or two children more than the rest. Even small children see this differentiation and wonder why the one or two get more touch. Touch is such an important communication variable that one has to use it in a fair manner in the classroom environment.

The younger children may also touch the teacher in places that are unacceptable for the older child to touch. Children usually learn the adult touch norms about age twelve. When a child is in the first grade, it is common for her or him to hug the teacher around the thigh. The teacher should be prepared for and accepting of such touching behavior. However, when the child is in the seventh grade or a sophomore in college, it is highly unusual and generally unacceptable to initiate such touch. In the upper grades, older children expect less touch and receive less. However, touch should still be used as a reinforcer. Older children can be touched on the back or shoulder for doing good work.

Teachers should remember that some students are touch-avoidant and are very uncomfortable when touched. A teacher who encounters a touch-avoidant student should leave him or her alone and not try to relax the student. In addition, some teachers are touch-avoidant and do not want to be touched. These teachers should not teach at the elementary levels. The touch-avoidant student or teacher might be perceived as nonimmediate and perhaps even aloof. If a person is touch-avoidant, other nonverbal cues can be used to communicate immediacy and establish an effective student-teacher relationship (Richmond, 1997).

Teachers or students who withdraw from another's touch might be perceived as nonimmediate or touch-avoidant. Teachers and students should be aware of the touch norms in schools and communities and be cautious about following them. Teachers should use touch as a form of reinforcement, not as punishment. Many classes such as physical education, art, and music allow for a great deal of touch. Teachers in these classes should use touch as a form of communication.

Environment

We acknowledge at the outset that many classrooms are not conducive to student-teacher interaction (Green, 1979; Ketcham, 1958; Richmond, 1997; Sommer, 1997; Todd-Mancillas, 1982). We also acknowledge that many schools have drab and dreary classrooms and very little can be done to improve the environment. Much of what we discuss here, however, can be adapted to any classroom in any school.

Attractive classrooms are much more likely to keep students and teachers attentive and to reduce hostility. Many studies have revealed that ugly environments produce hostile communication among participants. Think of the worst schoolroom you were ever taught in. Think of all its ugly aspects and how you felt while in that environment. The authors of this text have taught in a variety of ugly environments. It is more difficult to keep students' attention when the environment is ugly; too hot or cold; poorly lit; painted dingy yellow, dark brown, industrial green, or battleship-gray; or unclean. Darth Vader could have designed many classrooms in this country. They are dark, forbidding environments that say to students, "Don't plan on any fun here: shut up, sit, and listen." It is a shame that in a country so affluent, many classrooms are still in the Dark Ages. Teachers and students must continue to accept this. However, many teachers redecorate their rooms at their own expense to make the environment more conducive to learning and to enjoyment of learning.

SEATING.   There are optimal seating arrangements for different types of teaching. Traditional row and column arrangements (see Figure 13.1) are useful for listening, note-taking, and lecturing. Modular seating is best for group interaction; this arrangement allows the teacher to move from group to group to give assistance (see Figure 13.2). The circular, horseshoe, or open-square arrangement (Figure 13.3) is particularly useful for encouraging classroom discussion between students and teachers. A teacher's use of the above arrangements in different learning situations will improve student interest and student-teacher communication. Some of these classroom settings do, however, increase the noise level, which must also be considered.

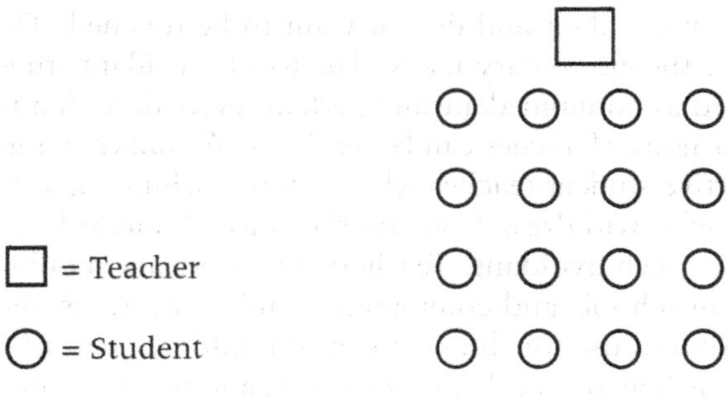

☐ = Teacher

◯ = Student

FIGURE 13.1
Traditional Seating

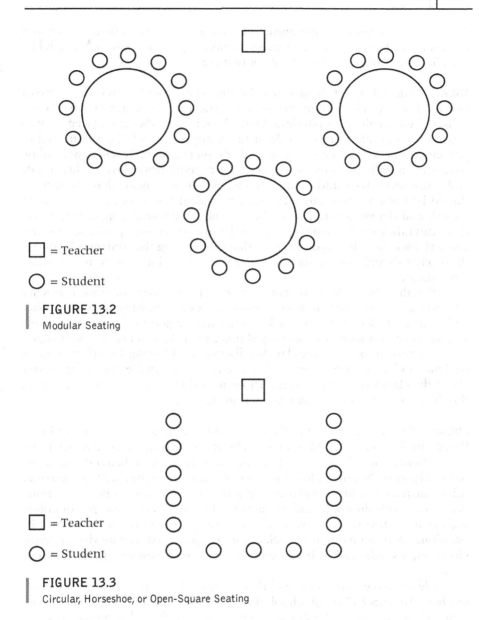

= Teacher

= Student

FIGURE 13.2
Modular Seating

= Teacher

= Student

FIGURE 13.3
Circular, Horseshoe, or Open-Square Seating

MUSIC. Music can be used to counteract student boredom and to establish a comfortable classroom atmosphere. We have found in our research that teachers can use music as an effective reinforcer for good behavior, as a reward for completing a task, and for relaxing the students. Elementary school teachers have long known the power of music in the classroom. They use it relax students, generate conversations, reward, excite, and lull students to sleep.

Teachers at any level can use music on occasion to create a better classroom environment. For example, if a teacher wants to spice up a unit on French history, he or she might play the music of that era.

TALK. "The only good classroom is the quiet classroom." This is the motto of many school systems. Many bright, energetic children enter Darth Vader's halls and eventually turn into little Darth Vaders after they are placed in drab classrooms and told to be quiet. Students at any age should be encouraged to participate in classroom discussions and talk on occasion. Teachers who allow some student talk are perceived by students as more responsive to their needs and more immediate and approachable. We do not mean that classrooms should be noisy without any purpose, but student talk is essential to student growth and development. The teacher should set up situations in which students can talk without being reprimanded. Group exercises, projects, and similar activities allow for student talk without decreasing the content. Of course, the teacher should not use such activities for content but as a means of teaching content.

Whether the students are younger or older, allowing for student-teacher interaction is an effective means of improving communication between teacher and student. Talk can also be used as a reward for good behavior. If students sit and listen and take notes as they should, then the teacher should assign a group exercise or open up the class for discussion. Allowing for talk time gives students a chance to relax and release tension, and makes them feel better about the classroom environment. Those who do not want to talk, however, should not be forced to or punished for not talking.

COLOR. Color can be used in the classroom to denote warmth or coldness. Recall the Ketcham (1958) study on school attractiveness we discussed earlier. Schools should never be painted dark brown, industrial green, or battleship-gray. Younger children probably function better with the warmer colors such as soft blues, yellows and pinks. Older students probably function better with the cooler colors such as blue and blue-green. Bright colors such as iridescent or neon reds, yellows, greens, and oranges should not be overdone. A room painted in such colors might overstimulate the students. However, a single wall of bright color may create a vibrant, active environment.

Clearly color and decor can influence the school environment. It can affect how students feel about school, the teacher, and the total learning environment. There are many schools where the art teacher, the industrial arts teacher, the custodians, the administrators, and some students get together to help paint the school's interior. For example, they paint the hallways in warm colors and then paint geometrical designs on the warm colors. These schools have found over the past ten years that students take more pride in their school than do students at other schools where no such effort has been made. The schools with the lively decors rarely have graffiti on the walls or smears or smudges. It is usual to see a student cleaning a wall if it gets marked. Student involvement

Different seating arrangements can make for different styles of teaching.

Source: Photo by C. Price Walt

in painting and decoration can help guarantee that students will take care of the classrooms and other school spaces.

LIGHTING. Lighting can also influence the relationship between teacher and student. A classroom that is poorly lit or too bright can cause fatigue and eye strain. Eventually, even boredom and hostility emerge. Thompson gave these guidelines for lighting in the classroom:

> *Maintain high levels of illumination.* When students must expend energy just to see, they will have little left to understand what is being said. All areas of the room should be balanced in brightness. Factory and assembly-line workers have their work well illuminated. Industry has known for a long time that eye fatigue plays havoc with production schedules. To avoid sharp contrast, the visual field around the task should be only one-third as bright as the work area. No part of the visual field should be brighter than the immediate

vicinity of the task. Avoid glare either from direct light sources or from reflecting surfaces. (p. 81)

TEMPERATURE AND HUMIDITY. Imagine sitting in a classroom and trying to absorb content when the temperature is 90 degrees with 90 percent humidity. About all you can do is sit very still and keep wiping the perspiration from your face. Many classrooms are kept too warm, both in the summer and in the winter. In the summer, they are too hot because they are not air-conditioned and the humidity is high. In the winter, they are hot and dry. Both classroom climates are disruptive to the learning and communication process between student and teacher. When a room is too hot, people become antsy and irritable.

The optimal classroom temperature is 66 to 72 degrees Fahrenheit. This assumes that the room is neither too dry nor too humid. Many classrooms do not have temperature controls, but if the room is painted a cool color, it will seem cooler. However, we know that when it's 90 degrees outside and 100 degrees inside, no one will feel cool even in a light-blue room.

During the winter, humidity should not fall below 30 percent or be allowed to rise above 50 percent. As humidity moves above or below these levels, student illness and absenteeism increase. Todd-Mancillas (1982) summarizes Green's climate results drawn from a study involving 3,600 students in grades one to eight in 11 different schools in Saskatoon, Saskatchewan, Canada:

> Results indicated that children attending schools with classroom humidity ranging between 22% and 26% experienced nearly 13% greater illness and absenteeism than children attending schools with classrooms having humidity levels ranging between 27% and 33%. . . . Green also cautions against excessive humidity, as allied research also indicates that increased respiratory infections result from humidity levels in excess of 50%. (p. 85)

If teachers cannot control the temperature in their classrooms, they should vary activities so that students do not notice the temperature as much. In other words, they should give the students plenty to do and think about other than the temperature. In cold months, if the room is too cold, they should have the students move around and talk a lot. In warmer months, if the room is too hot, they should have group discussions and activities that help direct attention away from the temperature.

FURNITURE. The furnishings in a classroom can often determine how students feel about the environment. Ugly furnishings do not improve communication between student and teacher. Granted, many schools do not have money to purchase new desks, chairs, equipment, and curtains. However, schools that are more attractive are generally better taken care of by the students. Teachers and students can improve the classroom environment by bringing in appealing artifacts. Hard architecture often interferes with a student's attention span and learning. Examples of hard architecture are hard chairs, sharp-edged tables and desks, and uncomfortable work tables. Soft architecture often encourages student attention and learning. Soft architecture sends signals of comfort and welcome. Examples of soft architecture are ergonomic chairs, chairs that are softer, chairs that lean back when we move, rounded tables, and other comfortable-looking classroom furniture. The instructor who makes optimal use of the space he or she has is likely to get along better with the students. Affect will improve for the teacher who cares about the classroom environment. Creative use of space, seating, lighting, color, sound, noise, temperature, and furnishings improve communication between student and instructor (Richmond, 1997).

SCENT. The odor a person exudes can encourage others to approach or avoid that person. Teachers should avoid wearing overpowering scents in the classroom. Overpowering scents can affect student attentiveness, learning, and health. Some students have allergies and cannot be near strong scents or odors. Teachers should be sensitive to this even if other students are not.

There is always one student in every class who has an offensive odor. Teachers need to learn not to avoid this student. Teachers still must be immediate with the student who doesn't smell like the others. A teacher we work with told us the following story: She sent home a note to the student's parents explaining that Joey had a body odor and it was causing a problem in the classroom. Joey's mother wrote back and said, "Joey ain't no rose, don't smell him, just learn him." Sometimes there is little or nothing anyone can do about scent except learn to live with it. Perhaps health teachers and physical education teachers can discuss odors with students, but other teachers probably cannot. However, all teachers can take care not to introduce noxious odors into the classroom. Some plants give off odors that some people cannot smell but others find overpowering. Take care to avoid having such plants in a classroom (Richmond, 1997).

TIME

Teachers must use time to their advantage. Time can be used to reward students for good behavior, control students, make the classroom more interesting, and learn about others. Teachers often spend too much time on one unit. Most adults can only listen effectively for about thirty minutes, so why should we expect children to pay attention for longer periods of time? Teachers must structure activities to meet students' time needs. Inflexible schedules are harmful to owl students. You'll recall that owls function best later in the day; whereas, sparrows function best early in the morning and fade in the afternoon. Therefore teachers must be sensitive to students' body schedules. Optimal learning occurs for the owl in the afternoon; whereas, optimal learning occurs for the sparrow in the morning. To the extent possible, teachers should vary the time in which subject matter is taught and the time when tests are given. Rigid schedules make for tight organization, but if they are not adapted to student differences, they are not tools for effective teaching or testing.

Students are less aroused during the lunch period if they have a recess before lunch. Allowing children to let off steam before eating reduces problems in the lunch room. Once the students have eaten, then they are ready to go back to the classroom. Teachers also should avoid punishing students by taking away their recess. Teachers who ignore this caution may be, in effect, punishing themselves. Students who have recess taken away cause bigger problems in later classes than they would normally. This happens because they missed the opportunity to burn off their excess energy. Sometimes a few minutes devoted to recess will save many minutes for instruction.

Instructors should allow for free time or talk time. If students complete projects early, let them have some time to do whatever they want. This also helps teach them responsibility. Teachers who use their time wisely have fewer classroom and student problems. They also have students who learn more and better. Teachers must be sensitive to the students' time needs. Around holidays, spring, and the beginning of school, students are more restless. The instructor must be more innovative and creative to keep their attention. Instructors can use time to understand their students better and to understand how to prepare lessons more effectively (Richmond, 1997).

OUTCOMES OF TEACHER IMMEDIACY

Throughout this chapter, we have discussed possible teacher and student nonverbal behavior that denotes immediacy or nonimmediacy. Obviously, the immediate teacher is perceived more positively than the nonimmediate teacher. Many of the results reported in this section are a direct result of research by Richmond and her associates. According to these researchers, there are significant advantages to be gained from teacher immediacy in the classroom. Increased teacher immediacy results in:

- Increased liking, affiliation, and positive affect on the part of the student. Immediate teachers are liked far more than nonimmediate teachers.
- Increased student affect for the subject matter. Students who become motivated to learn the subject matter because of the teacher's immediate behaviors will do well in the content and continue to learn long after the teacher who motivated them is out of the picture.
- Increased student cognitive learning. Students with immediate teachers attend more to the subject matter, concentrate more on the subject, retain more of the content, and when challenged can correctly recall more of the subject matter than students with nonimmediate teachers.
- Increased student motivation. It seems that the primary way that immediacy produces learning effects may be by increasing student motivation.
- Reduced student resistance to instructors' attempts to influence or modify behavior. Immediate teachers seem to have more referent, respect, or liking power; hence, students tend to comply with or conform to the wishes of the more immediate teachers. Nonimmediate teachers have more difficulty getting students to comply with or conform to their wishes.

- The teacher being perceived as a more competent communicator, one who listens and cares. Nonimmediate teachers are usually perceived as ineffective, if not incompetent, communicators.
- The teacher being able to reduce or alleviate student anxiety about the classroom situation. A more immediate teacher is perceived as a more caring, sensitive teacher; hence, the student feels less apprehensive about the overall instructional environment.
- Increased student-teacher communication and interaction. Some teachers might see this aspect as a negative. It is not. If students communicate more with their teachers, then the students might get the information they need.
- A reduced status differential between student and teacher. This does not mean the teacher is on the same level as the student. It simply means the student won't be so intimidated by the teacher's higher status. Therefore the student might be more willing to ask clarifying questions about the content without fear of the teacher.
- Higher evaluations from one's immediate supervisor. While this may seem unusual at first, it is really very simple to understand. Administrators like teachers who have good classes with few problems. Immediate teachers have good classes with fewer problems than nonimmediate teachers. Hence, administrators will find immediate teachers to be the more effective teachers.

In conclusion, immediacy behaviors are among the most valuable communication tools instructors have available to them. These nonverbal immediacy skills can help teachers and students have happier, more productive classroom experiences.

DIRECTIONS: The following statements describe the ways some people behave while talking with or to others. Please indicate in the space at the left of each item the degree to which you believe the statement applies **TO YOU**. Please use the following 5-point scale: 1 = Never; 2 = Rarely; 3 = Occasionally; 4 = Often; and 5 = Very Often.

_____ 1. I use my hands and arms to gesture while talking to people.

_____ 2. I touch others on the shoulder or arm while talking to them.

_____ 3. I use a monotone or dull voice while talking to people.

_____ 4. I look over or away from others while talking to them.

_____ 5. I move away from others when they touch me while we are talking.

_____ 6. I have a relaxed body position when I talk to people.

_____ 7. I frown while talking to people.

_____ 8. I avoid eye contact while talking to people.

_____ 9. I have a tense body position while talking to people.

(continued)

FIGURE 13.4
Self-Report of Nonverbal Immediacy

_____**10.** I sit close or stand close to people while talking with them.

_____**11.** My voice is monotonous or dull when I talk to people.

_____**12.** I use a variety of vocal expressions when I talk to people.

_____**13.** I gesture when I talk to people.

_____**14.** I am animated when I talk to people.

_____**15.** I have a bland facial expression when I talk to people.

_____**16.** I move closer to people when I talk to them.

_____**17.** I look directly at people while talking to them.

_____**18.** I am stiff when I talk to people.

_____**19.** I have a lot of vocal variety when I talk to people.

_____**20.** I avoid gesturing while I am talking to people.

_____**21.** I lean toward people when I talk to them.

_____**22.** I maintain eye contact with people when I talk to them.

_____**23.** I try not to sit or stand close to people when I talk with them.

_____**24.** I lean away from people when I talk to them.

_____**25.** I smile when I talk to people.

_____**26.** I avoid touching people when I talk to them.

SCORING PROCEDURE:

Step 1: Start with a score of 78. Add the scores from the following items: 1, 2, 6, 10, 12, 13, 14, 16, 17, 19, 21, 22, and 25.

Step 2: Add the scores from the following items: 3, 4, 5, 7, 8, 9, 11, 15, 18, 20, 23, 24, and 26.

Step 3: Subtract your score in Step 2 from your score in Step 1. This is your total score.

Expected alpha reliability: 0.87–0.92.

NORMS:

Females	Mean = 102.0	S.D. = 10.9	High = > 112	Low = < 92
Males	Mean = 93.8	S.D. = 10.8	High = > 104	Low = < 83

When using this instrument it is important to recognize that the difference in these self-reports between females and males is statistically significant and socially significant (that is, substantial variance in the scores on this instrument can be attributed to biological sex). Whether these differences are "real" (that is, females may actually be more nonverbally immediate than males) or a function of social desirability (that is, females think they should be more immediate than males think they should be) or a function of actual behavior has not yet been determined (as of November 2002).

FIGURE 13.4

(continued)

Potential Drawbacks of Teacher Immediacy

Immediacy has a plethora of positive results. However, the garden is not all roses; there are some thorns. Immediate teachers may encounter some personal or professional problems with their colleagues. They might be perceived as not having control over their classrooms. Immediate teachers have control over their classrooms; however, some of their peers may not see it.

Immediate teachers might be viewed by other teachers as pushovers. Immediacy does not mean "let the student do whatever he or she wants." It means "be approachable." Immediate teachers can still be firm and set standards.

Not everyone can be immediate in the same way. Select the behaviors you are most comfortable with and use those. To be immediate, you do not have to perform all the behaviors we have identified as immediate in this chapter, but you do need some of them. If you try to use behavior that makes you uncomfortable, you will appear awkward and uncomfortable rather than immediate. False immediacy is worse than none at all.

Glossary of Terminology

Primary function of teachers' verbal behavior to give content to improve students' cognitive learning.

Primary function of teachers' nonverbal behavior to improve students' affect or liking for the subject matter, teacher, and class and to increase desire to learn more about the subject matter.

CHAPTER 14

Intercultural Relationships

Source: Photo by C. Price Walt

Most people believe that we are in a world that is shrinking and that cultures are blending together more so than in the past. Because of the developments and advances in modern transportation and electronic communications systems, it is possible for people the world over to communicate more readily and over longer distances. Cultures from various parts of the world communicate with one another, but often with minimal success. Although our transportation and electronic systems are rapidly advancing, one could argue that they are only leading to more *mis*perceptions among the diverse peoples of the world. Our human systems generally have failed to keep up with the advances of our technical systems. This chapter reviews the distinctive characteristics of intercultural communication, discusses the relevance of nonverbal behavior to communication across cultures, and examines some nonverbal messages from various cultures.

As we become more likely to come into contact with people from cultures very different from our own, including many from subcultures that share some but not all of our own culture, there is a need for increased awareness about appropriate versus inappropriate behavior in intercultural contacts (Adler, 1974; Carbaugh, 1990; Gudykunst & Yun Kim, 1997; Klopf, 1998; Klopf & Ishii, 1984; Neuliep, 2002; Thomas-Maddox & Lowery-Hart, 1998; Ting-Toomey & Korzenny, 1991; Yousef, 1976). This is confirmed by the following accounts of misunderstandings.

The first illustration concerns an American named Henry Smith who had just returned from a business trip in El Salvador. He told his business partners that he understood and spoke Spanish and said he had had few problems communicating while in El Salvador. However, Smith related the following incident. He was invited to a businessman's home to socialize with him and his family. Throughout the evening, Smith kept talking about business; whereas, his Salvadoran host seemed mildly disconcerted at discussing business and would promptly move the conversation from business to the social realm. After several attempts at business talk, Smith relented and enjoyed the social environment. However, he could not understand why his host had refused to talk business during the social event at his home. Smith told his business partners that Salvadoran businessmen apparently do not know how to discuss business during social evenings in their homes, and that the businessman was not very savvy. All the while Smith was finding fault with the El Salvadoran, the Salvadoran had perceived Smith as pushy, aggressive, and insensitive. Unfortunately for Smith, his company lost the business of the Salvadoran businessman because Smith did not know the norms of the Salvadoran culture. The custom is that business is discussed in an office or over a meal in a restaurant, never in the home or around family. An occasion at a Salvadoran home is always a social one, never a business function. Salvadorans separate business from social functions, while North Americans often do not separate the two.

The second illustration took place in Turkey. Pete Martin was sent by his office to present a training seminar for the native personnel in the branch of a Fortune 500 corporation. Martin noticed that "smoking was everywhere." He could not deal with these conditions, so he simply informed the Turkish seminar participants that they could not smoke. After a short break, Martin returned to complete the seminar. His audience was still smoking. Reluctantly, he continued the seminar but "found the people rude and inconsiderate." Prior to the seminar, he had failed to learn that, in the Turkish culture, smoking is not prohibited, and no such area as a "smoke-free zone" exists. A person can smoke anywhere and at any time. Needless to say, the seminar was not a success for either Martin or the participants.

The third illustration took place in a classroom in California. Anna Maria Moore was shouting at little Ferlouke, an African-American child. She shouted,

"Look at me and listen when I talk to you! Is that clear?" Ferlouke proceeded to look up at her, then down at the floor, then turned and looked sideways while Moore stood by helplessly. In Ferlouke's culture, it is rude, inconsiderate, and disrespectful to look a person of higher authority, such as a teacher, in the eye. A student should always give respect by looking down, not at the instructor. The interaction was a difficult one for both Moore and Ferlouke.

In all three situations, Smith, Martin, and Moore appeared intolerant to their interactants. However, the reality was that they were unacquainted with the norms of the other cultures. They expected people to respond to them using general North American norms. People interacting with other cultures or subcultures need to be educated in some basic principles of intercultural communication. Perhaps the nonverbal aspects are more critical than the verbal aspects, because we readily recognize that other people speak languages different from our own. What we fail to recognize is that other people's nonverbal messages are even more different from our own than are their languages. Before we continue, we must define intercultural communication and look at some of its variations.

DEFINING INTERCULTURAL COMMUNICATION

Rich and Ogawa (1972) define **intercultural communication** simply as "communication between peoples of different cultures" (p. 24). Communication is intercultural when one interactant is from one culture and the other from another. Klopf and Park (1982) note, "One will encode a message based on her or his cultural background; the other will decode it from the framework of her or his culture" (p. 15). Klopf (1998) defines intercultural communication as "the communication between people of different cultures, . . . it occurs when a person (or persons) from one culture talks to a person (or persons) from another culture" (p. 39). He defines subcultures as "collections of people who possess conscious membership in identifiable units of an encompassing, larger cultural unit" (p. 36).

Although culture always influences interaction between people, the more the cultures of two people are alike, the less likely culture will cause problems in their interactions. People from cultures that have similar languages, hygiene, foods, rituals, folklore, etiquette, ethics, athletics, socioeconomic backgrounds, religion, schooling, geographic regions, and governments (Americans and English Canadians, for example) have a less difficult time communicating. The similarity between cultures makes communication easier. However, cultures that are quite different in terms of language, hygiene, foods, rituals, folklore, etiquette, ethics, athletics, socioeconomic backgrounds, religion, schooling, geographic region, and government have a more difficult time communicating (North American versus Asian cultures). As Klopf and Park (1982) suggest:

> Nevertheless, the possibility of misinterpretation always exists when messages encoded by persons of one culture are decoded by

persons of another. There is a need, therefore, to study intercultural communication to reduce or attempt to eliminate any misunderstandings that might result from cultural modification. (p. 16)

To avoid confusion, several variations of intercultural communication must be explained before we continue. We will use the definitions drawn by Klopf and Park (1982). *Cross-cultural* and *transcultural communication* are terms generally used interchangeably with intercultural communication. Ting-Toomey and Korzenny (1991) say, "cross-cultural interpersonal communication can be broadly defined as the comparative study of differences and similarities of relational communication patterns between two or more cultural communities" (p. 1). However, there are other terms that have different emphases. *International communication,* for example, is communication "between official representatives of nations and usually is political in nature" (p. 17). *Interracial communication* is communication between people "with racially identifiable physical differences, Koreans and Caucasians, for instance" (p. 17). This form may or may not be intercultural. Communication between a third-generation Korean American and a third-generation Italian American is interracial but probably not intercultural. Both have been acculturated into the North American culture and probably have similar values. Communication between a native Korean and an American-born Korean would be intercultural. *Interethnic communication* is communication between "people of the same race but not the same ethnic background" (p. 17). For example, English and French Canadians have the same predominant culture and race, yet they speak different languages and have different objectives and viewpoints. **Subcultures** are groups of people within a general culture who may be culturally different from one another yet share many of the characteristics of the general culture. Some examples within the general North American culture would be Texans, Mexican Americans, Irish Americans, senior citizens, gays, lesbians, persons with disabilities, residents of Beverly Hills, New Yorkers, and so on. A large proportion of the U.S. population identifies with both the general North American culture and one or more subcultures.

Despite all of these definitions, intercultural specialists suggest that certain universals are important to develop an understanding of communication practices across cultures. Hall's (1973) map of culture shows what he believes are its constituent parts, prominently featuring communication. His map has a hundred universals classified into these ten categories:

1. Communication: vocal qualifiers, kinesics, language
2. Society: class, caste, government
3. Work: formal work, maintenance, occupations
4. Sexes: masculinity versus femininity, biological sex, technical sex
5. Space: formal and informal, boundaries
6. Time: sequence, cycles, calendars
7. Enculturation: rearing, informal learning, education
8. Recreation: playing games, fun

┃ Let freedom RING!

9. Protection: formal and informal defenses, technical defenses
10. Material systems: contact with environment, motor habits, technology

Clearly communication behaviors, both verbal and nonverbal, are prevalent in all cultures and across cultures. To communicate effectively, we must understand the verbal as well as the nonverbal. Because intercultural communication is persistent, enduring, and omnipresent, we must become more aware of and acquainted with intercultural communication, particularly the influence of nonverbal communication. Furthermore, because cultures are composed of smaller units or subcultures, we often have to learn the larger culture first, and then the subculture, to be effective intercultural communicators.

Characteristics of Culture

Thomas-Maddox and Lowery-Hart (1998) suggest that culture has certain characteristics. First, culture is learned. They suggest that from a very early age, children in any culture are taught the attitudes, beliefs, values, behaviors, language, rituals, songs, history, stories, foods, preferences, and a plethora of other concepts by adults, peers, and others in the culture.

Second, culture is dynamic. Rarely do cultures remain static over time. Because of many interventions by outsiders and external forces, cultures are often forced to change even when they do not want to do so. When a populace moves from one geographic location to another, the original culture does not remain the same. There is a blending of ideas, attitudes, beliefs, and so on. Thomas-Maddox and Lowery-Hart note that with this dynamic trend comes the following orientations: "Some cultures embrace the change as exciting, while others are resistant because of the threat to tradition and stability" (p. 6).

Third, culture is pervasive and omnipresent. There are both "visible and invisible things which surround us that comprise our culture" (p. 7). These pervasive things often determine the language we speak, the clothes we wear, our bathing habits, the foods we consume, our religious beliefs, our behaviors toward men and women, and even our material possessions. For example, one common representation of typical American preferences is: "Baseball, hot dogs, apple pie, and Chevrolet." Perhaps not all Americans would agree that these elements are representative of the American culture.

Foundations of Culture

While large cultures differ from one another in seemingly infinite ways, they all have some common foundations. Most important of these are *xenophobia* and *ethnocentrism*. **Xenophobia** is the fear of strangers. This is a trait shared by most human beings regardless of their culture (Gudykunst & Yun Kim, 1997). Most of us fear what we do not understand, at least until we become more familiar with it and recognize that there is little danger. Communicating with strangers causes many people to withdraw and avoid intercultural contact or to approach it with considerable consternation. When people find themselves forced into communicating with people from another culture, their nonverbal reactions to each other are often interpreted by both sides as dislike and rejection.

The fact that xenophobia is common in most cultures causes some to suggest that this orientation is probably a function of humans' long period of evolution. In earlier times, fear of strangers likely was a factor in people's survival. Those who feared took action to protect themselves. Those who did not were more likely to be prey for strangers with evil intentions. Hence today's humans may be the descendants of those who feared strangers, because those who did not have that fear were less likely to have descendants. Whether this is the case, of course, we will never know. In any event, xenophobia is common among people across cultures and provides a powerful barrier to effective intercultural communication.

If you have not done so already, please complete the questionnaire in Figure 14.1 and compute your score. This scale measures what we call ethnocentrism. The term **ethnocentrism** is derived from two Greek words: *ethnos,* which is Greek for "nation," and *kentron,* which is Greek for "center." In combination, these words suggest that one sees one's own nation (or culture)

Directions: Below are 22 items that relate to the cultures of different parts of the world. Please indicate the degree to which you agree or disagree with each item, in the space before that item, using the following five-point scale: (5) Strongly agree; (4) Agree; (3) Undecided; (2) Disagree; (1) Strongly disagree. Work quickly and record your first reaction to each item. There are no right or wrong answers.

_____ 1. Most other cultures are backward compared to my culture.

_____ 2. My culture should be the role model for other cultures.

_____ 3. People from other cultures act strange when they come to my culture.

_____ 4. Lifestyles in other cultures are just as valid as those in my culture.

_____ 5. Other cultures should try to be more like my culture.

_____ 6. I am not interested in the values and customs of other cultures.

_____ 7. People in my culture could learn a lot from people in other cultures.

_____ 8. Most people from other cultures just don't know what's good for them.

_____ 9. I respect the values and customs of other cultures.

_____ 10. Other cultures are smart to look up to our culture.

_____ 11. Most people would be happier if they lived like people in my culture.

_____ 12. I have many friends from different cultures.

_____ 13. People in my culture have just about the best lifestyles of anywhere.

_____ 14. Lifestyles in other cultures are not as valid as those in my culture.

_____ 15. I am very interested in the values and customs of other cultures.

_____ 16. I apply my values when judging people who are different.

_____ 17. I see people who are similar to me as virtuous.

_____ 18. I do not cooperate with people who are different.

_____ 19. Most people in my culture just don't know what is good for them.

_____ 20. I do not trust people who are different.

_____ 21. I dislike interacting with people from different cultures.

_____ 22. I have little respect for the values and customs of other cultures.

Scoring Procedure:

Step 1: Add scores for items 4, 7, and 9.
Step 2: Add scores for items 1, 2, 5, 8, 10, 11, 13, 14, 18, 20, 21, and 22.
Step 3: Subtract the score of step 1 from 18.
Step 4: Add scores from Step 2 to Step 3. Result is your Ethno-Score.
Score should be between 15 and 75. Higher score = more ethnocentric.

FIGURE 14.1
Ethnocentrism Scale

as the center of the universe. All human infants are egocentric, which means they see themselves as the center of the universe, with all the other people circling around them. During their early years, the adults around them try to teach them that they are part of a group (family, community, etc.)—that the other people in the group are also important and should be respected. Hence the people in the child's culture become the center of the universe for that child. These people—through schools, community contacts, family and peer interactions, etc.—help intensify the maturing child's ethnocentrism by teaching him or her how to think and act; those ways, of course, being the ways that their culture considers appropriate. Simply put, cultures teach their children to be ethnocentric—to see the ways of their own culture to be the correct, normal, and appropriate. In the process, the children learn to be ethnocentric and to question anyone who does not behave in the ways of their culture.

Ethnocentrism is the foundation for group pride, patriotism, and the continuation of the culture itself. Unfortunately it also increases xenophobia, distrust of outsiders, an attitude of superiority toward people from other cultures (and communities, nations, etc.), and the belief that the ways of their own culture are normal, correct, and appropriate, while the ways of people from other cultures are abnormal, incorrect, and inappropriate. Hence, inadvertently (at least usually), children are raised to fear, dislike, and even hate people who are different (Neuliep & McCroskey, 1997; Neuliep, 2002).

Please examine your score for the ethnocentrism scale you completed. If your score is 30 or below, you have unusually low ethnocentrism. If your score is between 30 and 45, your level of ethnocentrism is typical of most people. If your score is above 45, you are quite ethnocentric. Of course, no scale of type is perfect. In the United States, for example, the society is now teaching people to be politically correct (PC). It is not PC to be highly ethnocentric, so you may have been hesitant to answer questions on the scale in ways that seemed to suggest you were not PC. If this seems a bit confusing, you are seeing the point clearly. The culture teaches us to be ethnocentric, and then it tells us that if we are ethnocentric, we are not being politically correct. This is not the case in many cultures, however. For many cultures, the more ethnocentric you are, the better. It is politically correct to hate outsiders in those cultures.

It is our position that ethnocentrism, while certainly having some positive aspects, raises a major barrier for a person who wants and/or needs to engage in effective intercultural communication. Nonverbal behaviors themselves are neutral. However, different cultures interpret those behaviors in very different ways and use, in some cases, very different nonverbal behaviors. Yet, all cultures see their way of nonverbally communicating as normal and have great difficulty trying to figure out how to interpret the nonverbal behaviors used by people from other cultures. The remainder of this chapter examines some examples of how difficult it is to deal with nonverbal intercultural communication.

NONVERBAL BEHAVIOR

A person's nonverbal behavior communicates the beliefs, attitudes, and values of that person's culture to others. Klopf and Park (1982) suggest that "What a person does nonverbally is always important in intercultural communication" (p. 73). Because nonverbal messages are always present, we must not ignore their importance or impact. Because we cannot learn the meaning of thousands of nonverbal behaviors, it is important that we at least "realize that the meanings are likely to change from culture to culture" (Klopf, 1998, p. 236). Today communication scholars are often educating people about the importance of effective cross-cultural communication. What if two countries have a serious nonverbal misunderstanding? Could it lead to war? Could it lead to economic sanctions?

Clearly, most nonverbal behaviors are not pan-cultural (the same for all cultures). Most meanings attributed to nonverbal behavior are based on the attributer's culture. The motivation for given behaviors is not universal. It varies from culture to culture. Thus, the meaning we can reasonably attribute to any given behavior is culturally determined. Nonverbal behavior is differentially learned from one culture to the next. How well one learns about her or his own nonverbal culture and understands the nonverbal culture of another determines how effective communication will be between people of different cultures. The remainder of this section reviews some intercultural nonverbal behaviors and what they are likely to communicate.

Appearance and Attractiveness

People judge others by their appearance and perceived attractiveness. However, what is attractive in one culture may not be attractive in another culture (Iliffe, 1960; Ishii, 1973, 1975; Klopf & Ishii, 1984; Martin, 1964). This has always been a source of communication misunderstandings. In ancient Rome—a culture of dark-haired people—the blonde-haired woman could either be royalty or a prostitute. Originally, only prostitutes had blonde hair. Then Messalina, the third wife of Emperor Claudius, started wearing blonde wigs. Soon many other women were wearing blonde wigs. It became nearly impossible to tell the prostitutes from royalty.

Roman men kept their hair short-cropped; whereas, slaves or barbarians had long hair. When the long-haired Europeans conquered Rome, they thought the men with short hair were slaves. Around the time of Charlemagne, AD 800, the French noblemen kept their hair short. At that same time, the Japanese shaved the tops of their heads, and Egyptians shaved off all of their hair.

For centuries, women have seemed to be more conscious of their appearance than men. In the United States, women spend far more than men on cosmetics and related items. Women worldwide have always tried to alter their appearance to adapt to their culture. For example, binding the feet of baby girls was a common practice in China for nearly a thousand years. The size of the woman's foot was related to how wealthy she was. The smaller the foot, the greater the wealth. The girl's family would place her shoe in the window so that suitors might see the size. To have one's feet bound was very painful. Infants would cry for weeks and months as their foot muscles and bones were compressed into smaller sizes. It is still common practice in some remote areas of China to bind women's feet.

How else do people manipulate their bodies to be attractive? How about reshaping heads? Mangbettu females in the Democratic Republic of the Congo have their heads wrapped tightly during early childhood so that they will become elongated. The Mayans flattened their heads by tying boards to each side of the head in early childhood. They would also file their teeth into points and place valuable jewels in them. Some Burmese girls have several inch-thick rings placed about their necks to lengthen them, and their necks sometimes reach 14 inches in length. In the Saras-Djinges tribe of Africa, girls have their lips stretched with wooden discs, sometimes to 14 inches around, and can consume only liquids. In Africa, the Masai use cow dung on their hair to make it stiff. Native American tribes used to paint their faces to represent various rituals; in some tribes they still do.

Before you conclude that behaviors such as these occur only in far-off lands, consider some North American fads. A popular fashion in North American culture is to have a small (sometimes larger) tattoo somewhere on the body. However, rather than enduring the pain of applying a permanent tattoo, some individuals use special paints for the body and paste-on tattoos. And then there is the practice of ear piercing. Although this was long the province of females in the United States, many males now do it as well. How about piercing the navel, the nose, the tongue, or sex organs? Those are now common fashions for our youth. Even serious surgical procedures are commonplace means of body manipulation in this culture, such as nose jobs, face-lifts, breast implants, hair transplants, liposuction, and the list goes on—all in the name of improved physical appearance.

American culture more readily accepts tall, large women than do some Asian countries. The average height of a woman in this country is about five feet six inches. This is considered very tall in Japan. Japanese women are small and petite. Many Chinese women have small builds, too. An American woman of average height looks like a giant in either country; she towers over both men and women. Preferred body type and height vary from culture to culture. Some cultures prefer hearty, hefty women who can do strenuous chores. Anorexic, waif-like women would be rejected in such cultures.

In short, physical appearance and attractiveness are highly influential in intercultural communication. Those who do not look like they belong to the culture will not be listened to, will not be able to persuade others, and therefore will not successfully communicate with others. Anyone who does not fit the physical norm of the culture will have trouble communicating in that culture. When we are in other cultures, we should try to respect and conform as much as possible to the norms of that culture.

Gesture and Movement

Axtell (1991) says, "gestures and body language are not only powerful communicators but . . . different cultures [also] use gestures and body language in dramatically different ways" (p. 1991). People of all cultures learn the gestures and movements of their particular culture (see Table 14.1). This idea is reinforced

---

▶ TABLE 14.1

Gestures and Body Movements from Axtell

Greetings

Americans—Good, firm grip, looking straight in the eye.
Middle East—*salaam* (right hand sweeps upward, first touching the heart, then the forehead, and finally up and outward, perhaps a slight nod of head and words, meaning "Peace be with you").
Eskimos—bang the other party with a hand on either the head or shoulder.
Maori tribespeople in New Zealand—rub noses.
Some East African tribes—spit at each other's feet.
South America—handshake and hearty clap on back.

Farewells

Americans—goodbye wave (hand up, palm out, wrist stiff) with a back and forth motion of forearm and hand.
Europeans—arm up and extended out, with the palm down and the hand bobbing up and down at wrist.
Italians and Greeks—arm extended, palm up, curling all the fingers back and forth toward themselves.

Beckoning

Americans—raise a hand (with index finger raised) about head high or a little higher, or raise the hand with the full open palm; wave back and forth to attract attention.
Much of Europe and many Latin American countries—extend the arm, hand out, palm down, and then make a scratching motion with the fingers.
Colombia—clap the hands lightly.

Insulting (Perhaps Obscene) Gestures (Meaning Equivalent)

Americans—Single middle finger salute.
Arabs—extending the hand, palm down, fingers splayed outward, with the middle finger directed down.
Russians—bend back the middle finger of one hand with the forefinger of the other.
Yugoslavia—bend the arm at the elbow, make a fist (with knuckles away from face) and shake the fist once.
North America, Latin America, and parts of Europe—the forearm jerk (right arm is bent at the elbow and the left hand comes chopping down into the crook of the elbow while the fist of the right hand is jerked upward).

Adapted from R. E, Axtell (1991). *Gestures; The do's and taboos of body language around the world.* New York: John Wiley & Sons.

by Morrison, Conaway, and Borden (1994) in *Kiss, Bow, or Shake Hands: How to Do Business in 60 Countries*. Their book gives a breakdown of how people in certain cultures speak, act, negotiate, and make decisions. It also reviews cultural, business, and time orientations. In a world of increasing globalization and cultural interaction, it is necessary to understand how others communicate (see Table 14.2). For example, North Americans use the OK hand sign to mean that everything is all right. Several years ago, a U.S. vice president visited a country in South America. While he was exiting the airplane, someone from below asked, "How was the trip?" The vice president did not think he could be heard over the crowd, so he used the OK sign. In the country he was visiting, however, the sign was interpreted the way "shooting the bird" is interpreted here. The local paper printed a picture of our vice president giving the equivalent of the bird to that country. Needless to say, the people of the country were not pleased (demonstrations, egg throwing, etc.).

Axtell (1991) suggests that gestures can also be a valuable form of public opinion polling. Axtell says that according to *People* magazine, at least one U.S. politician had this system of gauging his popularity: "I watch the crowds waving to me and I count the number of fingers they're using" (p. 16).

People from different parts of the world differ substantially in their gesturing (Axtell, Briggs, Corcoran, & Lamb, 1997; Brault, 1962; Jakobson, 1976; Saitz & Cervenka, 1972; Welch, 1979; Yousef, 1976). The biggest differences are in the use of emblems, which, you will recall, are gestures that can substitute for language equivalents. Cultures have very different emblems that they use to communicate the same meaning. Some emblems are shared by two cultures, but they represent different meanings. Also, there are emblems employed by one culture for which another culture may have no equivalent, and vice versa.

The use of our hands can mean many different things in different cultures. For example, an Ethiopian puts one finger to her or his lips to show silence when motioning to a child but uses four fingers when motioning silence to an adult; Ethiopians consider it disrespectful to use only one finger when motioning to an adult. In the United States, we use one finger to the lips for both children and adults. The OK sign references totally different meanings in different cultures. In Japan, it references money. It could represent female genitalia if a man used it in front of a woman he was attempting to seduce. When directed toward a man, it can be an indication about what the person making the gesture thinks of his masculinity. Therefore the OK emblem can be interpreted many different ways. It depends on the culture. It is also clear that this one emblem could create many communication misunderstandings across cultures. For example, one of the authors and a friend visited Brazil. Before leaving for Brazil, they read as much as they could about gestures that Brazilians saw as pleasing as well as those they saw as negative. The American OK sign turned sideways was used in Brazil to indicate what Americans indicate by using the middle finger. The friend was in need of buying a pair of sandals. He stopped at a local shoe store. The store owner spoke no English and the friend spoke no Portuguese. Yet the friend picked out a pair of sandals. When he

TABLE 14.2

Greetings, Gestures, Gifts, and Time

Country	Greetings	Gestures	Gifts	Time
1. Brazil	Effusive, extended handshakes.	OK sign is vulgar. Good luck is thumb between index and middle finger while in a fist.	Avoid purple/black = mourning. Knives = severing relationship. Buy lunch/dinner first meeting.	Dinners from 7–10 p.m. or until 2 a.m.
2. China	Nod, bow, or handshake.	Do not speak with hands. Point with open hand.	A banquet. High-quality pens, liquors, cognac.	Banquets start 6:30 & 7 p.m., last two hours.
3. Denmark	Handshakes firm & brief for both arriving/leaving.	OK sign is insult. In theater, enter with back to stage, not seated people.	Flowers, chocolates. Illustrated book of United States.	Be prompt. Expect to be at table a long time.
4. England	Handshake. Say "How do you do?"	Impolite to talk with hands in pocket. Give V with palm facing outward. Inward is insulting, rude.	Invite out for meal. Flowers, liquor, champagne, chocolates.	Lunch 12–2 p.m. Dinner 7–11 p.m. Be prompt.
5. France	Shake hands. Touch cheeks. Kissing the air.	Thumbs-up means OK. OK sign means zero. Don't chew gum in public.	Good taste is everything. Books, music, flowers, good liquors, chocolates.	Lunch lasts two hours. Dinner 8 or 9 p.m.
6. Germany	Shake hands firmly. Men may kiss woman's hand.	Formal/reserved. Little smiling. Few displays of affection.	Good quality but not exorbitant cost. Pens, calculators, or imported liquors.	No breakfast meetings. Be on time for lunch & dinner.
7. India	Know each ethnic religious group's norms. Do not hug, kiss, or touch in public. Handshake may work.	Never touch another's head. Beckon by holding hand out, palm downward, and making scooping motions with fingers. Arms akimbo will be viewed as anger.	Small gift of flowers or chocolate. No frangipani blossoms, associated with death.	Can be a few minutes late, unless official function.

(continued)

	Greeting	Gestures	Gifts	Pace
8. Italy	Shake hands when arriving or leaving. Handshakes may include grasping the arm with other hand. Women may kiss or touch cheeks of good friends. Men may embrace and slap each other on the back.	Talk with hands is good. Stroke fingertips under chin and thrust out = thumbing your nose at someone.	Business cards. Liquors or delicacies, or crafts from your homeland.	Pace is slower. Be patient and calm.
9. Japan	Very aware of Western habits. Handshake is good. Their handshakes may be soft or limp. Bow is the traditional greeting.	OK sign means money. High-context culture. All gestures carry meaning. Shrugging shoulders and winking means nothing to Japanese. Beckon to come is done with palm down.	Ceremony of gift giving is more important than gift. Japanese may give expensive gifts; we must accept them.	Be fashionably late for social occasions. Meals long but over by 11 p.m.
10. Saudi Arabia	Wait for Saudi to initiate greeting. Handshakes or kisses on each cheek. Women are not well received here.	Left hand is considered unclean. Gesture with right. Eat with right. Do not point—impolite. Keep feet on ground—never show bottom of foot to an Arab.	Saudi hospitality is legendary. We are not expected to bring gift.	Slower. Be very patient. Meetings start slowly. Decision making takes a long time.

Adapted from T. Morrison. W. H. Conway, and G. A. Borden (1994). *Kiss, bow, or shake hands: How to do business in 60 countries.* Holbrook, MA: Adams Media Corporation.

tried them on, however, they were the wrong size. He then used gestures to indicate he needed a larger size and the store owner complied. There was quite of bit of back-and-forth about the use of the American credit card, but finally the transaction was complete. The friend was so happy about the situation that he used the OK sign. Whether the store owner thought something negative about that is still unknown, but he could have, and this situation could have been avoided if the friend had remembered what he had learned about gestures in the Brazilian culture and had employed them properly.

According to Morsbach (1976), in Japan the little finger pointed straight up can refer to a girlfriend, wife, or mistress. Rapidly crossing the index fingers refers to a fight. Last, licking an index finger and then drawing it over an eyebrow is a way of suggesting that someone is a liar. Morsbach says that instead of the latter gesture, the word *mayutsuba* can be uttered in the appropriate context, which enables a Japanese person to imply lying and deception without saying the equivalent of the word *liar*.

The use of the head often creates communication misunderstandings. In some parts of eastern Europe, Africa, and Asia, a person nods her or his head when in disagreement and shakes her or his head when in agreement; whereas, in the United States we do the reverse. One of the authors of this textbook experienced this contrast in behaviors while lecturing to a large number of students several years ago. As he was lecturing, many students would nod in agreement. However, one student shook his head while the others were nodding. This confused the instructor, and after class he approached the student who had been shaking his head in apparent disagreement. He found out that the student was from a part of India where shaking one's head meant agreement. Therefore this student had agreed with the other students, and he was using the gesture appropriate for his culture to signify agreement.

In Japan, the head nod may only mean continued attention, not necessarily agreement. You might find that a Japanese person totally disagrees with you, but he or she will nod out of respect until you have finished speaking. Jakobson (1976) found that Bulgarians throw their heads back and then return their heads to an upright position for "no." Many westerners could misinterpret this to mean "yes." In Korea, shaking one's head from side to side indicates "I don't know." In U.S. culture, shrugging one's shoulders suggests "I don't know."

Certain meanings are derived from movements that require use of more body parts than just the head or hands. For example, the Japanese bow involves most of the body. There is a pecking order for who bows to whom and how deeply one bows. The rule is that women bow to men and juniors bow to seniors. The rules are more complicated than one would think. For example, how often one should bow, how long, and how deep all have to be considered in a relationship. Bows are usually reciprocated.

The bow is usually a form of greeting or respect. Americans typically learn to bow even when they have been in Japan for only a few hours. However, they seldom really learn the exact way of doing it. The Japanese would never criticize a guest in their country. They are simply amused by the

Americans trying to imitate them. When bowing, one must be careful to move one's head slightly to the right so as not to strike the other person's head. Americans often forget this. When bowing, people should lower their eyes and keep their palms flat against their thighs. The handshake as a form of greeting is a western import to Japan. Cosmopolitan Japanese and Americans often shake hands and bow simultaneously. Thais greet one another with a *Wai.* They hold their hands together (as if praying) in front of them and bow, while saying, "Sawadee." The gesture is used more now among the older citizens, but it still occurs between those of higher and lower status. The higher one's status being addressed, the higher the hands should be.

Brault (1962) found a complicated routine in France for communicating exquisiteness. The French pinch the fingers of the right hand together, point them toward and raise them to their lips, then kiss the fingers and raise them into the air. The chin is held high and the eyes closed slightly. Brault suggests that Americans use this routine for more than expressing exquisiteness. The French reserve it for acknowledging only very exquisite things.

Ishii (1973, 1975) explored the posture of the Japanese. He found that *teishisei,* or low posture, is a sign of acceptance or respect. People who have modest *teishisei* are often trusted, loved, and accepted. People who have *teishisei* and are quiet or smile often in public are seen as successful. Japanese do not stand up immediately to greet an American or European entering a room. Japanese women have been taught to keep low posture and remain quiet when greeting seniors. Japanese at American parties usually stay reserved and quiet and may sit quietly in a corner or talk to other Japanese guests.

Klopf and Park (1982) suggest that younger Japanese people no longer use the Asian form of squatting down to relax. Many in the older generation still do. Younger Japanese males sit in a chair with their legs crossed. In Kuwait, the more westernized men shake hands with other men in a greeting situation. A few Kuwaiti men will shake hands with western women, but many will not. They are simply not used to interacting with western women. A more traditional greeting between men in Kuwait follows this pattern: "Men grasp each other's right hand, placing the left hand on the other's right shoulder, and exchanging kisses on each cheek" (Morrison et al., 1994). Imagine how uncomfortable American men feel when approached with the traditional Kuwaiti greeting. When greeting or eating in Saudi Arabia, only use the right hand, even if you are left-handed. The left hand is reserved for hygiene duties and should never be used in eating or greeting another person.

In Romania, shaking hands occurs all the time, when greeting, meeting, leaving, and acknowledging. No matter how many times a Romanian sees another person during the day, a handshake is always exchanged. A man will wait for the woman to extend her hand before shaking it. Occasionally, more traditional Romanian men will kiss a woman's hand.

It is clear from the above discussion that gestures and body movements suggest different meanings from one culture to the next. It is also clear that successful communication across cultures can take place only if one understands the nonverbal behaviors of both cultures.

Face and Eye Behavior

In any culture, faces communicate emotions, personality, and obvious demographic characteristics such as age, ethnic group, nationality, and sex. Research done by Ekman, Friesen, and Ellsworth (1972), and by Izard (1969) suggests that the basic human emotions are transmitted by the same facial expressions across western Europe, South America, and even parts of New Guinea. The Ekman studies found that people worldwide can identify correctly the primary emotions of sadness, happiness, anger, surprise, disgust, interest, contempt, and fear. Izard found that both adults and children in a primitive culture of New Guinea could identify most of them, but they confused fear with surprise. Ekman found that people worldwide are fairly good encoders and decoders of the basic facial expressions. Ekman also showed that decoders from the United States, England, Germany, Spain, France, Greece, Switzerland, and Japan can interpret facial expressions as displaying the same emotion. He also found that these cultures are fairly accurate at judging the intensity of an emotion.

However, this does not mean that facial expressions are pan-cultural. Although many cultures recognize the primary facial expressions, we must remember that in every culture there will be culture-specific differences based on the context (Eibl-Eibesfeldt, 1972; Ekman, 1971, 1975, 2003; Ekman, Friesen, & Ellsworth, 1972; Iliffe, 1960; Keltner, 1997; Klopf, 1998; Rosenberg, 1997; Simons, 1997). For example, females in North America are allowed to be more expressive than females in Iran or Japan. The Japanese culture is conditioned to mask emotions. We have all heard the phrase "the inscrutable Japanese." They may not use many facial expressions, but they can recognize them. Children in North America can be more expressive and questioning than children in many Eastern cultures. Ekman (1971) suggests that it is "likely that there is much more cultural variability in blends of facial expression than in facial expressions of primary emotions" (p. 223).

According to Klopf and Park (1982), Koreans usually have fixed, rigid facial expressions when meeting new people. However, they are very warm and receptive to their friends. In public, Koreans are cold and distant, but in private they are warmer.

Klopf and Park have also discussed the smiling behavior of the Japanese. They suggest that the "Japanese smile is not always a spontaneous expression of amusement or friendliness as it is among Americans" (p. 88). The Japanese smile is an acculturated dimension of their culture. Japanese people are taught to smile as a form of etiquette and will smile even when it seems inappropriate. Klopf (1998) cites the following incident in history:

> The smile of the Japanese ambassador to the United States announcing the imminent attack on Pearl Harbor to American officials was completely misinterpreted by millions of Americans who saw newspaper photographs of the scene or read about it in the papers. The ambassador was observing Japanese custom when he

smiled. Children are taught in Japan to smile as a social duty even in case of sorrowful circumstances. Rather than show sorrow, cultural ritual requires the smile. The ambassador personally opposed the attack and did not like the news he was forced to deliver. Custom dictated that he smile. That smile was misunderstood by much of the world. It helped spur the American forces to a greater war effort. Photos of the smiling ambassador were tacked up in armament factories, military barracks, and the cockpits of American bombers to help motivate the nation to win the war. (p. 88)

Eibl-Eibesfeldt (1972) found some similarities across cultures in social greetings. He found that Europeans, South American Indians, Samoans, and South African bushmen will give an "eyebrow flash" when they are greeting a friend at a distance. An eyebrow flash involves moving the eyebrows up and down slightly while keeping the eyebrow raised at the highest level for about one-sixth of a second. This would look very strange to us in greeting. However, we use the eyebrow flash many times when we are surprised or are questioning something.

Eye behavior takes many forms in different cultures. In this culture, we are taught not to stare. It is considered impolite in most circumstances—a fact that tells us how important people feel eye behavior is. We have learned to use the unfocused stare when we need it. When we walk through a shopping mall and don't really want any eye contact, we use the unfocused stare. When we don't want to confront someone, we use an unfocused stare. Students use this on teachers in the classroom. The unfocused stare involves looking intently at nothing. In many cultures, staring is much more customary, particularly staring at strangers or attractive women. Americans traveling in such countries can become uncomfortable and often find the people in those cultures to be very impolite.

In our culture, eye contact is a significant part of the courtship dance of the male and female. Eye-to-body contact is the first step, eye-to-eye is the second step. If the female does not hold the male's eye contact, she has essentially said "go away." If the male cannot take the lack of eye contact as the cue, she will tell him in step three to get lost. Many people in this culture do not follow nonverbal cues. A male may continue staring. A female may respond when she should not.

In Japanese culture, the male and female engaging in courtship rarely look one another in the eye. Japanese males look elsewhere while they say romantic phrases. Japanese females usually act very shy and do not engage in much eye contact. In Japanese culture, eye contact is relevant, but in a different way than it is in American culture. In this culture, we place much value on direct eye contact. For example, if someone does not look us in the eye, we feel disliked, as if they were being inattentive to what we are saying, and we might even think that they were trying to deceive us.

It is not customary in Japan to look others in the eye. It makes Japanese people uneasy and uncomfortable to have much eye contact. Therefore Japanese and Americans often misperceive each other because the nonverbal behaviors are so distinct. The Japanese often look down or at other things when talking with each other. This is disturbing to Americans. However, in the Japanese culture, downcast or closed eyes at a meeting or conference are signs of attentiveness and agreement, not rejection and disagreement. Americans often misinterpret downcast or closed eyes as signs of disagreement, disinterest, or rejection.

In Nigerian culture, prolonged eye contact with a superior is considered disrespectful. Klopf (1998) and Klopf and Park (1982) cite the example of an American Peace Corps volunteer in Nigeria who kept telling his class to look at him. He had many problems with the students and their parents. He finally learned that in Nigeria, it is disrespectful for students to look at teachers. As an American, he needed and wanted eye contact from his students. The Nigerian students felt it very disrespectful to have prolonged eye contact with him, so they looked down.

Puerto Rican children are also taught as a sign of obedience and respect not to share eye contact with adults. To show respect in Asian cultures, one does not look the other in the eye. In addition, Asian men do not stare at women, and vice versa. A woman who makes her living on the streets is allowed to stare at men. In France, however, it is quite common for men to stare at women and to appraise their bodies.

Clearly facial expressions and eye contact communicate various meanings across cultures. We definitely need to educate ourselves as to these various meanings so that we can more fully understand people from other cultures and not offend them when communicating with them.

Vocal Behavior

Everything about our voices communicates. Our vocal variety, rate, volume, pauses, and even silence communicate. It is not only *how* we talk that matters, but also *whether* we talk.

The general U.S. culture respects talkativeness. People are evaluated more positively the more they talk, up to a very high amount. The Amish use the absence of talk as a punishment. They use silence as means of shunning, or punishing, someone for inappropriate behavior. Japanese culture, in contrast, respects quietness. The Japanese are a silent people, especially when listening to someone they respect. Sometimes they will not disagree with you even if they feel you are wrong. Silence, of course, should not be perceived as noncommunication. Silence can have a variety of functions, such as creating interpersonal distance, showing respect for others, punishing others, and avoiding embarrassment for others.

In many cultures, it is appropriate to make vocal noises of enjoyment while eating. It is not uncommon for Koreans and some Germans to belch at the dinner table (Hur & Hur, 1988). This signifies enjoyment of the meal. Americans and English find this behavior rude and intolerable. Koreans find it appropriate to blow one's nose at the dinner table, but this would be considered gross in many cultures. Japanese hiss or inhale their breath while talking to others as a sign of respect. It gives the other person time to think. This is difficult for westerners to deal with. On the other hand, westerners use many filled and unfilled pauses as well as *ah*s and *hum*s. This is difficult for the Japanese to respond to. Germans and Russians have very strong, demonstrative vocalic tones that say to Americans and Asians, "I am right; do not disagree." This prompts perceptions of rudeness and arrogance.

Thus it is easy to understand why people have difficulty communicating across cultures. Not only the languages but also the vocal behaviors differ substantially (Ishii, 1973, 1975; Klopf, 1998; Klopf & Ishii, 1984; Klopf & Park, 1982).

Space

Space talks. How we use space and territory tells something about our culture. On occasion, our culture dictates how we use space. South Americans, Greeks, Arabs, and Italians establish a much closer proximity when interacting than do North Americans. For example, Arabs like to be able to "breathe each other's breath" when talking. Shuter (1976, 1977) found that Costa Ricans establish closer proximity when communicating than Panamanians or Colombians do. Shuter also found that German men prefer greater distances when interacting; whereas, Italian men prefer closer distances. Jones (1971) found that Chinese in New York City interact at greater distances than Puerto Ricans and Italians do. In general, Asians, Pakistanis, Native Americans, North Americans, and northern Europeans prefer greater distances when talking than do southern Europeans, Arabs, and South Americans.

Space preference is influenced by cultural norms. Besides cultural norms, such things as economic background and density of population influence spatial norms. For example, it is not unusual in Japanese culture to find families sleeping in one bedroom even if they have extra bedrooms. Many sections of Japan are densely populated, but this does not seem to be the reason for families sleeping in one room. Japanese family norms dictate close family bonding. Therefore Japanese often sleep in one bedroom to have closeness. Of course larger families share more rooms.

The use of space by different cultures can communicate various meanings. For example, standing too far away from one who expects you to stand close might be perceived as aloofness or coldness. Standing too close to another person might be perceived as pushiness or aggressiveness. Klopf and Park (1982) make the point well:

> The South American automatically tries to step closer to the North American while the latter backs away. Each attempts to establish what he feels is the "correct" distance. In doing so, each produces a nonverbal message. The South American begins to believe that the North American is distant and remote and perhaps even downright unfriendly. In such an extreme situation, space becomes a powerful nonverbal communicator, and the verbal message tends to become completely overshadowed and virtually inconsequential. (p. 78)

Touch

Like space and other nonverbal behaviors, touch differs from culture to culture (Carbaugh, 1990; Frank, 1982; Gudykunst & Yun Kim, 1997; Neuliep, 2002; Klopf, 1998). Touch is a relevant form of communication in every culture. It has been said that touch may well be the most intimate form of communication in the U.S. culture. This is primarily because we are selective about where and whom we touch. U.S. culture is considered a noncontact-oriented culture. Despite the culture, touch can communicate love, caring, warmth, anger, happiness, sadness, or a variety of emotional states. This section reviews the various forms of touch and what they suggest in a variety of cultures.

Frank (1982) says that "each culture builds upon the early tactile experience of the infant and child a more or less elaborate series of patterns of adult conduct in which tactile surrogates and symbolic fulfillments are provided" (p. 288). For example, we teach our children how others say "don't touch," what certain touching means, and how to respond to touch. Frank suggests that it would take much "time and space to do more than mention the cultural patterning of person-to-person tactile communications" (p. 287). This is because of the variety of touching behaviors in cultures. He cites several such touching behaviors: handshake; removing a glove; dancing; rubbing noses or foreheads; clasping arms, shoulders, and waists; embracing knees; kissing; laying on of hands; slapping; and spanking.

Courtship takes place in every culture in the world, and the rituals for courtship vary from culture to culture. As noted earlier, the male is typically the pursuer in U.S. culture, and the female is typically the pursued. The type, amount, and duration of the touch between males and females determines how far the courtship will go. If the female does not respond to the male's arm around her waist, he should realize he has gone as far as he can go, at least for a while. The American female is more accessible to touch than the male. In Ireland, a couple may not hold hands until a considerable amount of acquaintance time has passed. Unmarried Muslim couples in Malaysia are forbidden to embrace or hold each other or have similar close contact. If they are caught, they face a substantial fine. The Japanese do not condone public displays of affection. Depending on the social status or class, some countries still require chaperones for the females. Cross-sexual contact is not widely used or accepted by adults in most Asian cultures. Tactile forms such as kissing, holding hands, patting, and hugging are reserved for private situations. Therefore there is little contact in Asian cultures between men and women in public. Sechrest (1969) studied cross-sexual student couples on college campuses. He found that the Asian cross-sexual couples touched less than the Caucasian couples.

Same-sex touching occurs in other cultures. However, our culture has made it almost taboo for males to touch other males except in very unusual circumstances. For example, when the U.S. men's basketball team won the gold medal at the Olympics in 1984, the men were hugging, kissing, and patting one another. If we saw two men hugging, kissing, and patting on Main Street, USA, many would assume that they were homosexual. In Korea, both men and women often hold hands, link arms, or walk hip to hip with the same sex. Walking close demonstrates friendship, not sexual interest. Touch that means affection between sexes is reserved for private places in Korean culture. In Japan, it is not uncommon to see men and women touching as they walk in the street. Young women even walk arm in arm, and boys touch and jostle each other on the street. Italian Americans touch more often than Anglo-Americans. It is common for African, Arab, and Southeast Asian males to hold hands as a sign of friendship. Among European females, the handshake is very common.

Touch plays an important role in the home. In a classic survey, Welch asked 2,200 children from ages seven to eleven how they were rewarded for good behavior. Almost two-thirds of the children said they were hugged. They also said they liked it. Kaleina (1979) reported that pets get more loving strokes than humans in the United States. He suggests that U.S. culture has more loving contact with its pets than its family members. In our culture, we allow our touch to decrease from early infancy on. Senior citizens receive less touch than any other group in our culture. Research suggests that the American mother has more vocal contact with her infant than tactile; whereas, the Japanese mother has more tactile contact with her infant than vocal. The Jewish and Italian subcultures in the United States probably give their children more tactile experiences than the Anglo subculture. In fact, mothers in the Anglo subculture are encouraged to leave their children alone or not touch them after a certain age, particularly the boys. Girls in the Anglo culture receive more touch from their parents than boys do.

Americans, Germans, and English are more offended by accidental touch by strangers than people in Asian cultures. This is because of the amount of space each culture is granted. Many Asian cultures have limited space, so they ignore, or at least are not offended by, accidental touch. However, Americans, Germans, and English are used to demanding more space and getting it, so they are often offended by the accidental touch of a stranger.

In general, we can classify cultures by their orientations toward tactile communication. The Caucasian North American, German, English, and many Asian cultures are generally noncontact-oriented. The Japanese exhibit less contact than any of the other cultures. Southern Europeans, Jews, Italians, Greek Americans, Arabs, and Puerto Ricans are generally more contact-oriented. Often this difference can create communication misunderstandings. When two people communicate who have different touch orientations, the communication can be misunderstood. Klopf and Park (1982) suggest, that "what is 'normal' for one group is not necessarily 'normal' for another." As a result, serious misunderstandings can occur. "An Anglo-American can be perceived as reserved and distant . . . an Italian-American or a Greek-American can be judged as too assertive and pushy" (pp. 90–91). It is not uncommon for men to pinch the buttocks of attractive women in parts of Italy. American women sometimes do not take such behavior as a compliment. It is clear that we need to understand and accept the touch norms of other cultures. Whenever we are in violation of cultural touch norms, we risk seriously offending a person from another culture.

Environment

People are always surrounded by the environment. Its smells, scents, colors, lighting, seating, and artifacts all influence our communication with one another. It is the same across cultures. When one enters a new culture, the environment assails one's perceptions. Imagine how you would feel taking a bath in a public place with other men, women, and children (Klopf, 1998; Samovar & Porter, 1976; Thomas-Maddox & Lowery-Hart, 1998). This is quite common in parts of Japan. Public baths are and have been an acceptable way of life for many Japanese; whereas, people in some other cultures take baths literally once a month. Let's look at another example. Imagine how people from another culture react to Las Vegas. Some view it as wasteful, frivolous, and brassy. Others see it as the most marvelous place in the world. It depends on what a culture values.

One of the authors recently visited Korea and was taken aback by the odor of garlic. He found out that garlic is the main ingredient in kimchee, one of Korea's national dishes. He was there for a week, and by the end of the week had adjusted to the odor, but it traveled all the way home with him and his luggage.

Air-conditioning is required in North American hotels and in hotels catering to Americans abroad. Most other countries do not have central air and heat to the degree it exists in the United States. However, people in many countries have learned that to keep the American tourist satisfied, they must have air-conditioning and heat. Even in countries such as England and France, people often do not have central heat or air in their own homes. Many hotels install central heat and air just to accommodate American tourists.

In the Philippines, many upper-class citizens have complete and elaborate bathrooms that do not function because they do not have modern sewage systems. To meet American standards, they have bathrooms in their homes that are not usable. They love to show Americans their bathrooms, but they are only for show.

When one is visiting another culture, it is essential to find out as soon as possible what is acceptable and what is not. It is easy to offend someone in another culture by attacking their environmental cues. For more reading on environmental influences read the informative magazine called *Feng Shui*.

Scent

We touched briefly on scent in the environment section. Scent communicates different things in different cultures. The greater North American culture is more concerned about smelling good than is any other culture. Many cultures accept bodily scents that we do not tolerate. Italians do not cover up their body scents. Many European women do not shave their legs or under their arms and consider it grotesque that North American women do. Some other cultures do not have the bathing facilities to stay as clean as we do, and others just do not take smelling good as seriously as North Americans do. They take sponge baths or simply try to not get dirty. Therefore their odors may be stronger than ours. In another culture, we have to be careful not to offend people by being too concerned about their personal hygiene habits. We must continue to communicate with them and accept their ways. After all, our ways and odors are strange to them.

Time

Time communicates and affects our communication with others (Horton, 1976; Ishii, 1973, 1975; Klopf, 1998; Shuter, 1977). Even in this culture we judge others based on their use of time. Southern people in the United States are more casual about time than northerners. This creates an immense amount of negative stereotyping. Northerners perceive southerners as slow, lazy, and dumb but really nice. Southerners perceive northerners to be pushy, aggressive, and too fast. Hawaiians and Mexican Americans are less concerned about time and meeting a time schedule than most North Americans. If such relatively small differences create negative perceptions, imagine how other cultural time orientations that are different can foster misperceptions.

Many Latin Americans and Arabs prefer to conduct several business meetings and activities simultaneously (when this is done via computer, we call it *multitasking*). Therefore, they will schedule several meetings at one time. This insults the American businessperson, who believes that you can do only one thing at a time. This misunderstanding of time can lead to negative perceptions. The Arabs and Latin Americans could perceive the American as demanding and selfish. The American could perceive the Latin Americans and Arabs as unconcerned about the business to be discussed.

In conversations, Americans talk faster and more, pause less often, fill silent pauses, and interject comments more often and more quickly than the Japanese do. The Japanese use silence more. To the Japanese, silence can be used as a means of respect for the other person or to show that one is thinking. To Americans, the talk time must be fast-paced. The Japanese like talk time to be well managed and thoughtful. Ishii (1975) surveyed businessmen and female secretaries in Japan about silence and eloquence. The survey revealed that 76 percent of the respondents believed that silent men were more likely to succeed than eloquent men. It also revealed that 65 percent of the secretaries would select silent men to marry. Thirty-six percent of those who felt they were eloquent would rather be perceived as silent; whereas, only 22 percent of the silent men wanted to be eloquent in the future.

Americans are very time-oriented, perhaps even more so than the Swiss, British, and Germans. Americans emphasize scheduling and segmentation. The clock is the controller. Americans, Swiss, and Germans hate to be kept waiting. They like people to be on time. They judge people by how punctual or late they are. In U.S. culture, we expect people to actually be early, not on time or late for an appointment. Latin Americans are usually late. In fact, it is a sign of respect to be late or to start things later than scheduled. If a Latin American sets a party for a given time, it will not begin until much later. The Japanese call before they visit. According to Klopf and Park (1982), the Japanese "may arrive not at a specified hour but anytime during the day" (p. 83).

Hall (1977) has pointed out the importance of high- and low-context cultures. Hall wrote, "HC (high-context) transactions feature preprogrammed information that is in the receiver and in the setting, with only minimal information in the transmitted message" (p. 101). And although one of the authors had read Hall years ago (decades ago), he had forgotten much about it. The text came into play when the author was invited to teach class at a university in Bangkok. The United States is a low-context culture, and Thailand is a high-context culture. First, the author thought there would be a written contract, but in fact there never was one. Anyone at the Thai university would know that, but not the author. The author repeatedly tried to determine such things as when the class meets, how long it meets, when he would obtain a class roll, and where he would turn in grades. Many of these things happened, but there was no schedule for them to happen. Incidentally, he never received a class roll. But classes met all day for eight days, chosen what the author considered to be almost at random. Eventually, the classes were taught, the students received grades, and the professor was paid. When a person from an LC (low-context) culture enters an HC culture, the person needs to learn to be a little more laid back and flexible. Many Americans are too structured and programmed in their own ways to adapt to the different approach. It works. But you must learn to adapt.

Obviously, in having contact with people from another culture, one can never take time for granted. It may be a serious breach of etiquette to treat time as one would in one's own culture. Be sure to find out—before such contact occurs, if possible—how the other culture's time system is arranged. Do not be surprised if it makes no sense to you. Just try to adapt as best you can.

GOALS TO SEEK

In today's world, it is highly likely that all of us will have contact with people from other cultures. Many educated Americans hold jobs that require extensive intercultural contact. From this chapter, it should be clear that learning to control our nonverbal communication behavior when we are interacting with a person from another culture is no simple task. It is difficult for us to decide how much effort to put into such learning unless we know it will be critical to our futures. Most people in the past have chosen to devote very little time indeed.

While traveling in Europe, one of the authors noted some graffiti scrawled on a restroom wall in Amsterdam. It read as follows:

Speaks three languages = trilingual

Speaks two languages = bilingual

Speaks one language = American

His own lack of skill in any language other than American English had been fully impressed on him in his early stops on his trip. The humor of the graffiti was tempered with a recognition of the truth it suggested. Very few Americans are truly bilingual. Far fewer are bicultural. Most have little understanding of nonverbal communication in any other culture.

Knowledge of a language does not provide an understanding of a culture. For example, many cultures speak Spanish, but the cultures differ from each other in extreme ways. The nonverbal behaviors of a culture are as important if not more so to understanding the culture as is the language of the culture. Many believe that the study of the nonverbal behavior of various cultures is as valuable to the American who may need to travel widely as is the study of foreign languages. People accept the fact that one cannot know all of the languages of the world. What they do not accept is rude and discourteous behavior—the nonverbal social blunders that occur when one is not familiar with the nonverbal norms of a given culture. In recognition of this fact, more business organizations are developing training programs for their employees who must venture abroad on behalf of the company.

There are essentially three types of people in today's world: *monocultural, bi-* or *multicultural,* and *acultural.* The vast majority of the people on earth fit in the first category: they are a product of a single culture and have little or no understanding or appreciation of any other culture. People in the second group are a product of one culture but have learned to adapt to the ways of one or more other cultures. Such people can flow from one culture to another and be accepted by the culture in which they find themselves. They have mastered not only the language but also the nonverbal behaviors of more than one culture. Most of us envy such people and wish we could be like them, but few of us are willing to devote the years of effort and study required to make that wish a reality.

The third category of people often is not recognized as different from the second, but it is very different. These people are acultural. By this we mean that they are not the product of any given culture. The best example of such a person is one who is born in and spends many years in one culture and then moves to another culture and spends many years in that culture. Many immigrants fall into this category. Sometimes their children do also. They may move back and forth between two cultures, but they are never fully accepted in any one because they cannot fully adapt their language or nonverbal behaviors in the transitions. They become hybrids that do not really fit anywhere except with similar hybrids. Many children of American military families who move all over the world report feeling that they are in this category.

Because many of us are destined to remain in our monocultural worlds, becoming bi- or multicultural is not a realistic goal, and—because we obviously do not want to give up our own culture to become acultural—we need to consider what goals we can set to help us to communicate with people from other cultures who may be just as monocultural as we are. Harris and Moran (1991), Klopf (1998), and Thomas-Maddox and Lowery-Hart (1998) have suggested skills we can learn that will aid in our cultural and diversity awareness:

1. Be nonjudgmental; avoid moralistic, value-laden evaluative statements; listen.
2. Be tolerant of differences and ambiguity; recognize differences.
3. Show respect; verbally and nonverbally convey positive regard and interest.

Symbols of diversity and different cultures

4. Personalize remarks; recognize your own values (say "I think," or "I believe").
5. Empathize; try to think as the other person would, or share his or her feelings and emotions.
6. Take turns; try to have some conversational turn-taking. Don't try to control the conversation; share and learn from one another.
7. Be patient. It takes time to fully understand others and for them to understand you.

8. Be less ethnocentric. Display less ethnocentrism.
9. Realize that diversity and diverse ways of communicating are here to stay. Let's learn and adapt.

Although such skills probably are best fostered by traveling and living for periods of time in another culture, we can also improve our skills by taking the time and effort to seek out people from other cultures in our own environment with whom we can interact. Remember, most people from other cultures are just as interested in learning about our culture and how to adapt to us as we are in learning about their culture and how to adapt to them. Such mutual learning can occur anywhere on the globe.

Glossary of Terminology

Ethnocentrism is the view that one's own culture is the center of the universe, that the ways of one's own culture are the normal, natural, and correct way of thinking about and doing things.

Intercultural communication is the communication between people of different cultures; it occurs when a person from one culture talks to a person from another.

Subculture a collection of people who possess conscious membership in an identifiable unit of an encompassing, larger cultural unit.

Xenophobia is the fear of confronting or communicating with strangers.

REFERENCES AND SELECTED READINGS

Chapter 1

Andersen, P. A. (1999). *Nonverbal communication: Forms and functions.* Mountain View, CA: Mayfield Publishing Company.

Andersen, P. A., Garrison, J. P., and Andersen, J. F. (1979). Implications of a neurophysiological approach for the study of nonverbal communication. *Human Communication Research, 6,* 74–89.

Beeman, M. J., and Chiarello, C. (1998). Complementary right- and left-hemisphere language comprehension. *Current Directions in Psychological Science, 7,* (1), 2–8.

Birdwhistell, R. L. (1970). *Kinesics and context: Essays on body motion communication.* Philadelphia: University of Pennsylvania Press.

Buck, R., and VanLear, A. (2002). Verbal and nonverbal communication: Distinguishing symbolic, spontaneous, and pseudo-spontaneous nonverbal behavior. *Journal of Communication, 52,* 522–541.

DeVito, J. A., and Hecht, M. L. (1990). *The nonverbal communication reader.* Prospect Heights, IL: Waveland Press.

Hall, E. T. (1966). *The hidden dimension.* Garden City, NY: A Doubleday Anchor Books.

Kendon, A. (2008). Some reflections on the relationship between 'gesture' and 'sign.' *Gesture, 8,* 348–366.

Knapp, M. L., and Hall, J. A. (1992). *Nonverbal communication in human interaction* (3rd ed.). New York: Holt, Rinehart & Winston.

LaFrance, M., and Mayo, C. (1978). *Moving bodies: Nonverbal communication in social relationships.* Monterey, CA: Brooks/Cole.

McCroskey, J. C. (2001). *An introduction to rhetorical communication* (8th ed.). Boston: Allyn and Bacon.

McCroskey, J. C., and Richmond, V. P. (1996). *Fundamentals of human communication.* Prospect Heights, IL: Waveland Press.

Mehrabian, A. (1971). *Silent messages: Implicit communication of emotions and attitudes* (5th ed.). Belmont, CA: Wadsworth.

Mehrabian, A., and Ferris, S.R. (1967). Inference of attitudes from nonverbal communication in two channels. *Journal of Consulting Psychology, 31,* 248–252.

Mehrabian, A., and Weiner, M. (1967). Decoding of inconsistent communications. *Journal of Personality and Social Psychology, 6,* 109–144.

Morris, D. (1983). *Bodywatching: A field guide to the human species.* New York: Crown Publishers Inc.

Philpot, J. S. (1983). *The relative contribution to meaning of verbal and nonverbal channels of communication: A meta-analysis.* (Unpublished master's thesis). University of Nebraska.

Richmond, V. P. (1996). *Nonverbal behavior in the classroom.* Edina, MN: Burgess International Group.

Richmond, V. P. (1997). *Nonverbal behavior in the classroom: A text, workbook, and study guide.* Acton, MA: Tapestry Press.

Richmond, V. P., and McCroskey, J. C. (1998). *Communication: Apprehension, avoidance, and effectiveness* (5th ed.). Scottsdale, AZ: Gorsuch Scarisbrick.

Richmond, V. P., and McCroskey, J. C. (2001). *Organizational communication for survival: Making work, work.* Boston: Allyn and Bacon.

Ruesch, J., and Kees, W. (1971). *Nonverbal communication: Notes on the visual perception of human relations.* (2nd ed.). Berkeley, CA: University of California Press.

Segerstrale, U., and Molnar, P. (1997a). *Nonverbal communication: Where nature meets culture.* Mahwah, NJ: Erlbaum.

Segerstrale, U., and Molnar, P. (1997b). Nonverbal communication: Crossing the boundary between culture and nature. In U. Segerstrale and P. Molnar (eds.). *Nonverbal communication: Where nature meets culture* (pp. 1–26). Mahwah, NJ: Erlbaum.

Chapter 2

Aiken, L. R. (1963). The relationships of dress to selected measures of personality in undergraduate women. *Journal of Social Psychology, 59,* 119–128.

Amsbary, J. H., Vogel, R., Hickson, M. III, Wittig, J. W., and Oakes, B. (1994). Smoking artifacts as indicators of homophily, attraction, and credibility: A replication. *Communication Research Reports, 11,* 161–167.

Andersen, P. A. (1999). *Nonverbal communication: Forms and functions.* Mountain View, CA: Mayfield Publishing Company.

Berscheid, E., and Walster, E. H. (1969). *Interpersonal attraction.* Reading, MA: Addison-Wesley.

Berscheid, E., and Walster, E. (1971, June). Adrenaline makes the heart grow fonder. *Psychology Today, 5,* 46–50, 62.

Berscheid, E., and Walster, E. (1972). Beauty and the best. *Psychology Today, 5,* 42–46, 74.

Berscheid, E., and Walster, E. H. (1978). *Interpersonal attraction* (2nd ed.). Reading, MA: Addison-Wesley.

Berscheid, E., Walster, E., and Bohrnstedt, G. (1973). Body image: The happy American body. *Psychology Today, 7,* 119–123, 126–131.

Bickman, L. (1974). The social power of a uniform. *Journal of Applied Social Psychology, 4,* 47–61.

Bixler, S., and Nix-Rice, N. (1997). *The new professional image.* Holbrook, MA: Adams Media Corporation.

Brislin, R. W., and Lewis, S. A. (1968). Dating and physical attractiveness: Replication. *Psychological Reports, 22,* 976.

Cash, T. F., and Janda, L. H. (1984). The eye of the beholder. *Psychology Today,* December, 46–52.

Chia, S. C. (2007). Third-person perceptions about idealized body image and weight-loss behavior. *Journalism and Mass Communication Quarterly, 84,* 677–694.

Compton, N. H. (1962). Personal attributes of color and design preferences in clothing fabrics. *Journal of Psychology, 54,* 191–195.

Corey, A. M. (2007). Body politics in online communication. *Texas Speech Communication Journal, 32,* 21–32.

Cortes, J. B., and Gatti, F. M. (1965). Physique and self-description of temperament. *Journal of Consulting Psychology, 29,* 434.

DeVito, J. A., and Hecht, M. L. (1990). *The nonverbal communication reader.* Prospect Heights, IL: Waveland Press.

Dion, K., Berscheid, E., and Walster, E. (1972). What is beautiful is good. *Journal of Personality and Social Psychology, 24,* 285–290.

Droogsma, R. A. (2007). Redefining hijab: American Muslim women' standpoints on veiling. *Journal of Applied Communication Research, 35,* 294-319.

Efran, M. G. (1974). The effect of physical appearance on the judgement of guilt, interpersonal attraction, and severity of recommended punishment in a simulated jury task. *Journal of Research in Personality, 8,* 45–54.

Esterling, C., Leslie, J., and Jones, M. (1992). Perceived importance and usage of dress codes among organizations that market professional services. *Public Person Management, 21,* 211–219.

Feiman, S., and Gill, G. W. (1978). Sex differences on physical attractiveness preferences. *Journal of Social Psychology, 105,* 43–52.

Feingold, A. (1992). Good looking people are not what we think. *Psychological Bulletin, 3,* 304–341.

Feingold, A., and Mazzella, R. (1998). Gender differences in body image are increasing. *Psychological Science, 9,* (3), 190–195.

Fischer-Mirkin, T. (1995). *Understanding the hidden meanings of women's clothing dress code.* New York: Clarkson Potter Publishers.

Fortenberry, J. H., McLean, J., Morris, P., and O'Connell, M. (1978). Mode of dress as a perception cue to deference. *Journal of Social Psychology, 104,* 139–140.

Frymier, A. B., and Wanzer M. B., (2006). Teacher and student affinity-seeking in the classroom. In T. P. Mottet, V. P. Richmond, and J. C. McCroskey. (eds.) *Handbook of instructional communication: Rhetorical and relational perspectives.* Boston: Allyn and Bacon.

Gashin, A., and Simmons, K. (2002). Mirror, mirror on the wall. . . . *USA Today Snapshots,* Life Section D, Tuesday, November 5.

Gorden, W.I., Tengler, C. D., and Infante, D. A. (1990). Women's clothing predispositions as predictors of dress at work, job satisfaction, and career advancement. In J.A. DeVito and M.L. Hecht. *The nonverbal communication reader* (pp. 155–162). Prospect Heights, IL: Waveland Press.

Gross, M. (1990). Admit it or not: Work dress codes are a fact of life. In J. A. DeVito and M.L. Hecht, *The nonverbal communication reader* (pp. 151–154). Prospect Heights, IL: Waveland Press.

Gudykunst, W. B., and Kim, Y. Y. (1992). *Communicating with strangers: An approach to intercultural communication* (2nd ed.). New York: Random House.

Guerrero, L. K., DeVito, J. A., and Hecht, M. L. (1999). *The nonverbal communication reader: Classic and contemporary readings* (2nd ed.). Prospect Heights, IL: Waveland Press.

Gundersen, D. F. (1987). Credibility and the police uniform. *Journal of Police Science and Administration, 15,* 192–195.

Gundersen, D. F. (1990). Uniforms: Conspicuous invisibility. In J. A. DeVito and M. L. Hecht, *The nonverbal communication reader* (pp. 172–178). Prospect Heights, IL: Waveland Press.

Hall, J. A. (1984). *Nonverbal sex differences: Communication, accuracy and expressive styles.* Baltimore, MD: Johns Hopkins University Press.

Harris, M. B. (1991). Sex differences in stereotypes of spectacles. *Journal of Applied Psychology, 21,* 1659–1680.

Haseltine, E. (2002, September). Beauty secret: What separates homely from comely? *Discover,* 88.

Heilman, M. E., and Stopeck, M. H. (1985). Being attractive, advantage or disadvantage? Performance-based evaluations and recommended personnel actions as a function of appearance, sex, and job type. *Organizational Behavior and Human Decision Processes, 35,* 202–215.

Henig, R. M. (1996, May/June). The price of perfection. *Civilization,* 56–61.

Henley, N. M. (1977). *Body politics: Power, sex, and nonverbal communication.* Englewood Cliffs, NJ: Prentice Hall.

Hewitt, J., and German, K. (1987). Attire and Attractiveness. *Perception and Motor Skills, 64,* 558.

Hickson, M. L., Stacks, D. W., and Moore, N. J. (2004). *Nonverbal communication: Studies and applications* (4th ed.). Los Angeles, CA: Roxbury.

Hoult, T. F. (1954). Experimental measurement of clothing as a factor in some social ratings of selected American men. *American Sociological Review, 19,* 324–328.

Johnston, J. E. (1994). *Appearance obsession: Learning to love the way you look*. Deerfield Beach, FL: Health Communications.

Jourard, S. M., and Secord, P. F. (1955). Body-cathexis and personality. *British Journal of Psychology, 46,* 130–138.

Kaiser, S. B. (1999). Women's appearance and clothing within organizations. In L. K. Guerrero, J. A. DeVito, and M. L. Hecht, *The nonverbal communication reader: Classic and contemporary readings* (2nd ed.), (pp. 106–113). Prospect Heights, IL: Waveland Press.

Kalick, S. M., Zebrowitz, L. A., Langlois, J. H., and Johnson, R. M. (1998). Does human facial attractiveness honestly advertise health? Longitudinal data on an evolutionary question. *Psychological Science, 9,* (1), 8–13.

Kaltenbach, P. (1991). Effects of diet advertising on women at-risk for the development of anorexia nervosa. *Dissertation Abstracts International, 51,* (10-B), 5031.

Keenan, A. (1976). Effects of the non-verbal behavior of interviewers on candidates' performance. *Journal of Occupational Psychology, 49,* 171–176.

Keenan, A., and Wedderburn, A. A. (1975). Effects of the non-verbal behavior of interviewers on candidates' impressions. *Journal of Occupational Psychology, 48,* 129–132.

Kiddie, T. (2009). Recent trends in business casual attire and their effects on student job seekers. *Business Communication Quarterly, 72 ,* 350–354.

Knapp, M. L., and Hall, J. A. (1992). *Nonverbal communication in human interaction* (3rd ed.). New York: Holt, Rinehart & Winston.

Knapp, M. K., and Vangelisti, A. (2000). *Interpersonal communication and human relationships* (4th ed.). Boston: Allyn and Bacon.

Korda, M. (1975). *Power: How to get it, How to use it*. New York: Ballantine.

Lannutti, P., and Camero, M. (2007). Women's perceptions of flirtatious nonverbal behavior: The effects of alcohol consumption and physical attractiveness.

Southern Communication Journal, 72, 21–35.

Lewis, K. E., and Bierly, M. (1990). Toward a profile of the female voter: Sex differences in perceived physical attractiveness and competence of political candidates. *Sex Roles, 22,* 1–11.

Lyon, D. W., Rainey, B. B., and Bullock, C. N. (2002). The effect of glasses on the self-concept of school-aged children. *Journal of Optometric Vision Development, 33,* 29–32.

McCroskey, J. C., Larson, C. E., and Knapp, M. L. (1971). *An introduction to interpersonal communication*. Englewood Cliffs, NJ: Prentice Hall.

McCroskey, J. C., and McCain, T. A. (1974). The measurement of interpersonal attraction. *Speech Monographs, 41,* 261–266.

McCroskey, J. C., and Richmond, V. P. (1996). *Fundamentals of human communication: An interpersonal perspective*. Prospect Heights, IL: Waveland Press.

McCroskey, J. C., Wrench, J. S., and Richmond, V. P. (2003). *Principles of public speaking*. Indianapolis, IN: The College Network.

Mehrabian, A. (1971a). *Silent messages: Implicit communication of emotions and attitudes* (5th ed.). Belmont, CA: Wadsworth.

Mehrabian, A. (1971b). Verbal and nonverbal interactions of strangers in a waiting situation. *Journal of Experimental Research in Personality, 5,* 127–138.

Mills, J., and Aronson, E. (1965). Opinion change as a function of the communicator's attractiveness and desire to influence. *Journal of Personality and Social Psychology, 1,* 173–177.

Mirivel, J. C. (2008). The physical examination in cosmetic surgery: Communication strategies to promote the desirability of surgery. *Health Communication, 23,* 153–170.

Molloy, J. T. (1975). *Dress for success*. New York: Warner Books.

Molloy, J. T. (1978). *The women's dress for success book*. New York: Warner Books.

Molloy, J. T. (1988). *The new dress for success book*. New York: Warner Books.

Moore, N. J., Hickson, M. III, and Stacks, M. J. (2010). *Nonverbal communication: Studies and applications*. (5th ed.). New York: Oxford University Press.

Morris, D. (1985). *Bodywatching*. New York: Crown.

Morris, T. L., Gorham, J., Cohen, S. H., and Huffman, D. (1996). Fashion in the classroom: Effects of attire on student perceptions of instructors in college classes. *Communication Education, 45*, (2), 135–148.

Mottet, T., and Richmond, V. P. (2002). Student nonverbal communication and its influence on teachers and teaching. In J. L. Chesebro and J.C. McCroskey, *Communication for teachers* (pp. 47–61). Boston: Allyn and Bacon.

Myers, P. N. Jr., and Biocca, F. A. (1999). The effect of television advertising and programming on body image distortions in young women. In L. K. Guerrero, J. A. DeVito, and M. L. Hecht, *The nonverbal communication reader: Classic and contemporary readings* (2nd ed.), (pp. 92–100). Prospect Heights, IL: Waveland Press.

Nix-Rice, N. (1996). *Looking good: A comprehensive guide to wardrobe development*. Holbrook, MA: Adams Media Corporation.

Park, S. Y. (2005). The influence of presumed media influence on women's desire to be thin. *Communication Research, 32*, 594–614.

Peluchette, J. V., and Karl, K. (2007). The impact of workplace attire on employee self-perceptions. *Human Resource Development Quarterly, 18*, 345–360.

Raiscot, J. (1983). *Jury selection, body language, and the visual trial*. Minneapolis, MN: AB Publications.

Raiscot, J. (1986). *Silent sales*. Minneapolis, MN: AB Publications.

Reyes, K. W. (1993, August). Eye of the beholder. *Modern Maturity*, 22–23.

Richmond, V. P. (1996). *Nonverbal communication in the classroom*. Edina, MN: Burgess International Group.

Richmond, V. P. (2000). *Image fixation measure*. Unpublished manuscript. West Virginia University. Morgantown, WV.

Richmond, V. P. (2002). Teacher nonverbal immediacy: Use and outcomes. In J.L. Chesebro and J.C. McCroskey, *Communication for teachers* (pp. 65–82). Boston: Allyn and Bacon.

Richmond, V. P., and Hickson, M. L. III. (2002). *Going public: A practical guide to public talk*. Boston: Allyn and Bacon.

Richmond, V. P., and McCroskey, J. C. (2000). The impact of supervisor and subordinate immediacy on relational and organizational outcomes. *Communication Monographs, 67*, 85–95.

Rosencranz, M. L. (1962). Clothing symbolism. *Journal of Home Economics, 54*, 18–22.

Rosenfeld, L. B., and Plax, T. G. (1977). Clothing as communication. *Journal of Communication, 27*, 24–31.

Sabatelli, R. M., and Rubin, M. (1986). Nonverbal expressiveness and physical attractiveness as mediators of interpersonal perceptions. *Journal of Nonverbal Behavior, 10*, 120–133.

Schlenker, B. R. (1980). *Impression management*. Monterey, CA: Brooks/Cole.

Sheldon, W. H. (1940). *The varieties of human physique*. New York: Harper and Brothers.

Sheldon, W. H. (1942). *The varieties of temperament*. New York: Hafner.

Sheldon, W. H. (1954). *Atlas of men: A guide for somatotyping the adult male of all ages*. New York: Harper.

Shriver, M. (2002). Jamie Lee Curtis keeps it real. *Dateline NBC, www.msnbc.com/news*, 10/9/2002, pp. 1–5.

Singer, M. S., and Singer, A. E. (1985). The effect of police uniforms on interpersonal perception. *Journal of Psychology, 119*, 157–161.

Singh, B. N. (1964). A study of certain personal qualities as preferred by college students in their marital partners. *Journal of Psychological Researchers, 8*, 37–48.

Stark, E. (1986, January). Bulimia: Not epidemic. *Psychology Today, 20,* 17.

Sterrett, J. H. (1978). The job interview: Body language and perceptions of potential effectiveness. *Journal of Applied Psychology, 63,* 389–390.

Stone, G., Singletary, M., and Richmond, V. P. (1999). *Clarifying communication theories: A hands-on approach.* Ames, IA: Iowa State University Press.

Sybers, R., and Roach, M. E. (1962). Clothing and human behavior. *Journal of Home Economics, 54,* 184–187.

Tanke, E. D. (1982). Dimensions of the physical attractiveness stereotype: A factor/analytic study. *Journal of Psychology, 110,* 63–74.

Taylor, L. C., and Compton, N. H. (1968). Personality correlates of dress conformity. *Journal of Home Economics, 60,* 653–656.

Tenzel, J. H., and Cizanckas, V. (1973). Uniform experiment. *Journal of Police Science and Administration, 1,* 421–424.

Terry, R. L. (1989) Eyeglasses and gender stereotypes. *Optometry and Visual Science, 66,* 694–697.

Terry, R. L., and Brady, C. S. (1976). Effects of framed spectacles and contact lenses on self-ratings of facial attractiveness. *Perceptual and Motor Skills, 42,* 789–790.

Terry, R. L., and Hall, C. A. (1989). Affective responses to eyeglasses: Evidence of a self difference. *Journal of the American Optometry Association, 60,* 609–611.

Terry, R. L., and Krantz, J. H. (1993). Dimensions of trait attributions associated with eyeglasses, men's facial hair, and women's hair length. *Journal of Applied Psychology, 23,* 1757–1769.

Terry, R. L., and Stockton, L. A. (1993). Eyeglasses and children's schemata. *Journal of Social Psychology, 133,* 425–438.

Thourlby, W. (1980). *You are what you wear.* New York: New American Library.

Vevea, N. (2008). Body art: Performing identity through tattoos and piercing. Conference Papers, International Communication Association, 1–26. Retrieved October 28, 2009 from Communicaton and Mass Media Complete database.

Walker, R. N. (1963). Body build and behavior in young children: II. Body build and parents' ratings. *Child Development, 34,* 1–23.

Walster, E. V., Aronson, E., Abrahams, D., and Rohmann, L. (1966). Importance of physical attractiveness in dating behavior. *Journal of Personality and Social Psychology, 4,* 508–516.

Webster, E. C. (1964). *Decision making in the employment interview.* Industrial Relations Center, McGill University.

Wells, W. D., and Siegel, B. (1961). Stereotyped somatotypes. *Psychological Reports, 8,* 77–78.

What women like in men. (1983, July 20). *USA Today.*

Widgery, R. N., and Ruch, R. S. (1981). Beauty and the Machiavellian. *Communication Quarterly, 29,* 297–301.

Wilson, G., and Nias, D. (1999). Beauty can't be beat. In L. K. Guerrero, J. A. DeVito, and M. L. Hecht, *The nonverbal communication reader: Classic and contemporary readings* (2nd ed.), (pp. 101–105). Prospect Heights, IL: Waveland Press.

Young, D. M., and Beier, E. G. (1977). The role of applicant non-verbal communication in the employment interview. *Journal of Employment Counseling, 14,* 154–165.

Chapter 3

Archer, D. (1991). *A world of gestures: Culture and nonverbal communication.* Video from the University of California, Center for Media and Independent Learning.

Argyle, M. (1975). *Bodily communication.* New York: International Universities Press.

Birdwhistell, R. L. (1952). *Introduction to kinesics: An annotation system for analysis of body motion and gesture.* Louisville, KY: University of Louisville Press.

Birdwhistell, R. L. (1970). *Kinesics and context: Essays on body motion communication.* Philadelphia: University of Pennsylvania Press.

Carney, D. R., Hall, J. A., and LeBeau, L. S. (2005). Beliefs about the nonverbal expression of social power. *Journal of Nonverbal Behavior, 29,* 105–123.

Caso, L., Maricchiolo, M., Bonaiuto, M., Vrij, A., and Mann, S. (2006). The impact of deception and suspicion on different hand movements. *Journal of Nonverbal Behavior, 30,* 1–19.

DePaulo, B. M. (1988). Nonverbal aspects of deception. *Journal of Nonverbal Behavior, 12,* 153–161.

DePaulo, B. M., and Kirkendol, S. E. (1988). The motivational impairment effect in the communication of deception. In J. Yuille (ed.), *Credibility assessment* (pp. 50–69). Belgium: Kluwer Academic Publishers.

Dittmann, A. T. (1971). Review of kinesics and context by R. L. Birdwhistell. *Psychiatry, 34,* 334–342.

Duncan, S. D. Jr. (1972). Some signals and rules for taking speaking turns in conversations. *Journal of Personality and Social Psychology, 23,* 283–292.

Duncan, S. D. Jr. (1974). On the structure of speaker-auditor interaction during speaking turns. *Language in Society, 2,* 161–180.

Ekman, P. (1976). Movements with precise meanings. *Journal of Communication, 26,* 14–26.

Ekman, P., and Friesen, W. V. (1969a). Nonverbal leakage and clues to deception. *Psychiatry, 32,* 88–106.

Ekman, P., and Friesen, W. V. (1969b). The repertoire of nonverbal behavior: Categories, origins, usage, and coding. *Semiotica, 1,* 49–98.

Ekman, P., and Friesen, W. V. (1972). Hand movements. *Journal of Communication, 22,* 353–374.

Ekman, P., and Friesen, W. V. (1974). Detecting deception from the body or face. *Journal of Personality and Social Psychology, 29,* 288–298.

Fast, J. (1970). *Body language.* New York: M. Evans.

Goffman, E. (1959). *The presentation of self in everyday life.* Garden City, NY: Doubleday-Anchor.

Goffman, E. (1967). *Interaction ritual.* Garden City, NY: Anchor Books.

Goleman, D. (1999). Can you tell when someone is lying to you? In L. K. Guerrero, J.A. DeVito, and M.L. Hecht (eds.), *The nonverbal communication reader: Classic and contemporary readings* (pp. 358–366). Prospect Heights, IL: Waveland Press.

Guerrero, L. K., DeVito, J. A., and Hecht, M. L. (1999). (eds.) *The Nonverbal Communication Reader: Classic and contemporary readings.* Prospect Heights, IL: Waveland Press.

Hall, J. A. (1996). Touch, status, and gender at professional meetings. *Journal of Nonverbal Behavior, 20,* 23–44.

Hall, J. A. (1998). How big are nonverbal sex differences? The case of smiling and sensitivity to nonverbal cues. In D. J. Canary and K. Dindia (eds.), *Sex differences and similarities in communication* (pp. 155–177). Mahwah, NJ: Erlbaum.

Henley, N. M. (1977). *Body politics: Power, sex, and nonverbal communication.* Englewood Cliffs, NJ: Prentice Hall.

Johnson, H. G., Ekman, P., and Friesen, W. V. (1975). Communicative body movements: American emblems. *Semiotica, 15,* 335–353.

Jones, S. M., and Wirtz, J. G. (2007). Sad monkey see, monkey do; Nonverbal matching in emotional support encounters. *Communication Studies, 58,* 71–86.

Kelly, S. D., Kravitz, C., and Hopkins, M. (2004). Neural correlates of bimodal speech and gesture comprehension. *Brain and Language, 89,* 253–260.

Kendon, A., and Ferber, A. (1973). A description of some human greetings. In R.P.

Michael and J.H. Crook (eds.), *Comparative ecology and behavior of primates*. London: Academic Press.

Knapp, M. L., and Hall, J.A. (1992). *Nonverbal communication in human interaction* (3rd ed.). New York: Holt, Rinehart & Winston.

Knapp, M. L., Hart, R.P., and Dennis, H.S. (1974). An exploration of deception as a communication construct. *Human Communication Research*, 1, 15–29.

Krauss, R. M. (1998). Why do we gesture when we speak? *Current Directions in Psychological Science*, 7, (2), 54–59.

Malandro, L. A., and Barker, L. (1983). *Nonverbal communication* (pp. 111–143). Reading, MA: Addison-Wesley.

McNeill, D. (2005). *Gesture and thought*. Chicago: University of Chicago Press.

Mehrabian, A. (1969a). Measures of achieving tendency. *Educational and Psychological Measurement*, 29, 445–451.

Mehrabian, A. (1969b). Significance of posture and position in the communicationof attitude and status relationships. *Psychological Bulletin*, 71, 359–372.

Mehrabian, A. (1971). *Silent messages: Implicit communication of emotions and attitudes* (5th ed.). Belmont, CA: Wadsworth.

Mehrabian, A. (1972). *Nonverbal communication*. Chicago: Aldine-Atherton.

McCroskey, J. C., and Richmond, V. P. (1996). *Fundamentals of human communication: An interpersonal perspective*. Prospect Heights, IL: Waveland Press.

Norton, R. (1983). *Communicator style: Theory, applications, and measures*. Beverly Hills, CA: Sage Publications.

Richmond, V. P. (1996). *Nonverbal communication in the classroom*. Acton, MA: Tapestry Press.

Richmond, V. P. (2002a). Teacher nonverbal immediacy: Uses and outcomes. In J.

L. Chesebro and J. C. McCroskey (eds.), *Communication for teachers* (pp. 65–82). Boston: Allyn and Bacon.

Richmond, V. P. (2002b). Socio-communicative style and orientation in instruction. In J. L. Chesebro and J. C. McCroskey (eds.), *Communication for teachers* (pp. 104–115). Boston: Allyn and Bacon.

Richmond, V. P., Smith, R. S., Heisel, A., and McCroskey, J. C. (2002). The association of physician socio-communicative style with physician credibility and patient satisfaction. *Communication Research Reports*, 19, 207–215.

Rogers, W. T. (1978). The contribution of kinesic illustrators toward the comprehension of verbal behavior within utterances. *Human Communication Research*, 5, 54–62.

Rosenfeld, H. M. (1966a). Approval-seeking and approval-inducing functions of verbal and nonverbal responses in the dyad. *Journal of Personality and Social Psychology*, 4, 597–605.

Rosenfeld, H. M. (1966b). Instrumental affiliative functions of facial and gestural expressions. *Journal of Personality and Social Psychology*, 4, 65–72.

Rosenfeld, H. M. (1982). Measurement of body motion and orientation. In K. R. Scherer and P. Ekman (eds.), *Handbook of methods in nonverbal behavior research* (pp. 199–286). New York: Cambridge University Press.

Scheflen, A. E. (1964). The significance of posture in communication systems. *Psychiatry*, 27, 316–331.

Scherer, K. R., and Ekman, P. (1982). (eds.) *Handbook of methods in nonverbal behavior research*. New York: Cambridge University Press.

Sousa-Poza, J. F., and Rohrberg, R. (1977). Body movement in relation to type of information (person- and nonperson-oriented) and cognitive style (field dependence). *Human Communication Research*, 4, (1), 19–29.

Stevanoni, E., and Salmon, K. (2005). Giving memory a hand: Instructing children to gesture enhances recall. *Journal of Nonverbal Behavior*, 29, 217–233.

Wachsmuth, I. (2006, November). Gestures offer insight. *Scientific American Mind, 17 (5)*, 20–25.

Chapter 4

Ambadar, Z., Cohn, J. F., and Reed, L. I. (2009). All smiles are not created equal: morphology and timing of smiles perceived as amused, polite, and embarrassed/nervous. *Journal of Nonverbal Behavior, 33*, 17–34.

Archer, D., Iritani, B., Kimes, D. D., and Barrios, M. (1983). Face-ism: Five studies of sex differences in facial prominence. *Journal of Personality and Social Psychology, 43, (4)*, 725–735.

Boucher, J. D., and Ekman, P. (1975). Facial areas and emotional information. *Journal of Communication, 25*, 21–29.

Bould, E., and Morris, N. (2008). Role of motion signals in recognizing subtle facial expressions of emotion. *British Psychological Society, 99*, 167–189.

Brownlow, S., and Zebrowitz, L. A. (1990). Facial appearance, gender, and credibility in television commercials. *Journal of Nonverbal Behavior, 14*, 51–59.

Carrere, S., and Gottman, J. (1999). Predicting divorce among newlyweds from the first three minutes of a marital conflict discussion. *Family Process, 38, (3)*, 293–301.

Darwin, C. (1998). *The expression of the emotions in man and animals.* (3rd ed.). New York: Oxford University Press.

Eibl-Eibesfeldt, I. (1970). *Ethology: The biology of behavior.* New York: Holt, Rinehart & Winston.

Eibl-Eibesfeldt, I. (1972). Similarities and differences between cultures in expressive movement. In R. A. Hinde (ed.), *Nonverbal communication* (pp. 297–314). Cambridge, UK: Cambridge University Press.

Ekman, P. (1972). Universals and cultural differences in facial expressions of emotions. In J. Cole (ed.), *Nebraska symposium on motivation* (pp. 207–283). Lincoln: University of Nebraska Press.

Ekman, P. (2003). *Emotions revealed: Recognizing faces and feelings to improve communication and emotional life.* New York: Henry Holt and Company.

Ekman, P., and Friesen, W. V. (1967). Head and body cues in the judgment of emotion: A reformulation. *Perceptual and Motor Skills, 24*, 711–724.

Ekman, P., and Friesen, W. V. (1969a). Nonverbal leakage and clues to deception. *Psychiatry, 32*, 88–106.

Ekman, P., and Friesen, W. V. (1969b). The repertoire of nonverbal behavior: Categories, origins, usage, and coding. *Semiotica, 1*, 49–98.

Ekman, P., and Friesen, W. V. (1975). *Unmasking the face: A guide to recognizing emotions from facial cues.* Englewood Cliffs, NJ: Prentice Hall.

Ekman, P., and Friesen, W. V. (1986). A new pan cultural expression of emotion. *Motivation and Emotion, 10*, 159–168.

Ekman, P., Friesen, W. V., and Ellsworth, P. (1972). *Emotion in the human face: Guidelines for research and an integration of findings.* New York: Pergamon Press.

Ekman, P., Friesen, W. V., and Tomkins, S. S. (1971). Facial affect scoring technique: A first validity study. *Semiotica, 3*, 37–58.

Ekman, P., and Heider, K. G. (1988). The universality of a contempt emotion: A replication. *Motivation and Emotion, 12*, 303–308.

Forgas, J., and East, R. (2008). How real is that smile? Mood effects on accepting or rejecting the veracity of emotional facial expressions. *Journal of Nonverbal Behavior, 32*, 157–170.

Gladwell, M. (2005). *Blink: The power of thinking without thinking.* New York: Little, Brown and Company.

Harper, R. G., Wiens, A. N., and Matarazzo, J. B. (1978). *Nonverbal communication: The state of the art* (pp. 77–118, 171–245). New York: John Wiley.

Haseltine, E. (2002a). Say cheese: Why a forced smile looks fake. *Discover*, August.

Haseltine, E. (2002b). Beauty secret: What separates homely from comely? *Discover*, September.

Haseltine, E. (2002c). Grin and bear it: Can a forced smile make you happy? *Discover*, November.

Heisel, A. D., Williams, D. K., and Valencic, K. M. (1999, April/May). *Intentional affect displays: Writing the face to read like a book*. Paper presented at the annual conference of the Eastern Communication Association, Charleston, WV.

Hickson, M. III, Stacks, D. W., and Moore, N. J. (2005). *Nonverbal communication: Studies and applications*. Los Angeles, CA: Roxbury.

Hugenberg, K., and Sczesny, S. (2006). On wonderful women and seeing smiles: Social categorization moderates the happy face response latency advantage. *Social Cognition, 24*, 516–539.

Johnson, H. G., Ekman, P., and Friesen, W. V. (1975). Communicative body movements: American emblems. *Semiotica, 15*, 335–353.

Kalick, S. M., Zebrowitz, L. A., Langlois, J. H., and Johnson, R. M. (1998). Does human facial attractiveness honestly advertise health? *Psychological Science, 9*, (1), 8–13.

Katsikitis, M., Pilowksy, I., and Innes, J. M. (1990). The quantification of smiling using a microcomputer-based approach. *Journal of Nonverbal Behavior, 14*, (1), 3–17.

Knapp, M. L., and Hall, J. A. (1992). *Nonverbal communication in human interaction* (3rd ed.). New York: Holt, Rinehart & Winston.

LeGault, M. R. (2006). *Think: Why crucial decisions can't be made in the blink of an eye*. New York: Threshold Editions.

McCroskey, J. C., and Richmond, V. P. (1986). *Fundamentals of human communication: An interpersonal perspective*. Prospect Heights, IL: Waveland Press.

Miles, L., and Johnston, L. (2007). Detecting happiness: Perceiver sensitivity to enjoyment and non-enjoyment smiles. *Journal of Nonverbal Behavior, 31*, 259–275.

Morris, D. (1985). *Body watching*. New York: Crown.

Murphy, N. A. (2005). Using thin slices for behavioral coding. *Journal of Nonverbal Behavior, 29*, 235–246.

Newcombe, N., and Lie, E. (1995). Overt and covert recognition of faces in children and adults. *Psychological Science, 6*, (4), 241–245.

Patterson, M. L. (2003). Evolution and nonverbal behavior: Functions and mediating processes. *Journal of Nonverbal Behavior, 27*, 201–207.

Pell, M. D. (2005). Nonverbal emotion priming: Evidence from the facial affect decision task. *Journal of Nonverbal Behavior, 29*, 45–73.

Richmond, V. P. (2002). Teacher nonverbal immediacy: Uses and outcomes. In J. L. Chesebro and J. C. McCroskey (eds.), *Communication for teachers* (pp. 65–82). Boston: Allyn and Bacon.

Russell, J. A., and Bullock, M. (1985). Multidimensional scaling of emotional facial expressions: Similarity from preschoolers to adults. *Journal of Personality and Social Psychology, 48*, 1290–1298.

Ruys, K. I. (2008). Emotion elicitor or emotion messenger? Subliminal priming reveals two faces of facial expressions. *Psychological Science, 19*, 593–600.

Sato, W., and Yoshikawa, S. (2007). Enhanced experience of emotional arousal in response to dynamic facial expressions. *Journal of Nonverbal Behavior, 31*, 119–135.

Schmidt, K. L., Amabadar, Z., Cohn, J. F., and Reed L. I. (2006). Movement differences between deliberate and spontaneous facial expressions: *Zygomaticus Major* action in smiling. *Journal of Nonverbal Behavior, 30*, 37–52.

Schmidt, K. L., Battacharya, S., and Denlinger, R. (2009). Comparisons of spontaneous and deliberate facial movement in smiles and eyebrow raises. *Journal of Nonvebal Behavior, 33*, 35–45.

Schubert, S. (2006). A look tells all. *Scientific American Mind, 17*, (5), 26–31.

Theobald, B-J., Mangini, I., Spies, J. R., Brick, T. R., Cohn, J. F., Boker, S. M., and Michael, M. (2009). Mapping and manipulating facial expression. *Language and Speech, 52*, 369–386.

Tomkins, S. S. (1962). *Affect, imagery, consciousness*, Vol. 1: *The positive affects*. New York: Springer.

Tomkins, S. S., and McCarter, R. (1964). What and where are the primary affects? Some evidence for a theory. *Perceptual and Motor Skills, 18*, 119–158.

Tucker, J. S., and Riggio, R. E. (1988). The role of social skills in encoding posed and spontaneous facial expressions. *Journal of Nonverbal Behavior, 12*, 87–97.

van Beek, Y., and Dubas, J. S. (2008). Age and gender differences in decoding non-basic facial expressions in late childhood and early adolescence. *Journal of Nonverbal Behavior, 32*, 37–52.

Wagner, H. L., MacDonald, C. J., and Manstead, A. S. R. (1986). Communication of individual emotions by spontaneous facial expressions. *Journal of Personality and Social Psychology, 50*, 737–743.

Walton, S. (2004). *A natural history of human emotions*. New York: Grove Press.

Weitz, S. (ed.) (1974). *Nonverbal communication: Readings with commentary*. New York: Oxford University Press.

Chapter 5

Argyle, M., and Cook, M. (1976). *Gaze and mutual gaze*. Cambridge, UK: Cambridge University Press.

Argyle, M., and Dean, J. (1965). Eye contact, distance, and affiliation. *Sociometry, 28*, 289–304.

Argyle, M., and Ingham, R. (1972). Gaze, mutual gaze, and proximity. *Semiotica, 6*, 32–49.

Bandler, R., and Grinder, J. (1979). *Frogs into princes*. Moab, UT: Real People Press.

Bakan, P. (1971). The eyes have it. *Psychology Today, 4*, 64–67, 96.

Bavelas, J. B., Coates, L., and Johnson, T. (2002). Listener responses as a collaborative process: The role of gaze. *Journal of Communication, 52*, 566–580.

Burkhardt, J. C., Weider-Hatfield, D., and Hocking, J. E. (1985). Eye contact contrast effects in the employment interview. *Communication Research Reports, 1*, 5–10.

Carvajal, F., and Iglesias, J. (2000). Looking behavior and smiling in down-syndrome infants. *Journal of Nonverbal Behavior, 24*, 225–236.

Dilts, R. B., Grinder, J., Bandler, R., DeLozier, J., and Cameron-Bandler, L. (1979). *Neuro-linguistic programming I*. Cupertino, CA: Meta Publications.

Dovidio, J. F., and Ellyson, S. L. (1985). Patterns of visual dominance behavior in humans. In S.L. Ellyson and J. F. Dovidio (eds.), *Power, dominance, and nonverbal behavior* (pp. 129–150). New York: Springer-Verlag.

Duncan, S. D. Jr. (1972). Some signals and rules for taking speaking turns in conversations. *Journal of Personality and Social Psychology, 23*, 283–292.

Ellsworth, P. C. (1975). Direct gaze as a social stimulus: The example of aggression. In P. Pliner, L. Krames, and T. Alloway (eds.), *Nonverbal communication of aggression* (pp. 53–76). New York: Plenum Press.

Exline, R. V. (1963). Explorations in the process of person perception: Visual interaction in relation to competition, sex, and need for affiliation. *Journal of Personality, 31*, 1–20.

Exline, R. V. (1971). Visual interaction: The glances of power and preference. In J. K. Cole (ed.), *Nebraska symposium on motivation* (pp. 162–205). Lincoln: University of Nebraska Press.

Exline, R. V., Ellyson, S. L., and Long, B. (1975). Visual behavior exhibited by males differing as to interpersonal control orientation in one- and two-way communication systems. In P. Pliner, L. Krames, and T. Alloway (eds.), *Nonverbal communication of aggression* (pp. 21–52). New York: Plenum Press.

Exline, R. V., and Fehr, B. J. (1982). The assessment of gaze and mutual gaze. In K. R. Scherer and P. Ekman (eds.), *Handbook of methods in nonverbal behavior research* (pp. 91–135). Cambridge, UK: Cambridge University Press.

Exline, R. V., Gray, D., and Schuette, D. (1965). Visual behavior in a dyad as affected by interview content and sex of respondent. *Journal of Personality and Social Psychology, 1,* 201–209.

Exline, R. V., and Winters, L. C. (1965). Affective relations and mutual glances in dyads. In S. S. Tomkins and C. E. Izard (eds.), *Affect, cognition, and personality: Empirical studies* (pp. 319–350). New York: Springer.

Gravitz, L. (2002). Lies and nothing but the lies. *Discover,* October, p. 13.

Goffman, E. (1959). *The presentation of self in everyday life.* Garden City, NY: Doubleday-Anchor.

Goffman, E. (1967). *Interaction ritual.* Garden City, NY: Anchor Books.

Hess, E. H. (1965). Attitude and pupil size. *Scientific American, 212,* 46–54.

Hess, E. H., and Polt, H. M. (1960). Pupil size as related to interest value of visual stimuli. *Science, 132,* 349–350.

Hess, E. H., Seltzer, A. L., and Schlien, J. M. (1965). Pupil responses of hetero- and homosexual males to pictures of men and women: A pilot study. *Journal of Abnormal Psychology, 70,* 165–168.

Heuig, J., Trippe, R. H., Hecht, H., Straube, T., and Miltner, W. H. R. (2008). Gender differences for specific body regions when looking at men and women. *Journal of Nonverbal Behavior, 32,* 67–78.

Hindmarch, I. (1970). Eyes, eye-spots, and pupil dilation in nonverbal communication. In I. Vine and M. von Cranach (eds.), *Social communication and movement* (pp. 299–321). New York: Academic Press.

Hood, B. M., Willen, J. D., and Driver, J. (1998). Adult's eyes trigger shifts of visual attention in human infants. *Psychological Science, 9,* (2), 131–134.

Kendon, A. (1967). Some functions of gaze-direction in social interaction. *Acta Psychologica, 26,* 22–63.

Knapp, M. L., and Hall, J. A. (1992). *Nonverbal communication in human interaction* (3rd ed.). Fort Worth, TX: Holt, Rinehart & Winston.

Levine, T R., Asada, K. J. K., and Park, H. S. (2006). The lying chicken and the gaze avoidant egg: Eye contact, deception, and causal order. *Southern Communication Journal, 71,* 401–411.

Levine, T. R., Kim, R. K., and Blair, J. P. (In)accuracy at detecting true and false confessions and denials: An initial test of a projected motive model of veracity judgments. *Human Communication Research, 36,* 82–102.

Metzinger, T. (2006). Exposing lies. *Scientific American Mind, 17*(5), 32–37.

Morris, D. (1985). *Body watching.* New York: Crown.

Richmond, V. P. (2002). Teacher nonverbal immediacy: Uses and outcomes. In J. L. Chesebro and J.C. McCroskey (eds.). *Communication for teachers* (pp. 65–82). Boston: Allyn and Bacon.

Scherwitz, L., and Helmreich, R. (1973). Interactive effects of eye contact and verbal content on interpersonal attraction in dyads. *Journal of Personality and Social Psychology, 25,* 6–14.

Theeuwes, J., Kramer, A. F., Hahn, S., and Irwin, D. E. (1998). Our eyes do not always go where we want them to go: Capture of the eyes by new objects. *Psychological Science, 9,* (5), 379–385.

Thompson, L. A., Aidinejad, M. R., and Ponte, J. (2001). Aging and effects of facial and prosodic *cues* on emotional intensity ratings and memory reconstructions. *Journal of Nonverbal Behavior, 25,* 101–125.

Tyler, J. M. (2009). Compensatory self-presentation in upward comparison situations. *Human Communication Research, 35,* 511–533.

Vlietstra, A. G., and Manske, S. H. (1981). Looks to adults, preferences for adult males and females, and interpretations of an adult's gaze by preschool children. *Merrill-Palmer Quarterly, 27,* 31–41.

Watson, O. M. (1970). *Proxemic behavior: A cross-cultural study.* The Hague: Monton.

Chapter 6

Addington, D. W. (1968). The relationship of selected vocal characteristics to personality perception. *Speech Monographs, 35,* 492–503.

Addington, D. W. (1971). The effect of vocal variations on ratings of source credibility. *Speech Monographs, 38,* 242–247.

Archer, D., and Akert, R. M. (1977). Words and everything else: Verbal and nonverbal cues in social interpretation. *Journal of Personality and Social Psychology, 35,* (6), 443–449.

Argyle, M. (1999). Nonverbal vocalizations. In L. K. Guerrero, J. A. DeVito, and M. L. Hecht (eds.), *The nonverbal communication reader: Classic and contemporary readings* (pp. 135–148). Prospect Heights, IL: Waveland Press.

Bachorowski, J., and Owren, M. J. (1995). Vocal expression of emotion: Acoustic properties of speech are associated with emotional intensity and context. *Psychological Science, 6,* (4), 219–224.

Berry, D. S. (1990). Vocal attractiveness and vocal babyishness: Effects on stranger, self and friend impressions. *Journal of Nonverbal Behavior, 14,* 141–153.

Berry, D. S., Hansen, J. S., Landry-Pester, J. C., and Meier, J. A. (1994). Vocal determinants of first impressions of young children. *Journal of Nonverbal Behavior, 18,* (3), 187–196.

Bradford, A., Farrar, D., and Bradford, G. (1974). Evaluation reactions of college students to dialect differences in the English of Mexican-Americans. *Language and Speech, 17,* 255–270.

Braithwaite, C.A. (1999). Cultural uses and interpretations of silence. In L. K. Guerrero, J. A. DeVito, and M. L. Hecht (eds.), *The nonverbal communication reader: Classic and contempo-* rary readings (pp. 163–172). Prospect Heights, IL: Waveland Press.

Bryant, G. A., and Haselton, M. G. (2009). Vocal cues of ovulation in human females. *Biology Letters, 5,* 12–15.

Camras, L. A., Sullivan, J., and Michel, G. (1993). Do infants express discrete emotions? Adults' judgments of facial, vocal, and body actions. *Journal of Nonverbal Behavior, 17,* (3), 171–185.

Christenfeld, N. (1995). Does it hurt to say um? *Journal of Nonverbal Behavior, 19,* 171–186.

Davitz, J. R. (ed.) (1964). *The communication of emotional meaning.* New York: McGraw-Hill.

Davitz, J. R., and Davitz, L. J. (1959). The communication of feelings by content-free speech. *Journal of Communication, 9,* 6–13.

Duncan, S. D. Jr. (1972). Some signals and rules for taking speaking turns in conversations. *Journal of Personality and Social Psychology, 23,* 283–292.

Duncan, S. D. Jr. (1973). Toward a grammar for dyadic conversation. *Semiotica, 9,* 29–46.

Duncan, S. D. Jr. (1974). On the structure of speaker-auditor interaction during speaking turns. *Language in Society, 2,* 161–180.

Durante, K. M., Li, N. P., and Haselton, M. G. (2008). Changes in women's choice of dress across the ovulatory cycle: Naturalistic and laboratory task-based evidence. *Personality and Social Psychology Bulletin, 34,* 1451–1460.

Gilbert, K. (2006). Voice messages: The science of your sound. *Psychology Today, 39* (6), 15.

Goldman-Eisler, F. (1968). *Psycholinguistics: Experiments in spontaneous speech.* New York: Academic Press.

Guerrero, L. K., DeVito, J. A., and Hecht, M. L. (eds.) (1999). *The nonverbal communication reader: Classic and contemporary readings* (pp. 163–172). Prospect Heights, IL: Waveland Press.

Hall, J. A. (1984). *Nonverbal sex differences: Communication accuracy and expressive style*. Baltimore, MD: Johns Hopkins University Press.

Hecht, M. A., and LaFrance, M. (1995). How (fast) can I help you? Tone of voice and telephone operator efficiency in interactions. *Journal of Applied Social Psychology, 25*, (23), 2066–2098.

Jaworski, A. (1999). The power of silence in communication. In L. K. Guerrero, J. A. DeVito, and M. L. Hecht (eds.), *The nonverbal communication reader: Classic and contemporary readings* (pp. 156–162). Prospect Heights, IL: Waveland Press.

Johnson, J. (1985, November). Laughs every day could keep the doctor away. *USA Weekend*, 23.

Jones, B. C., Feinberg, D. R., DeBruine, L. M., Little, A. C., and Vukovic, J. (2008). Integrating cues of social interest and voice pitch in men's preferences for women's voices. *Biology Letters, 4*, 192–194.

Kimble, C. E., and Seidel, S. D. (1991). Vocal signs of confidence. *Journal of Nonverbal Behavior, 15*, 99–105.

Knapp, M. L., and Hall, J. A. (1992). *Nonverbal communication in human interaction* (3rd ed.). New York: Holt, Rinehart & Winston.

Kramer, E. (1963). Judgment of personal characteristics and emotions from nonverbal properties of speech. *Psychological Bulletin, 60*, 408–420.

LaFrance, M., and Carmen, B. (1980). The nonverbal display of psychological androgyny. *Journal of Personality and Social Psychology, 38*, 36–49.

Lalljee, M. G., and Cook, M. (1969). An experimental investigation of the function of filled pauses in speech. *Language and Science, 12*, 24–28.

Liggon, C., Weston, J., Ambady, N., Colloton, M., Rosenthal, R., and Reite, M. (1992). Content-free voice analysis of mothers talking about their failure-to-thrive children. *Infant Behavior and Development, 15*, 507–511.

Markel, N. N. (1965). The reliability of coding paralanguage: Pitch, loudness, and tempo. *Journal of Verbal Learning and Verbal Behavior, 4*, 306–308.

Massaro, D. W., and Egan, P. B. (1996). Perceiving affect from the voice and the face. *Psychonomic Bulletin and Review, 3*, (2), 215–221.

McCroskey, J. C. (2001). *An introduction to rhetorical communication* (8th ed.). Englewood Cliffs, NJ: Prentice-Hall.

McCroskey, J. C., and Richmond, V. P. (1996). *Fundamentals of human communication: An interpersonal perspective* (pp. 169–214).

Mehrabian, A. (1968). Communication without words. *Psychology Today, 2*, 52–55.

Mehrabian, A., and Ferris, S. R. (1967). Inference of attitudes from nonverbal communication in two channels. *Journal of Consulting Psychology, 31*, 248–252.

Mehrabian, A., and Williams, M. (1969). Nonverbal concomitants of perceived and intended persuasiveness. *Journal of Personality and Social Psychology, 13*, 37–58.

Miller, G. R., and Hewgill, M. A. (1964). The effects of variations of nonfluency on audience ratings of source credibility. *Quarterly Journal of Speech, 50*, 36–44.

Miller, N., Maruyama, G., Beaber, R. J., and Valone, K. (1976). Speed of speech and persuasion. *Journal of Personality and Social Psychology, 34*, 615–624.

Mulac, A. (1976). Assessment and application of the revised speech dialect attitudinal scale. *Communication Monographs, 43*, 238–245.

Mulac, A., and Giles, H. (1996). You're only as old as you sound: Perceived vocal age and social meanings. *Health Communication, 8*, (3), 199–215.

Mulac, A., Hanley, T. D., and Prigge, D. Y. (1974). Effects of phonological speech foreignness upon three dimensions of attitude of selected American listeners. *Quarterly Journal of Speech, 60*, 411–420.

Newman, J. M. (1982). The sounds of silence in communicative encounters. *Communication Quarterly, 30*, 142–149.

Newman, L. L., and Smit, A. B. (1989). Some effects of variations in response time latency on speech rate, interruptions, and fluency in children's speech. *Journal of Speech and Hearing Research, 32*, 635–644.

O'Hair, D., Cody, M. J., and Behnke, R. R. (1985, Fall). Communication apprehension and vocal stress as indices of deception. *Western Journal of Speech Communication, 49*, 286–300.

Perlmutter, K. B., Paddock, J.R., and Duke, M. P. (1985). The role of verbal, vocal, and nonverbal cues in the communication of evoking message styles. *Journal of Research in Personality, 93*, 31–43.

Phillips, G. M., Kougl, K. M., and Kelly, L. (1985). *Speaking in public and private.* Indianapolis: Bobbs-Merrill Educational Publishing.

Plazewski, J. G., and Allen, V. L. (1985). The effect of verbal content on children's encoding of paralinguistic affect. *Journal of Nonverbal Behavior, 9*, (3), 147–159.

Poyatos, F. (1991). Paralinguistic qualifiers: Our many voices. *Language and Communication, 11*, (3), 181–195.

Richmond, V. P. (1996). *Nonverbal communication in the classroom.* Boston: Allyn and Bacon.

Richmond, V. P. (2002). Teacher nonverbal immediacy: Uses and outcomes. In J. L. Chesebro and J.C. McCroskey (eds.), *Communication for teachers* (pp. 65–82). Boston: Allyn and Bacon.

Sayer, J. E. (1979). The student's right to his own language: A response to Colquit. *Communication Quarterly, 27*, 44–46.

Scherer, K. R. (1982). Methods of research on vocal communication: Paradigms and parameters. In K. R. Scherer and P. Ekman (eds.), *Handbook of methods in nonverbal behavior research* (pp. 136–198). Cambridge, UK: Cambridge University Press.

Scherer, K. R., Koivumaki, J., and Rosenthal, R. (1972). Minimal cues in the vocal communication of affect: Judging emotions from content-masked speech. *Journal of Psycholinguistic Research, 1*, 269–285.

Scherer, K. R., and Osinsky, J. S. (1977). Cue utilization in emotion attribution from auditory stimuli. *Motivation and Emotion, 1*, 331–346.

Semic, B. (1999). Vocal attractiveness: What sounds beautiful is good. In L. K. Guerrero, J. A. DeVito, and M. L. Hecht (eds.), *The nonverbal communication reader: Classic and contemporary readings* (pp. 149–155). Prospect Heights, IL: Waveland Press.

Sereno, K. K., and Hawkins, G. J. (1967). The effects of variations in speaker's nonfluency upon audience ratings of attitude toward the speech topic and speaker's credibility. *Speech Monographs, 34*, 58–64.

Siegman, A. W., and Boyle, S. (1993). Voices of fear and anxiety and sadness and depression: The effects of speech rate and loudness on fear and anxiety and sadness and depression. *Journal of Abnormal Psychology, 102*, (3), 430–437.

Starkweather, J. A. (1961). Vocal communication of personality and human feelings. *Journal of Communication, 11*, 63–72.

Tannen, D. (1990). *You just don't understand: Women and men in conversation.* New York: William Morrow.

Tannen, D. (1994). *Gender and discourse.* Oxford: Oxford University Press.

Trager, G. L. (1958). Paralanguage: A first approximation. *Studies in Linguistics, 13*, 1–12.

Weitz, S. (1972). Attitude, voice and behavior. *Journal of Personality and Social Psychology, 24*, 14–21.

Wiemann, J. M., and Knapp, M. L. (1975). Turn-taking in conversations. *Journal of Communication, 25*, 75–92.

Williams, F. (1970). The psychological correlates of speech characteristics: On sounding disadvantaged. *Journal of Speech and Hearing Research, 13*, 472–488.

Woolbert, C. H. (1920). Effects of various modes of public reading. *Journal of Applied Psychology, 4*, 162–185.

Zuckerman, M., and Driver, R. E. (1989). What sounds beautiful is good: The vocal attractiveness stereotype. *Journal of Nonverbal Behavior, 13*, 67–81.

Chapter 7

Altman, I. (1975). *The environment and social behavior.* Monterey, CA: Brooks/Cole.

Ardrey, R. (1966). *The territorial imperative.* New York: Dell.

Athos, A. G. (1975). Time, space, and things. In A. G. Athos and R. E. Coffey (eds.), *Behavior in organizations: A multi-dimensional view* (pp. 69–81). Englewood Cliffs, NJ: Prentice-Hall.

Baxter, J. C. (1970). Interpersonal spacing in natural settings. *Sociometry, 33,* 444–456.

Becker, F. D. (1973). Study of spatial markers. *Journal of Personality and Social Psychology, 26,* 439–445.

Becker, F. D., and Mayo, C. (1971). Delineating personal distance and territory. *Environment and Behavior, 3,* 375–382.

Bell, P. A., and Barnard, W. A. (1984). Effects of heat, noise, and sex of subject on a projective measure of personal space permeability. *Perceptual and Motor Skills, 59,* 4–22.

Campbell, J. (2007). What's the role of *spatial* awareness in visual perception of objects? *Mind and Language, 22,* 548–562.

Carey, G. W. (1972, March/April). Density, crowding, stress, and the ghetto. *American Behavioral Scientist,* 495–507.

Conigliaro, L., Cullerton, K., Flynn, K., and Rueder, S. (1989). Stigmatizing artifacts and their effect on personal space. *Psychological Reports, 65,* 897–898.

Costa, M. (2010). Interpersonal distances in group walking. *Journal of Nonverbal Behavior, 34,* 15–26.

Edney, J. J. (1976). Human territories: Comment on functional properties. *Environment and Behavior, 8,* 31–47.

Ellis, R. (2009). Understanding interpersonal relationships in the Chinese context. *Journal of Intercultural Communication, 20,* 3–13.

Fisher, J. D., and Byrne, D. (1975). Too close for comfort: Sex difference in response to invasions of personal space. *Journal of Personality and Social Psychology, 32,* 15–21.

Fry, A. M., and Willis, F. N. (1971). Invasion of personal space as a function of the age of the invader. *Psychological Record, 21,* 385–389.

Galle, O. R., Grove, W. R., and McPherson, J. M. (1972). Population density and pathology: What are the relations for man? *Science, 176,* 23–30.

Gifford, R., and O'Connor, B. (1986). Nonverbal intimacy: Clarifying the role of seating distance and orientation. *Journal of Nonverbal Behavior, 10,* 207–214.

Goffman, E. (1971). *Relations in public: Microstudies of the public order.* New York: Harper Colophon Books.

Greenberg, C. I., and Firestone, I. J. (1977). Compensatory responses to crowding: Effects of personal space intrusion and privacy reduction. *Journal of Personality and Social Psychology, 9,* 637–644.

Guerrero, L. K., DeVito, J. A., and Hecht, M. L. (eds.) (1999). *The nonverbal communication reader: Classic and contemporary readings* (2nd ed.). Prospect Heights, IL: Waveland Press.

Hall, E. T. (1963). A system for the notation of proxemic behavior. *American Anthropology, 65,* 1003–1026.

Hall, E. T. (1966). *The hidden dimension.* Garden City, NJ: Doubleday.

Hall, E. T. (1968). Proxemics. *Current Anthropology, 9,* 83–108.

Hall, E. T. (1973). *The silent language.* Garden City, NJ: Doubleday.

Hall, E. T. (1983). Proxemics. In A. M. Katz and V. T. Katz (eds.), *Foundations of nonverbal communication: Readings, exercises, and commentary* (pp. 5–27). Carbondale: Southern Illinois University Press.

Harper, R. G., Wiens, A. N., and Matarazzo, J. D. (1978). *Nonverbal communication: The state of the art.* New York: John Wiley.

Hickson, M. III, and Roebuck, J. B. (2009). *Deviance and crime in colleges and universities.* Springfield, IL: C. C. Thomas.

Hickson, M. III, and Self, W. (2003). Biological foundations of territoriality: Nonverbal communication, language, and the law. *Journal of Intercultural Communication, 32,* 265–283.

Hickson, M. L. III, Stacks, D. W., and Moore, N. J. (2004). *Nonverbal communication: Studies and applications* (4th ed.). Los Angeles, CA: Roxbury.

Hughes, J., and Goldman, M. (1978). Eye contact, facial expression, sex, and the violation of personal space. *Perceptual and Motor Skills, 46,* 579–584.

Knapp, M. L., and Hall, J. A. (1992). *Nonverbal communication in human interaction* (3rd ed.). New York: Holt, Rinehart & Winston.

Lyman, S. M., and Scott, M. B. (1967). Territoriality: A neglected sociological dimension. *Social Problems, 15,* 236–249.

Madden, S. J. (1999). Proxemics and gender: Where's the spatial gap? South Dakota Journal of Speech and Theatre, 12, 41–46.

Malandro, L. A., Barker, L., and Barker, D. A. (1989). *Nonverbal communication.* New York: Random House.

McAndrew, F. T., Ryckman, R. M., Horr, W., and Soloman, R. (1978). The effects of invader placement of spatial markers on territorial behavior in a college population. *Journal of Social Psychology, 104,* 149–150.

Mehrabian, A. (1976). *Public places and private spaces: The psychology of work, play, and living environments.* New York: Basic Books.

Mehrabian, A., and Diamond, S. G. (1971). Seating arrangement and conversation. *Sociometry, 34,* 281–289.

Merkin, R. S. (2006). Power distance and face-work strategies. *Journal of Intercultural Communication Research, 35,* 139–160.

Moore, N. J., Hickson, M. III, and Stacks, M. J. (2010). *Nonverbal communication:* *Studies and applications.* (5th ed.). New York: Oxford University Press.

Morman, M. T., and Floyd, K. (2002). The "changing culture of fatherhood": Effects on affectionate communication, closeness, and satisfaction in men's relationships with their fathers and their sons. *Western Journal of Communication, 66,* 395–404.

Richmond, V. P., and McCroskey, J. C. (1998). *Communication: Apprehension, avoidance, and effectiveness* (5th ed.). Scottsdale, AZ: Gorsuch Scarisbrick.

Russo, N. (1967). Connotation of seating arrangements. *Cornell Journal of Social Relations, II,* 37–44.

Schaffer, D. R., and Sadowski, C. (1975). This table is mine: Respect for marked barroom tables as a function of gender of spatial marker and desirability of locale. *Sociometry, 38,* 408–419.

Scheflen, A. E. (1976). Micro-territories in human interaction. In A. Kendon, R. M. Harris, and M. R. Key (eds.), *Organization of behavior in face to face interaction* (pp. 159–174). Chicago: Mouton-Aldine.

Scherer, S. E. (1974). Proxemic behavior of primary school children as a function of their socioeconomic class and subculture. *Journal of Personality and Social Psychology, 29,* 800–805.

Shuter, R. (1976). Proxemics and tactility in Latin America. *Journal of Communication, 26,* 46–52.

Sommer, R. (1959). Studies in personal space. *Sociometry, 22,* 247–260.

Sommer, R. (1965). Further studies in small group ecology. *Sociometry, 28,* 337–348.

Sommer, R. (1969). *Personal space: The behavioral basis of design.* Englewood Cliffs, NJ: Prentice Hall.

Watson, O. M. (1970). *Proxemic behavior: A cross-cultural study.* The Hague: Mouton.

Watson, O. M. (1972). Conflicts and directions in proxemic research. *Journal of Communication, 22,* 443–459.

Willis, F. N. Jr. (1966). Initial speaking distance as a function of the speakers' relationship. *Psychonomic Science, 5,* 221–222.

Chapter 8

Baker, J. (1985). What your favorite color says about you. *Cosmopolitan, 232.*

Baron, R. A., and Bell, P. A. (1976). Aggression and heat: The influence of ambient temperature, negative affect, and a cooling drink on physical aggression. *Journal of Personality and Social Psychology, 33,* 245–255.

Birren, F. (1950). *Color psychology and color therapy: A factual study of the influence of color on human life.* New York: McGraw-Hill.

Bruneau, T. J. (1972, April). *Educational corridors: A field study and conceptualization of the nonverbal dimensions of spatiotemporal influences in a university hierarchy.* Paper presented at the annual convention of the International Communication Association, Atlanta.

Burton, R. (1976). *The language of smell.* Boston: Routledge and Kegan Paul.

Buslig, A. L. S. (1999). Stop signs: Regulating privacy with environmental features. In L. K. Guerrero, J. A. DeVito, and M. L. Hecht (eds.), *The nonverbal communication reader: Classic and contemporary readings* (pp. 241–249). Prospect Heights, IL: Waveland Press.

Cain, W. S. (1981). Educating your nose. *Psychology Today, 15,* 48–56.

Carr, S. J., and Dabbs, J. M., Jr. (1974). The effects of lighting, distance, and intimacy of topic on verbal and visual behavior. *Sociometry, 37,* 592–600.

Cook, M. (1970). Experiments on orientation and proxemics. *Human Relations, 23,* 61–76.

Gergen, K. J., Gergen, M. M., and Barton, W. H. (1973). Deviance in the dark. *Psychology Today, 7,* 129–130.

Gifford, R., and O'Connor, B. (1986). Nonverbal intimacy: Clarifying the role of seating distance and orientation. *Journal of Nonverbal Behavior, 10,* (4), 207–214.

Griffitt, W., and Veitch, R. (1971). Hot and crowded: Influences of population density and temperature on interpersonal affective behavior. *Journal of Personality and Social Psychology, 17,* 92–98.

Hall, E. T. (1966). *The hidden dimension.* Garden City, NY: Doubleday.

Hanson, J., and Hillier, B. (1982). Domestic space organization. *Architecture and Behavior, 2,* 5–25.

Hare, A. P., and Bales, R. F. (1963). Seating position and small group interaction. *Sociometry, 26,* 480–486.

Hayduk, L. A. (1994). Personal space: Understanding the simplex model. *Journal of Nonverbal Behavior, 18,* (3), 245–260.

Heaven scents (October, 2002). *Good Housekeeping,* pp. 24–30.

Hickson, M. III, and Stacks, D. W. (1993). NVC: *Nonverbal communication studies and applications.* Dubuque, IA: William C. Brown.

Hickson, M. L., III, Stacks, D. W., and Moore, N. J. (2004). *Nonverbal communication: Studies and applications* (4rd ed.). Los Angeles, CA: Roxbury.

Howard, B. (Winter 2002/2003). Winter blues. *Remedy,* pp. 40–47.

Howells, L. T., and Becker, S. W. (1962). Seating arrangement and leadership emergence. *Journal of Abnormal and Social Psychology, 64,* 148–150.

Huntington, E. (1915). *Civilization and climate.* New Haven: CT: Yale University Press.

Jackson, N. (2006). The architectural view: Perspectives on communication. *Visual Communication Quarterly, 13,* 32–45.

Ketcham, H. (1958). *Color planning for business and industry.* New York: Harper and Brothers.

Knapp, M. L. (1978). *Social intercourse: From greeting to goodbye.* Boston: Allyn and Bacon.

Knapp, M. L. (1980). *Essentials of nonverbal communication* (pp. 53–74). New York: Holt, Rinehart & Winston.

Koneya, M., and Barbour, A. (1976). *Louder than words . . . : Nonverbal communication.* Columbus, OH: Charles E. Merrill.

Korda, M. (1975). *Power! How to get it, how to use it.* New York: Random House.

Krupat, E., and Kubzansky, P. E. (1999). Designing to deter crime. In L. K. Guerrero, J. A. DeVito, and M. L. Hecht (eds.), *The nonverbal communication reader: Classic and contemporary readings* (pp. 250–254). Prospect Heights, IL: Waveland Press.

Lanagan, E. J. (1999). Environmental features in theme restaurants. In L. K. Guerrero, J. A. DeVito, and M. L. Hecht (eds.), *The nonverbal communication reader: Classic and contemporary readings* (pp. 255–263). Prospect Heights, IL: Waveland Press.

Luka, T., Berner, E. S., and Kanakis, C. (1977). Diagnosis by smell? *Journal of Medical Education, 52,* 349–350.

Maslow, A. H., and Mintz, N. L. (1956). Effects of aesthetic surroundings: I. Initial effects of three aesthetic conditions upon perceiving "energy" and "well-being" in faces. *Journal of Psychology, 41,* 247–254.

McClelland, D. (1976). *The achieving society.* New York: Van Nostrand Reinhold.

Mehrabian, A. (1976). *Public places and private spaces: The psychology of work, play, and living environments.* New York: Basic Books.

Miller, S., and Schlitt, J. K. (1985). *Interior space: Design concepts for personal needs.* New York: Praeger.

Mintz, N. L. (1956). Effects of aesthetic surroundings: II. Prolonged and repeated experience in a "beautiful" and "ugly" room. *Journal of Psychology, 41,* 459–466.

Molloy, J. T. (1983). *Molloy's live for success.* New York: Bantam Books.

Office in a capsule. (1994, August). *Progressive Architecture,* p. 2–7.

Ponte, L. (1982, June). Secret scents that affect behavior. *Reader's Digest,* 121–123.

Remland, M. S., Jones, T. S., and Brinkman, H. (1991). Proxemic and haptic behavior in three European countries. *Journal of Nonverbal Behavior, 15,* (4), 215–232.

Richmond, V. P. (1997). *Nonverbal communication in the classroom.* Acton, MA: Tapestry Press.

Russo, N. F. (1967). Connotations of seating arrangements. *Cornell Journal of Social Relations, 2,* 37–44.

Sommer, R. (1965). Further studies of small group ecology. *Sociometry, 28,* 337–348.

Sommer, R. (1969). *Personal space: The behavioral basis of design.* Englewood Cliffs, NJ: Prentice Hall.

Sommer, R. (1970). The ecology of privacy. In H. M. Proshansky, W. H. Ittleson, and L. G. Rivlin (eds.), *Environmental psychology: Man and his physical environment* (pp. 256–266). New York: Holt, Rinehart & Winston.

Sutton, T. (1985, March). Setting the tone. *Savvy,* 74–82.

Walberg, H. J. (1969). Physical and psychological distance in the classroom. *School Review, 77,* 64–70.

Wiener, H. (1979). Human exocrinology: The olfactory component of nonverbal communication. In S. Weitz (ed.), *Nonverbal communication: Readings with commentary* (2nd ed.), (pp. 338–345). New York: Oxford University Press.

Williams, R. (1954). *Lighting for color and form.* New York: Pitman.

Winter, R. (1976). *The smell book: Scents, sex, and society.* Philadelphia: Lippincott.

Zweigenhaft, R. L. (1976). Personal space in the faculty office: Desk placement and the student-faculty interaction. *Journal of Applied Psychology, 61,* 529–532.

Chapter 9

Adler, R., and Towne, N. (1975). *Looking out/looking in.* San Francisco: Reinhart Press.

Andersen, P. A., and Leibowitz, K. (1978). The development and nature of the construct touch avoidance. *Environmental Psychology and Nonverbal Behavior, 3,* 89–106.

Andersen, P. A., and Sull, K. K. (1985). Out of touch, out of reach: Tactile predispositions as predictors of interpersonal distance. *Western Journal of Speech Communication, 49,* 57–72.

Argyle, M. (1975). *Bodily communication.* New York: International Universities Press.

Barnlund, D. C. (1975). Communicative styles of two cultures: Public and private self in Japan and the United States. In A. Kendon, R. M. Harris, and M. R. Key (eds.), *Organization of behavior in face-to-face interaction.* The Hague: Mouton.

Boderman, A., Freed, D. W., and Kinnucan, M. T. (1972). Touch me, like me: Testing an encounter group assumption. *Journal of Applied Behavioral Science, 8,* 527–533.

Burgoon, J. K., and Saine, T. (1978). *The unspoken dialogue: An introduction to nonverbal communication.* Boston: Houghton Mifflin.

Clay, V. S. (1966). The effects of culture on mother-child tactile communication. (Ph.D. dissertation, Columbia University). *Dissertation Abstracts International,* 1967, 28, 1770B.

Davis, F. (1978, September 27). Skin hunger: An American disease. *Woman's Day,* 154–156.

Despert, J. L. (1941). Emotional aspects of speech and language development. *International Journal of Psychiatry and Neurology, 105,* 193–222.

Dolin, D. J., and Booth-Butterfield, M. (1993). Reach out and touch someone: Analysis of nonverbal comforting responses. *Communication Quarterly, 41,* (4), 383–393.

Fromme, D. K., Jaynes, W. E., Taylor, D. K., Hanold, E. G., Daniell, J., Rountree, J. R., and Fromme, M. L. (1989). Nonverbal behavior and attitudes toward touch. *Journal of Nonverbal Behavior, 13,* 3–13.

Glausiusz, J. (2002). Wired for a touch. *Discover,* December, p. 13.

Goldberg, S., and Rosenthal, R. (1986). Self-touching behavior in the job interview: Antecedents and consequences. *Journal of Nonverbal Behavior, 10,* 65–80.

Guerrero, L. K., and Andersen, P. A. (1994). Patterns of matching and initiation: Touch behavior and touch avoidance across romantic relationship stages. *Journal of Nonverbal Behavior, 18,* (2), 137–153.

Guerrero, L. K., and Andersen, P. A. (1999). Public touch behavior in romantic relationships between men and women. In L. K. Guerrero, J. A. DeVito, and M. L. Hecht (eds.), *The nonverbal communication reader: Classic and contemporary readings.* (2nd ed.), (pp. 202–210). Prospect Heights, IL: Waveland Press, Inc.

Hall, E. T. (1966). *The hidden dimension.* Garden City, NY: Doubleday.

Harlow, H. H., and Zimmerman, R. R. (1958). The development of affectional responses in infant monkeys. *Proceedings of the American Philosophical Society, 102,* 501–509.

Harlow, H. F., Harlow, M. K., and Hansen, E. W. (1963). The maternal affectional system of rhesus monkeys. In H. L. Rheingold (ed.), *Maternal behavior in mammals.* New York: John Wiley.

Harrison-Speake, K., and Willis, F. N. (1995). Ratings of the appropriateness of touch among family members. *Journal of Nonverbal Behavior, 19,* (2), 85–100.

Henley, N. M. (1973). Status and sex: Some touching observations. *Bulletin of the Psychonomic Society, 2,* 91–93.

Henley, N. M. (1977). *Body politics: Power, sex, and nonverbal communication.* Englewood Cliffs, NJ: Prentice Hall.

Heslin, R. (1974, May). *Steps toward a taxonomy of touching.* Paper presented to the annual meeting of the Midwestern Psychological Association, Chicago, IL.

Hite, S. (1977). What kind of loving does a woman want? *New Woman Magazine.* July-August, 75–76.

Johnson, K. L., and Edwards, R. (1991). The effects of gender and type of romantic touch on perceptions of relational commitment. *Journal of Nonverbal Behavior, 15,* 43–55.

Jones, S. E. (1999). Communicating with touch. In L. K. Guerrero, J. A., DeVito, and M. L. Hecht (eds.), *The nonverbal communication reader: Classic and contemporary readings* (pp. 192–201). Prospect Heights, IL: Waveland Press.

Jones, S. E., and Yarbrough, A. E. (1985). A naturalistic study of the meanings of touch. *Communication Monographs, 52,* 19–56.

Jourard, S. M. (1966a). An exploratory study of body-accessibility. *British Journal of Social and Clinical Psychology, 5,* 221–231.

Jourard, S. M. (1966b). *The transparent self: Self-disclosure and well-being.* Princeton, NJ: Van Nostrand.

Jourard, S. M. (1968). *Disclosing man to himself.* New York: Van Nostrand Reinhold.

Jourard, S. M. (1971). *The transparent self* (2nd ed.). New York: D. Van Nostrand.

Jourard, S. M., and Friedman, R. (1970). Experimenter-subject distance and self-disclosure. *Journal of Personality and Social Psychology, 15,* 278–282.

Knapp, M. L. (1978). *Social intercourse: From greeting to goodbye.* Boston: Allyn and Bacon.

Knapp, M. L., and Hall, J. A. (1992). *Nonverbal communication in human interaction* (3rd ed.). New York: Holt, Rinehart & Winston.

Kneidlinger, L. M., Maple, T. L., and Tross, S. A. (2001). Touching behavior in sport: Functional components, analyses of sex differences, and ethological considerations. *Journal of Nonverbal Behavior, 25,* 43–62.

Larsen, K. S., and LeRoux, J. (1984). A study of same-sex touching attitudes: Scale development and personality predictors. *The Journal of Sex Research, 20,* 264–278.

Maurer, D., and Maurer, C. (1988). *The world of the newborn.* New York: Basic Books.

Mehrabian, A. (1971). *Silent messages: Implicit communication of emotions and attitudes* (5th ed.). Belmont, CA: Wadsworth.

Montagu, M. R. A. (1978). *Touching: The human significance of the skin* (2nd ed.). New York: Columbia University Press.

Moore, N. J., Hickson, M. III, and Stacks, D. W. (2010). *Nonverbal communication: Studies and applications* (5th ed.). New York: Oxford University Press.

Morris, D. (1971). *Intimate behavior.* New York: Random House.

Morris, D. (1976). Please touch is message of Morris. In L. B. Rosenfeld and J. M. Civikly (eds.), *With words unspoken: The nonverbal experience* (pp. 129–132). New York: Holt, Rinehart & Winston.

Nguyen, T., Heslin, R., and Nguyen, M.L. (1975). The meanings of touch: Sex differences. *Journal of Communication, 25,* 92–103.

Nguyen, M. L., Heslin, R., and Nguyen, T. (1976). The meanings of touch: Sex and marital status differences. *Representative Research in Social Psychology, 7,* 13–18.

Patterson, M. L., Powell, J. L., and Lenihan, M. G. (1986). Touch, compliance, and interpersonal affect. *Journal of Nonverbal Behavior, 10,* 41–50.

Peters, R. M., Hackeman, E., and Goldreich, D. (2009). Diminutive digits discern delicate details: Fingertip size and the sex difference in tactile spatial acuity. *Journal of Neuroscience, 29,* 15756–15761.

Pines, M. (1984, December). Children's winning ways. *Psychology Today,* pp. 58–66.

Pisano, M. D., Wall, S. M., and Foster, A. (1985). Perceptions of nonreciprocal touch in romantic relationships. *Journal of Nonverbal Behavior, 10,* 29–40.

Remland, M. S., Jones, T. S., and Brinkman, H. (1991). Proxemic and haptic behavior in three European countries. *Journal of Nonverbal Behavior, 15,* (4), 215–232.

Richmond, V. P. (1997). *Nonverbal communication in the classroom.* Acton, MA: Tapestry Press.

Richmond, V. P. (2002). Teacher nonverbal immediacy: Uses and outcomes. In J. L. Chesebro and J. C. McCroskey (eds.), *Communication for teachers* (pp. 65–82). Boston: Allyn and Bacon.

Rosenfeld, L. B., and Civikly, J. M. (1976). *With words unspoken: The nonverbal experience.* New York: Holt, Rinehart & Winston.

Rosenfeld, L. B., Kartus, S., and Ray, C. (1976). Body accessibility revisited. *Journal of Communication, 26,* 27–30.

Roses, N. J., Olson, J. M., Borenstein, M. N., Martin, A., and Shores, A. L. (1992). Same-sex touching behavior: The modeling role of homophobic attitudes. *Journal of Nonverbal Behavior, 16,* (4), 249–259.

Schutz, W. (1971). *Here comes everybody.* New York: Harper & Row.

Shuter, R. (1976). Proxemics and tactility in Latin America. *Journal of Communication, 26,* 46–52.

Sigelman, C. K., and Adams, R. M. (1990). Family interactions in public: Parent-child distance and touching. *Journal of Nonverbal Behavior, 14* (2), 63–75.

Sloan, G. (2002). Passion at play. *USA Today,* December 13, pp. 1D–2D.

Sorensen, G. A., and Beatty, M. J. (1988). The interactive effects of touch and touch

avoidance on interpersonal evaluations. *Communication Research Reports, 5,* 84–90.

Smeltzer, L., Waltman, J., and Leonard, D. (1999). Proxemics and haptics in managerial communication. In L. K. Guerrero, J. A. DeVito, and M. L. Hecht (eds.), *The nonverbal communication reader: Classic and contemporary readings* (pp. 184–191). Prospect Heights, IL: Waveland Press.

Storrs, D., and Kleinke, C. L. (1990). Evaluation of high and equal status male and female touchers. *Journal of Nonverbal Behavior, 14,* 87–95.

Thayer, S. (1986). Touch: Frontier of intimacy. In S. Thayer (ed.), The psychology of touch. *Journal of Nonverbal Behavior* (special issue), *10,* 7–11.

Watson, W. H. (1975). The meanings of touch: Geriatric nursing. *Journal of Communication, 25,* 104–112.

Willis Jr., F. N., and Briggs, L. F. (1992). Relationship and touch in public settings. *Journal of Nonverbal Behavior, 16,* (1), 55–63.

Willis, F. N., and Hofman, G. E. (1975). Development of tactile patterns in relation to age, sex, and race. *Developmental Psychology, 11,* 8–66.

Chapter 10

Bloomfield, H. H., and Felder, L. (1985, June). Why are you always late for everything? *New Woman,* 67–69.

Brophy, B. (1985, October). Conquering the time crunch. *USA Weekend,* 22.

Cinelli, L. A., and Ziegler, D. J. (1990). Cognitive appraisal of daily hassles in college students showing type A or type B behavior patterns. *Psychological Reports, 67,* 83–88.

Cooperrider, K., and Nunez, R. (2009). Across time, across the body: Transversal temporal gestures. *Gesture, 9,* 181–206.

Fine, G. A. (1990). Organizational time: Temporal demands and the experience of work in restaurant. *Social Forces, 69,* 95–114.

Gonzalez, A., and Zimbardo, P. G. (1999). Time in perspective. In L. K. Guerrero, J. A. DeVito, and M. L. Hecht (eds.). *The nonverbal communication reader: Classic and contemporary readings* (2nd ed.) (pp. 227–236). Prospect Heights, IL: Waveland Press.

Hall, E. T. (1972). Proxemics: The study of man's spatial relations. In L. A. Samovar and R. E. Porter (eds.), *Intercultural communication: A reader* (pp. 205–220). Belmont, CA: Wadsworth.

Hall, E. T. (1973). *The silent language.* Garden City, NY: Doubleday.

Hall, E. T. (1976). *Beyond culture.* Garden City, NY: Anchor Press/Doubleday.

Hall, E. T. (1984). *The dance of life: The other dimension of time.* New York: Anchor Books.

Hall, E. T., and Hall, M. R. (1990). Monochronic and polychronic time. In L. K. Guerrero, J. A. DeVito, and M. L. Hecht (eds.). *The nonverbal communication reader: Classic and contemporary readings* (2nd ed.), (pp. 237–240). Prospect Heights, IL: Waveland Press.

Howard, B. (Winter 2002/2003). Winter blues. *Remedy,* pp. 24–30.

Lakein, A. (1973). *How to get control of your time and your life.* New York: New American Library.

Levine, R. (1989). The pace of life. *Psychology Today, October,* 42–46.

Managing your time: Think quality, not quantity. (June 24, 1999). *Office hours.* The Economics Press, Issue No. 405.

Moore, N. J., Hickson, M., and Stacks, D. W. (2010). Nonverbal communication: Studies and applications. (5th ed.). New York: Oxford University Press.

Moskowitz, D. S., Brown, K. W., and Cote, S. (1997). Reconceptualizing stability: Using time as a psychological dimension. *Current Directions in Psychological Science, 6,* (5), 127–132.

Perry, A. R., Kane, K. M., Bernesser, K. J., and Spicker, P. T. (1990). Type A behavior, competitive achievement-striving, and cheating among college students. *Psychological Reports, 66,* 449–465.

Potter, B. A. (1980). *Beating job burnout.* New York: Ace Books.

Richmond, V. P. (1997). *Nonverbal communication in the classroom.* Acton, MA: Tapestry Press.

Chapter 11

Addington, D. W. (1968). The relationship of selected vocal characteristics to personality perception. *Speech Monographs, 35,* 492–503.

Bate, B., and Bowker, J. (1997). *Communication and the sexes* (2nd ed.). Prospect Heights, IL: Waveland Press.

Bem, S. L. (1974). The measurement of psychological androgyny. *Journal of Consulting and Clinical Psychology, 42,* 155–162.

Berman, P. W., and Smith, V. L. (1984). Gender and situational differences in children's smiles, touch, and proxemics. *Sex Roles, 10,* 347–356.

Bernard, J. S. (1968). *The sex game.* New York: Atheneum.

Birdwhistell, R. L. (1970). *Kinesics and context: Essays on body motion communication.* Philadelphia: University of Pennsylvania Press.

Buck, R., Miller, R. E., and Caul, W. F. (1974). Sex, personality and physiological variables in the communication of affect via facial expression. *Journal of Personality and Social Psychology, 30,* 587–596.

Bugental, D. E., Love, L. R., and Gianetto, R. M. (1971). Perfidious feminine faces. *Journal of Personality and Social Psychology, 17,* 314–318.

Canary, D. J., and Dindia, K. (1998). *Sex differences and similarities in communication: Critical essays and empirical investigations of sex and gender in interaction.* Mahwah, NJ: Erlbaum.

Dittmann, A. T. (1972). Developmental factors in conversational behavior. *Journal of Communication, 22,* 404–423.

Duck, S. (1998). *Human relationships* (3rd ed.). London: Sage Publications.

Eakins, B. W., and Eakins, R. G. (1978). *Sex differences in human communication.* Boston: Houghton-Mifflin.

Freedman, J. L. (1971). The crowd: Maybe not so madding after all. *Psychology Today, 5,* 58–61, 86.

Gamble, T. K., and Gamble, M. W. (2003). *The gender communication connection.* Boston: Houghton Mifflin.

Grady, K. E., Miransky, L. J., and Mulvey, M. A. (1976). *A nonverbal measure of dominance.* Paper presented at the meeting of the American Psychological Association, Washington, DC.

Hall, J. A. (1984). *Nonverbal sex differences: Communication accuracy and expressive style.* Baltimore: The Johns Hopkins University Press.

Hall, J. A., and Halberstadt, A. G. (1986). Smiling and gazing. In J. S. Hyde and M. Linn (eds.), *The psychology of gender: Advances through meta-analysis* (pp. 136–158). Baltimore: Johns Hopkins University Press.

Heisel, M. J., and Mongrain, M. (2004). Facial expressions and ambivalence: Looking for conflict in all the right faces. *Journal of Nonverbal Behavior, 28,* 35–51.

Henley, N. M. (1977). *Body politics: Power, sex, and nonverbal communication.* Englewood Cliffs, NJ: Prentice Hall.

Henley, N. M. (1995). Body politics revisited: What do we know today? In P. J. Kalbfleisch and M. J. Cody (eds.), *Gender, power, and communication in human relationships.* Hillsdale, NJ: Erlbaum.

Hickson, M. L. III, Stacks, D. W., and Moore, N. J. (2004). *Nonverbal communication: Studies and applications* (4th ed.). Los Angeles, CA: Roxbury.

Jones, S. E. (1986). Sex differences in touch communication. *Western Journal of Speech Communication, 50,* 227–241.

Jourard, S. M. (1966). An exploratory study of body-accessibility. *British Journal of Social and Clinical Psychology, 5,* 221–231.

Jourard, S. M. (1968). *Disclosing man to himself.* New York: Van Nostrand Reinhold.

Jourard, S. M., and Rubin, J. E. (1968). Self-disclosure and touching: A study of two modes of interpersonal encounter and their interrelation. *Journal of Humanistic Psychology, 8,* 39–48.

Kalbfleisch, P. J., and Cody, M. J. (1995). Power and communication in the relationships of women and men. In P. J. Kalbfleisch and M. J. Cody (eds.), *Gender, power, and communication in human relationships* (pp. 3–26). Hillsdale, NJ: Erlbaum.

Knapp, M. L., and Hall, J. A. (1992). *Nonverbal communication in human interaction* (3rd ed.). New York: Holt, Rinehart and Winston.

LaFrance, M., and Mayo, C. (1978). *Moving bodies: Nonverbal communication in social relationships* (pp. 155–170). Monterey, CA: Brooks/Cole.

Lee, V., and Wagner, H. (2002). The effect of social presence on the facial and verbal expression of emotion and the interrelationships among emotion components. *Journal of Nonverbal Behavior, 26,* 3–25.

Lomranz, J., Shapira, A., Choresh, N., and Gilat, Y. (1975). Children's personal space as a function of age and sex. *Developmental Psychology, 11,* 541–545.

Lyons, M., Wanzer, M. B., and Richmond, V. P. (1998). Amount of communication as a symptom of distressed marriages based on reports of divorced individuals. *Communication Research Reports, 15,* (3), 327–330.

McAndrew, F. T., and Warner, J. E. (1986). Arousal seeking and the maintenance of mutual gaze in same- and mixed-sex dyads. *Journal of Nonverbal Behavior, 10,* 168–172.

McCroskey, J. C., and Richmond, V. P. (1996). *Fundamentals of human communication: An interpersonal perspective.* Prospect Heights, IL: Waveland Press.

Mehrabian, A. (1971). *Silent messages: Implicit communication of emotions and attitudes* (5th ed.). Belmont, CA: Wadsworth.

Mehrabian, A. (1972). *Nonverbal communication.* Chicago: Aldine.

Mehrabian, A., and Diamond, S. G. (1971). The effects of furniture arrangement, props, and personality on social interaction. *Journal of Personality and Social Psychology, 20,* 18–30.

Morris, D. (1971). *Intimate behavior.* New York: Random House.

Mulac, A. Studley, L. B., Wiemann, J. W., and Bradac, J. J. (1987). Male/female gaze in same-sex and mixed-sex dyads: Gender-linked differences and mutual influence. *Human Communication Research, 13,* 323–344.

Nguyen, T., Heslin, R., and Nguyen, M. L. (1975). The meanings of touch: Sex differences. *Journal of Communication, 25,* 92–103.

Piercy, M. (1973). *Small changes.* New York: Doubleday.

Ray, G. B., and Floyd, K. (2006). Nonverbal expressions of liking and disliking in initial interaction: Encoding and decoding perspectives. *Southern Communication Journal, 71,* 45–65.

Reninger, L. A., Wade, T. J., and Grammer, K. (2004). Getting the female glance: Patterns and consequences of male nonverbal behavior in courtship contexts. *Evolution and Human Behavior, 25,* 416–431.

Richmond, V. P., Beatty, M. J., and Dyba, P. (1988). Language patterns and gender role orientation among students in grades 3–12. *Communication Education, 37,* 142–149.

Richmond, V. P., Gorham, J., and Furio, B. (1987). Affinity-seeking communication in collegiate female-male relationships. *Communication Quarterly, 35,* 334–348.

Richmond, V. P., and Lyons, M. (1995). Amount of communication in marital dyads as a function of dyadic and individual marital satisfaction. *Communication Research Reports, 13,* 152–159.

Richmond, V. P., and Lyons, M. (1997). Communication and decision-making styles, power base usage, and satisfaction in marital dyads. *Communication Quarterly, 45,* 410–426.

Richmond, V. P., and Martin, M. M. (1998). Socio communicative style and socio communicative orientation. In J. C. McCroskey, J. A. Daly, M. M. Martin, and M. J. Beatty. *Communication and personality: Trait perspectives* (pp. 133–148). Hillsdale, NJ: Erlbaum.

Richmond, V. P., and McCroskey, J. C. (1989). An investigation of self-perceived communication competence and personality orientations. *Communication Research Reports, 6,* 28–36.

Richmond, V. P., and McCroskey, J. C. (1990). Reliability and separation of factors in the assertiveness-responsiveness measure. *Psychological Reports, 67,* 449–450.

Richmond, V. P., and McCroskey, J. C. (1998). *Communication: Apprehension, avoidance, and effectiveness* (5th ed.). Boston: Allyn and Bacon.

Rosenthal, R., Hall, J. A., DiMatteo, R., Rogers, R. L., and Archer, D. (1979). *Sensitivity to nonverbal communication: The PONS test.* Baltimore: The Johns Hopkins University Press.

Scheflen, A. E. (1965). Quasi-courtship behavior in psychotherapy. *Psychiatry, 28,* 245–257.

Silveira, J. (1972). Thoughts on the politics of touch. *Women's Press, 1,* 1–3.

Smith, M. L., Cottrell, G. W., Gosselin, F., and Schyns, P. G. (2005). Transmitting and decoding facial expressions. *Psychological Science, 16,* 184–189.

Sternglanz, R. W., and DePaulo, B. M. (2004). Reading nonverbal cues of emotion: The advantages and liabilities of relationship closeness. *Journal of Nonverbal Behavior, 28,* 245–266.

Tannen, D. (1994). *Talking from 9 to 5: Women and men in the workplace. Language, sex, and power.* New York: Avon Books.

Tiefer, L. (1979). The kiss. *Human Nature, 1,* 2–8.

Trees, A. R., and Manusov, V. (1998). Managing face concerns in criticism: Integrating nonverbal behaviors as a dimension of politeness in female friendship dyads. *Human Communication Research, 24,* (4), 564–583.

Widgery, R. N., and Webster, B. (1969). The effects of physical attractiveness upon perceived initial credibility. *Michigan Speech Journal, 4,* 9–15.

Willis, F. N., Jr. (1966). Initial speaking distance as a function of the speaker's relationship. *Psychonomic Science, 5,* 221–222.

Chapter 12

Bixler, S., and Nix-Rice, N. (1997). *The new professional image.* Holbrook, MA: Adams Media Corporation.

Bovee, C. L., and Thill, J. V. (1983). *Business communication today.* New York: Random House.

Cash, T. F., and Kilcullen, R. N. (1985). The eye of the beholder: Susceptibility to sexism and beautyism in the evaluation of managerial applicants. *Journal of Applied Social Psychology, 15,* 591–605.

Cohen, L. R. (1983, January–February). Nonverbal (Mis) communication between managerial men and women. *Business Horizons,* 14–17.

Flippo, E. (1974). *Management: A behavioral approach.* Boston: Allyn and Bacon.

Gendrin, D. M., and Rucker, M. L. (2008). Revisiting sexual harassment: Are there perceived cultural differences between Asian and American college students? *Human Communication, 11,* 431–443.

Gordon, R. L. (1975). *Interviewing: Strategy, techniques, and tactics.* Homewood, IL: The Dorsey Press.

Hall, E. T. (1966). *The hidden dimension.* Garden City, NY: Doubleday.

Hall, E. T. (1973). *The silent language.* Garden City, NY: Doubleday.

Heckel, R. V. (1973). Leadership and voluntary seating choice. *Psychological Reports, 32,* 141–142.

Henley, N. M. (1977). *Body politics: Power, sex, and nonverbal communication.* Englewood Cliffs, NJ: Prentice Hall.

Hickson, M. L. III, Grierson, R. D., and Linder, B. C. (1991). A communication perspective on sexual harassment: Affiliative nonverbal behaviors in asynchronous relationships. *Communication Quarterly, 39,* (2), 111–118.

Hickson, M. L. III, Powell, L., Turner, J., Neiva, E., and Adams, C. T. (2002). The somatic marker as a "short cut" to verbal immediacy. *Communication Research Reports, 19,* 389–398.

Hickson, M. L. III, Stacks, D. W., and Moore, N. J. (2004). *Nonverbal communication: Studies and applications* (4th ed.). Los Angeles, CA: Roxbury.

Hickson, M. L. III, Stacks, D. W., and Padgett-Greely, M. (1998). *Organizational communication in the personal context: From interview to retirement.* Boston: Allyn and Bacon.

Hunsaker, P. L. (1980, March–April). Communicating better: There's no proxy for proxemics. *Business,* pp. 41–48.

Jorgenson, D. O. (1975). Field study of the relationship between status and discrepancy and proxemics behavior. *Journal of Social Psychology, 97,* 173–179.

Kaiser, S. B. (1997). Women's appearance and clothing within organizations. In S.B. Kaiser (2nd ed.) *The social psychology of clothing: Symbolic appearances in context.* Fairchild Publications/Capital Cities Media.

Korda, M. (1975). *Power! How to get it, how to use it.* New York: Ballantine.

LaFrance, M., and Mayo, C. (1978). *Moving bodies: Nonverbal communication in social relationships* (pp. 95–105). Monterey, CA: Brooks/Cole.

Lott, D. F., and Sommer, R. (1967). Seating arrangements and status. *Journal of Personality and Social Psychology, 7,* 90–95.

McCaskey, M. B. (1979, November–December). The hidden messages managers send. *Harvard Business Review,* pp. 135–148.

Mehrabian, A. (1971). *Silent messages: Implicit communication of emotions and attitudes* (5th ed.). Belmont, CA: Wadsworth.

Mehrabian, A. (1976). *Public places and private spaces: The psychology of work, play, and living environments.* New York: Basic Books.

Molloy, J. T. (1975). *Dress for success.* New York: Warner Books.

Molloy, J. T. (1977). *The woman's dress for success book.* Chicago: Follett.

Molloy, J. T. (1988). *New dress for success.* New York: Warner.

Molloy, J. T. (1996). *New women's dress for success.* New York: Warner.

Moore, N. J, Hickson, M. III, and Stacks, D. W. (2010). *Nonverbal communication: Studies and applications.* New York: Oxford University Press.

Oldham, G. R., and Rotchford, N. L. (1983). Relationships between office characteristics and employee reactions: A study of the physical environment. *Administrative Science Quarterly, 28,* 542–556.

Powell, L., and Hickson, M. III (2000). Power imbalance and anticipation of conflict resolution: Positive and negative attributes of perceptual recall. *Communication Research Reports, 17,* 181–190.

Remland, M. S. (1984). Leadership impressions and nonverbal communication in a superior-subordinate interaction. *Communication Quarterly, 32,* 41–48.

Richmond, V. P. (2002). Sociocommunicative style and orientation in instruction. In J. L. Chesebro and J. C. McCroskey (eds.), *Communication for teachers* (pp. 104–115). Boston: Allyn and Bacon.

Richmond, V. P., Davis, L. M., Saylor, K., and McCroskey, J. C. (1984). Power strategies in organizations: Communication techniques and messages. *Human Communication Research, 11,* 85–108.

Richmond, V. P., and Martin, M. M. (1998). Sociocommunicative style and socio-communicative orientation. In J. C. McCroskey, J. A. Daly, M. M. Martin, and M. J. Beatty (eds.). *Communication and personality: Trait perspectives* (pp. 133–148). Hillsdale, NJ: Erlbaum.

Richmond, V. P., and McCroskey, J.C. (1998). *Communication: Apprehension, avoidance, and effectiveness* (5th ed.). Boston: Allyn and Bacon.

Richmond, V. P., and McCroskey, J. C. (2000). The impact of supervisor and subordinate immediacy on relational and organizational outcomes. *Communication Monographs, 67,* 85–95.

Richmond, V. P., and McCroskey, J. C. (2001). *Organizational communication for survival: Making work, work* (2nd ed.). Boston: Allyn and Bacon.

Richmond, V. P., McCroskey, J. C., and Davis, L. M. (1986). The relationship of supervisor use of power and affinity-seeking strategies with subordinate satisfaction. *Communication Quarterly, 34,* 178–193.

Richmond, V. P., Smith, R., Heisel, A., and McCroskey, J. C. (1998). The impact of communication apprehension and fear of talking with a physician on perceived medical outcomes. *Communication Research Reports, 15,* 344–353.

Richmond, V. P., Smith, R., Heisel, A., and McCroskey, J. C. (2001). Nonverbal immediacy in the physican/patient relationship. *Communication Research Reports, 18,* 211–216.

Richmond, V. P., Smith, R., Heisel, A., and McCroskey, J. C. (2002). The association of physician sociocommunicative style with physician credibility and patient satisfaction. *Communication Research Reports, 19,* (3), 207–215.

Richmond, V. P., Wagner, J. P., and McCroskey, J. C. (1983). The impact of perceptions of leadership style, use of power, and conflict management style on organizational outcomes. *Communication Quarterly, 31,* 27–36.

Robinson, J. D. (1998). Getting down to business: Talk, gaze, and body orientation during openings of doctor-patient consultations. *Human Communication Research, 25,* (1), 97–123.

Sommer, R. (1969). *Personal space: The behavioral basis of design.* Englewood Cliffs, NJ: Prentice Hall.

Chapter 13

Ambady, N., and Rosenthal, R. (1993). Half a minute: Predicting teacher evaluations from thin slices of nonverbal behavior and physical attractiveness. *Journal of Personality and Social Psychology, 64,* 431–441.

Andersen, J. F. (1979). Teacher immediacy as a predictor of teaching effectiveness. In D. Nimmo (ed.), *Communication Yearbook 3* (pp. 543–559). New Brunswick, NJ: Transaction Books.

Andersen, J. F. (1986). Instructor nonverbal communication: Listening to our silent messages. In J. M. Civikly (ed.), *Communicating in college classrooms: New directions for teaching and learning* (pp. 41–49). San Francisco: Jossey-Bass.

Andersen, P. A. (1985). Nonverbal immediacy in interpersonal communication. In A. W. Siegman and S. Feldstein (eds.), *Multichannel integrations of nonverbal behavior* (pp. 1–36). Hillsdale, NJ: Erlbaum.

Andersen, P., and Andersen, J. (1982). Nonverbal immediacy in instruction. In L. L. Barker (ed.), *Communication in the classroom: Original essays* (pp. 98–102). Englewood Cliffs, NJ: Prentice Hall.

Andersen, P. A., and Leibowitz, K. (1978). The development and nature of the construct touch avoidance. *Environmental Psychology and Nonverbal Behavior, 3,* 89–106.

Barr, A. S. (1929). *Characteristic differences in the teaching performance of good and poor teachers of social studies.* Bloomington, IL: Public School Publishing Company.

Baringer, D. K., and McCroskey, J. C. (2000). Immediacy in the classroom: Student immediacy. *Communication Education, 49,* (2), 178–186.

Buhr, T. A., Clifton, T. I., and Pryor, B. (1994). Effects of speaker's immediacy on receivers' information processing. *Perceptual and Motor Skills, 79,* 779–783.

Chesebro, J. L., and McCroskey, J. C. (1998). The relationship of teacher clarity and teacher immediacy with students' experiences of state receiver apprehension. *Communication Quarterly, 46,* (4), pp. 446–456.

Chesebro, J. L., and McCroskey, J. C. (2001). The relationship of teacher clarity and immediacy with student state receiver apprehension, affect, and cognitive learning. *Communication Education, 50,* (1), 59–68.

Chesebro, J. L., and Wanzer, M. B. (2006). Instructional message variables. In T. P. Mottet, V. P. Richmond, and J. C. McCroskey (eds.). *Handbook of instructional communication: Rhetorical and relational perspectives.* Boston: Allyn and Bacon.

Christophel, D. M. (1990). The relationships among teacher immediacy behaviors, student motivation, and learning. *Communication Education, 39,* 323–340.

Frymier, A. B. (1993). The impact of teacher immediacy on students' motivation: Is it the same for all students? *Communication Quarterly, 41,* (4), 454–464.

Frymier, A. B. (1994). A model of immediacy in the classroom. *Communication Quarterly, 42,* 133–144.

Frymier, A. B., and Wanzer, M. B. (2006). Teacher and student affinity-seeking in the classroom. In T. P. Mottet, V. P. Richmond, and J. C. McCroskey (eds.). *Handbook of instructional communication: Rhetorical and relational perspectives* (pp. 195–211). Boston: Allyn and Bacon.

Gorham, J., Cohen, S. H., and Morris, T. L. (1997). Fashion in the classroom II: Instructor immediacy and attire. *Communication Research Reports, 14,* (1), 11–23.

Gorham, J., Cohen, S. H., and Morris, T. L. (1999). Fashion in the classroom III: Effects of instructor attire and immediacy in natural classroom interactions. *Communication Quarterly, 47,* (3), 281–299.

Green, G. H. (1979). Ah-choo! Humidity can help. *American School and University*, 52, 64–65.

Kearney, P., Plax, T. G., Richmond, V. P., and McCroskey, J. C. (1984). Power in the classroom IV: Teacher communication techniques as alternatives to discipline. In D. Nimmo (ed.), *Communication Yearbook 4* (pp. 724–746). Beverly Hills, CA: Sage.

Kearney, P., Plax, T. G., Richmond, V. P., and McCroskey, J. C. (1985). Power in the classroom III: Teacher communication techniques and messages. *Communication Education*, 34, 19–28.

Kelly, S. D., and Goldsmith, L. H. (2004). Gesture and right hemisphere involvement in evaluating lecture material. *Gesture*, 4, 25–42.

Ketcham, H. (1958). *Color planning for business and industry*. New York: Harper and Brothers.

Kougl, K. (1997). *Communicating in the classroom*. Prospect Heights, IL: Waveland Press.

McCroskey, J. C. (1992). *Communication in the classroom*. Acton, MA: Tapestry Press.

McCroskey, J. C., and Richmond, V. P. (1983). Power in the classroom I: Teacher and student perceptions. *Communication Education*, 32, 175–184.

McCroskey, J. C., and Richmond, V. P. (1992). Increasing teacher influence through immediacy. In V.P. Richmond and J. C. McCroskey (eds.), *Power in the classroom: Communication, control, and concern* (pp. 101–119). Hillsdale, NJ: Erlbaum.

McCroskey, J. C., and Richmond, V. P. (1996). *Fundamentals of human communication: An interpersonal perspective*. Prospect Heights, IL: Waveland Press.

McCroskey, J. C., Richmond, V. P., Plax, T. G., and Kearney, P. (1985). Power in the classroom V: Behavior alteration techniques, communication training and learning. *Communication Education*, 34, 214–226.

McCroskey, J. C., Richmond, V. P., and Stewart, R. A. (1986). *One on one: The foundations of interpersonal communication*. Englewood Cliffs, NJ: Prentice Hall.

McCroskey, J. C., Sallinen, A., Fayer, J. M., Richmond, V. P., and Barraclough, R. A. (1996). Nonverbal immediacy and cognitive learning: A cross-cultural investigation. *Communication Education*, 45, (3), 200–211.

McPherson, M. B., Kearney, P., and Plax, T. G. (2006). College teacher misbehaviors. In T. P. Mottet, V. P. Richmond, and J. C. McCroskey. (eds.). *Handbook of instructional communication: Rhetorical and relational perspectives* (pp. 213–234). Boston: Allyn and Bacon.

Mehrabian, A. (1966). Immediacy: An indicator of attitudes in linguistic communication. *Journal of Personality*, 34, 26–34.

Mehrabian, A. (1971). *Silent messages: Implicit communication of emotions and attitudes* (5th ed.). Belmont, CA: Wadsworth.

Moore, A., Masterson, J. T., Christophel, D. M., and Shea, K. A. (1996). College teacher immediacy and student ratings of instruction. *Communication Education*, 45, 29–39.

Moore, N. J., Hickson, M., and Stacks, D. W. (2010). *Nonverbal communication: Studies and applications*. (5th ed.). New York: Oxford University Press.

Morris, T. L., Gorham, J., Cohen, S. H., and Huffman, D. (1996). Fashion in the classroom: Effects of attire on student perceptions of instructors in college classes. *Communication Education*, 45, 135–148.

Mottet, T. P., Beebe, S. A., and Fleuriet, C. A. (2006). Students' influence messages. In T. P. Mottet, V. P. Richmond, and J. C. McCroskey. (eds.). *Handbook of instructional communication*. Boston: Allyn and Bacon.

Mottet, T. P., Beebe, S. A., and Fleuriet, C. A. (2006). Students' influence messages. In T. P. Mottet, V. P. Richmond, and J. C. McCroskey. (eds.). *Handbook of instructional communication: Rhetorical and relational perspectives* (pp. 143–165). Boston: Allyn and Bacon.

Mottet, T., and Richmond, V. P. (1998). An inductive analysis of verbal immediacy: Alternative conceptualization of relational verbal approach/avoidance strategies. *Communication Quarterly, 46,* (1) 25–40.

Mottet, T., and Richmond, V. P. (2002). Student nonverbal communication and its influence on teachers and teaching. In J. L. Chesebro and J. C. McCroskey (eds.), *Communication for teachers* (pp. 47–61). Boston: Allyn and Bacon.

Mottet, T. P., Richmond, V. P., and McCroskey, J. C. (2006). Assessing instructional communication. In T. P. Mottet, V. P. Richmond, and J. C. McCroskey. (eds.). *Handbook of instructional communication: Rhetorical and relational perspectives* (pp. 143–165). Boston: Allyn and Bacon.

Plax, T. G., Kearney, P., McCroskey, J. C., and Richmond, V. P. (1986). Power in the classroom VI: Verbal control strategies, nonverbal immediacy, and affective learning. *Communication Education, 35,* 43–55.

Richmond, V. P. (1990). Communication in the classroom: Power and motivation. *Communication Education, 39,* 181–195.

Richmond, V. P. (1997). *Nonverbal communication in the classroom: A text, workbook, and study guide.* Acton, MA: Tapestry Press.

Richmond, V. P. (1999). Extended learning. In A. L. Vangelisti, J. A. Daly, and G. W. Friedrich (eds.). *Teaching communication: Theory, research, and methods* (2nd ed.) (pp. 497–506). Mahwah, NJ: Erlbaum.

Richmond, V. P. (2002a). Teacher nonverbal immediacy: Uses and outcomes. In J. L. Chesebro and J. C. McCroskey (eds.). *Communication for teachers* (pp. 65–82). Boston: Allyn and Bacon.

Richmond, V. P. (2002b). Sociocommunicative style and orientation in instruction. In J. L. Chesebro and J. C. McCroskey (eds.). *Communication for teachers* (pp. 105–115). Boston: Allyn and Bacon.

Richmond, V. P., Gorham, J. S., and McCroskey, J. C. (1986). The relationship between selected immediacy behaviors and cognitive learning. In M. L. McLaughlin (ed.), *Communication Yearbook 10.* Beverly Hills, CA: Sage.

Richmond, V. P., and Hickson, M. III. (2002). *Going public: A practical guide to public talk.* Boston: Allyn and Bacon.

Richmond, V. P., Lane, D. R., and McCroskey, J. C. (2006). Teacher immediacy and the teacher-student relationship. In T. P. Mottet, V. P. Richmond, and J. C. McCroskey. (eds.). *Handbook of instructional communication: Rhetorical and relational perspectives* (pp. 167–193). Boston: Allyn and Bacon.

Richmond, V. P., and Martin, M. M. (1998). Sociocommunicative style and sociocommunicative orientation. In J. C. McCroskey, J. A. Daly, M. Martin, and M. J. Beatty. *Communication and personality: Trait perspectives* (pp. 133–148). Hillsdale, NJ: Erlbaum.

Richmond, V. P., and McCroskey, J. C. (1984). Power in the classroom II: Power and learning. *Communication Education, 33,* 125–136.

Richmond, V. P., and McCroskey, J. C. (1990). Reliability and separation of factors on the assertiveness-responsiveness measure. *Psychological Reports, 67,* 449–450.

Richmond, V. P., and McCroskey, J. C. (1998). *Communication: Apprehension, avoidance, and effectiveness* (5th ed.). Boston: Allyn and Bacon.

Richmond, V. P., and McCroskey, J. C. (2000). The impact of supervisor and subordinate immediacy on relational and organizational outcomes. *Communication Monographs, 67,* 85–95.

Richmond, V. P., and McCroskey, J. C. (2001). *Organizational communication for survival: Making work, work* (2nd ed.). Boston: Allyn and Bacon.

Richmond, V. P., McCroskey, J. C., Kearney, P., and Plax, T. G. (1987). Power in the classroom VII: Linking behavioral alteration techniques to cognitive learning. *Communication Education, 36,* 1–12.

Richmond, V. P., McCroskey, J. C., Plax, T. G., and Kearney, P. (1986). *Teacher immediacy training and student learning.* Paper presented at the annual convention of the Speech Communication Association, Chicago.

Richmond, V. P., Smith, R., Heisel, A., and McCroskey, J. C. (1998). The impact of communication apprehension and fear of talking with a physician on perceived medical outcomes. *Communication Research Reports, 15,* 344–353.

Richmond, V. P., Smith, R., Heisel, A., and McCroskey, J. C. (2001). Nonverbal immediacy in the physician/patient relationship. *Communication Research Reports, 18,* 211–216.

Richmond, V. P., Smith, R., Heisel, A., and McCroskey, J. C. (2002). The association of physician sociocommunicative style with physician and patient satisfaction. *Communication Research Reports, 19,* (3), 207–215.

Richmond, V. P., Wrench, J., and Gorham, J. S. (1998). *Communication, learning, and affect in instruction.* Acton, MA: Tapestry Press.

Richmond, V. P., Wrench, J., and Gorham, J. (2001). *Communication, learning, and affect in instruction.* Acton, MA: Tapestry Press.

Roach, K. D. (1997). Effects of graduate teaching assistant attire on student learning, misbehaviors, and ratings of instruction. *Communication Quarterly, 45,* (3), 125–141.

Roach, K. D., Richmond, V. P., and McCroskey, J. C. (2006). Teachers' influence messages. In T. P. Mottet, V. P. Richmond, and J. C. McCroskey. (eds.). *Handbook of instructional communication: Rhetorical and relational perspectives* (pp. 117–139). Boston: Allyn and Bacon.

Rocca, K. A., and McCroskey, J. C. (1999). The interrelationship of student ratings of instructors' immediacy, verbal aggressiveness, homophily, and inter-personal attraction. *Communication Education, 48,* (4), 308–316.

Sidelinger, R. J., and McCroskey, J. C. (1997). Communication correlates of teacher clarity in the college classroom.

Communication Research Reports, 14, (1), 1–10.

Smith, H. A. (1979). Nonverbal communication in teaching. *Review of Educational Psychology, 49,* 631–672.

Sommer, R. (1977). Classroom layout. *Theory into Practice, 16,* 174–175.

Thomas, C. E., Richmond, V. P., and McCroskey, J. C. (1994). The association between immediacy and socio-communicative style. *Communication Research Reports, 11,* 107–115.

Thompson, J. J. (1973). *Beyond words: Nonverbal communication in the classroom.* New York: Citation Press.

Thweatt, K. S., and McCroskey, J. C. (1996). Teacher nonimmediacy and misbehavior: Unintentional negative communication. *Communication Research Reports, 13,* (2), 198–204.

Thweatt, K. S., and McCroskey, J. C. (1998). The impact of teacher immediacy and misbehaviors on teacher credibility. *Communication Education, 47,* (4), 348–358.

Todd-Mancillas, W. R. (1982). Classroom environments and nonverbal communication. In L. L. Barker (ed.), *Communication in the classroom: Original essays* (pp. 7797). Englewood Cliffs, NJ: Prentice Hall.

Wiemann, M. O., and Wiemann, J. M. (1975). *Nonverbal communication in the elementary classroom.* Urbana, IL: ERIC Clearinghouse on Reading and Communication Skills.

Chapter 14

Adler, P. S. (1974). Beyond cultural identity: Reflections on cultural and multicultural man. *Topics in Culture Learning, 2,* 23–40.

Axtell, R. E. (1991). *Gestures: The do's and taboos of body language around the world.* New York: John Wiley.

Axtell, R. E., Briggs, T., Corcoran, M., and Lamb, M. B. (1997). *Do's and taboos around the world for women in business.* New York: John Wiley.

Brault, G. J. (1962). Kinesics and the classroom: Some typical French gestures. *French Review, 36,* 374–382.

Carbaugh, D. (1990). *Cultural communication and intercultural contact.* Hillsdale, NJ: Erlbaum.

Eibl-Eibesfeldt, I. (1972). *Similarities and differences between cultures in expressive moments.* In R. A. Hinde (ed.), *Non-verbal communication.* London: Cambridge University Press.

Ekman, P. (1971). Universals and cultural differences in facial expressions of emotion. In *Nebraska Symposium on Motivation* (pp. 207–283). Lincoln: University of Nebraska Press.

Ekman, P. (1975, September). Face muscles talk every language. *Psychology Today, 9,* 35–39.

Ekman, P. (2003). *Emotions revealed: Recognizing faces and feelings to improve communication and emotional life.* New York: Henry Holt.

Ekman, P., Friesen, W. V., and Ellsworth, P. (1972). *Emotion in the human face.* New York: Pergamon Press.

Faigan, G. (1990). *The artist's complete guide to facial expression.* New York: Watson-Guptill.

Frank, L. K. (1982). Cultural patterning of tactile experiences. In L. A. Samovar and R. E. Porter (eds.), *Intercultural communication: A reader* (3rd ed.), (pp. 285–289). Belmont, CA: Wadsworth.

Gudykunst, W. B., and Yun Kim, Y. (1997). *Communicating with strangers: An approach to intercultural communication* (3rd ed.). New York: McGraw-Hill.

Hall, E. T. (1973). *The silent language.* Greenwich, CT: Fawcett.

Hall, E. T. (1977). *Beyond culture.* Garden City, NY: Anchor.

Harris, P. R., and Moran, R. T. (1991). *Managing cultural differences* (3rd ed.). Houston, TX: Gulf Publishing.

Horton, J. (1976). Time and cool people. In L. A. Samovar and R.E. Porter (eds.), *Intercultural communication: A reader* (2nd ed.), (pp. 274–287). Belmont, CA: Wadsworth.

Hur, S. V., and Hur, B. S. (1988). *Culture shock! Korea.* Singapore: Times Books International.

Iliffe, A. H. (1960). A study of preferences in feminine beauty. *British Journal of Psychology, 51,* 267–273.

Ishii, S. (1973). Characteristics of Japanese nonverbal communicative behavior. Communication, 2. Cited in D. W. Klopf and S. Ishii (1984). *Communicating effectively across cultures.* Tokyo: NANOUN-DO.

Ishii, S. (1975). The American male viewed by Japanese female students of English: A stereotype image. Speech Education, 3. Cited in D. W. Klopf and S. Ishii (1984). *Communicating effectively across cultures.* Tokyo: NANOUN-DO.

Izard, C. E. (1969). The emotions and emotion constructs in personality and culture research. In R. B. Cattell (ed.), *Handbook of modern personality theory.* Chicago: Aldine.

Jakobson, R. (1976). Nonverbal signs for "Yes" and "No." In L. A. Samovar and R. E. Porter (eds.), *Intercultural communication: A reader* (2nd ed.), (pp. 235–240). Belmont, CA: Wadsworth.

Jones, S. E. (1971). A comparative proxemics analysis of dyadic interaction in selected subcultures of New York City. *Journal of Social Psychology, 84,* 35–44.

Jourard, S. M. (1968). *Disclosing man to himself.* New York: Van Nostrand Reinhold.

Kaleina, G. (March 3, 1979). More than other folks, pets get loving strokes. *Arizona Republic,* p. c2.

Keltner, D. (1997). The forms and functions of embarrassment In P. Ekman and E. Rosenberg (eds.). *What the face reveals: Basic and applied studies of spontaneous expression using the Facial Action Coding System (FACS).* New York: Oxford University Press.

Klopf, D. W. (1998). *Intercultural encounters: The fundamentals of intercultural communication* (4th ed.). Englewood, CO: Morton.

Klopf, D. W., and Ishii, S. (1984). *Communicating effectively across cultures.* Tokyo: NANOUN-DO.

Klopf, D. W., and Park, M. S. (1982). *Cross-cultural communication: An introduction to the fundamentals.* Seoul, Korea: Han Shin Publishers.

Martin, J. G. (1964). Racial ethnocentrism and judgment of beauty. *Journal of Social Psychology, 63,* 59–63.

Morrison, T., Conaway, W. A., and Borden, G. A. (1994). *Kiss, bow, or shake hands: How to do business in 60 countries.* Holbrook, MA: Adams Media Corporation.

Morsbach, H. (1976). Aspects of nonverbal communication in Japan. In L. A. Samovar and R. E. Porter (eds.), *Intercultural communication: A reader.* Belmont, CA: Wadsworth.

Neuliep, J. W. (2002). *Intercultural communication: A contextual approach.* Boston: Houghton Mifflin Company.

Neuliep, J. W., and McCroskey, J. C. (1997). The development of a U.S. and generalized ethnocentrism scale. *Communication Research Reports, 14,* (4), 385–398.

Rich, A. L., and Ogawa, D. M. (1972). Intercultural and interracial communication: An analytical approach. In L. A. Samovar and R. E. Porter (eds.). *Intercultural communication: A reader.* Belmont, CA: Wadsworth.

Rosenberg, E. L. (1997). The study of spontaneous facial expressions in psychology. In P. Ekman and E. Rosenberg (eds.). *What the face reveals: Basic and applied studies of spontaneous expression using the Facial Action Coding System (FACS).* New York: Oxford University Press.

Ruben, B. D. (1977). Human communication and cross-cultural effectiveness. *International and Intercultural Communication Annual, 4.*

Saitz, R. L., and Cervenka, E. J. (1972). *Handbook of gestures: Colombia and the United States.* The Hague: Morton.

Samovar, L. A., and Porter, R. E. (eds.), (1976). *Intercultural communication: A reader* (2nd ed.). Belmont, CA: Wadsworth.

Sechrest, L. (1969). Nonreactive assessment of attitudes. In E. P. Willems and H. L. Rausch (eds.). *Naturalistic viewpoints in psychological research.* New York: Holt, Rinehart and Winston.

Shuter, R. (1976). Proxemics and tactility in Latin America. *Journal of Communication, 26,* 46–52.

Shuter, R. (1977). A field study of nonverbal communication in Germany, Italy, and the United States. *Communication Monographs, 44,* 298–305.

Simons, R. C. (1997). FACS in the study of the latah syndrome. In P. Ekman and E. Rosenberg (eds.). *What the face reveals: Basic and applied studies of the spontaneous expression using the Facial Action Coding System (FACS).* New York: Oxford University Press.

Thomas-Maddox, C., and Lowery-Hart, R. (1998). *Communicating with diverse students: A text and workbook.* Acton, MA: Tapestry Press.

Ting-Toomey, S., and Korzenny, F. (1991). *Cross-cultural interpersonal communication.* Newbury Park, CA: Sage Publications.

Welch, M. S. (1979, July). Touching: Kissing, hugging, stroking, patting, grabbing, tickling, tweaking, brushing. *Glamour,* 70–71.

Wickline, V. B., Bailey, W., and Nowicki, S. (2009). Cultural in-group advantage: Emotion recognition in African American and European American faces and voices. *Journal of Genetic Psychology, 170,* 5–29.

Yousef, F. S. (1976). Nonverbal behavior: Some intricate and diverse dimensions in intercultural communication. In L. A. Samovar and R. E. Porter (eds.), *Intercultural communication: A reader.* (2nd ed.), (pp. 230–235). Belmont, CA: Wadsworth.

PHOTO CREDITS

INDEX